READINGS ABOUT

The Social Animal

A Series of Books in Psychology

EDITORS: Richard C. Atkinson
Jonathan Freedman
Richard F. Thompson

READINGS ABOUT
The Social Animal

Edited by
Elliot Aronson
THE UNIVERSITY OF TEXAS AT AUSTIN

W. H. FREEMAN AND COMPANY
San Francisco

Library of Congress Cataloging in Publication Data
Aronson, Elliot, comp.
   Readings about the social animal.

1. Social psychology — Addresses, essays, lectures.
I. Title. [DNLM: 1. Psychology, Social — Collected
works. HM 251 A7691 1972]
HM251.A789   301.1'08   72-12664   ISBN 0-7167-0833-7

Printed in the United States of America

International Standard Book Number: 0-7167-0833-7

1   2   3   4   5   6   7   8   9   10

To all of the kids —
past, present, and future

Preface

In my textbook *The Social Animal,* I attempted to paint a clear picture of
the current state of our social psychological knowledge and how such knowledge might be applied to alleviate some problems plaguing us in the world
today. The book was intended to be concise and was written in a brisk and
lively manner. It was almost totally unencumbered by graphs, charts, tables,
statistical analysis, or detailed methodological discussions. Although that
kind of presentation makes for an easy and enjoyable introduction to the
world of social psychology, many of my readers expressed a need to delve
more deeply into the details of the research which formed the backbone of
The Social Animal. The present volume is designed to fill that need; thus,
it is aimed primarily at accompanying *The Social Animal.* With this in mind,
I selected the readings in such a way that they would both complement and
supplement the material contained in that text. Not only are the sections in
the present volume organized so as to coincide with chapters in *The Social
Animal,* but, in addition, the specific readings represent an attempt to am-
plify and elaborate on the major themes covered in that book.

In editing this book, I was especially careful to choose readings that
would provide a mixture of classic and contemporary research. Such a
combination enables the reader to be exposed to the old and the new in
one volume. Some of the articles were already classics when I first read
them as a student. Others were still in press when I decided to include them
after having read them in the form of prepublication reports. Some well-
known pieces of work, such as Solomon Asch's conformity experiment and

Stanley Milgram's experiment on obedience, are included. In other cases, a ground-breaking experiment that is discussed in *The Social Animal* is replaced in this collection of readings by a more recent experiment along the same lines because the latter serves to clarify the original findings. For example, the experiment by Elliot Aronson and Judson Mills, published in 1959, that was the first to demonstrate the effects of a severe initiation on increasing the attractiveness of a group, does not appear in this collection. Rather, the initiation phenomenon is presented in the form of a subsequent experiment by Harold Gerard and Grover Mathewson that pins down and extends the theoretical explanation offered in the earlier work. By the same token, the classic experiment on "counterattitudinal advocacy" by Leon Festinger and Merrill Carlsmith, although discussed in *The Social Animal,* is replaced in this collection by a more elaborate and clearer experiment subsequently performed by J. Merrill Carlsmith, Barry Collins, and Robert Helmreich.

There is another way of classifying the articles in this collection: most of the articles are reports of specific experiments as originally published in technical journals; others are more general pieces summarizing several experiments on a given topic written by one of the major contributors to that area. A specific research report, though not always easy to read, has the advantage of providing the detail necessary for enabling the reader to gain some understanding of exactly what goes into an experiment. The summary article is usually less technical and, therefore, easier to read. Moreover, it offers a more panoramic overview of the area by the people who know it best; in effect, it enables the reader to look over a researcher's shoulder and see how he or she views an array of experiments on a given topic.

Elliot Aronson

September 1972

Contents

The Authors

Vernon L. Allen
University of Wisconsin

Elliot Aronson
University of Texas
Austin

Solomon E. Asch
Rutgers University

Steven R. Asher
University of Wisconsin

Albert Bandura
Stanford University

Robert A. Baron
Purdue University

Leonard Berkowitz
University of Wisconsin

Ellen Berscheid
University of Minnesota

Robert R. Blake
Scientific Methods, Inc.
Austin, Texas

David Boye
University of Minnesota

J. Merrill Carlsmith
Stanford University

Barry E. Collins
University of California
Los Angeles

James M. Dabbs, Jr.
University of Michigan

Michael Jay Diamond
University of Hawaii

Karen K. Dion
  University of Toronto

Raymond Ditrichs
  Northern Illinois University

Edward Donnerstein
  Florida State University
  Tallahassee

Marcia Donnerstein
  Florida State University
  Tallahassee

Anthony N. Doob
  University of Toronto

Leon Festinger
  New School for Social Research

Scott C. Fraser
  University of Washington

Jonathan L. Freedman
  Columbia University

Harold B. Gerard
  University of California
  Los Angeles

Robert L. Helmreich
  University of Texas
  Austin

Irving L. Janis
  Yale University

Edward E. Jones
  Duke University

Michael Kahn
  University of California
  Santa Cruz

Donald Kaye
  Columbia Employment Agency
  New York City

Paul Kirschner
  Yale University

Thomas K. Landauer
  Bell Telephone Laboratories
  Murray Hill, New Jersey

Bibb Latané
Ohio State University
Columbus

Monroe Lefkowitz
New York State Department of Mental Health
Albany

Melvin J. Lerner
University of Waterloo
Waterloo, Ontario

Howard Leventhal
Yale University

Robert M. Liebert
State University of New York
Stony Brook

Darwyn Linder
Arizona State University

Nathan Maccoby
Stanford University

Grover C. Mathewson
University of California
Riverside

David R. Mettee
University of Denver

Stanley Milgram
City University of New York

Jane Srygley Mouton
Scientific Methods, Inc.
Austin, Texas

Richard Page
University of Rochester

Thomas F. Pettigrew
Harvard University

Judith Rodin
Columbia University

Dorothea Ross
Stanford University

Sheila A. Ross
Stanford University

Irwin Rubin
Massachusetts Institute of Technology

Jerrold L. Shapiro
   University of Hawaii

Muzafer Sherif
   Pennsylvania State University

Harold Sigall
   University of Maryland

Carolyn H. Simmons
   Lexington, Kentucky

Seymore Simon
   Northern Illinois University

Soleng Tom, Jr.
   Stanford University

Judith A. Turner
   University of Iowa

Elaine Walster
   University of Wisconsin

READINGS ABOUT

The Social Animal

I

CONFORMITY AND OBEDIENCE

1

Opinions and Social Pressure

Solomon E. Asch

Exactly what is the effect of the opinions of others on our own? In other words, how strong is the urge toward social conformity? The question is approached by means of some unusual experiments.

That social influences shape every person's practices, judgments and beliefs is a truism to which anyone will readily assent. A child masters his "native" dialect down to the finest nuances; a member of a tribe of cannibals accepts cannibalism as altogether fitting and proper. All the social sciences take their departure from the observation of the profound effects that groups exert on their members. For psychologists, group pressure upon the minds of individuals raises a host of questions they would like to investigate in detail.

How, and to what extent, do social forces constrain people's opinions and attitudes? This question is especially pertinent in our day. The same epoch that has witnessed the unprecedented technical extension of communication has also brought into existence the deliberate manipulation of opinion and the "engineering of consent." There are many good reasons why, as citizens and as scientists, we should be concerned with studying the ways in which human beings form their opinions and the role that social conditions play.

Studies of these questions began with the interest in hypnosis aroused by the French physician Jean Martin Charcot (a teacher of Sigmund Freud) toward the end of the nineteenth century. Charcot believed that only hysterical patients could be fully hypnotized, but this view was soon challenged by two other physicians, Hyppolyte Bernheim and A. A. Liébault, who demonstrated that they could put most people under the hypnotic spell. Bernheim proposed that hypnosis was but an extreme form of a normal psychological process which became known as "suggestibility." It was shown that monotonous reiteration of instructions could induce in normal persons in the waking state involuntary bodily changes such as swaying or rigidity of the arms, and sensations such as warmth and odor.

It was not long before social thinkers seized upon these discoveries as a basis for explaining numerous social phenomena, from the spread of opinion to the formation of crowds and the following of leaders. The sociologist Gabriel Tarde summed it all up in the aphorism: "Social man is a somnambulist."

When the new discipline of social psychology was born at the beginning of this century, its first experiments were essentially adaptations of the suggestion demonstration. The technique generally followed a simple plan. The subjects, usually college students, were asked to give their opinions or preferences concerning various matters; some time later they were again asked to state their choices, but now they were also informed of the opinions held by authorities or large groups of their peers on the same matters. (Often the alleged consensus was fictitious.) Most of these studies had substantially the same result: confronted with opinions contrary to their own, many subjects apparently shifted their judgments in the direction of the views of the majorities or the experts. The late psychologist Edward L. Thorndike reported that he had succeeded in modifying the esthetic preferences of adults by this procedure. Other psychologists reported that people's evaluations of the merit of a literary passage could be raised or lowered by ascribing the passage to different authors. Apparently the sheer weight of numbers or authority sufficed to change opinions, even when no arguments for the opinions themselves were provided.

Now the very ease of success in these experiments arouses suspicion. Did the subjects actually change their opinions, or were the experimental victories scored only on paper? On grounds of common sense, one must question whether opinions are generally as watery as these studies indicate. There is some reason to wonder whether it was not the investigators who, in their enthusiasm for a theory, were suggestible, and whether the ostensibly gullible subjects were not providing answers which they thought good subjects were expected to give.

The investigations were guided by certain underlying assumptions, which today are common currency and account for much that is thought and said about the operations of propaganda and public opinion. The assumptions are that people submit uncritically and painlessly to external manipulation by suggestion or prestige, and that any given idea or value can be "sold" or "unsold" without reference to its merits. We should be skeptical, however, of the supposition that the power of social pressure necessarily implies uncritical submission to it: independence and the capacity to rise above group passion are also open to human beings. Further, one may question on psychological grounds whether it is possible as a rule to change a person's judgment of a situation or an object without first changing his knowledge or assumptions about it.

In what follows I shall describe some experiments in an investigation of the effects of group pressure which was carried out recently with the help of a number of my associates. The tests not only demonstrate the operations of group pressure upon individuals but also illustrate a new kind of attack on the problem and some of the more subtle questions that it raises.

A group of seven to nine young men, all college students, are assembled in a classroom for a "psychological experiment" in visual judgment. The experimenter informs them that they will be comparing the lengths of lines. He shows two large white cards. On one is a single vertical black line—the standard whose length is to be matched. On the other card are three vertical lines of various lengths. The subjects are to choose the one that is of the same length as the line on the other card. One of the three actually is of the

FIGURE 1.1
Experiment is repeated in the Laboratory of Social Relations at Harvard University. Seven student subjects are asked by the experimenter (*right*) to compare the length of lines (*see Fig. 1.2*). Six of the subjects have been coached beforehand to give unanimously wrong answers. The seventh (*sixth from the left*) has merely been told that it is an experiment in perception. (Photograph by William Vandivert.)

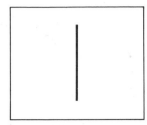 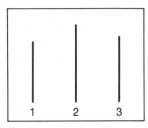

FIGURE 1.2
Subjects were shown two cards. One bore a standard line. The other bore three lines, one of which was the same length as the standard. The subjects were asked to choose this line.

same length; the other two are substantially different, the difference ranging from three quarters of an inch to an inch and three quarters.

The experiment opens uneventfully. The subjects announce their answers in the order in which they have been seated in the room, and on the first round every person chooses the same matching line. Then a second set of cards is exposed; again the group is unanimous. The members appear ready to endure politely another boring experiment. On the third trial there is an unexpected disturbance. One person near the end of the group disagrees with all the others in his selection of the matching line. He looks surprised, indeed incredulous, about the disagreement. On the following trial he disagrees again, while the others remain unanimous in their choice. The dissenter becomes more and more worried and hesitant as the disagreement continues in succeeding trials; he may pause before announcing his answer and speak in a low voice, or he may smile in an embarrassed way.

What the dissenter does not know is that all the other members of the group were instructed by the experimenter beforehand to give incorrect answers in unanimity at certain points. The single individual who is not a party to this prearrangement is the focal subject of our experiment. He is placed in a position in which, while he is actually giving the correct answers, he finds himself unexpectedly in a minority of one, opposed by a unanimous and arbitary majority with respect to a clear and simple fact. Upon him we have brought to bear two opposed forces: the evidence of his senses and the unanimous opinion of a group of his peers. Also, he must declare his judgments in public, before a majority which has also stated its position publicly.

The instructed majority occasionally reports correctly in order to reduce the possibility that the naive subject will suspect collusion against him. (In only a few cases did the subject actually show suspicion; when this happened, the experiment was stopped and the results were not counted.. There are 18 trials in each series, and on 12 of these the majority responds erroneously.

How do people respond to group pressure in this situation? I shall report first the statistical results of a series in which a total of 123 subjects from three institutions of higher learning (not including my own, Swarthmore College) were placed in the minority situation described above.

Two alternatives were open to the subject: he could act independently, repudiating the majority, or he could go along with the majority, repudiating the evidence of his senses. Of the 123 put to the test, a considerable percentage yielded to the majority. Whereas in ordinary circumstances individuals matching the lines will make mistakes less than 1 percent of the time, under group pressure the minority subjects swung to acceptance of the misleading majority's wrong judgments in 36.8 percent of the selections.

Of course individuals differed in response. At one extreme, about one quarter of the subjects were completely independent and never agreed with the erroneous judgments of the majority. At the other extreme, some individuals went with the majority nearly all the time. The performances of individuals in this experiment tend to be highly consistent. Those who strike out on the path of independence do not, as a rule, succumb to the majority even over an extended series of trials, while those who choose the path of compliance are unable to free themselves as the ordeal is prolonged.

The reasons for the startling individual differences have not yet been investigated in detail. At this point we can only report some tentative generalizations from talks with the subjects, each of whom was interviewed at the end of the experiment. Among the independent individuals were many who held fast because of staunch confidence in their own judgment. The most significant fact about them was not absence of responsiveness to the majority but a capacity to recover from doubt and to reestablish their equilibrium. Others who acted independently came to believe that the majority was correct in its answers, but they continued their dissent on the simple ground that it was their obligation to call the play as they saw it.

Among the extremely yielding persons we found a group who quickly reached the conclusion: "I am wrong, they are right." Others yielded in order "not to spoil your results." Many of the individuals who went along suspected that the majority were "sheep" following the first responder, or that the majority were victims of an optical illusion; nevertheless, these suspicions failed to free them at the moment of decision. More disquieting were the reactions of subjects who construed their difference from the majority as a sign of some general deficiency in themselves, which at all costs they must hide. On this basis they desperately tried to merge with the majority, not realizing the longer-range consequences to themselves. All the yielding subjects underestimated the frequency with which they conformed.

Which aspect of the influence of a majority is more important—the size of the majority or its unanimity? The experiment was modified to examine

this question. In one series the size of the opposition was varied from one to fifteen persons. The results showed a clear trend. When a subject was confronted with only a single individual who contradicted his answers, he was swayed little: he continued to answer independently and correctly in nearly all trials. When the opposition was increased to two, the pressure became substantial: minority subjects now accepted the wrong answer 13.6 percent of the time. Under the pressure of a majority of three, the subjects' errors jumped to 31.8 percent. But further increases in the size of the majority apparently did not increase the weight of the pressure substantially. Clearly the size of the opposition is important only up to a point.

Disturbance of the majority's unanimity had a striking effect. In this experiment the subject was given the support of a truthful partner — either another individual who did not know of the prearranged agreement among the rest of the group, or a person who was instructed to give correct answers throughout.

The presence of a supporting partner depleted the majority of much of its power. Its pressure on the dissenting individual was reduced to one-fourth: that is, subjects answered incorrectly only one-fourth as often as under the pressure of a unanimous majority (Fig. 1.6). The weakest persons did not yield as readily. Most interesting were the reactions to the partner. Generally the feeling toward him was one of warmth and closeness; he was credited with inspiring confidence. However, the subjects repudiated the suggestion that the partner decided them to be independent.

Was the partner's effect a consequence of his dissent, or was it related to his accuracy? We now introduced into the experimental group a person who was instructed to dissent from the majority but also to disagree with the subject. In some experiments the majority was always to choose the worst of the comparison lines and the instructed dissenter to pick the line that was closer to the length of the standard one; in others the majority was consistently intermediate and the dissenter most in error. In this manner we were able to study the relative influence of "compromising" and "extremist" dissenters.

Again the results are clear. When a moderate dissenter is present, the effect of the majority on the subject decreases by approximately one-third,

Figure 1.3
Experiment proceeds as follows: In the top picture, the subject (*center*) hears rules of experiment for the first time. In the second picture, he makes his first judgment of a pair of cards, disagreeing with the unanimous judgment of the others. In the third, he leans forward to look at another pair of cards. In the fourth, he shows the strain of repeatedly disagreeing with the majority. In the fifth, after twelve pairs of cards have been shown, he explains that "he has to call them as he sees them." This subject disagreed with the majority on all twelve trials. Seventy-five percent of experimental subjects agree with the majority in varying degrees. (Photograph by William Vandivert.)

10

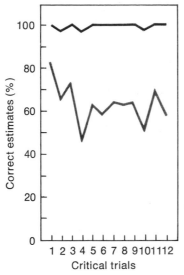

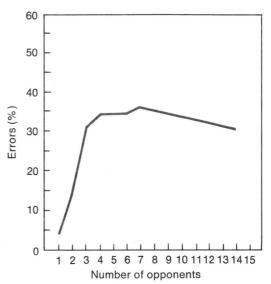

FIGURE 1.4
Error of 123 subjects, each of whom compared lines in the presence of six to eight opponents, is plotted in the gray curve. The accuracy of judgment not under pressure is indicated in black.

FIGURE 1.5
Size of majority that opposed them had an effect on the subjects. With a single opponent, the subject erred only 3.6 percent of the time; with two opponents he erred 13.6 percent; with three, 31.8 percent; with four, 35.1 percent; with six, 35.2 percent; with seven, 37.1 percent; with nine, 35.1 percent; with fifteen, 31.2 percent.

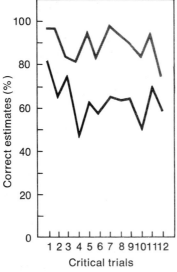

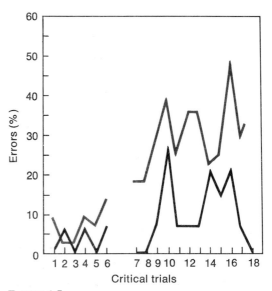

FIGURE 1.6
Two subjects supporting each other against a majority made fewer errors (*gray curve*) than one subject did against a majority (*black curve*).

FIGURE 1.7
Partner left subject after six trials in a single experiment. The gray curve shows the error of the subject when the partner "deserted" to the majority. The black curve shows error when partner merely left the room.

and extremes of yielding disappear. Moreover, most of the errors the subjects do make are moderate, rather than flagrant. In short, the dissenter largely controls the choice of errors. To this extent the subjects broke away from the majority even while bending to it.

On the other hand, when the dissenter always chose the line that was more flagrantly different from the standard, the results were of quite a different kind. The extremist dissenter produced a remarkable freeing of the subjects; their errors dropped to only 9 percent. Furthermore, all the errors were of the moderate variety. We were able to conclude that dissent *per se* increased independence and moderated the errors that occurred, and that the direction of dissent exerted consistent effects.

In all the foregoing experiments each subject was observed only in a single setting. We now turned to studying the effects upon a given individual of a change in the situation to which he was exposed. The first experiment examined the consequences of losing or gaining a partner. The instructed partner began by answering correctly on the first six trials. With his support the subject usually resisted pressure from the majority: eighteen of twenty-seven subjects were completely independent. But after six trials the partner joined the majority. As soon as he did so, there was an abrupt rise in the subjects' errors. Their submission to the majority was just about as frequent as when the minority subject was opposed by a unanimous majority throughout.

It was surprising to find that the experience of having had a partner and of having braved the majority opposition with him had failed to strengthen the individuals' independence. Questioning at the conclusion of the experiment suggested that we had overlooked an important circumstance; namely, the strong specific effect of "desertion" by the partner to the other side. We therefore changed the conditions so that the partner would simply leave the group at the proper point. (To allay suspicion it was announced in advance that he had an appointment with the dean.) In this form of the experiment, the partner's effect outlasted his presence. The errors increased after his departure, but less markedly than after a partner switched to the majority.

In a variant of this procedure the trials began with the majority unanimously giving correct answers. Then they gradually broke away until on the sixth trial the naive subject was alone and the group unanimously against him. As long as the subject had anyone on his side, he was almost invariably independent, but as soon as he found himself alone, the tendency to conform to the majority rose abruptly.

As might be expected, an individual's resistance to group pressure in these experiments depends to a considerable degree on how wrong the majority is. We varied the discrepancy between the standard line and the other lines systematically, with the hope of reaching a point where the error of the majority would be so glaring that every subject would repudiate it and choose independently. In this we regretfully did not succeed. Even when the difference between the lines was seven inches, there were still some who yielded to the error of the majority.

The study provides clear answers to a few relatively simple questions, and it raises many others that await investigation. We would like to know the degree of consistency of persons in situations which differ in content and structure. If consistency of independence or conformity in behavior is shown to be a fact, how is it functionally related to qualities of character and personality? In what ways is independence related to sociological or cultural conditions? Are leaders more independent than other people, or are they adept at following their followers? These and many other questions may perhaps be answerable by investigations of the type described here.

Life in society requires consensus as an indispensable condition. But consensus, to be productive, requires that each individual contribute independently out of his experience and insight. When consensus comes under the dominance of conformity, the social process is polluted and the individual at the same time surrenders the powers on which his functioning as a feeling and thinking being depends. That we have found the tendency to conformity in our society so strong that reasonably intelligent and well-meaning young people are willing to call white black is a matter of concern. It raises questions about our ways of education and about the values that guide our conduct.

Yet anyone inclined to draw too pessimistic conclusions from this report would do well to remind himself that the capacities for independence are not to be underestimated. He may also draw some consolation from a further observation: those who participated in this challenging experiment agreed nearly without exception that independence was preferable to conformity.

References

ASCH, S. E. Effects of group pressure upon the modification and distortion of judgments. *Groups, leadership, and men,* Harold Guetzdow (ed.). Carnegie Press, 1951.

ASCH, SOLOMON E. *Social psychology.* Prentice-Hall, Inc., 1952.

MILLER, N. E., AND DOLLARD, J. *Social learning and imitation.* Yale University Press, 1941.

2

Status Factors in Pedestrian Violation of Traffic Signals

*Monroe Lefkowitz, Robert R. Blake, and
Jane Srygley Mouton*

A social factor of importance in determining the reaction a given prohibition will evoke—whether conformance or violation—is the respondent's knowledge of the behavior the restriction has produced in others (1). More people will conform when they see others conforming to a restriction, while knowledge that violations occur will increase the probability of infraction. The validity of these statements for a typical situation involving a prohibition has been demonstrated by an experiment dealing with reactions to signs forbidding entry to a building (2). When test subjects saw that another person violated the sign, they also violated it significantly more frequently than when they saw that another person had reacted in compliance with the prohibition.

PROBLEM

The power of others to increase or decrease the strength of a prohibition is probably a function of "who the others are." Blake and Mouton (1) proposed that the perceived status of the person whose behavior serves as a model will be an important factor in determining the rate of violation. "High status figures known to violate a given law will have greater influence in weakening it than if only low status people are known to be violators. The same holds for conformance. When high status individuals are known to accept the prohibition it should have the effect of making the law more acceptable than if only low status people are known to conform."

The present paper is concerned with testing the validity of the statements relating status of the violator who serves as a model to the reaction a prohibition provokes in others. Perceived status quality of the person whose behavior toward a prohibition served as model for others was systematically varied. The basic hypothesis was that a naive subject facing a prohibition will more likely violate or conform when a high status person serves as a model for conformance or violation than when a low status person does so.

EXPERIMENTAL SITUATION

Prohibition Situation

The prohibition was a pedestrian traffic signal that flashed from "wait" to "walk" alternatively with the red, amber, and green signals regulating the flow of motor traffic. During every fifty-five-second interval, the "wait" signal flashed for forty seconds and the "walk" for fifteen. Observations were made during the "wait" signal when the sign forbade movement across the street.

A counterbalanced design was employed with respect to daily time periods for observations and locations of the "wait-walk" signals. Data were collected on three successive afternoons during the hours from 12 to 1, 2 to 3, and 4 to 5, respectively. The "wait-walk" signals were located at three street corners at right angles to the main thoroughfare in the central commercial section of Austin, Texas. An observer located approximately 100 feet away from the corner recorded the data. Police officers were not on duty at the locations during the time intervals when data were collected, but arrangements for conducting the experiments had been made with the Traffic Department of the Austin Police Department.

Subjects

With the exception of children and physically handicapped people, the 2103 pedestrians passing the three locations during the three test intervals served as subjects.

Covariations in Perceived Status of and Violation by the Model

Two aspects of social background were covaried in the experimental design suggested by Helson's adaptation-level theory (3). One was the behavior of an experimenter's model who either complied with or violated the "wait" signal. The second was the perceived status of the experimenter's model. The experimenter's model was a thirty-one-year-old male. By changing his clothing the model's perceived status was either high or low. For half the conformance reactions and half the violation responses, the experimenter's model was dressed in clothing intended to typify a high status person, with a freshly pressed suit, shined shoes, white shirt, tie and straw hat. Well-worn scuffed shoes, soiled patched trousers and an unpressed blue denim shirt served to define the model as a low status person for the remaining half of the conforming and violating conditions. The rate of pedestrian violation observed during the same time intervals and at the same test locations with the experimenter's model absent served as the neutral or control condition.

The experimental design permitted both social background factors to be varied simultaneously. For example, at 12:00 noon on one day the experimenter's model, dressed in one status attire, conformed to the "wait" stimulus by crossing the street when the signal changed to "walk." The procedure was repeated for each of five trials, with the number of subjects conforming or violating recorded. Following these trials, pedestrians were observed for five additional trials under the neutral condition in which the experimenter's model was absent. The experimenter's model returned to the scene dressed in the other status attire and violated the "wait" signal by crossing the street once at approximately the midpoint of each "wait" interval for the same number of trials. The inverse order for conforming and violating trials was followed the next day, and so on.

Criteria for Scoring Violation

Two criteria were used in assessing whether pedestrians were violating the "wait" signal. Only subjects standing with the experimenter's model before he crossed the street were included in the data. Pedestrians reaching or passing the white line in the center of the street while the signal still flashed "wait" were recorded as violators. By using the center line as the criterion for scoring violation and conformity, errors of judgment as to pedestrian intent were reduced to a minimum. All others meeting the first criterion but not the second were recorded as conforming with the prohibition.

RESULTS

Results from the several experimental and control conditions are presented in Tables 2.1 and 2.2 Examination of column totals demonstrates that the presence of a model of either high or low perceived status complying with the signal prohibition did not increase the rate of pedestrian conformance beyond that observed for the control condition. Since the rate of conformance under neutral conditions was so high (99 percent), the present study did not permit a valid test of the proposition that seeing another person conform increased rate of conformity ($\chi^2 = 1.30$, 1 df). However, the presence of a model of either high or low perceived status violating the prohibition increased the pedestrian violation rate above that for the control condition. The χ^2 (48.04, 1 df) between control and experimental conditions is significant beyond the 1 percent level of confidence. This finding is consistent with results from the comparable part of the experiment dealing with the violation of a sign forbidding the entry of a building (2).

The relationship between status and violation is shown in cell frequencies across rows of Table 2.1. When a perceived high status model was seen to violate the prohibition, 14 percent of pedestrians violated the signal restricting movement. The χ^2 of 44.59 (1 df) for the difference in pedestrian violation between the high status violation and the control condition, and the χ^2

TABLE 2.1
Reactions of test subjects to experimental treatments and control conditions

Status attire of experimenter's model	Reactions of experimenter's model							
	Conforming		Control*		Violating		Total	
	Pedestrian conforms	Pedestrian violates	Pedestrian conforms	Pedestrian violates	Pedestrian conforms	Pedestrian violates	Pedestrian conforms	Pedestrian violates
High N**	351	3	347	3	250	40	948	46
%†	99	01	99	01	86	14	95	05
Low N	420	1	395	5	276	12	1091	18
%	100	00	99	01	96	04	98	02
Total N	771	4	742	8	526	52	2039	64
%	99	01	99	01	91	09	97	03

*The entries in the high and low status rows represent control observations made under conditions identical with the observations for the high and low status conditions except that the experimenter's model was absent.
**The unequal N's are due to slight variations in the flow of pedestrians under counterbalanced test conditions.
†Figures rounded to the nearest percentage.

TABLE 2.2
χ^2 values for differences between conditions

Conditions	χ^2	*df*	Level of significance
Conforming model vs. control	1.30	1	–
Violating model vs. control	48.04	1	.01
High status violating model vs. control	44.59	1	.01
Low status violating model vs. control	3.88	1	.05
High status condition: violating model vs. conforming model	44.56	1	.01
Low status condition: violating model vs. conforming model	16.22	1	.01
Violating condition: high status model vs. low status model	16.61	1	.01

of 44.56 (1 *df*) for the difference between perceived high status violation and perceived high status conformance are both significant beyond the 1 percent level. The results demonstrate that when a high status person violated a prohibition, there was a significant increase in the rate of violation by pedestrians. An examination of differences in pedestrian violations that were provoked by a violating person of low status contrasted with both a low status person who conforms ($\chi^2 = 16.22$, 1 *df*) and also with the control condition where the low status person was absent ($\chi^2 = 3.88$, 1 *df*) leads to the conclusion that the low status violator increased the pedestrian violation rate beyond that typical for either of the other two conditions. Such findings demonstrate that with a person whose perceived status quality was either high or low acting as a model by violating a prohibition, the pedestrian violation rate was increased significantly beyond that occurring when the model either conformed or was absent.

From the standpoint of the hypothesis stated in the introduction, the significant comparison is that between violation rates when the status of the violator was shifted from low to high. Changing the status of the violator from low to high through creating differences in attire increased pedestrian violations from 4 percent to 14 percent. The χ^2 of 16.61 (1 *df*) for this difference in violation rate is significant at the 1 percent level. Such findings point to the conclusion that if a situation contains a violator, a significantly greater number of pedestrians will violate the signal when the status model is high rather than low. This finding confirms the prediction given in the introduction. The behavior of others is not of equal weight in determining the readiness to violate a prohibition. Rather the higher the status of the perceived violator the greater the reduction in conformance to a prohibition by pedestrians in the same situation.

SUMMARY

Pedestrians violated the prohibition of an automatic traffic signal more often in the presence of an experimenter's model who violated the prohibition than when the latter conformed or was absent. Significantly more violations occurred among pedestrians when the nonconforming model was dressed to represent high social status than when his attire suggested lower status.

References

1. BLAKE, R. R., AND MOUTON, JANE S. Present and future implications of social psychology for law and lawyers. *Symposium Issue, Emory Univ. J. Public Law,* 1955, **3,** 352–369.
2. FREED, A. M., CHANDLER, P. J., MOUTON, JANE S., AND BLAKE, R. R. Stimulus and background factors in sign violation. *J. Pers.,* 1955, **23,** 499.
3. HELSON, H. Adaptation-level as a basis for a quantitative theory of frames of reference. *Psychol. Rev.,* 1948, **55,** 297–313.

3

Behavioral Study of Obedience

Stanley Milgram

This article describes a procedure for the study of destructive obedience in the laboratory. It consists of ordering a naive S to administer increasingly more severe punishment to a victim in the context of a learning experiment. Punishment is administered by means of a shock generator with thirty graded switches ranging from Slight Shock to Danger: Severe Shock. The victim is a confederate of the E. The primary dependent variable is the maximum shock the S is willing to administer before he refuses to continue further. Twenty-six Ss obeyed the experimental commands fully, and administered the highest shock on the generator. Fourteen Ss broke off the experiment at some point after the victim protested and refused to provide further answers. The procedure created extreme levels of nervous tension in some Ss. Profuse sweating, trembling and stuttering were typical expressions of this emotional disturbance. One unexpected sign of tension — yet to be explained — was the regular occurrence of nervous laughter, which in some Ss developed into uncontrollable seizures. The variety of interesting behavioral dynamics observed in the experiment, the reality of the situation for the S, and the possibility of parametric variation within the framework of the procedure, point to the fruitfulness of further study.

Obedience is as basic an element in the structure of social life as one can point to. Some system of authority is a requirement of all communal living, and it is only the man dwelling in isolation who is not forced to respond, through defiance or submission, to the commands of others. Obedience, as a determinant of behavior, is of particular relevance to our time. It has been reliably established that from 1933–1945 millions of innocent persons were systematically slaughtered on command. Gas chambers were built, death

Reprinted with permission from the author and *The Journal of Abnormal and Social Psychology,* Vol. 67, No. 4, 1963. Copyright 1963 by the American Psychological Association.

This research was supported by a grant (NSF G–17916) from the National Science Foundation. Exploratory studies conducted in 1960 were supported by a grant from the Higgins Fund at Yale University. The research assistance of Alan C. Elms and Jon Wayland is gratefully acknowledged.

camps were guarded, daily quotas of corpses were produced with the same efficiency as the manufacture of appliances. These inhumane policies may have originated in the mind of a single person, but they could only be carried out on a massive scale if a very large number of persons obeyed orders.

Obedience is the psychological mechanism that links individual action to political purpose. It is the dispositional cement that binds men to systems of authority. Facts of recent history and observation in daily life suggest that for many persons obedience may be a deeply ingrained behavior tendency, indeed, a prepotent impulse overriding training in ethics, sympathy, and moral conduct. C. P. Snow (1961) points to its importance when he writes:

> When you think of the long and gloomy history of man, you will find more hideous crimes have been committed in the name of obedience than have ever been committed in the name of rebellion. If you doubt that, read William Shirer's "Rise and Fall of the Third Reich." The German Officer Corps were brought up in the most rigorous code of obedience . . . in the name of obedience they were party to, and assisted in, the most wicked large scale actions in the history of the world [p. 24].

While the particular form of obedience dealt with in the present study has its antecedents in these episodes, it must not be thought all obedience entails acts of aggression against others. Obedience serves numerous productive functions. Indeed, the very life of society is predicated on its existence. Obedience may be ennobling and educative and refer to acts of charity and kindness, as well as to destruction.

General Procedure

A procedure was devised which seems useful as a tool for studying obedience (Milgram, 1961). It consists of ordering a naive subject to administer electric shock to a victim. A simulated shock generator is used, with 30 clearly marked voltage levels that range from 15 to 450 volts. The instrument bears verbal designations that range from Slight Shock to Danger: Severe Shock. The responses of the victim, who is a trained confederate of the experimenter, are standardized. The orders to administer shocks are given to the naive subject in the context of a "learning experiment" ostensibly set up to study the effects of punishment on memory. As the experiment proceeds the naive subject is commanded to administer increasingly more intense shocks to the victim, even to the point of reaching the level marked Danger: Severe Shock. Internal resistances become stronger, and at a certain point the subject refuses to go on with the experiment. Behavior prior to this rupture is considered "obedience," in that the subject complies with the commands of the experimenter. The point of rupture is the act of disobedience. A quantitative value is assigned to the subject's performance based on the maximum intensity shock he is willing to administer before he refuses to participate further. Thus for any particular subject and for any particular experimental condition the degree of obedience may be specified with a numerical value. The crux of the study is to systematically vary the factors believed to alter the degree of obedience to the experimental commands.

The technique allows important variables to be manipulated at several points in the experiment. One may vary aspects of the source of command, content and form of command, instrumentalities for its execution, target object, general social setting, etc. The problem, therefore, is not one of designing increasingly more numerous experimental conditions, but of selecting those that best illuminate the *process* of obedience from the sociopsychological standpoint.

Related Studies

The inquiry bears an important relation to philosophic analyses of obedience and authority (Arendt, 1958; Friedrich, 1958; Weber, 1947), an early experimental study of obedience by Frank (1944), studies in "authoritarianism" (Adorno, Frenkel-Brunswik, Levinson, and Sanford, 1950; Rokeach, 1961), and a recent series of analytic and empirical studies in social power (Cartwright, 1959). It owes much to the long concern with *suggestion* in social psychology, both in its normal forms (e.g., Binet, 1900) and in its clinical manifestations (Charcot, 1881). But it derives, in the first instance, from direct observation of a social fact; the individual who is commanded by a legitimate authority ordinarily obeys. Obedience comes easily and often. It is a ubiquitous and indispensable feature of social life.

METHOD

Subjects

The subjects were 40 males between the ages of 20 and 50, drawn from New Haven and the surrounding communities. Subjects were obtained by a newspaper advertisement and direct mail solicitation. Those who responded to the appeal believed they were to participate in a study of memory and learning at Yale Univeristy. A wide range of occupations is represented in the sample. Typical subjects were postal clerks, high school teachers,

TABLE 3.1
Distribution of age and occupational types in the experiment

Occupations	20–29 years n	20–39 years n	40–50 years n	Percentage of total (occupations)
Workers, skilled and unskilled	4	5	6	37.5
Sales, business, and white-collar	3	6	7	40.0
Professional	1	5	3	22.5
Percentage of total (age)	20	40	40	

Note: Total $N = 40$.

salesmen, engineers, and laborers. Subjects ranged in educational level from one who had not finished elementary school, to those who had doctorate and other professional degrees. They were paid $4.50 for their participation in the experiment. However, subjects were told that payment was simply for coming to the laboratory, and that the money was theirs no matter what happened after they arrived. Table 3.1 shows the proportion of age and occupational types assigned to the experimental condition.

Personnel and Locale

The experiment was conducted on the grounds of Yale University in the elegant interaction laboratory. (This detail is relevant to the perceived legitimacy of the experiment. In further variations, the experiment was dissociated from the university, with consequences for performance.) The role of experimenter was played by a 31-year-old high school teacher of biology. His manner was impassive, and his appearance somewhat stern throughout the experiment. He was dressed in a gray technician's coat. The victim was played by a 47-year-old accountant, trained for the role; he was of Irish-American stock, whom most observers found mild-mannered and likable.

Procedure

One naive subject and one victim (an accomplice) performed in each experiment. A pretext had to be devised that would justify the administration of electric shock by the naive subject. This was effectively accomplished by the cover story. After a general introduction on the presumed relation between punishment and learning, subjects were told:

But actually, we know *very little* about the effect of punishment on learning, because almost no truly scientific studies have been made of it in human beings.

For instance, we don't know how *much* punishment is best for learning—and we don't know how much difference it makes as to who is giving the punishment, whether an adult learns best from a younger or an older person than himself—or many things of that sort.

So in this study we are bringing together a number of adults of different occupations and ages. And we're asking some of them to be teachers and some of them to be learners.

We want to find out just what effect different people have on each other as teachers and learners, and also what effect *punishment* will have on learning in this situation.

Therefore, I'm going to ask one of you to be the teacher here tonight and the other one to be the learner.

Does either of you have a preference?

Subjects then drew slips of paper from a hat to determine who would be the teacher and who would be the learner in the experiment. The drawing was rigged so that the naive subject was always the teacher and the accomplice always the learner. (Both slips contained the word "Teacher.") Immediately after the drawing the teacher and learner were taken to an adjacent room and the learner was strapped into an "electric chair" apparatus.

The experimenter explained that the straps were to prevent excessive movement while the learner was being shocked. The effect was to make it impossible for him to escape from the situation. An electrode was attached to the learner's wrist, and electrode paste was applied "to avoid blisters and burns." Sujects were told that the electrode was attached to the shock generator in the adjoining room.

In order to improve credibility the experimenter declared, in response to a question by the learner: "Although the shocks can be extremely painful, they cause no permanent tissue damage."

Learning task. The lesson administered by the subject was a paired-associate learning task. The subject read a series of word pairs to the learner, and then read the first word of the pair along with four terms. The learner was to indicate which of the four terms had originally been paired with the first word. He communicated his answer by pressing one of four switches in front of him, which in turn lit up one of four numbered quadrants in an answer-box located atop the shock generator.

Shock generator. The instrument panel consists of 30 lever switches set in a horizontal line. Each switch is clearly labeled with a voltage designation that ranges from 15 to 450 volts. There is a 15-volt increment from one switch to the next going from left to right. In addition, the following verbal designations are clearly indicated for groups of four switches going from left to right: Slight Shock, Moderate Shock, Strong Shock, Very Strong Shock, Intense Shock, Extreme Intensity Shock, Danger: Severe Shock. (Two switches after this last designation are simply marked XXX.)

Upon depressing a switch: a pilot light corresponding to each switch is illuminated in bright red; an electric buzzing is heard; an electric blue light, labeled "voltage energizer," flashes; the dial on the voltage meter swings to the right; various relay clicks are sounded.

The upper left-hand corner of the generator is labeled Shock Generator, Type ZLB, Dyson Instrument Company, Waltham, Mass. Output 15 Volts — 450 Volts.

Details of the instrument were carefully handled to insure an appearance of authenticity. The panel was engraved by precision industrial engravers, and all components were of high quality. No subject in the experiment suspected that the instrument was merely a simulated shock generator.[1]

Sample shock. Each naive subject is given a sample shock on the shock generator, prior to beginning his run as teacher. This shock is always 45 volts, and is applied by pressing the third switch of the generator. The shock is applied to the wrist of the naive subject, and has its source in a 45-volt battery wired into the generator. This further convinces the subject of the authenticity of the generator.

Shock instructions. The subject is told to administer a shock to the learner each time he gives a wrong response. Moreover — and this is the key command — the subject is instructed to "move one level higher on the shock generator each time the learner flashes a wrong answer." He is also instructed to announce the voltage level before administering a shock. This serves to continually remind subjects of the increasing intensity of shocks administered to the learner.

Preliminary and regular run. Pretests revealed that the procedure of reading words and administering shocks requires some practice before it can be handled smoothly. Therefore, immediately preceding the regular run, the

---

[1]A related technique, making use of a shock generator, was reported by Buss (1961) for the study of aggression in the laboratory. Despite the considerable similarity of technical detail in the experimental procedures, both investigators proceeded in ignorance of the other's work. Milgram provided plans and photographs of his shock generator, experimental procedure, and first results in a report to the National Science Foundation in January 1961. This report received only limited circulation. Buss reported his procedure six months later, but to a wider audience. Subsequently, technical information and reports were exchanged. The present article was first received in the editor's office on December 27, 1961; it was resubmitted with deletions on July 27, 1962.

teacher is given a preliminary series of 10 words to read to the learner. There are 3 neutral words in the practice series (i.e., words that the learner answers correctly), so that shocks are administered for 7 of the words, with the maximum shock at 105 volts (moderate shock). Almost all subjects master the procedure by the time the preliminary run is over.

Subjects are then presented with a second list, and are told that the procedure is the same as for the first list; the experimenter adds, however:

> When you get to the bottom of the list, repeat it over again, and continue giving shocks, until the learner has learned all the pairs correctly.

The experimenter instructs the subject to

> start from 15 volts and increase the shock level one step each time the learner gives a wrong answer.

Feedback from the victim. In all conditions the learner gives a predetermined set of responses to the word pair test, based on a schedule of approximately three wrong answers to one correct answer. In the present experimental condition no vocal response or other sign of protest is heard from the learner until Shock Level 300 is reached. When the 300-volt shock is administered, the learner pounds on the wall of the room in which he is bound to the electric chair. The pounding can be heard by the subject. From this point on, the learner's answers no longer appear on the four-way panel.

At this juncture, subjects ordinarily turn to the experimenter for guidance. The experimenter instructs the subject to treat the absence of a response as a wrong answer, and to shock the subject according to the usual schedule. He advises the subjects to allow 5–10 seconds before considering no response as a wrong answer, and to increase the shock level one step each time the learner fails to respond correctly. The learner's pounding is repeated after the 315-volt shock is administered; afterwards he is not heard from, nor do his answers reappear on the four-way signal box.

Experimenter feedback. At various points in the experiment the subject may turn to the experimenter for advice on whether he should continue to administer shocks. Or he may indicate that he does not wish to go on. It was important to standardize the experimenter's responses to these inquiries and reactions.

If the subject indicated his unwillingness to go on, the experimenter responded with a sequence of "prods," using as many as necessary to bring the subject into line.

> Prod 1: Please continue. *or* Please go on.
> Prod 2: The experiment requires that you continue.
> Prod 3: It is absolutely essential that you continue.
> Prod 4: You have no other choice, you *must* go on.

The prods were always made in sequence: Only if Prod 1 had been unsuccessful, could Prod 2 be used. If the subject refused to obey the experimenter after Prod 4, the experiment was terminated. The experimenter's tone of voice was at all times firm, but not impolite. The sequence was begun anew on each occasion that the subject balked or showed reluctance to follow orders.

Special prods. If the subject asked if the learner was liable to suffer permanent physical injury, the experimenter said:

> Although the shocks may be painful, there is no permanent tissue damage, so please go on. [Followed by Prods 2, 3, and 4 if necessary.]

If the subject said that the learner did not want to go on, the experimenter replied:

> Whether the learner likes it or not, you must go on until he has learned all the word pairs correctly. So please go on. [Followed by Prods 2, 3, and 4 if necessary.]

Dependent Measures

The primary dependent measure for any subject is the maximum shock he administers before he refuses to go any further. In principle this may vary from 0 (for a subject who refuses to administer even the first shock) to 30 (for a subject who administers the highest shock on the generator). A subject who breaks off the experiment at any point prior to administering the thirtieth shock level is termed a *defiant* subject. One who complies with experimental commands fully, and proceeds to administer all shock levels commanded, is termed an *obedient* subject.

Further records. With few exceptions, experimental sessions were recorded on magnetic tape. Occasional photographs were taken through one-way mirrors. Notes were kept on any unusual behavior occurring during the course of the experiments. On occasion, additional observers were directed to write objective descriptions of the subjects' behavior. The latency and duration of shocks were measured by accurate timing devices.

Interview and dehoax. Following the experiment, subjects were interviewed; open-ended questions, projective measures, and attitude scales were employed. After the interview, procedures were undertaken to assure that the subject would leave the laboratory in a state of well being. A friendly reconciliation was arranged between the subject and the victim, and an effort was made to reduce any tensions that arose as a result of the experiment.

RESULTS

Preliminary Notions

Before giving an account of the experimental results, it is instructive to consider how persons predict others will perform when commanded to administer powerful shocks to another person. Fourteen Yale seniors, all psychology majors, were provided with a detailed description of the experimental situation. They were asked to reflect carefully on it, and to predict the behavior of 100 hypothetical subjects. More specifically, they were instructed to plot the distribution of obedience of "100 Americans of diverse occupations, and ranging in age from 20 to 50 years," who were placed in the experimental situation.

There was considerable agreement among the respondents on the expected behavior of hypothetical subjects. All respondents predicted that only an insignificant minority would go through to the end of the shock series. (The estimates ranged from 0 to 3 percent; i.e., the most "pessimistic" member of the class predicted that of 100 persons, 3 would continue through to the most potent shock available on the shock generator—450 volts.) The class mean was 1.2 percent. The question was also posed informally to colleagues of the author, and the most general feeling was that few if any subjects would go beyond the designation Very Strong Shock.

Result of Experiment I

Subjects accept situation. With few exceptions subjects were convinced of the reality of the experimental situation, that they were administering shocks to another person, and the most potent shocks were extremely painful. In the post-experimental interview subjects were asked: "How painful to the learner were the last few shocks that you administered to him?" Subjects were instructed to indicate their answers on a printed 14-point scale ranging from "Not at all painful" to "Extremely painful." The modal response was 14 (Extremely painful) with the mean at 13.42.

Signs of extreme tension. Many subjects showed signs of nervousness in the experimental situation, and especially upon administering the more powerful shocks. In a large number of cases the degree of tension reached extremes that are rarely seen in sociopsychological laboratory studies. Subjects were observed to sweat, tremble, stutter, bite their lips, groan, and dig their fingernails into their flesh. These were characteristic rather than exceptional responses to the experiment.

One sign of tension was the regular occurrence of nervous laughing fits. Fourteen of the 40 subjects showed definite signs of nervous laughter and smiling. The laughter seemed entirely out of place, even bizarre. Full-blown, uncontrollable seizures were observed for 3 subjects. On one occasion we observed a seizure so violently convulsive that it was necessary to call a halt to the experiment. The subject, a 46-year-old encyclopedia salesman, was seriously embarrassed by his untoward and uncontrollable behavior. In the post-experimental interviews subjects took pains to point out that they were not sadistic types, and that the laughter did not mean they enjoyed shocking the victim.

Distribution of scores. It had been conjectured that persons would not, in general, agree to administer shocks beyond the level designated as Very Strong Shock. The distribution of maximum shocks for this experiment is shown in Table 3.2. The obtained distribution of scores deviates radically from the prediction.

Upon command of the experimenter, each of the 40 subjects went beyond the expected breakoff point. No subject stopped prior to administering Shock Level 20. (At this level—300 volts—the victim kicks on the wall and no longer provides answers to the teacher's multiple-choice questions.)

Of the 40 subjects, 5 refused to obey the experimental commands beyond the 300-volt level. Four more subjects administered one further shock, and then refused to go on. Two broke off at the 330-volt level, and 1 each at 345, 360, and 375 volts. Thus a total of 14 subjects defied the experimenter. It is instructive to reprint their remarks at the point of defiance, as transcribed from the tape recordings:

> [0124] I think he's trying to communicate, he's knocking . . . Well it's not fair to shock the guy . . . these are terrific volts. I don't think this is very humane . . . Oh, I can't go on with this; no, this isn't right. It's a hell of an experiment. The guy is suffering in there. No, I don't want to go on. This is crazy. [Subject refused to administer more shocks.]

> [0123]He's banging in there. I'm gonna chicken out. I'd like to continue, but I can't do that to a man . . . I'm sorry I can't do that to a man. I'll hurt his heart. You take your check . . . No really, I couldn't do it.

These subjects were frequently in a highly agitated and even angered state. Sometimes, verbal protest was at a minimum, and the subject simply got up from his chair in front of the shock generator, and indicated that he wished to leave the laboratory.

Of the 40 subjects, 26 obeyed the orders of the experimenter to the end, proceeding to punish the victim until they reached the most potent shock available on the shock generator. At that point, the experimenter called a halt to the session. (The maximum shock is labeled 450 volts, and is two steps beyond the designation: Danger: Severe Shock.) Although obedient subjects continued to administer shocks, they often did so under extreme stress. Some expressed reluctance to administer shocks beyond the 300-volt

TABLE 3.2
Distribution of breakoff points

Verbal designation and voltage indication	Number of subjects for whom this was maximum shock
Slight Shock	
15	0
30	0
45	0
60	0
Moderate Shock	
75	0
90	0
105	0
120	0
Strong Shock	
135	0
150	0
165	0
180	0
Very Strong Shock	
195	0
210	0
225	0
240	0
Intense Shock	
255	0
270	0
285	0
300	5
Extreme Intensity Shock	
315	4
330	2
345	1
360	1
Danger: Severe Shock	
375	1
390	0
405	0
420	0
XXX	
435	0
450	26

level, and displayed fears similar to those who defied the experimenter; yet they obeyed.

After the maximum shocks had been delivered, and the experimenter called a halt to the proceedings, many obedient subjects heaved sighs of relief, mopped their brows, rubbed their fingers over their eyes, or nervously fumbled cigarettes. Some shook their heads, apparently in regret. Some subjects had remained calm throughout the experiment, and displayed only minimal signs of tension from beginning to end.

DISCUSSION

The experiment yielded two findings that were surprising. The first finding concerns the sheer strength of obedient tendencies manifested in this situation. Subjects have learned from childhood that it is a fundamental breach of moral conduct to hurt another person against his will. Yet, 26 subjects abandon this tenet in following the instructions of an authority who has no special powers to enforce his commands. To disobey would bring no material loss to the subject; no punishment would ensue. It is clear from the remarks and outward behavior of many participants that in punishing the victim they are often acting against their own values. Subjects often expressed deep disapproval of shocking a man in the face of his objections, and others denounced it as stupid and senseless. Yet the majority complied with the experimental commands. This outcome was surprising from two perspectives: first, from the standpoint of predictions made in the questionnaire described earlier. (Here, however, it is possible that the remoteness of the respondents from the actual situation, and the difficulty of conveying to them the concrete details of the experiment, could account for the serious underestimation of obedience.)

But the results were also unexpected to persons who observed the experiment in progress, through one-way mirrors. Observers often uttered expressions of disbelief upon seeing a subject administer more powerful shocks to the victim. These persons had a full acquaintance with the details of the situation, and yet systematically underestimated the amount of obedience that subjects would display.

The second unanticipated effect was the extraordinary tension generated by the procedures. One might suppose that a subject would simply break off or continue as his conscience dictated. Yet, this is very far from what happened. There were striking reactions of tension and emotional strain. One observer related:

I observed a mature and initially poised businessman enter the laboratory smiling and confident. Within 20 minutes he was reduced to a twitching, stuttering wreck, who was rapidly approaching a point of nervous collapse. He constantly pulled on his earlobe, and twisted his hands. At one point he pushed his fist into his forehead and muttered: "Oh God, let's stop it." And yet he continued to respond to every word of the experimenter, and obeyed to the end.

Any understanding of the phenomenon of obedience must rest on an analysis of the particular conditions in which it occurs. The following features of the experiment go some distance in explaining the high amount of obedience observed in the situation.

1. The experiment is sponsored by and takes place on the grounds of an institution of unimpeachable reputation, Yale University. It may be reasonably presumed that the personnel are competent and reputable. The importance of this background authority is now being studied by conducting a series of experiments outside of New Haven, and without any visible ties to the university.

2. The experiment is, on the face of it, designed to attain a worthy purpose—advancement of knowledge about learning and memory. Obedience occurs not as an end in itself, but as an instrumental element in a situation that the subject construes as significant, and meaningful. He may not be able to see its full significance, but he may properly assume that the experimenter does.

3. The subject perceives that the victim has voluntarily submitted to the authority system of the experimenter. He is not (at first) an unwilling captive impressed for involuntary service. He has taken the trouble to come to the laboratory presumably to aid the experimental research. That he later becomes an involuntary subject does not alter the fact that, initially, he consented to participate without qualification. Thus he has in some degree incurred an obligation toward the experimenter.

4. The subject, too, has entered the experiment voluntarily, and perceives himself under obligation to aid the experimenter. He has made a commitment, and to disrupt the experiment is a repudiation of this initial promise of aid.

5. Certain features of the procedure strengthen the subject's sense of obligation to the experimenter. For one, he has been paid for coming to the laboratory. In part this is canceled out by the experimenter's statement that:

> Of course, as in all experiments, the money is yours simply for coming to the laboratory. From this point on, no matter what happens, the money is yours.[2]

---

[2]Forty-three subjects, undergraduates at Yale University, were run in the experiment without payment. The results are very similar to those obtained with paid subjects.

6. From the subject's standpoint, the fact that he is the teacher and the other man the learner is purely a chance consequence (it is determined by drawing lots) and he, the subject, ran the same risk as the other man in being assigned the role of learner. Since the assignment of positions in the experiment was achieved by fair means, the learner is deprived of any basis of complaint on this count. (A similar situation obtains in Army units, in which — in the absence of volunteers — a particularly dangerous mission may be assigned by drawing lots, and the unlucky soldier is expected to bear his misfortune with sportsmanship.)

7. There is, at best, ambiguity with regard to the prerogatives of a psychologist and the corresponding rights of his subject. There is a vagueness of expectation concerning what a psychologist may require of his subject, and when he is overstepping acceptable limits. Moreover, the experiment occurs in a closed setting, and thus provides no opportunity for the subject to remove these ambiguities by discussion with others. There are few standards that seem directly applicable to the situation, which is a novel one for most subjects.

8. The subjects are assured that the shocks administered to the subject are "painful but not dangerous." Thus they assume that the discomfort caused the victim is momentary, while the scientific gains resulting from the experiment are enduring.

9. Through Shock Level 20 the victim continues to provide answers on the signal box. The subject may construe this as a sign that the victim is still willing to "play the game." It is only after Shock Level 20 that the victim repudiates the rules completely, refusing to answer further.

These features help to explain the high amount of obedience obtained in this experiment. Many of the arguments raised need not remain matters of speculation, but can be reduced to testable propositions to be confirmed or disproved by further experiments.[3]

The following features of the experiment concern the nature of the conflict which the subject faces.

10. The subject is placed in a position in which he must respond to the competing demands of two persons: the experimenter and the victim. The conflict must be resolved by meeting the demands of one or the other; satisfaction of the victim and the experimenter are mutually exclusive. Moreover, the resolution must take the form of a highly visible action, that of continuing to shock the victim or breaking off the experiment. Thus the subject is forced into a public conflict that does not permit any completely satisfactory solution.

---

[3] A series of recently completed experiments employing the obedience paradigm is reported in Milgram (1964).

11. While the demands of the experimenter carry the weight of scientific authority, the demands of the victim spring from his personal experience of pain and suffering. The two claims need not be regarded as equally pressing and legitimate. The experimenter seeks an abstract scientific datum; the victim cries out for relief from physical suffering caused by the subject's actions.

12. The experiment gives the subject little time for reflection. The conflict comes on rapidly. It is only minutes after the subject has been seated before the shock generator that the victim begins his protests. Moreover, the subject perceives that he has gone through but two-thirds of the shock levels at the time the subject's first protests are heard. Thus he understands that the conflict will have a persistent aspect to it, and may well become more intense as increasingly more powerful shocks are required. The rapidity with which the conflict descends on the subject, and his ealization that it is predictably recurrent may well be sources of tension to him.

13. At a more general level, the conflict stems from the opposition of two deeply ingrained behavior dispositions: first, the disposition not to harm other people, and second, the tendency to obey those whom we perceive to be legitimate authorities.

References

ADORNO, T., FRENKEL-BRUNSWIK, ELSE, LEVINSON, D. J., AND SANFORD, R. N. *The authoritarian personality.* New York: Harper, 1950.

ARENDT, H. What was authority? In C. J. Friedrich (ed.), *Authority.* Cambridge: Harvard Univer. Press, 1958. Pp. 81–112.

BINET, A. *La suggestibilité.* Paris: Schleicher, 1900.

BUSS, A. H. *The psychology of aggression.* New York: Wiley, 1961.

CARTWRIGHT, S. (ed.) *Studies in social power.* Ann Arbor: University of Michigan Institute for Social Research, 1959.

CHARCOT, J. M. *Oeuvres complètes.* Paris: Bureaux du Progrès Médical, 1881.

FRANK, J. D. Experimental studies of personal pressure and resistance. *J. gen. Psychol.,* 1944, **30,** 23–64.

FRIEDRICH, C. J. (ed.) *Authority.* Cambridge: Harvard Univer. Press, 1958.

MILGRAM, S. Dynamics of obedience. Washington: National Science Foundation, 25 January 1961. (Mimeo)

MILGRAM, S. Some conditions of obedience and disobedience to authority. *Hum. Relat.,* 1965, **18,** 57–76.

ROKEACH, M. Authority, authoritarianism, and conformity. In I. A. Berg and B. M. Bass (eds.), *Conformity and deviation.* New York: Harper, 1961. Pp. 230–257.

SNOW, C. P. Either-or. *Progressive,* 1961(Feb.), 24.

WEBER, M. *The theory of social and economic organization.* Oxford: Oxford Univer. Press, 1947.

4

A Lady in Distress:
Inhibiting Effects of Friends and
Strangers on Bystander Intervention

Bibb Latané and Judith Rodin

One hundred twenty male undergraduates waiting either alone, with a friend, or with a stranger, overheard a woman fall and cry out in pain. Two-person groups were less likely to offer help to the injured woman than were subjects who overheard the emergency while alone. Pairs of friends were less inhibited from intervening than were strangers and helped significantly faster. In this ambiguous situation, each bystander may look to others for guidance before acting misinterpret their apparent lack of concern, and decide the situation is not serious. Friends seem less likely to misinterpret each other's initial inaction than strangers.

"There's safety in numbers," according to an old adage, and modern city dwellers seem to believe it. They shun deserted streets, empty subway cars, and lonely walks in dark parks, preferring instead to go where others are or to stay at home. When faced with stress, most individuals seem less afraid when they are in the presence of others than when they are alone (Wrightsman, 1959). Dogs are less likely to yelp when they face a strange situation with other dogs (Scott and Fuller, 1965); even rats are less likely to defecate and freeze when they are placed in a frightening open field with other rats (Latané, 1969; Latané and Glass, 1968).

A feeling so widely shared must have some basis in reality. Is there safety in numbers? If so, why? Two reasons are often suggested: Individuals are less likely to find themselves in trouble if there are others about, and even if they do find themselves in trouble, others are likely to help them deal with it.

Reprinted with permission from the authors and *The Journal of Experimental Social Psychology,* Vol. 5, 1969. Copyright 1969 by Academic Press, Inc.

This research was supported by National Science Foundation Grant GS1239 to Bibb Latané and was conducted while Judith Rodin held an N.D.E.A. Title IV Fellowship.

Ecologists have long puzzled over the adaptive functions of such phenomena as schooling in fish and flocking in birds. Such congregations seem ideally designed to make life easy for predators; yet they are widespread in nature. Why? Predators may be inhibited by fear from attacking large troops of animals (Lorenz, 1966), and they may be "confused" by the presence of many individuals, unable to focus on any one (Allee, 1951; Shaw, 1962). Similar processes may operate in humans. Roving psychopaths are probably more likely to hit isolated farm dwellings than urban apartment houses. Rapists do not usually work in Times Square.

Even if trouble comes, individuals may feel more certain of getting help if others are present. In 1871, Charles Darwin, in *The Descent of Man*, wrote "As man is a social animal it is almost certain that . . . he would from an inherited tendency be willing to defend, in concert with others, his fellow men; and be ready to aid them in any way, which did not too greatly interfere with his own welfare or his own strong desires." We may quarrel with Darwin's assertion of an *inherited* tendency, but most of us seem eady to assume that others are willing to help us in our distress.

While it is certainly true that a victim is unlikely to receive help if nobody knows of his plight, recent research casts doubt on the suggestion that he will be more likely to receive help if more people are present. In fact, experiments by Darley and Latané (1968) and by Latané and Darley (1968) show the opposite to be true. In the former study, students overhearing someone in the midst of a serious nervous seizure were more likely to attempt help, and did so sooner, if they thought they were the only person present and aware of the emergency than if they thought other people were also listening to it. In the latter study, subjects alone in a waiting room were more likely to report a possible fire than were subjects waiting in groups. In both these experiments, an emergency was less likely to be reported the more people who witnessed it.

The results of these studies may provide some insight into such widely publicized and distressing incidents as the murder of Kitty Genovese, a murder which 38 people witnessed from the safety of their apartments but did nothing to prevent. As in our laboratory studies, the presence of others served in a variety of ways to inhibit taking positive action.

These incidents have been widely cited as examples of "apathy" and "dehumanization" stemming from the urbanization of our society. These glib phrases may contain some truth since startling cases like the Genovese murder often occur in large cities, but such terms may also be misleading. The studies above suggest that situational factors, specifically factors involving the immediate social environment, may be of greater importance in determining an individual's reaction to an emergency than such vague cultural or personality concepts as "apathy" or "alienation due to urbanization."

If the social inhibition effects demonstrated by Latané and Darley and by Darley and Latané are general, they may explain why the failure to intervene seems to be more characteristic of large cities than rural areas. Bystanders to urban emergencies are more likely to be, or at least think they are, in the presence of other bystanders than witnesses of non-urban emergencies.

A second way in which urban emergencies differ from emergencies in other settings is that, in the former, bystanders are not likely to know each other. It is possible that the kinds of social inhibition and diffusion of responsibility generated by the presence of strangers may not arise from the presence of friends. Groups of friends may be even more able and willing to intervene in an emergency than single individuals. It is the purpose of the present experiment to test these possibilities, and to do so in a new emergency setting. In addition to demonstrating possible differences between friends and strangers, this will further test the generalities of social inhibition effects.

METHOD

Subjects waited either alone, with a friend, or with a stranger to participate in a market research study. As they waited, they heard someone fall and apparently injure herself in the room next door. Whether they tried to help and how long they took to do so were the main dependent variables of the study.

Subjects. One hundred fifty-six male Columbia undergraduates between the ages of eighteen and twenty-one were selected at random from the college dormitory list. They were telephoned and offered $2.00 to participate in a survey of game and puzzle preferences conducted at Columbia by the Consumer Testing Bureau (CTB), a market research organization. Each person contacted was asked to find a friend who would also be interested in participating. Only those students who recommended friends, and the friends they suggested, were used as subjects. Fourteen percent of the students called were unwilling to participate and 9 percent with appointments did not come, leaving 120 who served in the study.

Procedure. Subjects were met at the door by the market research representative and taken to the testing room. On the way they passed the CTB office and through its open door they were able to see a desk and bookcases piled high with papers and filing cabinets. They entered the adjacent testing room which contained a table and chairs and a variety of games, and they were given a preliminary background information and game preference questionnaire to fill out.

The representative told subjects that she would be working next door in her office for about ten minutes while they completed the questionnaires, and left by opening the collapsible curtain which divided the two rooms. She made sure that subjects were aware that the curtain was unlocked and easily opened and that it provided means of entry to her office. The representative stayed in her office, shuffling papers, opening drawers, and making enough noise to remind the subjects of her presence. Four minutes after leaving the testing area, she turned on a high fidelity stereophonic tape recorder.

The emergency. If the subject listened carefully, he heard the representative climb on a chair to reach for a stack of papers on the bookcase. Even if he were not listening carefully, he heard a loud crash and a scream as the chair collapsed and she fell to the floor. "Oh, my God, my foot . . . I . . . I . . . can't move it. Oh . . . my ankle," the representative moaned. "I . . . can't get this . . . thing . . . off me." She cried and moaned for about a minute longer, but the cries gradually got more subdued and controlled. Finally she muttered something about getting outside, knocked around the chair as she pulled herself up, and thumped to the door, closing it behind her as she left. The entire incident took 130 seconds.

If a subject intervened, the post-experimental interview was begun immediately. If he did not intervene, the representative waited one minute after the end of the tape and then entered the testing room through the door, visibly limping. The representative asked all subjects about the noises next door, their reactions to them, and the reasons for the course of action they had taken, and then explained in detail the true purposes of the experiment. At the end of the interview, subjects were paid and asked to fill out an anonymous questionnaire concerning their feelings about the experiment. Reasons for secrecy were discussed and all subjects readily agreed.

Measures. The main dependent variables of the study were whether the subject took action to help the victim and how long it took him to do so. There were actually several modes of interaction available. A subject could open the screen dividing the two rooms, leave the testing room and enter the CTB office by the door, find someone else, or, most simply, call out to see if the representative needed help.

Design of the experiment. Four experimental groups were used. In one condition (Alone, $N = 26$), each subject was by himself in the testing room while he filled out the questionnaire and heard the fall. In a second condition (Stooge, $N = 14$), a stranger, actually a confederate of the experimenter, was also present. The confederate had instructions to be as passive as possible and to answer questions put to him by the subject with a brief gesture or remark. During the emergency, he looked up, shrugged his shoulders, and continued working on his questionnaire. Subjects in the third condition (Strangers, $N = 20$ pairs) were placed in the testing room in pairs. Each subject in the pair was unacquainted with the other before entering the room and they were not introduced. Only one subject in this condition spontaneously introduced himself to the other. In a final condition (Friends, $N = 20$ pairs), each subject had been scheduled with a friend and remained with him throughout the experiment.

RESULTS

Check on manipulation. In the post-experimental interview, subjects were asked to describe what they thought had taken place next door. All thought the market research representative had fallen and hurt her foot. Less than 5 percent reported any suspicion that they had been listening to a tape recording. All subjects in the Two Strangers condition reported that they were unacquainted before the experiment.

Mode of intervention. Across all experimental groups, the majority of subjects who intervened did so by pulling back the room divider and coming into the CTB office (61 percent). Few subjects came the round-about way through the door to offer their assistance (14 percent), and a surprisingly small number (24 percent) chose the easy solution of calling out to offer help. No one tried to find someone else to whom to report the accident. Thus all interveners offered some kind of direct assistance to the injured woman. Since experimental conditions did not differ in the proportions choosing various modes of intervention, the comparisons below will deal only with the total proportions of subjects offering help.

Alone vs. Stooge conditions. Seventy percent of all subjects who heard the fall while alone in the waiting room offered to help the victim before she left the room. By contrast, the presence of a nonresponsive bystander markedly inhibited helping. Only 7 percent of subjects in the Stooge condition intervened. These subjects seemed upset and confused during the emergency and frequently glanced at the passive confederate who continued working on his questionnaire. The difference between the Alone and Stooge conditions is, of course, highly significant ($\chi^2 = 13.92$, $p < .001$).[1]

---

[1] All statistical tests in this paper are two-tailed.

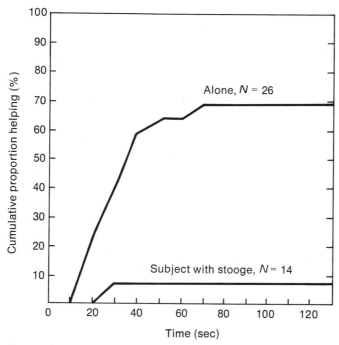

FIGURE 4.1
Cumulative proportion helping in the Alone and Stooge conditions.

Figure 4.1 presents the cumulative proportion of subjects who had intervened by any point in time following the accident. For example, Fig. 4.1 shows that by the end of 60 seconds, 64 percent of Alone subjects and only 7 percent of subjects tested with a stooge had intervened. The shapes of these curves indicate that even had the emergency lasted longer than 130 seconds, little further intervention would have taken place. In fact, over the experiment as a whole, 90 percent of all subjects who ever intervened did so in the first half of the time available to them.

It is clear that the presence of an unresponsive bystander strongly inhibited subjects from offering to help the injured woman. Let us look now at whether this effect depends upon some specific characteristic or unnatural behavior of the passive confederate. Will the same social inhibition occur when two naive subjects are tested together?

Alone vs. Two Strangers. Once one person in a group of two bystanders has intervened, the situation confronting the other bystander changes. It is no longer necessary for him to act (and indeed, nobody did so). For this reason, we took the latency of the *first* person's response as our basic measure. This procedure, however, complicates a simple comparison between the Alone

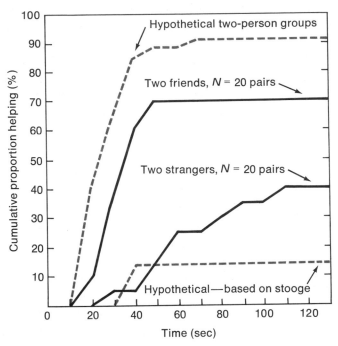

FIGURE 4.2
Cumulative proportion helping in the Friends and Strangers
conditions and hypothetical baselines.

and Two Strangers conditions. Since there are twice as many people available to respond in the latter condition, we should expect an increased probability that at least one person would intervene by chance alone.

To compare the two groups, we computed a hypothetical baseline from the Alone distribution. This was achieved by mathematically combining all possible "groups" of two scores obtained from subjects in the Alone condition, and taking the distribution of the fastest scores in each "group" for the hypothetical baseline. This baseline is graphed in Fig. 4.2, and represents the *expected* cumulative proportion of pairs in which at least one person helps if the members of the pairs are entirely independent (i.e., behave exactly like Alone subjects). Since 70 percent of Alone subjects intervened, we should expect that at least one person in 91 percent of all two-person groups would offer help, even if members of a pair had no influence upon each other.[2]

In fact, the results show that members of a pair had a strong influence on each other. In only 40 percent of the groups of subjects in the Two Strangers condition did even one person offer help to the injured woman. Only 8 sub-

---

[2]The probability that at least one member of a group will help by a given time is $1 - (1 - p)^n$ where n is the number of people in the group and p is the probability of a single individual helping by that time.

jects of the 40 who were run in this condition intervened. This response rate is significantly below the hypothetical base rate ($\chi^2 = 11.34$, $p < .001$). Figure 4.2 shows that at every point in time, fewer subjects in the Two Strangers condition had intervened than would be expected on the basis of the Alone response rate ($p < .01$ by Kolmogorov-Smirnov). This result demonstrates that the presence of another person strongly inhibits individuals from responding and that this inhibition is not a function of some artificiality of a stooge's behavior.

Strangers vs. Stooge. The response rate of 40 percent in the Two Strangers condition appears to be somewhat higher than the 7 percent rate in the Stooge condition. Making a correction similar to that used for the Alone scores, the expected response rate based on the Stooge condition is 13 percent. This is significantly lower than the response rate in the Strangers condition ($p < .05$ by binomial test).

The results above strongly replicate the finding by Latané and Darley (1968) in a different experimental setting: Smoke trickling into a waiting room. In both experiments, subjects were less likely to take action if they were in the presence of passive confederates than if they were alone, and in both studies, this effect showed up even when groups of naive subjects were tested together. This congruence of findings from different experimental settings supports their validity and generality: It also helps rule out a variety of explanations suitable to either situation alone. For example, the smoke may have represented a threat to the subject's own personal safety. It is possible that subjects in groups were less likely to respond than single subjects because of a greater concern to appear "brave" in the face of a possible fire. This explanation, however, does not fit the present experiment in which the same pattern of results appeared. In the present experiment, non-intervention cannot signify bravery.

Comparison of the two experiments also suggests that the absolute number of nonresponsive bystanders may not be a critical factor in producing social inhibition of intervention. One passive confederate in the present experiment was as effective as two in the smoke study; pairs of strangers in the present study inhibited each other as much as did trios in the former study.

Let us look now at our final experimental condition in which pairs of friends were tested together.

Alone vs. Two Friends. Pairs of friends often talked about the questionnaire before the accident, and sometimes discussed a course of action after the fall. Even so, in only 70 percent of the pairs did even one person intervene.

While, superficially, this appears as high as the Alone condition, again there must be a correction for the fact that two people are free to act. When compared to the 91 percent base rate of hypothetical two-person groups, friends do inhibit each other from intervening ($\chi^2 = 2.84, p < .10$). Friends were less likely, and they were also slower, to intervene than would be expected on the basis of the Alone rate ($p < .05$ by Kolmogorov-Smirnov).

Friends vs. Strangers. Although pairs of friends were inhibited from helping when compared to the Alone condition, they were significantly faster to intervene than were pairs of strangers ($U = 96, p < .01$). The median latency of the first response from pairs of friends was 36 seconds; the median pair of strangers did not respond at all within the arbitrary 130-second duration of the emergency.

One sort of alternative explanation which plagues comparisons of friends and strangers in many experiments was ruled out by the present procedure. If some subjects are asked to recruit friends, and others are not, different degrees of commitment may be aroused. In this experiment, all subjects either recruited friends or were recruited by them, equalizing commitment across conditions.

From the victim's viewpoint. In order to determine whether an individual's likelihood of responding is affected by the presence of other people, we have compared scores in the Friends and Strangers conditions with a hypothetical base rate computed from the distribution of responses in the Alone condition. By this procedure, we have shown that an individual is less likely to respond when he is with either a friend or a stranger. But what of the victim? Under what conditions is she most likely to get help? For this question, the use of hypothetical baselines is unjustified. The results show that the victim is no better off if two friends hear her cry for help than if only one person does. When the bystanders are strangers, social inhibition was so strong that the victim actually got help significantly faster the fewer people who heard her distress (Alone vs. Strangers, $U = 112, p < .01$). In this instance, she would be foolish indeed to count on safety in numbers.

Post-experimental interview. Although the interview began differently for the interveners and noninterveners, all subjects were encouraged to discuss the accident and their reactions to it in some detail before they were told about the tape and the purpose of the experiment.

Subjects who intervened usually claimed that they did so either because the fall sounded very serious or because they were uncertain what had occurred and felt they should investigate. Many talked about intervention as the "right thing to do" and asserted they would help again in any situation.

Many of the noninterveners also claimed that they were unsure what had happened (59 percent), but had decided it was not too serious (46 percent). A number of subjects reported that they thought other people would or could help (25 percent), and three said they refrained out of concern for the victim—they did not want to embarrass her.[3] Whether to accept these explanations as reasons or rationalizations is moot—they certainly do not explain the differences among conditions. The important thing to note is that noninterveners did not seem to feel that they had behaved callously or immorally. Their behavior was generally consistent with their interpretation of the situation. Subjects almost uniformly claimed that in a "real" emergency, they would be among the first to help the victim.

Interestingly, when subjects were asked whether they had been influenced by the presence or action of their co-worker, they were either unwilling or unable to believe that they had. Subjects in the passive confederate condition reported, on the average, that they were "very little" influenced by the stooge. Subjects in the Two Strangers condition claimed to having been only "a little bit" influenced by each other, and friends admitted to "moderate" influenced. Put another way, only 14, 30 and 70 percent of the subjects in these three conditions admitted to at least a "moderate" degree of influence ($\chi^2 = 12.2$, 2 *df*, $p < .01$). These claims, of course, run directly counter to the experimental results, in which friends were the least inhibited and subjects in the Stooge condition most inhibited by the other's actions.

Reactions to the experiment. After the post-experimental interview, debriefing, and payment of the promised $2.00, subjects were asked to fill out a final questionnaire concerning their mood and their reactions to the experiment. Subjects were convincingly assured that their answers would be entirely anonymous and the experimenter departed. On an adjective check list, 85 percent of the subjects said they were "interested," 77 percent "glad to have taken part," 59 percent "concerned about the problem," 33 percent "surprised," 24 percent "satisfied," 18 percent "relieved," 12 percent "happy," 2 percent "confused," 2 percent "annoyed," 1 percent "angry at myself," and 0 percent "angry at the experimenter," "afraid," or "ashamed."[4] One hundred percent said they would be willing to take part in similar experiments in the future, 99 percent that they understood what the experiment was really about, 99 percent that the deceptions were necessary, and 100 percent that they were justified. On a 5-point scale, 96 percent found the experiment either "very interesting" or "interesting," the two extreme points. The only sign of a difference in reaction between interveners and noninterveners was that 47 percent of the former and only 24 percent of the latter

---

[3]Noninterveners reported an average of 1.9 different reasons.
[4]Subjects checked an average of 3.1 adjectives.

checked the most extreme interest ($\chi^2 = 4.64$, $p < .05$). In general, then, reactions to the experiment were highly positive.

DISCUSSION

The idea of "safety in numbers" receives no support from the results of this experiment. When it was first designed, our major worry was that everyone would act, or at least call out to offer help to the injured woman. Yet on almost 40 occasions, she limped away from her accident without even the offer of help. In general she fared fairly well when only one person heard her distress. Her luck was much worse when several did. Although in the combined group conditions, 23 people offered help, 49 did not. What is there about a group setting which caused such ungentlemanly behavior? Two lines of explanation seem plausible. The first involves the workings of social influence processes (Latané and Darley, 1968), and the second the concept of "diffusion of responsibility" (Darley and Latané, 1968). Let us consider each of these lines of explanation and see how they fit the present case.

A bystander to an emergency must first come to some general interpretation of the situation, and then, on the basis of this interpretation, he may choose what to do. Many emergencies are rather ambiguous: It is unclear whether anything is really wrong or whether anything can be done about it. In a previous experiment, smoke might have represented fire, but it might have been nothing more than steam from a radiator. In the present experiment, a crash and the sounds of sobbing might have indicated a girl with a badly injured leg, but it might have meant nothing more than a slight sprain and a good deal of chagrin.

In deciding what interpretation to put on a particular configuration of emergency symptoms, a bystander will be influenced by his experience and his desires as well as by what he sees. In addition, if other people are present, he will be guided by their apparent reactions in formulating his own impressions. Unfortunately, their apparent reactions may not be a good indication of their true feelings. Apparent passivity and lack of concern on the part of other bystanders may indicate that they feel the emergency is not serious, but it may simply mean that they have not yet had time to work out their own interpretation or even that they are assuming a bland exterior to hide their inner uncertainty and concern. The presence of other bystanders provides an audience to any action he may undertake. In public, Americans generally wish to appear poised and in control of themselves. Thus it is possible for a state of "pluralistic ignorance" to develop, in which each bystander is led by the *apparent* lack of concern of the others to interpret the situation as being less serious than he would if he were alone. To the extent that he does not feel the situation is an emergency, of course, he will be unlikely to take any helpful action.

Even if an individual does decide that an emergency is actually in process and that something ought to be done, he still is faced with the choice of whether he himself will intervene. His decision will presumably be made in terms of the rewards and costs associated with the various alternative courses of action open to him. The presence of other people can alter these rewards and costs—perhaps most importantly, they can alter the cost of not acting. If only one bystander is present at an emergency, he bears 100 percent of the responsibility for dealing with it; he will feel 100 percent of the guilt for not acting; he will bear 100 percent of any blame others may level for nonintervention. If others are present, the onus of responsibility is diffused, and the individual may be more likely to resolve his conflict between intervening and not intervening in favor of the latter alternative.

Both the "social influence" and "diffusion of responsibility" explanations seem valid, and there is no reason why both should not be jointly operative. Neither alone can account for all the data. For example, the "diffusion" explanation cannot account for the significant difference in response rate between the Strangers and Stooge conditions—there should be equal diffusion in either case. The difference can more plausibly be attributed to the fact that strangers typically did not show such complete indifference to the accident as did the stooge. The diffusion process also does not seem applicable to results from the Smoke situation (Latané and Darley, 1968). Responsibility for pretecting oneself should not diffuse. On the other hand, social influence processes cannot account for results in the Seizure situation (Darley and Latané, 1968). Subjects in that experiment could not communicate with one another and thus could not be influenced by each other's reactions.

Although both processes probably operate, they may not do so at the same time. To the extent that social influence leads an individual to define the situation as nonserious and not requiring action, his responsibility is eliminated, making diffusion unnecessary. Only if social influence is unsuccessful in leading subjects to misinterpret the situation should diffusion play a role. Indirect evidence supporting this analysis comes from observation of nonintervening subjects in the various emergency settings. In settings involving face-to-face contact among bystanders, as in the present study and in the Smoke situation, noninterveners typically redefined the situation and did not see it as a serious emergency. Consequently, they avoided the moral choice of whether or not to take action. During the post experimental interviews, subjects in these experiments seemed relaxed and self-assured. In the Seizure situation, on the other hand, face-to-face contact was prevented, social influence could not help subjects define the situation as nonserious, and they were faced with the moral dilemma of whether to intervene. Although the imagined presence of other people led many subjects to delay intervention, their conflict was exhibited in the post experimental interviews. If anything, subjects who did not intervene seemed more emotionally aroused than did subjects who reported the emergency.

How can we fit friend-stranger differences into this framework? There are several possibilities. It may be that people are less likely to fear possible embarrassment in front of friends than before strangers, and that friends are less likely to misinterpret each other's inaction than are strangers. If so, social influence may be less likely to lead friends to decide there is no emergency. It also may be that individuals are less likely to lay off responsibility on their friends than on strangers, reducing the effectiveness of responsibility diffusion. There is some evidence consistent with both these possibilities.

When strangers overheard the emergency, they seemed noticeably confused and concerned, attempting to interpret what they heard and to decide on a course of action. They often glanced furtively at one another, apparently anxious to discover the other's reaction yet unwilling to meet eyes and betray their own concern. Friends, on the other hand, seemed better able to convey their concern nonverbally, and often discussed the incident and arrived at a mutual plan of action. Although these observations are admittedly impressionistic, they are consistent with a further piece of data. During the emergency, a record was kept of whether the bystanders engaged in verbal conversation. Unfortunately, no attempt was made to code the amount or content of what was said, but it is possible to break down whether there was any talking at all. Only 29 percent of subjects attempted any conversation with the stooge; while 60 percent of the pairs of strangers engaged in some conversation, mostly desultory and often unrelated to the accident. Although the latter rate seems higher than the former, it really is not, since there are two people free to initiate a conversation rather than just one. Friends, on the other hand, were somewhat more likely to talk than strangers. Eighty-five percent of the pairs did so ($p < .15$ by Fisher's Exact test). Friends, then, may show less mutual inhibition than strangers because they are less likely to develop a state of "pluralistic ignorance."

Friends may also be less likely to diffuse responsibility than strangers. In a variation on the Seizure situation, Darley and Darley[5] recruited pairs of friends to serve as subjects at the same time. During the course of the emergency, friends could have no contact with each other and thus could have no direct influence on each other. Even so, subjects tested with friends were quicker to intervene than subjects tested with strangers.

[5]Personal communication.

CONCLUSIONS

The results of this experiment, in conjunction with those of previous studies in this series, suggest that social inhibition effects may be rather general over a variety of emergency situations. In three different experiments, bystanders have been less likely to intervene if other bystanders are present. The nature of the other bystander seems to be important: A nonreactive confederate provides the most inhibition, a stranger provides a moderate amount, and a friend the least. Overall, the results are consistent with a multiprocess model of intervention: The effect of other people seems to be mediated both through the interpretations that bystanders place on the situation, and through the decisions they make once they have come up with an interpretation. The results suggest situational reasons why our large cities may be less safe than smaller towns: Even if there be an equal likelihood of getting involved in an emergency, the presence of many strangers may prevent you from getting help. There may be safety in numbers, but these experiments suggest that if you are involved in an emergency, the best number of bystanders is one.

In a less sophisticated era, Rudyard Kipling prayed "That we, with Thee, may walk uncowed by fear or favor of the crowd; that, under Thee, we may possess man's strength to comfort man's distress." It appears that the latter hope may depend to a surprising extent upon the former.

References

ALLEE, W. C. *The Social life of animals.* Boston: Beacon Press, 1951.

DARLEY, J. M., AND LATANÉ, B. Bystander intervention in emergencies: Diffusion of responsibility. *Journal of Personality and Social Psychology,* 1968, **8,** 377–383.

LATANÉ, B. Gregariousness and fear in the laboratory rat. *Journal of Experimental Social Psychology,* 1969, **5,** 61–69.

LATANÉ, B., AND DARLEY, J. M. Group inhibition of bystander intervention in emergencies. *Journal of Personality and Social Psychology,* 1968, **10,** 215–221.

LATANÉ, B., AND GLASS, D. C. Social and nonsocial attraction in rats. *Journal of Personality and Social Psychology,* 1968, **9,** 142–146.

LORENZ, KONRAD. *On aggression.* New York: Harcourt, Brace and World, 1966.

SCOTT, J. P., AND FULLER, J. L. *Genetics and the social behavior of the dog.* Chicago: University of Chicago Press, 1965.

SHAW, E. The schooling of fishes. *Scientific American,* 1962, **206,** No. 6, 128–138.

WRIGHTSMAN, LAWRENCE, S., JR. The effects of small group membership on level of concern. Unpublished doctoral dissertation, University of Minnesota, 1959. *Dissertation Abstracts,* 1959, **20,** 1473–1474.

II

MASS COMMUNICATION, PROPAGANDA, AND PERSUASION

5

Facilitating Effects of "Eating-While-Reading" on Responsiveness to Persuasive Communications

Irving L. Janis, Donald Kaye, and Paul Kirschner

This experiment was designed to test the hypothesis that food, as an extraneous gratification accompanying exposure to a persuasive communication, will increase acceptance, even though the donor of the food is not the source of the communication and does not endorse it. Two replicating experiments were carried out with 216 male college students. In both experiments there were 3 groups of Ss, assigned on a random basis to the following conditions, which involved exposure to: (a) 4 persuasive communications while eating desirable food; (b) the same 4 communications with no food present; (c) no relevant communications (control condition). Both experiments provide confirmatory evidence, indicating that more opinion change tends to be elicited under conditions where the Ss are eating while reading the communications. The theoretical implications are discussed with respect to psychological processes involved in changing attitudes.

It is commonly assumed that people are more likely to yield to persuasion at a time when they are eating or drinking than at a time when they are not engaged in any such gratifying activity. Salesmen, business promoters, and lobbyists often try to "soften up" their clients by inviting them to talk things over at a restaurant or cafe. Representatives of opposing economic or political groups, when unable to settle their disputes while seated formally around a conference table, may find themselves much more amenable to mutual influence, and hence more conciliatory, while seated comfortably around a dinner table.

Reprinted with permission from the authors and *The Journal of Personality and Social Psychology,* Vol. 1, No. 2, 1965. Copyright 1965 by the American Psychological Association.

This experimental investigation was conducted under the auspices of the Yale Studies in Attitude and Communication, which is supported by a grant from the Rockefeller Foundation.

Little systematic research has been done, as yet, to determine the conditions under which pleasant stimulation will augment the acceptance of persuasive communications. One might expect that when the communicator is the perceived source of the gratifying stimulation, a more favorable attitude toward him will ensue, which would tend to lower the recipient's resistance to his persuasive efforts (see Hovland, Janis, and Kelley, 1953, pp. 19–55). But a more complicated situation often arises at educational symposia, political conventions, cocktail parties, and informal dinners where: (*a*) the donor (that is, the person who is perceived as being responsible for the gratification) is *not* the communicator and (*b*) the donor does *not* endorse the persuasive communications that happen to be presented at the particular time when the recipients are being indulged. If a positive gain in effectiveness is found to occur under these conditions, where the gratifying activity is entirely extraneous to the content, source, or endorsement of the communications, a number of important theoretical questions will arise—questions concerning some of the basic processes of attitude change which will require systematic experimental analysis. For example, when eating has a facilitating effect on acceptance of persuasive messages, does it always depend entirely upon the heightened motivation of the recipients to conform with the donor's wishes? If so, a positive outcome under nonendorsement conditions will be paradoxical unless it turns out that there is a general tendency for people to assume, consciously or unconsciously, that the donor would like them to be influenced by whatever communications are presented (even though he explicitly says that he does not endorse the point of view being expressed). Or does the extraneous gratification operate as a source of reinforcement independently of the recipient's attitude toward the donor? If this is the case, we might be led to assume that the food corresponds to an "unconditioned stimulus," and its facilitating effects might be accounted for in terms of the laws of conditioning.

The latter theoretical possibility is suggested by Razran's (1940) brief research note, published 25 years ago, in which he gave a summary statement of the following two experimental observations: (*a*) an increase in ratings of "personal approval" occurred when a series of sociopolitical slogans were presented to experimental subjects while they were enjoying a free lunch and (*b*) a decrease in such ratings occurred when the slogans were presented while the subjects were being required to inhale a number of unpleasant, putrid odors. In his report, however, Razran does not mention certain important details, such as whether the experimenter was the donor of the free lunch and whether he said anything to the subjects about his personal attitude toward the slogans.

So far as the authors have been able to ascertain, no subsequent experiments have been published pertinent to checking Razran's observations. Nor has any published research been found bearing on the related questions of whether or not (and under what limiting conditions) extraneous pleasant or unpleasant stimulation can affect the degree to which a recipient will accept a series of persuasive arguments that attempt to induce him to change a personal belief or preference.

As a preliminary step toward reopening experimental research on the above-mentioned set of theoretical problems, the present study was designed to investigate the alleged phenomenon of enhanced communication effectiveness arising from "eating-while-reading." The research was designed primarily to answer the following question: If an experimenter gives the subjects desirable food and drink but states explicitly that the persuasive messages to be presented are ones with which he does not necessarily agree, will there be a significant increase in acceptance from the gratifying activity of eating that accompanies exposure to the communications?

METHOD AND PROCEDURE

Experimental Design

The basic design involved randomly assigning the subjects to two different experimental conditions. One was a condition in which a substantial quantity of food was offered to the subjects during the time they were engaged in reading a series of four persuasive communications. Upon entering the experimental room, the subjects found the experimenter imbibing some refreshments (peanuts and Pepsi-Cola) and they were offered the same refreshments with the simple explanation that there was plenty on hand because "I brought some along for you too." The contrasting "no-food" condition was identical in every respect except that no refreshments were in the room at any time during the session.

The same measures of opinion change were used in the two experimental groups and also in a third group of *unexposed controls,* who were included in the study in order to obtain a base line for ascertaining the effectiveness of each communication per se. The subjects randomly assigned to the control condition were given the same pre- and postcommunication questionnaires, separated by the same time interval as in the other two experimental conditions, but without being exposed to any relevant communications.

The Communications and the Opinion Measures

On the basis of extensive pretesting, we prepared four communications, each of which advocated an unpopular point of view and had been found to be capable of inducing a significant degree of opinion change. These communications were attributed to fictitious authors who were described as journalists or news commentators. The main conclusions, all of which involved quantitative predictions or preferences about future events, were as follows:

1. It will be more than twenty-five years before satisfactory progress can be expected in the search for a cure for cancer.
2. The United States Armed Forces do not need additional men and can be reduced to less than 85 percent of their present strength.
3. A round-trip expedition to the moon will be achieved within the next decade.[1]
4. Within the next three years, three-dimensional films will replace two-dimensional films in practically all movie theaters.

In order to assess opinion changes, four key questions were included in both the pre- and the postcommunication questionnaires, each of which asked the subject to express his opinion in the form of a quantitative estimate (for example, "How many years do you think it will be before an extremely effective cure is found for cancer so that cancer will no longer be a major cause of death? About — years.")

Experiments I and II: Similarities and Differences

The same experimental design, described above, was used in two separate experiments, during successive semesters at the same college. In all essential features the first (Experiment I) was identical with the second (Experiment II) in that exactly the same experimental variations were used along with the same instructions, the same communications, and the same pre- and postcommunication questionnaires. But the two experiments differed in several minor ways. The main difference was that in Experiment I the time interval between the precommunication questionnaire and exposure to the communications was about two months; whereas in Experiment II the precommunication questionnaire was given at the beginning of the experimental session, immediately preceding the communications.

In Experiment I, the initial questionnaire was administered in regular undergraduate class sessions. It was introduced as a "survey of student opinions" and the key questions were embedded among numerous filler questions on a variety of other controversial issues. After a period of two months, the subjects were contacted by telephone and asked to be unpaid volunteers for a study on reading preferences. The vast majority volunteered and each subject was seen in a private interview session, at the beginning of which he was randomly assigned to the "food with communication" condition or the "no food with communication" condition or the unexposed control condition.

---

[1]This study was carried out before the major developments in space flights had occurred, at a time when few people were optimistic about the rate of technical progress in this field. In response to the moon-flight question on the initial questionnaire, almost all the students gave estimates of ten years or more before a successful round-trip flight could be expected.

After answering the final set of postcommunication questions, each subject was briefly interviewed concerning his reactions to the experimental situation.

In Experiment II, the same essential procedures were used exept for the fact that the precommunication questionnaire was given at the beginning of the experimental session. Another minor difference was that the unexposed controls were given some extracts from a popular magazine on irrelevant topics, which took approximately the same reading time as the four persuasive communications. Moreover, unlike the unexposed controls in Experiment I, those in Experiment II were give the same food in the same way as in the main experimental condition, so that they too were eating while reading the (irrelevant) articles.

In addition to the three conditions that were set up to replicate the essential features of Experiment I, a fourth experimental condition was introduced in Experiment II in order to investigate a subsidiary problem, namely, the effects of extraneous *unpleasant* stimuli. The fourth experimental group, while reading the four persuasive communications, was exposed to an unpleasant odor (produced by a hidden bottle of butyric acid), for which the experimenter disclaimed any responsibility.

In both experiments, the experimenter explained that the purpose was to assess the students' reading preferences. He asserted that the did *not* endorse the communications and casually mentioned that he happened to agree with certain of the ideas expressed and not with others (without specifying which). He asked the subjects to read the articles as though they were at home reading a popular magazine. In line with the alleged purpose, the postcommunication questionnaire in both Experiments I and II included 20 filler questions asking for interest ratings of the articles (for example, ratings of how much interest they would expect the average college student to have in each topic).

Subjects

A total of 216 Yale undergraduate students were used in the two experiments. In Experiment I, 35 men were in the unexposed control group, 32 in the "no food with communication" condition, and 33 in the "food with communication" condition. In Experiment II, the corresponding numbers were 23, 31, and 31, respectively. There were also 31 subjects in the fourth experimental group exposed to the "unpleasant" condition.

RESULTS

In both experiments, observations of the subjects' eating behavior in the "food" condition showed that every one of them ate at least one handful of peanuts and drank at least one-half glass of the soft drink. The main findings concerning the effects of eating desirable food on the acceptance of the four persuasive communications are shown in Table 5.1. In general, the results indicate that "eating-while-reading" has a facilitating effect on the amount of opinion change. In Experiment I, the differences between the food and no-food conditions are consistently in the predicted direction for all four communications, two of which are significant at the .05 level. (All *p* values are one-tailed and were obtained on the basis of the formula for assessing the difference between two net percentage changes, given by Hovland, Lumsdaine, and Sheffield, 1949.) The results for Experiment II show differences in the same direction for three of the four communications, two of which are significant at the .10 level. There is a very small, nonsignificant difference in the reverse direction on the fourth communication.

The *p* values based on the combined data from both experiments, shown in the last column of Table 5.1, can be regarded as a satisfactory summary of the overall outcome inasmuch as: (*a*) the numbers of cases in each experiment are almost equal; and (*b*) the two experiments differed only in minor features that are irrelevant to the main comparison under investigation. The combined data show that all four communications produced differences in the predicted direction and for three of them the differences are large enough to be statistically significant. Thus, the results support the conclusion that, in general, the extraneous gratification of eating while reading a series of persuasive communications tends to increase their effectiveness.

That each communication was effective in inducing a significant degree of opinion change, whether presented under food or no-food conditions, is indicated by the comparative data from the unexposed controls. In both experiments, the control group showed very slight positive changes, if any, on each of the four key questions and the amount of change was always significantly less than the corresponding net change shown by the food and no-food experimental groups.[2] There were no consistent differences between the control group in Experiment I and the one in Experiment II, which indicates that the different time intervals between the before and after measures and

---

[2]In all but one instance, the net change shown by the unexposed controls was not significantly different from zero. The one exception occurred in the control group in Experiment I with respect to the first issue (cancer cure), on which a significant net change of −34 percent was found. This change, however, was in the reverse direction from that advocated by the communication (probably as a consequence of optimistic publicity concerning new advances in cancer research that appeared in the newspapers during the months between the before and after questionnaires). Thus, on this item, as well as on the other three, the control group showed significantly less change in the expected direction than the two experimental groups.

An analysis of responses to the precommunication questionnaire from both experiments showed that initially, on each of the four key opinion questions, there were only very slight, nonsignificant differences among the experimental and control groups. None of the results in Table 5.1 and none of the other observed differences in amount of opinion change are attributable to initial differences.

TABLE 5.1
Opinion changes induced by exposure to four persuasive communications under two
different conditions: "Food" versus "No Food" given by the experimenters

Communication topic	Percentage opinion change					
	Experiment I		Experiment II		Combined data from Experiments I and II	
	No food (N = 31)	Food (N = 33)	No food (N = 31)	Food (N = 31)	No food (N = 63)	Food (N = 64)
1. Cure for cancer						
Positive change	68.7	81.8	80.7	93.5	74.6	87.4
Negative change	21.8	12.1	3.2	0.0	12.7	6.3
No change	9.5	6.1	16.1	6.5	12.7	6.3
Total	100.0	100.0	100.0	100.0	100.0	100.0
Net change	46.9	69.7	77.5	93.5	61.9	81.1
p	= .11		<.10		<.05	
2. Preferred size of U.S. Armed Forces						
Positive change	65.6	81.8	29.0	51.6	47.6	67.2
Negative change	9.4	0.0	0.0	0.0	4.8	0.0
No change	25.0	18.2	71.0	48.4	47.6	32.8
Total	100.0	100.0	100.0	100.0	100.0	100.0
Net change	56.2	81.8	29.0	51.6	42.8	67.2
p	<.05		<.05		<.01	
3. Round trip to moon						
Positive change	53.2	75.9	48.4	58.0	50.8	67.2
Negative change	21.9	12.1	19.4	12.9	20.6	12.5
No change	24.9	12.0	32.2	29.1	28.6	20.3
Total	100.0	100.0	100.0	100.0	100.0	100.0
Net change	31.3	63.8	29.0	45.1	30.2	54.7
p	= .05		= .20		<.05	
4. Three dimensional movies						
Positive change	68.7	75.9	74.2	77.4	71.5	76.6
Negative change	21.8	12.1	0.0	6.5	11.1	9.4
No change	9.5	12.0	25.8	16.1	17.4	14.0
Total	100.0	100.0	100.0	100.0	100.0	100.0
Net change	46.9	63.8	74.2	70.9	60.4	67.2
p	= .20		= .40		<.20	

the other minor procedural differences between the two experiments had no direct effect on the opinion measures.

The condition of unpleasant stimulation introduced into Experiment II had no observable effect on the amount of opinion change. The net changes obtained from the group exposed to the foul odor ($N = 31$) were as follows: cancer cure, 67.7 percent; size of armed forces, 25.8 percent; round trip to moon, 38.7 percent; three-dimensional movies, 64.5 percent. These values differ only very slightly from those obtained from the group exposed to the no-food condition in Experiment II (see Table 5.1); none of the differences is large enough to approach statistical significance. As expected, however, all the net changes for the unpleasant odor condition are smaller than those for the food condition and in two of the four instances the differences are statistically significant at beyond the .05 level.

DISCUSSION

Our finding that the extraneous gratifying activity of eating tended to increase the degree to which the accompanying persuasive messages were accepted may prove to have important implications for the psychology of attitude change, especially if subsequent research shows that the gains tend to be persistent, giving rise to sustained modifications of personal beliefs or preferences. Since the control group in Experiment II (which received food along with irrelevant communications) showed net opinion changes that were practically zero and were significantly less than those shown by the main experimental group, the food alone appears to have had no direct effect on any of the opinion measures. Hence the observed outcome seems to implicate psychological processes involved in the *acceptance* of persuasive influences.

Our results on the positive effects of food are similar to Razran's (1940) findings on the increase in favorable ratings of sociopolitical slogans induced by a free lunch. Razran has indicated that he regards his observations as evidence of Pavlovian conditioning, resulting from the contiguity of the conditioned stimuli (the slogans) and the unconditioned pleasant stimuli (food). Before accepting any such interpretation, however, further investigations are needed to check systematically on the possibility that the change in acceptability is brought about by creating a more favorable attitude toward the donor. We attempted to minimize this possibility in both Experiments I and I by having the experimenter give the subjects an introductory explanation in which he clearly stated that he was not sponsoring the persuasive communications. Despite this attempt, however, the subjects may have ignored or forgotten his remarks and assumed that he was sponsoring them. We have no evidence bearing directly on this matter, but we did note that in the informal interviews conducted at the end of each experimental session, many more favorable comments about the experimenter were made by the subjects who had been in the food condition than by those who had been in the no-food condition.

Our failure to confirm Razran's findings on the negative effects of *unpleasant* stimulation might be accounted for in terms of attitude toward the experimenter. In Razran's experiment, the experimenter "required" the subjects to sniff the putrid odors, and hence he might have been directly blamed for the unpleasant stimulation; whereas in our Experiment II, the unpleasant odor was presented as an accidental occurrence for which the experimenter was not responsible. Further experimental analysis is obviously needed to determine if the effects of pleasant and unpleasant stimulation observed in our experiment are dependent upon whether or not the experimenter is perceived as the causal agent.

The fact that the experimenter himself participated in eating the food might have influenced the subjects' perceptions of the general atmosphere of the reading session and hence needs to be investigated as a possible variable, independently of the subjects' food consumption. The limiting conditions for positive effects from "eating-while-reading" also require systematic investigation, particularly in relation to unpleasant interpersonal stimuli, such as those provoking embarrassment, outbreaks of hostility, or other forms of emotional tension that could counteract the positive atmosphere created by the availability of desirable food.

It is also important to find out whether variations in the experimenter's endorsement of the communications play a crucial role in determining the facilitating effects of the proferred food. For example, if subsequent research shows that the experimenter's positive versus negative endorsements make a difference, then an explanation in terms of increased motivation to please the donor will be favored, rather than a simple conditioning mechanism, and a more complicated explanation will be required to account for the positive effects obtained under conditions where the experimenter explicitly detaches himself from sponsorship of the communications.[3] These implications are mentioned to illustrate the new lines of research suggested by comparing the results from the present experiment with those from Razran's earlier study.

---

[3]The potential importance of positive versus negative endorsement by the experimenter as an interacting variable was suggested by some unexpected results obtained in a pilot study by Dabbs and Janis, which was carried out as a preliminary step toward replicating the present experiment under conditions where the experimenter indicates that he personally *disagrees* with the persuasive communications. The pilot study results led us to carry out a new experiment in which we compared the effects of eating-while-reading under two different endorsement conditions (the experimenter agreeing or disagreeing with the communications). A report on the effects of the interacting variables, as revealed by the data from the Dabbs and Janis experiment, is currently being prepared for publication.

References

HOVLAND, C. I., JANIS, I. L., AND KELLEY, H. H. *Communication and persuasion.* New Haven: Yale Univer. Press, 1953.

HOVLAND, C. I., LUMSDAINE, A. A., AND SHEFFIELD, F. D. *Experiments on mass communication.* Princeton: Princeton Univer. Press, 1949.

RAZRAN, G. H. S. Conditioned response changes in rating and appraising sociopolitical slogans. *Psychological Bulletin,* 1940, **37,** 481.

6

Communicator Credibility and Communication Discrepancy as Determinants of Opinion Change

Elliot Aronson, Judith A. Turner, and J. Merrill Carlsmith

The theory of cognitive dissonance suggests that opinion change is a function of a specific complex interaction between the credibility of the communicator and the discrepancy of the communication from the initial attitude of the recipient. In a laboratory experiment, Ss who read a communication that was attributed to a highly credible source showed greater opinion change when the opinion of the source was presented as being increasingly discrepant from their own. In sharp contrast to this was the behavior of Ss who were exposed to the same communication —attributed to a source having only moderate credibility. In this condition, increasing the discrepancy increased the degree of opinion change only to a point; as discrepancy became more extreme, however, the degree of opinion change decreased. The results support predictions from the theory and suggest a reconciliation of previously contradictory findings.

Recent experiments in the area of communication and persuasion have shown that a number of variable affect the success of an influence attempt. One such variable is the credibility of the communicator. Experimental results have shown unequivocally that there is a positive relationship between the credibility of the communicator and the extent of opinion change (Arnet, Davidson, and Lewis, 1931; Haiman, 1949; Hovland and Weiss, 1952; Kelman and Hovland, 1953; Kulp, 1934). Another variable of obvious importance is the extent of the discrepancy between the opinion advocated by the communicator and the precommunication opinion of the recipient. However, experiments dealing with this variable have yielded contradictory results.

Reprinted with permission from *The Journal of Abnormal and Social Psychology,* Vol. 67, No. 1, 1963. Copyright 1963 by the American Psychological Association.

This research was conducted at Harvard University. It was supported by a grant from the National Science Foundation (NSF-G-16838) to Elliot Aronson; the research was conducted while Merrill Carlsmith was on the tenure of a National Science Foundation fellowship.

Several investigators have found that the degree of induced opinion change varies as a positive function of the degree of discrepancy (Cohen, 1959; Goldberg, 1954; Hovland and Pritzker, 1957; Zimbardo, 1960). However, other investigators have found evidence for resistance to change when the discrepancy is extreme (Cohen, 1959; Fisher and Lubin, 1958; Hovland, Harvey, and Sherif, 1957).

Some attempts have been made to explain these inconsistent findings. Hovland et al. (1957), for example, have suggested that there is a linear relationship between discrepancy and opinion change only when the audience is not highly involved with the topic of the communication. They assert that when involvement is high, the function is curvilinear—that with great discrepancies there is little opinion change.

A different explanation, based upon the theory of cognitive dissonance (Festinger, 1957), was proposed by Festinger and Aronson (1960). They suggested that the apparently inconsistent findings could be explained by an interaction between discrepancy and credibility. According to Festinger and Aronson, when an individual finds that an opinion advocated by a credible communicator is discrepant from his own opinion he experiences dissonance. His cognition that he holds a particular opinion is dissonant with his cognition that a credible communicator holds a somewhat different opinion. The greater the discrepancy between his own opinion and the opinion advocated by the communicator, the greater the dissonance. Generally, a person might reduce this dissonance in at least four ways: He could change his own opinion to bring it closer to that of the communicator; change the communicator's opinion to bring it closer to his own opinion; seek support for his opinion by finding other people who hold similar opinions; derogate the communicator—that is, make the opinion of the communicator nonapplicable to his own by discounting the ability of the communicator to have a valuable opinion on the topic. However, in most experimental influence situations, a communication is delivered either by a noninteracting speaker or in the form of a written message. Hence, it is impossible for the recipient to influence the communicator's opinion. In addition, the recipient is usually a member of a noninteracting audience. Hence, he is unable to seek immediate social support. Therefore, in this type of situation, the recipient may reduce dissonance by changing his own opinion or by derogating the communicator.

The magnitude of dissonance increases as a function of the discrepancy. Thus, if dissonance were reduced by opinion change alone, then the degree of opinion change would increase as a direct function of the extent of discrepancy. But dissonance can also be reduced by derogating the communicator; as with opinion change, the tendency to derogate the communicator should likewise increase as a direct function of the extent of the discrepancy. Moreover, it seems reasonable to assume that at the extremes, opinion changes and derogation of the communicator are clear alternatives. A person is not likely to change his opinion in the direction of a communicator whom he has sharply derogated; similarly, he is not likely to derogate a communicator who had induced a major change in his opinion.[1]

What conditions will maximize dissonance reduction through opinion change rather than derogation? Credibility seems to be crucial. If a communicator has perfect credibility, he cannot be derogated (by definition). Here, dissonance can be reduced only by opinion change. In this situation, dissonance theory would predict that degree of opinion change would vary as a direct function of the extent of discrepancy. This prediction received support from an experiment by Zimbardo (1960). In this experiment, if the communicator was the best friend of the recipient, she was able to induce the greatest opinion change when the discrepancy was the greatest; this was true even when the advocated position was described previously by the recipient as unreasonable and indefensible.

At the other extreme, if a communicator has no credibility, he can be derogated completely (by definition). In this case, there would be no opinion change regardless of the degree of discrepancy, since a discrepant statement would not arouse dissonance.

Consider a communicator of mild credibility. Here, both opinion change and derogation can be used to reduce dissonance. If a communication is relatively close to the opinion of the recipient, the existing dissonance can be reduced easily by a slight shift in opinion. On the other hand, if the discrepancy is great, a person can reduce dissonance much more easily by derogating the communicator. That is, if the position advocated by a mildly credible communicator is extreme, it may appear quite unrealistic to the recipient. If this were the case, it is unlikely that he would change his attitude very much. Instead, he might reduce dissonance by deciding that the communicator is unrealistic — or stupid, naive, untruthful, etc.

This experiment was designed to investigate the conditions under which changing one's opinion and derogating the communicator are chosen as alternative methods of reducing the dissonance which is created when an individual is exposed to an opinion which is discrepant from his own. Suppose subjects are exposed to persuasive communications at various distances from their original positions, and for some subjects the communicator is presented as highly credible (virtually indisparageable), while for other subjects the communicator is presented as mildly credible (easily disparageable). For each level of communicator credibility, we may predict a different function relating discrepancy to opinion change. Thus, it should be possible to construct a family of curves reflecting opinion change as a function of communicator credibility and degree of discrepancy. In the ideal

---

[1]This is true *only* at the extremes. Theoretically if neither opinion change nor derogation is extreme, dissonance may be reduced by a combination of both processes.

case—the case of a communicator who is perfectly indisparageable—opinion change should be a linear function of discrepancy. The larger the degree of opinion change advocated, the greater the dissonance, and hence, the greater the opinion change. As the communicator becomes less credible, and derogation becomes a possible avenue of dissonance reduction, we predict that the curve will decline near the extreme end. As the discrepancy becomes large, derogation will be an easier method of dissonance reduction than opinion change, and, consequently, there would be little or no opinion change and great derogation of the communicator. As the communicator becomes even less credible, the curve representing opinion change will begin to decline at a point closer to the origin (zero discrepancy). Finally, in the ideal case of zero credibility, the curve should be completely flat. Moreover, the curve for a highly credible communicator should be higher at all points of discrepancy. This follows because a highly credible communicator can arouse greater dissonance and hence induce greater opinion change; dissonance introduced by a communicator of low credibility can be more easily reduced by disparaging the communicator than by changing opinions. (See Fig. 6.1 for theoretical and actual curves.)

PROCEDURE

In order to test these hypotheses, an experiment was designed which had the following characteristics:

1. The subjects were exposed to a persuasive communication which was identical for all groups except for the extent of the discrepancy and the credibility of the communicator.
2. The task was such that the original opinions of the subjects fell at the same position on some continuum so that the amount of change advocated could be determined independently of the initial position of the subject.
3. The subsequent opinions of the subjects as well as the amount of derogation of the communicator were measured.

The subjects were 112 female college students[2] who were paid volunteers for "an experiment in esthetics." They met in small groups, ranging in size from two to seven. The subjects were told that the experimenter was interested in studying how people evaluate poetry. They were first asked to rank order nine stanzas from obscure modern poems, all of which contained alliteration. The criterion for ranking was stated ambiguously: "the way the poet

---

[2]Actually, 115 subjects participated in the experiment. The data from 3 were discarded because the experimental sanction against intercommunication was not observed; one of the subjects announced loudly (within earshot of the others) that she disagreed with the author of the essay.

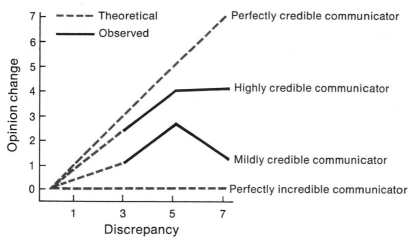

FIGURE 6.1
Opinion change as a function of credibility and extent of discrepancy—theoretical and observed curves.

uses form to aid in expressing his meaning." Next, each subject was asked to read a two-page essay entitled "The Use of Alliteration in Poetry." This communication consisted mostly of general statements about the uses and abuses of alliteration in poetic writing. The final half page consisted of an illustration of the points made in the essay; that is, the ideas stated in the essay were applied in the evaluation of a particular stanza. For each subject, the stanza that was used as an illustration was the one that she had originally ranked as the eighth-best stanza.

For approximately one-third of the subjects there was a small discrepancy between her opinion of the stanza and the communicator's opinion; for approximately one-third of the subjects there was a moderate discrepancy; and for approximately one-third of the subjects there was an extreme discrepancy. The discrepancy was created by having the communication state that the poem was better than the subject had indicated in her first ranking. The slight discrepancy was established by introducing the stanza as average; the communication asserted that half of the stanzas were better, half worse. The medium discrepancy was established by introducing the stanza as one of the better examples; it was stated that two of the others were superior. The large discrepancy was established by introducing the stanza as the best example of the use of alliteration in the sample. In summary, the subjects were faced with a discrepancy of either three, five, or seven rank-order positions between their ranking of the crucial stanza and that of the communicator.

In each of these three conditions, some of the subjects read communications supposedly written by a highly credible source—an expert on poetry;

the others read virtually identical essays, supposedly written by a student. T. S. Eliot was chosen as the expert or highly credible source. It was assumed that his importance as both a poet and a critic would be well known to the subjects and, therefore, that it would be relatively difficult for them to discount his judgment of the poems. In the mildly credible condition, the communication was attributed to a Miss Agnes Stearns, who was described as a student at Mississippi State Teachers College. The subjects were told that Miss Stearns planned to become a high school English teacher—that she had composed the essay and had asked the experimenter (her cousin) to show it to the subjects. In all conditions, subjects were told that the experimenter was interested in seeing whether the communication would help them to evaluate poetry.

After the subjects had read the essay, they were told that their initial ranking was used merely to acquaint them with the poetry and with the ranking procedure. The experimenter explained that now that they were familiar with the ranking technique, they should carefully rank the poems a second time according to the same criterion. Finally, they were asked to evaluate the essay by indicating on a seven-point scale the strength of their agreement or disagreement with 14 evaluative statements about the essay and the author (e.g., the coherence of the essay, the reasonableness of the author, etc.). These evaluative statements constituted our measure of disparagement.

At the end of the session, the purpose of the experiment and the need for deception were discussed.

RESULTS

According to the theory, the highly credible communicator should produce greater opinion change when he advocates a more extreme position. The greater the discrepancy between his opinion and the opinion of the recipient, the greater the opinion change. On the other hand, the mildly credible communicator should produce greater opinion change with increasing discrepancy only up to a point; as his position becomes more extreme, recipients will resort to disparagement rather than opinion change as a means of reducing dissonance.

Table 6.1 shows the mean opinion change in each of the six conditions. It is apparent that the highly credible communicator was more successful in inducing opinion change than the mildly credible communicator at every point of discrepancy. Moreover, in the High Credibility condition, opinion

TABLE 6.1
Mean opinion change

Communicator	Discrepancy			Differences between conditions of discrepancy for each communicator[b]		
	Small	Medium	Large	Small-medium	Medium-large	Small-large
Highly credible	2.50 (16)[a]	4.06 (16)	4.14 (14)	2.25*	0.11	2.45*
Mildly credible	1.19 (21)	2.56 (23)	1.41 (22)	2.42**	2.06*	0.39

Condition	Differences between communicators for each condition of discrepancy[b]		
	Small	Medium	Large
High credibility — mild credibility	2.49**	2.22*	4.37†

[a]*n* 's appear in parentheses.   [b]*t* values.   *$p < .05$, two-tailed.   **$p < .02$.   †$p < .001$.

change increases with degree of discrepancy. The mildly credible communicator is not only less able to induce opinion change, but actually induces less change with a large discrepancy than with a moderate discrepancy.

Figure 6.1 shows a family of theoretical and actual curves for this situation. The degree of discrepancy is plotted on the abscissa, and the degree of opinion change is plotted on the ordinate. We have predicted a different curve for each degree of communicator credibility. The 45-degree line is a theoretical curve representing the "perfectly credible" communicator, perhaps unattainable experimentally. In response to such a communicator, disparagement is impossible, so that opinion change is the only means of reducing dissonance. The horizontal line is a theoretical curve representing the "perfectly incredible" communicator. In this case, the recipient would experience no dissonance regardless of the extent of the discrepancy between his opinion and that advocated by the communicator. The other two curves show intermediate degrees of credibility. These curves are empirical, representing the opinion change of the subjects in this experiment. As the communicator is made less credible, the curve is lowered at all points (since more disparagement takes place at all points, reducing some of the dissonance). Similarly, as the communicator is made less credible, the curve reaches its maximum sooner (as disparagement replaces opinion change as the major method of reducing dissonance).

TABLE 6.2
Derogation of the communicator

Communicator	Discrepancy		
	Small	Medium	Large
Highly credible	31.75	29.31	32.43
Mildly credible	60.10	58.04	56.00

To some extent, the results involving the derogation of the communicator lend support to this analysis. The results pertinent to derogation are presented in Table 6.2. It is clear that subjects derogated the mildly credible communicator to a greater extent than the highly credible communicator. This was the case irrespective of the degree of the discrepancy; for each condition of discrepancy, the difference between the derogation of the highly credible and mildly credible communicators is highly significant. These results are not unequivocal, however. As can be seen from inspection of Table 6.2, there was no difference in derogation among the various conditions of discrepancy in the Mildly Credible condition. These data do not support our theoretical analysis. That is, although we have demonstrated that credibility and discrepancy do interact to produce opinion change as predicted, our analysis suggests systematic differences in the derogation of the communicator within the Mildly Credible condition. Specifically, it was predicted that in the Mildly Credible condition, with high discrepancy, derogation would be used in lieu of opinion change as a means of reducing dissonance. Thus, if our analysis is correct, subjects in this condition appear to have ended the experiment carrying a barrel full of dissonance. This is an unenviable circumstance—for the theorists as well as the subjects. There appears to be no easy theoretical explanation for this datum. Methodologically, it is possible that our measure of derogation was not a very good one. It may have been sensitive enough to induce the subjects to playback the instructions, leaving those in the Mildly Credible condition more derogatory than those in the Highly Credible condition. But our measure may not have been sensitive enough to reflect fine distinctions within the Mildly Credible condition. Similarly, it is well known that college students are often reluctant to make extremely negative statements about a fellow student. That is, in the Mildly Credible condition, there may have been a ceiling effect in the disparagement scale; the degree of derogation may have been maximal even when the communicator's position was not discrepant. Thus, subjects in this condition may have privately derogated the communicator without expressing it in writing. Although these methodological explanations are convenient from our point of view, they are hardly conclusive. Further research may suggest alternative explanations for these particular results.

Reconciliation of Results with Previous Findings

The main body of results supports the theoretical analysis and suggests a reconciliation of previous contradictory findings. It is a reasonable assumption that each of the previous experiments examined only one of the family of theoretical functions outlined above. We may at least tentatively support such an assumption by a brief analysis of the disparageability of the communicators used in these studies.

Let us first examine some studies which found a linear relationship between opinion change and degree of discrepancy. As previously mentioned, Zimbardo (1960) used as a communicator a person who was not only a close friend of the subject, but one who was also a proven expert in the area of the communication. Clearly, this communicator was highly credible. Hovland and Pritzker (1957) described their communicator as "respected by the recipient, and hence an authoritative source of opinion." Goldberg (1954) used, as an expert, the combined previous judgments of the subject himself and one or more peers. It seems reasonable that such a combined judgment (of from two to four people, *including* the subject himself) would be difficult to disparage.

In contrast, Hovland et al. (1957), who found decreasing opinion change with an extreme discrepancy, used a communicator without describing him to the subject. To quote the authors, there was "ambiguity about the credibility of the communicator." Fisher and Lubin (1958), who found a similar effect, used a single unexpert peer as a communicator. It seems apparent that such a communicator was relatively easy to disparage.

In Cohen's (1959) experiment the communicator was defined only by a description of the communication. When the communication was described as "difficult and subtle," "arguments . . . related in a complex fashion," Cohen found increasing opinion change with increasing discrepancy. However, when the communication was described as "easy to grasp," he found less opinion change with high discrepancy. It may be assumed that a communicator who has been able to compose a complex, difficult, and subtle argument is perceived as more intelligent and, hence, more credible than a communicator whose argument is simple and easy to grasp. Moreover, it is difficult to disparage a communicator after one has been told that one might not be able to understand the communication, since disliking the communication may be tantamount to failing to understand it.

References

ARNET, C. C., DAVIDSON, HELEN H., AND LEWIS, H. N. Prestige as a factor in attitude change. *Sociol. soc. Res.,* 1931, **16,** 49–55.

COHEN, A. R. Communication discrepancy and attitude change. *J. Pers.,* 1959, **27,** 386–396.

FESTINGER, L. *A theory of cognitive dissonance.* Evanston, Ill.: Row, Peterson, 1957.

FESTINGER, L., AND ARONSON, E. The arousal and reduction of dissonance in social contexts. In D. Cartwright and A. Zander (eds.), *Group dynamics: Research and theory.* (2nd ed.) Evanston, Ill.: Row, Peterson, 1960. Pp. 214–231.

FISHER, S., AND LUBIN, A. Distance as a determinant of influence in a two-person serial interaction situation. *J. abnorm. soc. Psychol.,* 1958, **56,** 230–238.

GOLDBERG S. C. Three situational determinants of conformity to social norms. *J. abnorm. soc. Psychol.,* 1954, **49,** 325–329.

HAIMAN, F. S. An experimental study of the effects of ethos in public speaking. *Speech Monogr.,* 1949, **16,** 190–202.

HOVLAND, C. I., HARVEY, L. J., AND SHERIF, M. Assimilation and contrast effects in reactions to communication and attitude change. *J. abnorm. soc. Psychol.,* 1957, **55,** 244–252.

HOVLAND, C. I., AND PRITZKER, H. A. Extent of opinion change as a function of change advocated. *J. abnorm. soc. Psychol.,* 1957, **54,** 257–261.

HOVLAND, C. I., AND WEISS, W. The influence of source credibility on communication effectiveness. *Publ. Opin. Quart.,* 1952, **15,** 635–650.

KELMAN, H. C., AND HOVLAND, C. I. "Reinstatement" of the communicator in delayed measurement of opinion change. *J. abnorm. soc. Psychol.,* 1953, **48,** 327–335.

KULP, D. H. Prestige as measured by single-experience changes and their permanency. *J. educ. Res.,* 1934, **27,** 663–672.

ZIMBARDO, P. G. Involvement and communication discrepancy as determinants of opinion conformity. *J. abnorm. soc. Psychol.,* 1960, **60,** 86–94.

7

Effects of Varying the Recommendations in a Fear-Arousing Communication

James M. Dabbs, Jr., and Howard Leventhal

It has been suggested that divergent effects of fear arousal on attitude change can be caused by variations in the recommendations in a persuasive communication. In a three-way factorial design Ss were presented with communications manipulating fear of tetanus and the perceived effectiveness and painfulness of inoculation against tetanus. Inoculation was recommended for all Ss. It was expected that more Ss would take shots described as highly effective and not painful, and that this tendency would change as level of fear was increased. The manipulations of effectiveness and painfulness were perceived as intended, but they did not affect intentions to take shots or shot-taking behavior. The fear manipulation influenced both intentions and behavior, with higher fear producing greater compliance with the recommendations.

A number of studies have investigated the effects of fear arousal on persuasion. Although the majority report that fear increases persuasion, the picture is not completely clear. Facilitating effects of fear on persuasion have been reported in studies of dental hygiene practices (Haefner, 1965; Leventhal and Singer, 1966; Singer, 1965), tetanus inoculations (Leventhal, Jones, and Trembly, 1966; Leventhal, Singer, and Jones, 1965), safe driving practices (Berkowitz and Cottingham, 1960; Leventhal and Niles, 1965), and cigarette smoking (Insko, Arkoff, and Insko, 1965; Leventhal and Watts, 1966; Niles, 1964). However, under increasing levels of fear Janis and Feshbach (1953)

Reprinted with permission from the authors and *The Journal of Personality and Social Psychology*, Vol. 4, No. 5, 1966. Copyright 1966 by the American Psychological Association.

The present study was supported in part by United States Public Health Service Grant CH00077–04 to Howard Leventhal. The authors wish to thank John S. Hathaway and James S. Davie of the Yale University Department of University Health for their many contributions to the research.

observed no increase in acceptance of beliefs about the proper type of tooth-brush to use, and Leventhal and Niles (1964) observed some decrease in acceptance of a recommendation to stop smoking. All these results are based on verbal measures of *attitude* change.

The picture is even less clear when one considers actual *behavior* change. The study on tetanus by Leventhal et al. (1965) reports that some minimal amount of fear is necessary for behavior change, but that further increases in fear do not affect change. The later study by Leventhal et al. (1966) reports a slight tendency for increases in fear to increase behavior change. In the studies of dental hygiene practices, Janis and Feshbach (1953) reported decreased behavior change under high fear, while Singer (1965) found no main effect of fear. In the study on smoking by Leventhal and Watts (1966) high fear simultaneously increased compliance with a recommendation to cut down on smoking and decreased compliance with a recommendation to take an X-ray.

The present study attempted to account for some of these divergent findings. It is reasonable to expect that the behavior being recommended by a persuasive communication is of critical importance (Leventhal, 1965). Recommendations that are seen as effective in controlling danger may be accepted more readily as fear is increased, while ineffective recommendations may be rejected rationally or may produce reactions of denial (Janis and Feshbach, 1953) or aggression (Janis and Terwilliger, 1962). Additionally, rejection of a recommended behavior may occur if subjects have become afraid of the behavior itself (Leventhal and Watts, 1966).

Recommendations presented as part of fear-arousing communications vary in their effectiveness in controlling danger and in the unpleasantness associated with them. For example, brushing the teeth offers no guarantee of preventing decay, while taking a chest X-ray can lead to the unpleasant discovery of lung cancer. An audience might well reject recommendations which are ineffective in warding off danger or which are difficult, painful, or apt to bring unpleasant consequences. Recommendation factors have been invoked post hoc to explain research findings, but have not been manipulated and studied directly.

In the present study fear was manipulated by presenting differing discussions of the danger of tetanus. Inoculations and booster shots were recommended for protection against tetanus. Under high and low levels of fear, inoculation was portrayed so that it would be seen as more or less *effective* in preventing tetanus and more or less *painful* to take (these manipulations were orthogonal). Subjects' intentions to take shots and their actual shot-taking behavior were used to measure compliance with the recommendations.

It was expected that compliance would be greater when shots were highly effective or not painful. These factors might produce simple main effects or they might interact with level of fear. It seemed more likely that the latter would be the case — that increased fear would make subjects either more or less sensitive to differences in the recommendations.

METHOD

Subjects and Design

Letters were sent to all Yale College seniors asking them to participate in a study to be conducted jointly by the John Slade Ely Center, a local research organization, and the Department of University Health. The study was presented as a survey of student health practices at Yale and an evaluation of some health-education materials. An attempt was then made to contact all seniors by telephone for scheduling.

Of approximately 1000 students who received letters, 274 were scheduled and run in the experiment. Seventy-seven of these were excluded because they had been inoculated since the preceding academic year, and 15 were excluded because of suspicion, involvement in compulsory inoculation programs, allergic reactions to inoculation, or religious convictions against inoculation. The final usable N was 182.

Each subject received a communication which was intended to manipulate perceived effectiveness and painfulness of inoculation. Three levels of fear (including a no-fear control level), two levels of effectiveness, and two levels of pain were combined in a $3 \times 2 \times 2$ factorial design. The n's for the resulting 12 conditions ranged from 11 to 20, with smaller n's in the no-fear control conditions.

Procedure

Experimental sessions were conducted in a classroom with groups ranging in size from 1 to 12. Subjects within each session were randomly assigned to conditions. Control (no-fear) conditions were run separately because of the brevity of the control communications.

Questionnaires containing medical items and personality premeasures were administered at the beginning of the session. Subjects then read a communication on tetanus and gave their reactions to it in a second questionnaire. They were assured that all their responses would be kept confidential.

Communications

Communications were ten-page pamphlets which discussed the danger of tetanus and the effectiveness and painfulness of inoculation.[1] All pamphlets gave specific instructions on how to become inoculated and were similar in style and content to those used by Leventhal et al. (1965) and Leventhal et al. (1966).

Fear. Low-fear material described the very low incidence of tetanus and indicated that bleeding from a wound usually flushes the poison-producing bacilli out of the body. A case history was included which reported recovery from tetanus following mild medication and throat-suction procedures. High-fear material indicated that tetanus can be contracted through seemingly trivial means and that if contracted the chances of death are high. A high-fear case history was included which reported death from tetanus despite heavy medication and surgery to relieve throat congestion. Black-and-white photographs were included in the low-fear material and color photographs in the high-fear material. The discussion of tetanus and case history were omitted entirely from control (no-fear) communications.

Effectiveness. The effectiveness manipulation stressed either the imperfections or the unusual effectiveness of inoculation. Low-effectiveness material stated that inoculation is generally effective and about as adequate as the measures available to deal with other kinds of danger. It pointed out, however, that no protection is perfect and that there is a possibility that even an inoculated person will contract tetanus. High-effectiveness material described inoculation as almost perfect and as far superior to methods available to deal with other kinds of danger. It emphasized that inoculation reduces the chances of contracting tetanus, for all practical purposes, to zero. All communications reported that a new type of inoculation was available at the Department of University Health which would provide protection against tetanus for a period of 10 years.

Pain. To produce fear of the recommended behavior, it was pointed out that inoculation against tetanus has always been painful. Subjects were told that the new inoculation requires a deep intramuscular injection of tetanus

---

[1]Communications have been deposited with the American Documentation Institute. Order Document No. 9011 from ADI Auxiliary Publications Project, Photoduplication Service, Library of Congress, Washington, D.C. 20540. Remit in advance $2.00 for microfilm or $3.75 for photocopies and make checks payable to: Chief, Photoduplication Service, Library of Congress.

toxoid and alum precipitate, making the injection even more painful than before and the local reaction longer lasting. The discussion of pain was presented to subjects as a forewarning so that the discomfort would not take them by surprise. This discussion was omitted from pamphlets in the no-pain conditions.

Specific instructions on how to get a shot and a map showing the location of the Department of University Health were included in all pamphlets. Subjects were encouraged to get a shot or at least to check on whether or not they needed one.

Measures

Most questions on the pre- and postcommunication questionnaires were answered on 7-point rating scales. The precommunication questionnaire contained medical questions and four personality measures (susceptibility, coping, anxiety, and self-esteem). The susceptibility measure was made up of three items which asked subjects how susceptible they felt toward common illnesses, toward unusual diseases, and toward illness and disease in general. Three items used to measure coping asked subjects whether they tended to tackle problems actively or to postpone dealing with them. The problems concerned subjects' health habits, their everyday lives as students, and their decisions regarding summer activities. The anxiety scale was made up of 10 true-false items from the Taylor (1953) Manifest Anxiety scale.

The self-esteem measure was similar to that used by Dabbs (1964). Subjects rated themselves on 20 adjectives and descriptive phrases and then rated each of the 20 items as to its desirability. Eight items were classified as desirable and 12 as undesirable on the basis of mean ratings from the entire sample of subjects. Using this group criterion of desirability, each subject's self-esteem score was defined as the sum of his ratings of himself on the undesirable items subtracted from the sum of his ratings on the desirable items. (It was subsequently discovered that 12 subjects in the present study had participated in the earlier study by Dabbs, and the correlation between their self-esteem scores in the two studies was .62, $p < .01$. This correlation, despite a lapse of 3 years and changes in the measuring instrument, suggests this type of measure is reasonably stable.)

The postcommunication questionnaire included checks on each of the experimental manipulations, a 10-item mood adjective check list, and questions on intentions to take shots, the importance of shots, and the likelihood of contracting tetanus. The subject's evaluation of the pamphlet and the date and place of his last tetanus shot were obtained on this questionnaire.

TABLE 7.1
Compliance with recommendations

	Control (no fear)	Low fear	High fear
Mean intentions to take shots	4.12	4.73	5.17
Proportion of Ss taking shots	.06	.13	.22
N	48	62	72

A measure of behavioral compliance with the recommendations was obtained from shot records of the Department of University Health. Subjects were counted as complying if they took tetanus shots between the experimental sessions and the end of the semester, about one month later. When contacted by letter and phone, no subjects reported receiving shots at places other than the Department of University Health. A few reported that they had tried to take shots and had been told they did not need any. These subjects were counted as having taken shots, but their data are presented separately in footnote 2.

RESULTS

Main Effects of the Manipulations

Compliance with the recommendations was unaffected by the manipulations of effectiveness and pain. The manipulation of fear, however, influenced both intentions to take shots ($F_{2,179} = 4.85$, $p < .01$) and actual shot-taking behavior[2] ($F = 3.39$, $p < .05$). The effects were linear (Table 7.1), with compliance being greatest under high fear. The consistency of subjects' responses is indicated by high biserial correlations between intention and behavior measures within high-fear ($r_b = .62$, $p < .01$) and low-fear ($r_b = .68$, $p < .01$) conditions; no correlation was computed for the control conditions since only three control subjects took shots.

[2] "Shot-taking behavior" combines 20 subjects who took shots and 7 who reported trying to take shots. These two categories are distributed similarly across the fear treatment conditions: 2, 6, and 12 subjects took shots; and 1, 2, and 4 subjects tried to do so.

An arc sine transformation of the proportions in Table 7.1 was used (Winer, 1962). This made it possible to test the significance of the differences between groups against the *baseline variance* of the transformation (see Gilson and Abelson, 1965). Base-line variance has a theoretical value which does not depend on computations from observed data. In the present case this value is given by the reciprocal of the harmonic mean number of cases on which each proportion is based, or $1/59 = .0169$.

TABLE 7.2
Other reactions to fear manipulation

	Control	Low fear	High fear	F^a
Fear[b]	7.74	9.25	12.19	21.50**
Feelings of nausea	1.27	1.24	1.90	7.95**
Feelings of interest	4.48	4.70	5.39	6.12**
Evaluation of the severity of tetanus	4.64	4.83	5.34	3.86*
Feelings of susceptibility to tetanus	3.46	3.99	4.25	3.31*
Evaluation of the importance of shots	5.85	6.16	6.52	6.44**
Desire for more information about tetanus	3.08	2.68	3.57	3.90*

[a]F ratios are computed from three-way analyses of variance. In each analysis $df = 2/170$ (approximately).
[b]"Fear" represents the sum of three items: feelings of fear, fear of contracting tetanus, and fear produced by the pamphlet.
　*$p < .05$.
　**$p < .01$.

Table 7.2 shows that the fear manipulation increased feelings of fear, as it was intended to do. It also increased feelings of interest and nausea, belief in the severity of tetanus and the importance of taking shots, and desire to have additional information. None of these measures were affected by the manipulations of effectiveness or pain.

Both effectiveness and pain were successfully manipulated. Check questions showed that subjects in the high-effectiveness conditions felt inoculation was more effective than did those in the low-effectiveness conditions ($\bar{X}_{high} = 6.7$, $\bar{X}_{low} = 5.8$, $F_{1,170} = 105.85$, $p < .01$). Subjects in the pain conditions felt shots would be more painful ($\bar{X}_{pain} = 4.1$, $\bar{X}_{no\ pain} = 2.3$, $F_{1,170} = 74.56$, $p < .01$) and reported more "mixed feelings" about taking shots ($F_{1,170} = 7.20$, $p < .01$) than did subjects in the no-pain conditions. But the clear perception of differences in effectiveness did not affect subjects' intentions to take shots, nor did increasing the anticipated painfulness of shots decrease intentions to take them. In fact, there was a slight tendency for painfulness to strengthen intentions to be inoculated ($F_{1,170} = 2.72$, $p = .10$).

Correlations Among Responses

Only within the high-fear condition did reported fear correlate with intentions to take shots ($r = .23$, $p < .01$). A scatterplot of scores revealed that the high-fear condition increased the range of reported fear and that the positive correlation could be attributed to subjects in the extended portion

TABLE 7.3
Correlations between anger and intentions to take
shots under varying portrayal of recommendations

	Effectiveness	
	Low	High
Pain		
Low	−.29	.15
High	−.52	−.18

of the range (those scoring higher than 13 on a 19-point composite scale). These extreme subjects all showed strong intentions to take shots, while other subjects in the high-fear condition sometimes did and sometimes did not intend to take shots. This pattern suggests that fear and acceptance of a recommendation are more closely associated when fear is relatively high, though acceptance may occur at any level of reported fear.

Unlike fear, anger was negatively associated with intent to take shots. The over-all within-class correlation between anger and intentions was −.18 ($p < .05$). This correlation remained essentially the same within different levels of the fear treatment, but became increasingly negative as the recommendation was portrayed as less effective and more painful (Table 7.3). Both the row and column differences in Table 7.3 are significant[3] (for rows, $CR = 2.02$, $p < .05$; for columns, $CR = 2.81$, $p < .01$). It should be emphasized that these are correlational differences only. Low effectiveness and high pain did not increase the mean level of anger or decrease intentions (or decrease actual shot taking). The ranges of anger and intention scores also did not differ among the four conditions.

Personality Differences

None of the premeasures on personality (susceptibility, coping, anxiety, self-esteem) were significantly correlated with intentions to take shots, nor did the correlations vary systematically across the 12 experimental conditions. However, differences were observed when subjects were split at the median into groups high and low on self-esteem. Figure 7.1 shows intentions to take shots among high- and low-self-esteem subjects. The only significant effect within this data (other than the main effect of fear) is the interaction between self-esteem and fear level ($F_{2,166} = 4.74$, $p < .01$). Subjects low in

[3]Significance of these differences was tested after applying Fisher's z' transformation to the correlation coefficients.

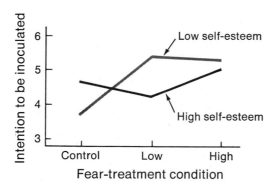

FIGURE 7.1
Self-esteem differences in reactions to the
communications on tetanus.

self-esteem increased their intentions to take shots from control to low-fear
conditions, then showed no further increase under high fear. Subjects high
in self-esteem, on the other hand, showed increased intentions only from
low- to high-fear conditions.

DISCUSSION

A positive relationship between fear arousal and persuasion was observed.
Increases in the intensity of the fear manipulation were associated with increases in attitude and behavior change, with high correlations between
intentions to take shots and actual shot taking. These findings are similar to
those of Leventhal et al. (1966), who reported a slight tendency for shot taking to increase as fear was raised from low to high levels.

Subjects' beliefs about the effectiveness of inoculation did not affect their
compliance; they responded equally well to recommendations portrayed as
low and high in effectiveness. This may be because even the low-effective
recommendation was rated relatively high in effectiveness (5.8 on a 7-point
scale). However, the manipulation was sufficient for subjects to perceive
significant differences between low and high effectiveness, and the failure
of this variable to influence compliance suggests caution in using it to recon-
cile divergent results of studies on fear arousal and persuasion (Janis and
Leventhal, 1967; Leventhal, 1965; Leventhal and Singer, 1966).

The description of pain produced mixed feelings about shots, but did not
prevent subjects from taking them. Perhaps this is because the discomfort
of inoculation is negligible in comparison with the pain of tetanus itself. A
stronger manipulation of anticipated "painfulness" was unintentionally in-

troduced in the study by Leventhal and Watts (1966), who created fear of smoking by showing a film in which a chest X-ray led to the discovery of cancer and to surgical removal of a lung. The authors suggested that decreased X-ray taking in this condition was more likely caused by fear of the consequences of an X-ray than by defensive reactions to the fear-arousing material on cancer. The present findings do not invalidate their conclusion, but they limit the range of situations to which such an explanation might apply. Subjects apparently do not respond to small variations in the effectiveness or unpleasantness of a recommended course of action. Unless a compelling deterrent exists, people who anticipate danger prefer to do something rather than nothing.

This last statement is qualified by differences in the behavior of high- and low-self-esteem subjects. Low-self-esteem subjects showed high compliance with the recommendations in both high- and low-fear conditions, while high-self-esteem subjects showed high compliance only in the high-fear condition. In addition, personality measures of self-esteem and coping were significantly correlated ($r = .49$, $p < .01$) in the present study, as they were in the study reported by Dabbs (1964). One might conclude that high-self-esteem subjects are more active and aggressive in dealing with their environment and have developed more skill in meeting dangers with appropriate protective actions. Thus, they may recognize inoculation to be more appropriate when the danger of tetanus is greater, while low-self-esteem subjects may accept the position of the communication that inoculation is appropriate regardless of the magnitude of danger. An alternative possibility is that some differences characteristically associated with self-esteem simply disappear when there is an urgent need to combat danger (as there was with the high-fear communication).

In the conditions where inoculation was depicted as ineffective or painful, anger was negatively associated with intentions to be inoculated. It is possible that increased anger in these conditions would have lowered compliance. But since anger and compliance did not covary as the fear treatment was increased, there appears to be no causal relationship between them. It seems more likely that anger does not decrease compliance, but that under certain conditions it provides the justification for noncompliance. Under other conditions—as when recommended behaviors are highly effective, not painful, and not a reasonable target for anger—noncompliance may have to be justified in some other manner.

All the present findings could have been influenced by several factors which were not varied. For example, all subjects received the manipulations of perceived danger, effectiveness, and pain in the same order. Learning about the dangers of tetanus first may have caused some subjects to ignore differences in the effectiveness and painfulness of inoculation. In addition, all subjects were asked after reading the communications whether or not they intended to be inoculated. One might expect that stating an intention to be inoculated would commit the subject to following this course of behavior later on. However, the findings of Leventhal et al. (1965) and Leventhal et al. (1966) indicate that specific instructions must be present before intentions will be translated into behavior. Since all subjects in the present study did receive specific instructions, the high correlations between intentions and behavior may be due to this factor.

Finally, while fear and persuasion were associated, the evidence of any causal relationship between them is tenuous. As in most studies of fear arousal and attitude change, the communications used were complex ones. They discussed the damage tetanus can cause and the likelihood of contracting it. They differed in fearfulness, interest, and feelings of nausea evoked. They also differed in length, type of language used, and amount of information about tetanus. With such confounding it is impossible to attribute increases in attitude change solely to increases in fear. This is an inherent difficulty when fear is manipulated by the use of differing descriptions of danger. Another approach should be developed by anyone wishing to manipulate fear independently of other aspects of a persuasive communication.

References

BERKOWITZ, L., AND COTTINGHAM, D. R. The interest value and relevance of fear-arousing communications. *Journal of Abnormal and Social Psychology*, 1960, **60**, 37–43.

DABBS, J. M., JR. Self-esteem, communicator characteristics, and attitude change. *Journal of Abnormal and Social Psychology*, 1964, **69**, 173–181.

GILSON, C., AND ABELSON, R. P. The subjective use of inductive evidence. *Journal of Personality and Social Psychology*, 1965, **2**, 301–310.

HAEFNER, D. P. Arousing fear in dental health education. *Journal of Public Health Dentistry*, 1965, **25**, 140–146.

INSKO, C. A., ARKOFF, A., AND INSKO, V. M. Effects of high and low fear-arousing communications upon opinions toward smoking. *Journal of Experimental Social Psychology*, 1965, **1**, 256–266.

JANIS, I. L., AND FESHBACH, S. Effects of fear-arousing communications. *Journal of Abnormal and Social Psychology*, 1953, **48**, 78–92.

JANIS, I. L., AND LEVENTHAL, H. Human reactions to stress. In E. Borgatta and W. Lambert (eds.), *Handbook of personality theory and research*. New York: Rand McNally, 1967.

JANIS, I. L., AND TERWILLIGER, R. An experimental study of psychological resistances to fear-arousing communications. *Journal of Abnormal and Social Psychology*, 1962, **65**, 403–410.

LEVENTHAL, H. Fear communications in the acceptance of preventive health practices. *Bulletin of the New York Academy of Medicine,* 1965, **41,** 1144–1168.

LEVENTHAL, H., JONES, S., AND TREMBLY, G. Sex differences in attitude and behavior change under conditions of fear and specific instructions. *Journal of Experimental Social Psychology,* 1966, **2,** 387–399.

LEVENTHAL, H., AND NILES, P. A field experiment on fear arousal with data on the validity of questionnaire measures. *Journal of Personality,* 1964, **32,** 459–479.

LEVENTHAL, H., AND NILES, P. Persistence of influence for varying durations of threat stimuli. *Psychological Reports,* 1965, **16,** 223–233.

LEVENTHAL, H., AND SINGER, R. P. Affect arousal and positioning of recommendations in persuasive communications. *Journal of Personality and Social Psychology,* 1966, **4,** 137–146.

LEVENTHAL, H., SINGER, R. P., AND JONES, S. Effects of fear and specificity of recommendations upon attitudes and behavior. *Journal of Personality and Social Psychology,* 1965, **2,** 20–29.

LEVENTHAL, H., AND WATTS, J. C. Sources of resistance to fear-arousing communications on smoking and lung cancer. *Journal of Personality,* 1966, **34,** 155–175.

NILES, P. The relationships of susceptibility and anxiety to acceptance of fear-arousing communications. Unpublished doctoral dissertation, Yale University, 1964.

SINGER, R. P. The effects of fear-arousing communications on attitude change and behavior. Unpublished doctoral dissertation, University of Connecticut, 1965. *Dissertation Abstracts,* 1966, **26,** 5574.

TAYLOR, J. A. A personality scale of manifest anxiety. *Journal of Abnormal and Social Psychology,* 1953, **48,** 285–290.

WINER, B. J. *Statistical principles in experimental design.* New York: McGraw-Hill, 1962.

8

On Resistance to Persuasive Communications

Leon Festinger and Nathan Maccoby[1]

Three separate experiments were done at different universities to test the hypothesis that a persuasive communication that argues strongly against an opinion to which the audience is committed will be more effective if the audience is somewhat distracted from the communication so that they cannot adequately counterargue while listening. Two films were prepared, each containing the same communication arguing strongly against fraternities. One was a normal film of the speaker making a speech. The other film, with the same track, had an utterly irrelevant and highly distracting visual presentation. Fraternity men were more influenced by the distracting presentation of the persuasive communication than by the ordinary version. There was no difference between the two for nonfraternity men. In general, the hypothesis concerning the effect of distraction was supported.

Some time ago Allyn and Festinger (1961) reported an experiment which showed that if subjects are forewarned concerning the content of a communication arguing against an opinion they hold strongly, they tend to reject the speaker more and are influenced less than if they are not forewarned. Since the ideas which form the basis for the present article emerge in part from that experiment, it is necessary to examine it in some detail.

Allyn and Festinger, in their experiment, used high school students as subjects on the assumption that high school students, at or approaching the age at which they could obtain licenses to drive automobiles (age sixteen

Reprinted with permission from the authors and *The Journal of Abnormal and Social Psychology,* Vol. 68, No. 4, 1964. Copyright 1964 by the American Psychological Association.

The studies reported in this paper were supported by funds from Grant Number G-11255 from the National Science Foundation to Leon Festinger and by funds from Stanford University Institute for Communication Research to Nathan Maccoby.

[1]The authors wish to express their thanks and appreciation to Ernest W. Rose and Henry Breitrose for their help in planning the experiments, devising and preparing the experimental materials, and in conducting the actual experiments.

in California), would be rather strongly committed to opinions that teen-agers were good and capable drivers. This assumption was, of course, largely correct. For the experiment a sizable number of these high school students were assembled in the high school auditorium where they heard a person, announced to them as an authority on the subject, deliver a speech denouncing teen-age drivers and arguing that the only thing to do was to keep teen-agers off the road for as long as possible. The subjects were then asked several questions to measure their opinions about driving by teen-agers.

Two conditions were run in this experiment. As each subject entered the auditorium, he was given a booklet. For half of the subjects, the cover page on this booklet told them that they were to hear a speech against teen-age driving and that they should listen carefully since they would be asked questions about the speaker's opinions. This was the "forewarned" condition. For the other half of the subjects, the cover page told them that they would hear a person make a speech (nothing about the content of the speech) and that they should listen carefully because, afterwards, they would be asked questions about the speaker's personality.

The results of the experiment showed that in the "forewarned" condition, the students were relatively uninfluenced by the speaker and rejected him more than in the "personality" condition where the speaker successfully influenced their attitudes. The authors of the experiment interpret this result as implying that, if persons who are rather committed to a given opinion are forewarned that their opinion will be attacked, they are better able to marshal their defenses and, hence, are more successful in rejecting the speaker and in resisting his persuasions.

At first glance, this seems like a plausible interpretation of the result and fits many common-sense conceptions such as "forewarned is forearmed" and the like. Further consideration of the matter, however, produces some concern about the adequacy of this interpretation. The difference between the "forewarned" and the "personality-orientation" conditions was created by what they read on the face sheet of the booklet. After having read this, the speech commenced. Virtually the first words out of the speaker's mouth were a vigorous denunciation of teen-agers in automobiles. In other words, after the first few sentences of the speech, the personality-orientation subjects were *also* forewarned. Indeed, in terms of being forewarned, the only difference between conditions seems to have been a matter of when the forewarning took place, at the beginning of the speech or two to three minutes earlier. If does seem somewhat implausible for such a small time difference to have produced the result reported in the experiment.

But if we do not like the explanation offered by Allyn and Festinger, the problem is then created as to how one would, plausibly, explain the results they obtained. In order to arrive at such an explanation, let us first try to understand the cognitive behavior of a person who, strongly committed to an opinion, listens to a vigorous, persuasive communication that attacks that opinion. Certainly, such a listener is not passive. He does not sit there listening and absorbing what is said without any counteraction on his part. Indeed, it is most likely that under such circumstances, while he is listening to the persuasive communication, he is very actively, inside his own mind, counterarguing, derogating the points the communicator makes, and derogating the communicator himself. In other words, we can imagine that there is really an argument going on, one side being vocal and the other subvocal.

Let us imagine that one could somehow prevent the listener from arguing back while listening to the persuasive communication. If one created such a passive listener, it seems reasonable to expect that the persuasive communication would then have more of an impact. The listener, not able to counterargue, would be more influenced and would be less likely to reject the communication. And perhaps this is exactly what was really done in the experiment reported by Allyn and Festinger. The group that was not forewarned was also told to pay attention to the speaker's personality. In other words, a good deal of their attention was focused on a task which had little to do with the persuasive communication itself. It may be that, under such circumstances, they still listen to, and hear, the content of the speech that is being delivered but, with a good deal of their attention focused on something irrelevant, they are less able to counterargue while they are listening.

If this interpretation is correct, then the forewarning variable is irrelevant, at least in this particular experiment. The critical variable would be the extent to which the attention of the person was distracted from the persuasive communication while listening to it. If the attention of the listener were distracted sufficiently to make it quite difficult for him to counterargue, but not so much as to interfere with his hearing of the speech, this would represent a maximally effective influence situation.

How can we test the validity of this interpretation? The simplest procedure which suggested itself to us was to choose an issue such that we could easily identify a group of people strongly committed to a given position on that issue, devise a persuasive communication strongly attacking this committed position, and present this persuasive communication to these people under two different conditions, one where their attention was focused on the communication and one where they were distracted on a completely irrelevant basis. We decided to use attitudes toward college fraternities as the issue since fraternity members were likely to be strongly committed to a favorable opinion on this matter. We also decided to use as pure a form of distraction as we could think of so as to reduce the plausibility of alternative interpretations. We settled on a procedure whereby the subjects were visually distracted while listening to a speech.

METHOD

Experimental Materials and Procedure

A persuasive communication arguing strongly against college fraternities was prepared in the form of a color, 16-millimeter sound film. The film was about twelve minutes long. The first two minutes told the audience that this film was Part 4 of a series on university life, this part dealing with college fraternities. The visual showed various scenes of campus buildings and students walking on college campuses. These scenes then dissolved to a scene of a young college professor[2] who, after stating that he himself had been a member of a fraternity in college, proceeded to argue for almost 10 minutes that fraternities encouraged cheating and dishonesty, encouraged social snobbishness and racial discrimination, were antithetical to the purposes of a university and should be abolished. This film was used to present the persuasive communication to subjects in those experimental conditions in which the attention of the audience was to be focused on the communication.

A second film was prepared to present the same persuasive communication under distraction conditions. We chose to use, as the basic vehicle, an existing short color film *Day of the Painter* produced by Little Movies, Incorporated, which had sound effects and music but no dialogue or narration and which was very amusing and rather absorbing to watch. This film was edited somewhat to shorten it to match the length of the other film. It opened with the identical titles and preliminary visuals used in the original film, and the identical sound track from the persuasive-communication film superimposed over it. Thus, this film for the distraction conditions of the experiment was identical visually for the first two minutes with the nondistracting film. Instead of the scene shifting to the young college professor making a speech, however, the visual of this distracting film dissolved to the amusing and absorbing short film. The sound tracks on the two films were identical throughout. In short, in the distraction conditions, the subjects heard the same persuasive communication while watching a completely irrelevant and highly interesting movie.

Experiments using these film materials were conducted at three different academic institutions: the University of Minnesota, San Jose State College, and the University of Southern California. In all three institutions the procedure employed was similar. Subjects were assigned at random to a particular room. In each room the subjects were given the identical verbal introduction which told them they were to see a film about fraternities, that

---

[2]We wish to express our thanks to William McCord for preparing and delivering the persuasive communication in the film.

the presentation was a rather unusual one, and that we would appreciate their paying close attention since we would want to ask them some questions about it later. In one room they were then shown the straight film version of the persuasive communication while in the other room the subjects saw the distracting version. Following the showing of the film, the subjects were asked to answer a number of questions designed to measure their attitudes toward fraternities and their perception of the expertness and fairness of the speaker. When the questionnaires had been completed and collected, the total procedure, its purposes and our hypotheses were explained in detail to all subjects.

After having prepared the film materials, our first step was to try them out on a preliminary basis with students at Stanford University. The results were very encouraging. We then ran the experiment at the University of Minnesota using two groups, fraternity men who saw the straight version and fraternity men who saw the distracting version of the film. The identical design was next used at San Jose State College. Finally we ran a more complete design at the University of Southern California which involved six conditions: Fraternity men and nonfraternity men, one-third of each seeing the straight version, one-third the distraction version, and one-third answering the questionnaire before seeing any film.

RESULTS

We will present the data and discuss the results separately and in the sequence in which the experiments were actually conducted for the three different academic institutions.

University of Minnesota Experiment

At the University of Minnesota[3] 65 fraternity men participated in the experiment. Thirty-three of them saw the straight film version of the persuasive communication and 32 saw the distracting version. The questionnaire which they answered after having seen the film had six questions oriented toward measuring their attitude toward fraternities. These questions were:

1. In your opinion, what should be done with American college fraternities (5-point scale from "definitely should be abolished" to "their power in university life should be increased")?

---

[3]We would like to thank Ben Willerman and Elliot Aronson for their help and cooperation in arranging for the conduct of the experiment at the University of Minnesota.

2. On the whole, how do you feel about the ways in which fraternities influence university life (5-point scale from "excellent influence" to "very poor influence")?

3. How do you personally feel about fraternities (8-point scale from "dislike fraternities strongly" to "like fraternities very much")?

4. As far as you know, how do fraternity men's grades compare with comparable independent men's grades in most universities and colleges (5-point scale from "fraternity men do much better" to "independent men do much better")?

5. How do you feel about the nature of the contribution to American college life that fraternities make (4-point scale from "fraternities contribute nothing" to "fraternities contribute considerably")?

6. What effect, if any, do fraternities have on those students who are not chosen by them (4-point scale from "very harmful effect" to "no harmful effect")?

All answers to these questions were scored so that the larger number represented a more favorable attitude toward fraternities. The maximum profraternity score possible was 31. The more influenced they were by the persuasive communication, the lower should their score be.

The questionnaire also contained two questions to obtain a measure of the extent to which they rejected the speaker. These questions were:

1. In your opinion, how well qualified to discuss fraternities was the lecturer in this film (3-point scale from "very well qualified" to "not well qualified")?

2. In your opinion, how fair was the presentation about fraternities (4-point scale from "quite fair" to "quite biased")?

These two questions were summed to provide a rejection measure. Maximum rejection of the speaker would be represented by a score of 7.

Table 8.1 presents the data on attitude toward fraternities and rejection of the speaker for each of the two conditions at the University of Minnesota. It is clear from the table that the differences between conditions were negligible. The slight difference that does exist is in the direction of having been more influenced in the distraction condition and rejecting the speaker less in that condition, but the difference is disappointingly small.

One reason for continuing our investigation was an explanation offered by those familiar with the situation at the University of Minnesota for the failure to obtain any difference. It was suggested that the fraternity system at Minnesota is very weak and, for many years now, has been under constant attack and pressure from the University. It was suggested that the fraternity men at the University of Minnesota have already heard all the antifraternity arguments many, many times and, consequently, their counterarguments

TABLE 8.1
Average ratings for fraternity men at
University of Minnesota

Condition	Attitude toward fraternities	Rejection of speaker
Ordinary (N = 33)	26.2	6.0
Distraction (N = 32)	26.0	5.8

are all formed and ready. Hence, distraction may not have had the effect which we anticipated.

True or not, we proceeded to do our experiment again, this time in an institution where the fraternity system was strong and prestigeful and was *not* under attack and pressure.

San Jose State College Experiment

At San Jose State College[4] 99 fraternity men participated in the experiment. Fifty-one of them saw the straight film version and 48 saw the distracting version of the persuasive communication. The procedure and the questionnaire were identical in all respects to the experiment done at the University of Minnesota. Table 8.2 presents the data collected at San Jose.

An examination of the data in Table 8.2 shows that they clearly support our theoretical expectations. The subjects who heard the persuasive communication under distracting conditions are significantly less favorable to fraternities ($t = 3.63, p < .01$) and reject the speaker less ($t = 2.80, p < .01$).

These results are, of course, consistent with the notion that, if distracted while listening to the persuasive communication, the subject is less able to counterargue against the communication and against the speaker. As a result, under these circumstances he is less likely to reject the speaker and is more influenced by the communication than subjects who focused all their attention on the persuasive communication. However, this interpretation of the data is not quite unambiguous in the absence of a control group. It is quite conceivable, for example, that the ordinary presentation of the persuasive communication aroused so much resentment and anger in the fraternity men who were listening that a boomerang effect could have ensued. That is, in the ordinary condition they may have moved away from the position advocated by the speaker. For our interpretation to be strongly supported, it would be well to show that the distraction presentation results in effective

[4]We would like to thank Robert Martin, Dean, for his help and cooperation in arranging for the conduct of the experiment at San Jose State College.

TABLE 8.2
Average ratings for fraternity men at
San Jose State College

Condition	Attitude toward fraternities	Rejection of speaker
Ordinary (N = 51)	25.7	6.0
Distraction (N = 48)	24.0	5.5

influence which is not only significantly greater than the ordinary presentation condition but also represents significant change from a control group
whose attitudes were measured before seeing any film. We thus decided to
repeat the experiment once more using a more complete experimental
design.

University of Southern California Experiment

The University of Southern California[5] was selected as the site for the
experiment because, among other things, the fraternity system there was
important on the campus, fraternities were prestigeful and had not been too
much under attack in recent years. In short, we attempted to select a situation which would be comparable to San Jose State College rather than like
the University of Minnesota.

The plan at the University of Southern California was to have three conditions: those who saw the straight presentation, those who saw the distracting version, and those who saw no film at all — these latter constituting
a control group to give us an indication of attitudes prior to exposure to the
persuasive communication. We also decided to do the experiment here using
both fraternity and nonfraternity men in order to provide further clarification of the theoretical interpretation of the results. It will be recalled that the
idea behind the experiment was that people will actively counterargue while
listening to a persuasive communication which attacks an opinion to which
they are committed. The distraction condition is intended to interfere with
this activity of counterarguing while listening. If this is the correct interpretation, one should find that the distracting presentation is indeed more
effective in influencing fraternity men but one should not find it any more
effective in influencing nonfraternity men. After all, many, if not most, of
the nonfraternity men will already tend to agree with the speaker and, al-

[5]We wish to thank James Finn, Harold Gluth, Robert Heinick, Francis Joyce, and Bernard
Kanter at the University of Southern California.

though their opinions may not be as extreme as those represented in the persuasive communication, there is little reason to expect nonfraternity men to be motivated to counterargue while listening. Thus, the distraction version of the film should not provide any advantage in effectiveness over the straight version.

The experiment was carried out as planned with 179 fraternity men and 114 independents. In order to have the two samples as comparable as possible, the samples were restricted to sophomores, juniors, and seniors, since relatively few freshmen already belong to fraternities. Subjects were randomly assigned to one of three rooms, fraternity and nonfraternity men being mixed in each room. In one room, after the same introduction as in the previous studies, they saw the straight version of the persuasive communication; in another they saw the distracting version; and in the third room they were asked to answer the questionnaire before seeing the film.

The questionnaire was changed somewhat for this experiment. Questions 1 and 2 were extended to 6-point scales; Question 3 was contracted to a 7-point scale; Questions 5 and 6 were omitted and in their place they were asked to indicate on a 7-point scale their "overall reaction to college fraternities"; Question 4 on the original questionnaire was retained unchanged. The two questions measuring rejection of the speaker had the scales extended to 5- and 6-point scales in place of the original 3- and 4-point scales. Thus, on this revised questionnaire, the maximum profraternity attitude would be represented again by a score of 31. Maximum rejection of the speaker and the communication would be represented by a score of 11. Table 8.3 presents the results of the experiment at the University of Southern California.

Let us first examine the data from the fraternity men to see how they compare with the data collected at San Jose. It is clear that, once more, the distracting persuasive communication has resulted in a less favorable attitude toward fraternities and less rejection of the speaker than the ordinary,

TABLE 8.3
Averages for fraternity men and independents at the University of Southern California

Condition	Fraternity men		Independents	
	Attitude to fraternities	Rejection of speaker	Attitude to fraternities	Rejection of speaker
Control	24.8 (N = 59)	–	17.4 (N = 37)	–
Ordinary film version	24.6 (N = 59)	8.6	16.3 (N = 34)	7.4
Distracting film	23.5 (N = 61)	8.0	16.1 (N = 43)	7.5

nondistracting version. Although the differences are not quite as significant as they were at San Jose, they are quite adequate considering the fact of replication. The difference between the two experimental conditions on attitude toward fraternities is significant at the 6 percent level ($t = 1.88$), and the difference in rejection of the speaker is sig ificant at the 5 percent level ($t = 1.97$). In other words, we have replicated and confirmed the San Jose result.

It is also clear in Table 8.3 that the straight film version does not produce a boomerang effect. Rather, it produces virtually no effect at all. The difference between the control condition and the ordinary film version is neglible. On the other hand, those who saw the distracting version of the persuasive communication have indeed been influenced significantly ($t = 1.94$).

Let us now turn our attention to the results on the nonfraternity men. First of all, it is clear and not surprising that there is a huge initial difference between their attitude toward fraternities and the attitudes of fraternity men. In other words, the independents do agree more initially with the speaker in the film and should not be expected to counterargue while listening. And, indeed, it may be seen that there are only negligible differences either in attitude toward fraternities or in rejection of the speaker between those who saw the ordinary version and those who saw the distracting version of the persuasive communication. Both of these conditions seem to have been somewhat influenced although the differences from the control condition are not significant ($t = 1.17$ and $t = 1.08$).

Relation Between the Attitude and Rejection Measures

It is of interest to examine the relation which exists between attitude toward fraternities after seeing the persuasive-communication film and the extent to which the speaker is rejected. It is generally accepted that the extent to which a person is influenced by a persuasive communication is related to the extent to which he accepts the speaker as trustworthy, expert, unbiased, and the like. There is, for example, a fair amount of research which shows that if the source of a communication is regarded as untrustworthy, the communication is less effective in influencing people. And in the data we have presented above, we also find that in the distraction condition, where we find more effective influence, we also find less rejection of the speaker.

In terms of the reaction of one individual to a persuasive communication, however, the direction of the empirical relation we would expect is less clear. On the one hand, we would still expect that if a person, listening to a persuasive communication, succeeds in utterly derogating and rejecting the communicator and his arguments, he would not have been influenced. On the other hand, since changing one's opinion and derogating the communicator are both modes of coping with the impact of the persuasive communication, one might expect that a person on whom the communication has a strong impact might do both of them to some extent rather than one to the exclusion of the other. Thus, if within any experimental condition one correlated the amount of change of opinion with the amount of rejection of the speaker, the size and direction of the correlation would depend on whether or not these two reactions were alternate forms of coping with the situation or whether they were both simultaneously available to the same person.

The data from our three experiments are rather interesting in this respect. Table 8.4 presents the correlations between attitude toward fraternities and rejection of the speaker for fraternity men in each of our two conditions in the three universities. It will be recalled that a larger number indicated greater profraternity sentiment and indicated greater rejection of the speaker. Hence, a positive correlation between these two variables indicates that the less the person was influenced by the persuasive communication, the more he rejects the speaker.

An examination of the figures in the table makes it clear that there is a consistent difference in the magnitude of the correlations between the two conditions. While all of the correlations are positive, none of them is significantly different from zero for those subjects who saw the ordinary, straight version of the film and had their attention focused on the persuasive communication. On the other hand, all of the correlations for those subjects who saw the distracting film are significantly different from zero at the 5 percent level or better. While none of the differences between the correlations is significant for any one of the experiments, the consistency of the result lends considerable weight to the conclusion that they are different.

We did not anticipate this finding and we must regard it as tentative but suggestive. It may be that in the distraction condition, not being able to effectively counterargue, subjects are influenced by the communication unless they are able to derogate and reject the speaker. In the condition where they

TABLE 8.4
Correlations between attitude and rejection of speaker
for fraternity men

Academic institution	Experimental condition	
	Ordinary film	Distracting film
University of Minnesota	+.04	+.36
San Jose State College	+.18	+.37
University of Southern California	+.16	+.39

are able to counterargue, the result suggests that they are able to resist influence by other means even if they do not reject the speaker. If this tentative interpretation of the magnitudes of these correlations is correct, one could perhaps summarize it by saying that, to the extent one does not counterargue while listening to a persuasive communication, there will be a positive correlation between rejecting the speaker and being able to resist influence. Such a hypothesis would, of course, suggest that one should also find such positive correlations for the nonfraternity men in the experiment at the University of Southern California. After all, there is little reason for the nonfraternity men to be motivated to counterargue even when seeing the straight, ordinary version of the film. The correlation between attitude and rejection for the independents who saw the ordinary version is, indeed, +.45, a significant correlation. Things are not, however, as clear-cut as one might like to have them. The comparable correlation for the independents who saw the distracting film is −.02, certainly not consistent with what we might expect from our tentative hypothesis. Perhaps the distracting film introduces other variables for the independent men who would not counterargue anyhow, or perhaps our suggested hypothesis to account for the correlations is not quite correct. We will leave it at this, a suggestion which may be worthwhile to explore more adequately in the future.

Possible Alternative Interpretations

An experiment can never rule out all possible alternative explanations of the findings and, perhaps, the best support for one particular interpretation is to say that the experiment was designed with that interpretation in mind and, indeed, it came out as predicted. Nevertheless, it is useful to look briefly at the plausibility of some other explanations. Two such possible explanations readily come to mind and we will examine them each.

1. It is conceivable that the so-called "distracting" version of the communication was actually not distracting. In fact, it may have produced the reverse effect, namely, because of the attempt to distract, the subjects may have concentrated harder on listening to the speech. If this did occur, it could explain the results for the fraternity men—the more closely they listened, the more they were influenced. There are two sources of data relevant to this possible explanation. In the experiment done at the University of Southern California the questionnaire contained one page on which the subjects were asked to "list the main criticisms of fraternities which the speaker made." If the greater influence among fraternity men in the distracting condition was due to *more* careful attention on their part to the verbal content, we might expect this to reveal itself on this question. Analysis of the answers

to this question, however, reveals no superior retention of arguments for those viewing the distracting film. In fact, the mean number of arguments repeated by those viewing the ordinary version was slightly higher (3.9) than for those exposed to the distracting version (3.7).

Another relevant source of data comes from comments written by subjects in a space provided for "general comments." The following are some rather typical comments obtained from subjects who had seen the distracting version of the persuasive communication:

> The presentation was interesting because, although I had already seen that film, and was interested in the monologue which was against something I am in favor of, I would still find myself watching the film instead of listening fully.
>
> It was extremely difficult to pay close attention to both the audio and visual parts of the film. It would seem that attention would be determined by whether you wanted to defend fraternities or enjoy the visual part.
>
> I could see only a slight correlation between the acting and the commentary. Trying to understand the action detracted from the commentary.
>
> I could not see any tie in between what was being said and what was being shown. It was very hard to concentrate on what was being said without completely looking away from the movie.

There seems to be little question but that the distracting film was really distracting.

2. It is possible that the effect obtained for the fraternity men is simply the result of reward and reinforcement. The visual portion of the distracting film was a highly amusing thing and, consequently, those in the distracting condition heard the message while they were being rewarded or entertained and, hence, were more influenced. It is difficult, of course, to marshal data relevant to such a possible explanation. There are two things which can be said, however, to indicate a lack of plausibility. No spontaneous comments were obtained which indicated that they actually enjoyed the film. Comments that dealt with the issue almost always indicated some irritation with the difficulty of both watching and listening. This is clear to anyone who has seen the film used in the distracting condition. The visual portion commands attention but the experience is not as entertaining as it would have been with its original sound track. The other point that can be made in reference to this possible interpretation is that, if it is true, it is difficult to understand why the independents at the University of Southern California do not respond in the same way to the same reinforcing mechanism. It seems difficult to believe that the distracting film would be reinforcing for fraternity men but not for independents.

We, ourselves, have not been able to think of other possible explanations which even superficially promise plausibility. For example, the experience of those subjects who see the distracting film must certainly constitute an unusual, and rather strange experience for them. There does not seem to be, however, any plausible reason for assuming that simply the unusual and strange would be more effective in influencing people in this context. The data strongly suggest that our own explanation has validity.

Reference

ALLYN, JANE, AND FESTINGER, L. The effectiveness of unanticipated persuasive communications. *J. abnorm. soc. Psychol.,* 1961, **62,** 35–40.

III

SELF-JUSTIFICATION

9

Cognitive Dissonance

Leon Festinger

It is the subject of a new theory based on experiments showing that the grass is usually not greener on the other side of the fence and that grapes are sourest when they are in easy reach.

There is an experiment in psychology that you can perform easily in your own home if you have a child three or four years old. Buy two toys that you are fairly sure will be equally attractive to the child. Show them both to him and say: "Here are two nice toys. This one is for you to keep. The other I must give back to the store." You then hand the child the toy that is his to keep and ask: "Which of the two toys do you like better?" Studies have shown that in such a situation most children will tell you they prefer the toy they are to keep.

This response of children seems to conflict with the old saying that the grass is always greener on the other side of the fence. Do adults respond in the same way under similar circumstances or does the adage indeed become true as we grow older? The question is of considerable interest because the adult world is filled with choices and alternative courses of action that are often about equally attractive. When they make a choice of a college or a car

FIGURE 9.1
The grass is not always greener on the other side of the fence.

or a spouse or a home or a political candidate, do most people remain satisfied with their choice or do they tend to wish they had made a different one? Naturally any choice may turn out to be a bad one on the basis of some objective measurement, but the question is: Does some psychological process come into play immediately after the making of a choice that colors one's attitude, either favorably or unfavorably, toward the decision?

To illuminate this question there is another experiment one can do at home, this time using an adult as a subject rather than a child. Buy two presents for your wife, again choosing things you are reasonably sure she will find about equally attractive. Find some plausible excuse for having both of them in your possession, show them to your wife and ask her to tell you how attractive each one is to her. After you have obtained a good measurement of attractiveness, tell her that she can have one of them, whichever she chooses. The other you will return to the store. After she has made her choice, ask her once more to evaluate the attractiveness of each of them. If you compare the evaluations of attractiveness before and after the choice, you will probably find that the chosen present has increased in attractiveness and the rejected one decreased.

Such behavior can be explained by a new theory concerning "cognitive dissonance." This theory centers around the idea that if a person knows various things that are not psychologically consistent with one another, he will, in a variety of ways, try to make them more consistent. Two items of information that psychologically do not fit together are said to be in a dissonant relation to each other. The items of information may be about behavior, feelings, opinions, things in the environment and so on. The word "cognitive" simply emphasizes that the theory deals with relations among items of information.

Such items can of course be changed. A person can change his opinion; he can change his behavior, thereby changing the information he has about it; he can even distort his perception and his information about the world around him. Changes in items of information that produce or restore consistency are referred to as dissonance-reducing changes.

Cognitive dissonance is a motivating state of affairs. Just as hunger impels a person to eat, so does dissonance impel a person to change his opinions or his behavior. The world, however, is much more effectively arranged for hunger reduction than it is for dissonance reduction. It is almost always possible to find something to eat. It is not always easy to reduce dissonance. Sometimes it may be very difficult or even impossible to change behavior or opinions that are involved in dissonant relations. Consequently, there are circumstances in which appreciable dissonance may persist for long periods.

To understand cognitive dissonance as a motivating state, it is necessary to have a clearer conception of the conditions that produce it. The simplest definition of dissonance can, perhaps, be given in terms of a person's expectations. In the course of our lives we have all accumulated a large number of expectations about what things go together and what things do not. When such an expectation is not fulfilled, dissonance occurs.

For example, a person standing unprotected in the rain would expect to get wet. If he found himself in the rain and he was not getting wet, there would exist dissonance between these two pieces of information. This unlikely example is one where the expectations of different people would all be uniform. There are obviously many instances where different people would not share the same expectations. Someone who is very self-confident might expect to succeed at whatever he tried, whereas someone who had a low opinion of himself might normally expect to fail. Under these circumstances what would produce dissonance for one person might produce consonance for another. In experimental investigations, of course, an effort is made to provide situations in which expectations are rather uniform.

Perhaps the best way to explain the theory of cognitive dissonance is to show its application to specific situations. The rest of this article, therefore, will be devoted to a discussion of three examples of cognitive dissonance. I shall discuss the effects of making a decision, of lying and of temptation. These three examples by no means cover all the situations in which dissonance can be created. Indeed, it seldom happens that everything a person

Figure 9.2
Consequences of making a decision between two reasonably attractive alternatives.

knows about an action he has taken is perfectly consistent with his having taken it. The three examples, however, may serve to illustrate the range of situations in which dissonance can be expected to occur. They will also serve to show the kinds of dissonance-reduction effects that are obtained under a special circumstance: when dissonance involves the person's behavior and the action in question is difficult to change.

Let us consider first the consequences of making a decision. Imagine the situation of a person who has carefully weighed two reasonable attractive alternatives and then chosen one of them—a decision that, for our purposes, can be regarded as irrevocable. All the information this person has concerning the attractive features of the rejected alternative (and the possible unattractive features of the chosen alternative) are now inconsistent, or dissonant, with the knowledge that he has made the given choice. It is true that the person also knows many things that are consistent or consonant with the choice he has made, which is to say all the attractive features of the chosen alternative and unattractive features of the rejected one. Nevertheless, some dissonance exists and after the decision the individual will try to reduce the dissonance.

There are two major ways in which the individual can reduce dissonance in this situation. He can persuade himself that the attractive features of the rejected alternative are not really so attractive as he had originally thought, and that the unattractive features of the chosen alternative are not really unattractive. He can also provide additional justification for his choice by exaggerating the attractive features of the chosen alternative and the unattractive features of the rejected alternative. In other words, according to the theory the process of dissonance reduction should lead, after the decision, to an increase in the desirability of the chosen alternative and a decrease in the desirability of the rejected alternative.

This phenomenon has been demonstrated in a variety of experiments. A brief description of one of these will suffice to illustrate the precise nature of the effect. In an experiment performed by Jon Jecker of Stanford University, high school girls were asked to rate the attractiveness of each of twelve "hit" records. For each girl two records that she had rated as being only moderately attractive were selected and she was asked which of the two she would like as a gift. After having made her choice, the girl again rated the attractiveness of all the records. The dissonance created by the decision could be reduced by increasing the attractiveness of the chosen record and decreasing the attractiveness of the rejected record. Consequently, a measurement of dissonance reduction could be obtained by summing both of these kinds of changes in ratings made before and after the decision.

Different experimental variations were employed in this experiment in order to examine the dynamics of the process of dissonance reduction. Let us look at three of these experimental variations. In all three conditions the girls, when they were making their choice, were given to understand there was a slight possibility that they might actually be given both records. In one condition they were asked to rerate the records after they had made their choice but before they knew definitely whether they would receive both records or only the one they chose. The results for this condition should indicate whether dissonance reduction begins with having made the choice or whether it is suspended until the uncertainty is resolved. In a

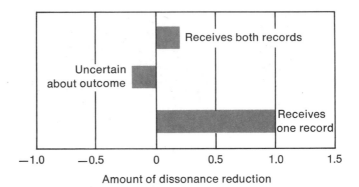

FIGURE 9.3
Dissonance reduction is a psychological phenomenon found to occur after a person has made a choice between two approximately equal alternatives. The effect of the phenomenon is to enhance the attractiveness of the chosen object or chosen course of action. The chart summarizes the results of an experiment in which high-school girls rated the attractiveness of twelve "hit" records before and after choosing one of them as a gift. Substantial dissonance reduction occurred under only one of three experimental conditions described in the text. Under two other conditions, no systematic reduction was observed.

second condition the girls were actually given both records after their choice and were then asked to rerate all the records. Since they had received both records and therefore no dissonance existed following the decision, there should be no evidence of dissonance reduction in this condition. In a third condition the girls were given only the record they chose and were then asked to do the rerating. This, of course, resembles the normal outcome of a decision and the usual dissonance reduction should occur.

Figure 9.3 shows the results for these three conditions. When the girls are uncertain as to the outcome, or when they receive both records, there is no dissonance reduction—that is, no systematic change in attractiveness of the chosen and rejected records. The results in both conditions are very close to zero—one slightly positive, the other slightly negative. When they receive only the record they chose, however, there is a large systematic change in rating to reduce dissonance. Since dissonance reduction is only observed in this last experimental condition, it is evident that dissonance reduction does not occur during the process of making a decision but only after the decision is made and the outcome is clear.

Let us turn now to the consequences of lying. There are many circumstances in which, for one reason or another, an individual publicly states something that is at variance with his private belief. Here again one can expect dissonance to arise. There is an inconsistency between knowing that one really believes one thing and knowing that one has publicly stated something quite different. Again, to be sure, the individual knows things that are

FIGURE 9.4
Further consequences of making a difficult decision.

consonant with his overt, public behavior. All the reasons that induced him to make the public statement are consonant with his having made it and provide him with some justification for his behavior. Nevertheless, some dissonance exists and, according to the theory, there will be attempts to reduce it. The degree to which the dissonance is bothersome for the individual will depend on two things. The more deviant his public statement is from his private belief, the greater will be the dissonance. The greater the amount of justification the person has for having made the public statement, the less bothersome the dissonance will be.

How can the dissonance be reduced? One method is obvious. The individual can remove the dissonance by retracting his public statement. But let us consider only those instances in which the public statement, once made, cannot be changed or withdrawn; in other words, in which the behavior is irrevocable. Under such circumstances the major avenue for reduction of the dissonance is change of private opinion. That is, if the private opinion were changed so that it agreed with what was publicly stated, obviously the dissonance would be gone. The theory thus leads us to expect that after having made an irrevocable public statement at variance with his private belief, a person will tend to change his private belief to bring it into line with his public statement. Furthermore, the degree to which he changes his private belief will depend on the amount of justification or the amount of pressure for making the public statement initially. The less the original justification or pressure, the greater the dissonance and the more the person's private belief can be expected to change.

An experiment recently conducted at Stanford University by James M. Carlsmith and me illustrates the nature of this effect. In the experiment, college students were induced to make a statement at variance with their own belief. It was done by using students who had volunteered to participate in an experiment to measure "motor performance." The purported experiment lasted an hour and was a boring and fatiguing session. At the end of the hour the experimenter thanked the subject for his participation, indicating that the experiment was over. The real purpose of the hour-long session, however, was to provide each subject with an identical experience about which he would have an unfavorable opinion.

At the end of the fatiguing hour the experimenter enlisted the subject's aid in preparing the next person for the experiment. The subject was led to believe that, for experimental purposes, the next person was supposed to be given the impression that the hour's session was going to be very interesting and lots of fun. The subject was persuaded to help in this deception by telling the next subject, who was waiting in an adjoining room, that he himself had just finished the hour and that it had indeed been very interesting and lots of fun. The first subject was then interviewed by someone else to determine his actual private opinion of the experiment.

Two experimental conditions were run that differed only in the amount of pressure, or justification given the subject for stating a public opinion at variance with his private belief. All subjects, of course, had the justification of helping to conduct a scientific experiment. In addition to this, half of the

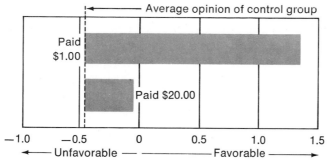

FIGURE 9.5
Consequences of lying are found to vary, depending on whether
the justification for the lie is large or small. In this experiment,
students were persuaded to tell others that a boring experience
was really fun. Those in one group were paid only $1 for their
cooperation; in a second group, $20. The low-paid students,
having least justification for lying, experienced most dissonance
and reduced it by coming to regard the experience favorably.

subjects were paid $1 for their help — a relatively small amount of money;
the other subjects were paid $20 — a rather large sum for the work involved.
From the theory we would expect that the subjects who were paid only $1,
having less justification for their action, would have more dissonance and
would change their private beliefs more in order to reduce the dissonance.
In other words, we would expect the greatest change in private opinion
among the subjects given the least tangible incentive for changing.

Figure 9.5 shows the results of the experiment. The broken line in the
chart shows the results for a control group of subjects. These subjects
participated in the hour-long session and then were asked to give their
private opinion of it. Their generally unfavorable views are to be expected
when no dissonance is induced between private belief and public statement.
It is clear from the chart that introducing such dissonance produced a change
of opinion so that the subjects who were asked to take part in a deception
finally came to think better of the session than did the control subjects. It
is also clear that only in the condition where they were paid a dollar is this
opinion change appreciable. When they were paid a lot of money, the justification for misrepresenting private belief is high and there is correspondingly
less change of opinion to reduce dissonance.

Another way to summarize the result is to say that those who are highly
rewarded for doing something that involves dissonance change their opinion
less in the direction of agreeing with what they did than those who are given
very little reward. This result may seem surprising, since we are used to
thinking that reward is effective in creating change. It must be remembered,
however, that the critical factor here is that the reward is being used to
induce a behavior that is dissonant with private opinion.

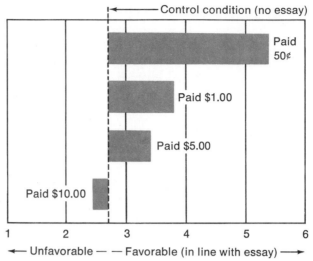

FIGURE 9.6
Graded change of opinion was produced by paying subjects
various sums for writing essays advocating opinions contrary to
their beliefs. When examined later, students paid the least had
changed their opinion the most to agree with what they had
written. Only the highest-paid group held to their original opinion
more strongly than did a control group.

To show that this result is valid and not just a function of the particular
situation or the particular sums of money used for reward, Arthur R. Cohen
of New York University conducted a similar experiment in a different context. Cohen paid subjects to write essays advocating an opinion contrary
to what they really believed. Subjects were paid either $10, $5, $1 or 50
cents to do this. To measure the extent to which dissonance was reduced by
their changing their opinion, each subject was then given a questionnaire,
which he left unsigned, to determine his private opinion on the issue. The
extent to which the subjects reduced dissonance by changing their opinion
to agree with what they wrote in the essay is shown in Figure 9.6. Once
again it is clear that the smaller the original justification for engaging in the
dissonance-producing action, the greater the subsequent change in private
opinion to bring it into line with the action.

The final set of experiments I shall discuss deals with the consequences
of resisting temptation. What happens when a person wants something and
discovers that he cannot have it? Does he now want it even more or does
he persuade himself that it is really not worth having? Sometimes our common general understanding of human behavior can provide at least crude
answers to such questions. In this case, however, our common understanding is ambiguous, because it supplies two contradictory answers. Everyone
knows the meaning of the term "sour grapes"; it is the attitude taken by a

person who persuades himself that he really does not want what he cannot have. But we are also familiar with the opposite reaction. The child who is not allowed to eat candy and hence loves candy passionately; the woman who adores expensive clothes even though she cannot afford to own them; the man who has a hopeless obsession for a woman who spurns his attentions. Everyone "understands" the behavior of the person who longs for what he cannot have.

Obviously one cannot say one of these reactions is wrong and the other is right; they both occur. One might at least, however, try to answer the question: Under what circumstances does one reaction take place and not the other? If we examine the question from the point of view of the theory of dissonance, a partial answer begins to emerge.

Imagine the psychological situation that exists for an individual who is tempted to engage in a certain action but for one reason or another refrains.

FIGURE 9.7
The effect of rewards on lying.

An analysis of the situation here reveals its similarity to the other dissonance-producing situations. An individual's knowledge concerning the attractive aspects of the activity toward which he was tempted is dissonant with the knowledge that he had refrained from engaging in the activity. Once more, of course, the individual has some knowledge that is consonant with his behavior in the situation. All the pressures, reasons and justifications for refraining are consonant with his actual behavior. Nevertheless, the dissonance does exist, and there will be psychological activity oriented toward reducing this dissonance.

As we have already seen in connection with other illustrations, one major way to reduce dissonance is to change one's opinions and evaluations in order to bring them closer in line with one's actual behavior. Therefore,

FIGURE 9.8
Temptation accompanied by a severe threat.

FIGURE 9.9
Temptation accompanied by a mild threat.

FIGURE 9.10
Consequences of resisting temptation when deterence varies.

when there is dissonance produced by resisting temptation, it can be reduced by derogating or devaluing the activity toward which one was tempted. This derivation from the theory clearly implies the sour-grapes attitude, but both theory and experiment tell us that such dissonance-reducing effects will occur only when there was insufficient original justification for the behavior. Where the original justification for refraining from the action was great, little dissonance would have occurred and there would have been correspondingly little change of opinion in order to reduce dissonance. Therefore, one might expect that if a person had esisted temptation in a situation of strong prohibition or strong threatened punishment, little dissonance would have been created and one would not observe the sour-grapes effect. One would expect this effort only if the person resisted temptation under conditions of weak deterrent.

This line of reasoning leaves open the question of when the reverse effect occurs—that is, the situation in which desire for the "unattainable" object is increased. Experimentally is is possible to look at both effects. This was done by Elliot Aronson and J. M. Carlsmith, at Stanford University, in an experiment that sheds considerable light on the problem. The experiment was performed with children who were about four years old. Each child was individually brought into a large playroom in which there were five toys on a table. After the child had had an opportunity to play briefly with each toy, he was asked to rank the five in order of attractiveness. The toy that the child liked second best was then left on the table and the other four toys were spread around on the floor. The experimenter told the child that he had to leave for a few minutes to do an errand but would be back soon. The experimenter then left the room for ten minutes. Various techniques were employed to "prohibit" the child from playing with the particular toy that he liked second best while the experimenter was out of the room.

For different children this prohibition was instituted in three different ways. In one condition there was no temptation at all; the experimenter told the child he could play with any of the toys in the room and then took the second-best toy with him when he left. In the other two conditions temptation was present: the second-best toy was left on the table in the experimenter's absence. The children were told they could play with any of the toys in the room except the one on the table. The children in one group were threatened with mild punishment if they violated the prohibition, whereas those in the other group were threatened with more severe punishment. (The actual nature of the punishment was left unspecified.)

During his absence from the room the experimenter observed each child through a one-way mirror. None of the children in the temptation conditions played with the prohibited toy. After ten minutes were up the experimenter returned to the playroom and each child was again allowed to play briefly with each of the five toys. The attractiveness of each toy for the child was again measured. By comparing the before and after measurements of the attractiveness of the toy the child originally liked second best, one can assess the effects of the prohibition. The results are shown in Figure 9.11.

When there was no temptation — that is, when the prohibited toy was not physically present — there was of course no dissonance, and the preponderant result is an increase in the attractiveness of the prohibited toy. When the temptation is present but the prohibition is enforced by means of a severe threat of punishment, there is likewise little dissonance created by refraining, and again the preponderant result is an increase in the attractiveness of the prohibited toy. In other words, it seems clear that a prohibition that is enforced in such a way as not to introduce dissonance results in a greater desire for the prohibited activity.

The results are quite different, however, when the prohibition is enforced by only a mild threat of punishment. Here we see the result to be expected from the theory of dissonance. Because the justification for refraining from playing with the toy is relatively weak, there is appreciable dissonance between the child's knowledge that the toy is attractive and his actual behavior. The tendency to reduce this dissonance is strong enough to more than overcome the effect apparent in the other two conditions. Here, as a result

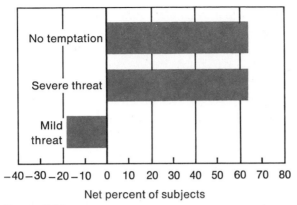

-40 -30 -20 -10 0 10 20 30 40 50 60 70 80

Net percent of subjects

FIGURE 9.11
Consequences of temptation were explored by prohibiting
children from playing with a desirable toy. Later, the
children were asked to re-evaluate the attractiveness of the
forbidden toy. In one case, the prohibition was enforced
by removing the toy from the child's presence. In the
second case, the prohibition took the form of a threat of
severe punishment; in the third case, a threat of mild
punishment. The chart shows the net percentage of
children who thought the forbidden toy more attractive
after the experiment than before. ("Net percent" means
the percentage who found the toy more attractive minus
the percentage who found it less so.) Evidently, only those
threatened mildly experienced much dissonance, and they
reduced it by downgrading the toy's desirability. Others
thought the toy more desirable.

of dissonance reduction, we see an appreciable sour-grapes phenomenon.

The theory of cognitive dissonance obviously has many implications for
everyday life. In addition to throwing light on one's own behavior, it would
seem to carry useful lessons for everyone concerned with understanding
human behavior in a world where everything is not black and white.

References

FESTINGER, LEON. *A theory of cognitive dissonance.* Row, Peterson & Company, 1957.
FESTINGER, LEON, AND CARLSMITH, JAMES M. Cognitive consequences of forced com-
pliance. *Journal of Abnormal and Social Psychology,* Vol. 58, No. 2, pp. 203–210;
March, 1959.
FESTINGER, LEON, RIECKEN, HENRY W., AND SCHACTER, STANLEY. *When prophecy
fails.* University of Minnesota Press, 1956.
YARYAN, RUBY B., AND FESTINGER, LEON. Preparatory action and belief in the probable
occurrence of future events. *Journal of Abnormal and Social Psychology,* Vol. 63,
No. 3, pp. 603–606; November, 1961.

10

The Effects of Severity of Initiation on Liking for a Group: A Replication

Harold B. Gerard and Grover C. Mathewson

This experiment represents an attempt to rule out a number of alternative explanations of an effect found in a previous experiment by Aronson and Mills. This effect, that the more a person suffers in order to obtain something, the greater will be the tendency for him to evaluate it positively, was predicted from dissonance theory. By modifying the original experiment in a number of ways, and applying additional treatment variations, these other hypotheses were effectively ruled out, thus lending considerable additional support to the original "suffering-leading-to-liking" hypothesis.

The experiment by Aronson and Mills (1959), in which a positive relationship was found between the severity of initiation into a group and subsequent liking for that group, is open to a variety of interpretations other than the one the authors give. The purpose of the experiment to be reported here was an attempt to rule out some of the more cogent of these alternative interpretations.

The observation that people often tend to value highly things for which they have suffered or expended a great deal of effort can be interpreted as having been due to dissonance reduction. The hypothesized process involved assumes that knowledge held by the person that he had suffered or

Reprinted with permission from the authors and *The Journal of Experimental Social Psychology*, Vol. 2, 1966. Copyright 1966 by Academic Press, Inc.

This experiment was conducted by the junior author as part of an undergraduate senior tutorial. We gratefully acknowledge the financial support provided by grant No. MH 1181701 from the National Institute of Mental Health and grant No. GS 392 from the National Science Foundation.

expended a great deal of effort for a desired goal is inconsistent with knowledge that the goal or certain aspects of it are worthless. Such inconsistencies produce psychological dissonance which is unpleasant and the individual will attempt to reduce this unpleasantness by cognitive work. In this case he can either distort his beliefs about the amount of suffering or effort he expended by coming to believe that it was less than he had previously thought or he can distort his belief about the worthlessness of aspects of the goal by coming to believe that these aspects were really not worthless. In their study, Aronson and Mills attempted to create a laboratory situation in which the latter hypothesized process could be examined. Let us review that experiment in some detail so that we may then point up the basis for the other interpretations of the data.

The subjects were college coeds who were willing to volunteer for a series of group discussions on the psychology of sex. The ostensible purpose of the study was presented to the subject as having to do with the investigation of group dynamics. Before any prospective member could join one of the discussion groups she was given a "screening test" to determine her suitability for the group. The severity of this screening test (or initiation) was varied; in the "severe" treatment the subject read obscene literature and a list of dirty words out loud to the experimenter (who was a male), whereas in the "mild" condition the subject read sexual material of an innocuous sort. The subject was told that the screening test had been necessary in order to weed out people who were too shy to discuss topics related to sex. After the initiation, each experimental subject was informed that she had passed the test and was therefore eligible for membership in the group. She was led to believe that the group she was to join had been formed several weeks ago and that she was to take the place of a girl who had to drop out. Her "participation" in her first meeting with the group was limited to "overhearing" via headphones what was presented to her as an ongoing discussion by the group on aspects of sexual behavior in animals. The reason she was given for not being able to participate actively in the discussion was that the other three girls had prepared for the discussion by reading a book on the sexual behavior of animals. It was also suggested to her that overhearing the discussion without participating in it would give her an opportunity to get acquainted with how the group operates. What she heard was not an ongoing discussion but was instead a standardized recorded discussion on the sexual behavior of animals that was extremely boring and banal. The discussion was contrived to be worthless in order to maximize the dissonance of the subject in the "severe" initiation group, since the knowledge that she had suffered to get into the group would be dissonant with finding out that the discussion was worthless.

After hearing the taped recording, the subject was asked to evaluate the discussion and the participants on a number of semantic differential-type scales. A control group was also run in which the subjects evaluated the discussion without having received any initiation whatsoever. The findings of the experiment supported the derivation from dissonance theory, namely that the subjects in the "severe" treatment evaluated the discussion more favorably than did the "mild" or control subjects. A dissonance theory interpretation conceives of the "severe" initiation as confronting the subject with the "problem" of having suffered for something that was later found to be worthless and the prediction is based upon how that problem is "solved." One of the reasons why the results are important and provocative is that they are exactly opposite to what a strict application of secondary reinforcement theory would predict in which it would be expected that the unpleasantness of the initiation would "rub off" and generalize to the discussion.

While the results are consistent with dissonance theory, they lend themselves to a variety of other, quite plausible interpretations. For example, there is an entire *family* of interpretations that derives from the fact that the content of the initiation and the content of the discussion are so closely related, both having to do with sex. One could argue that the initiation aroused the girls sexually to a greater extent in the "severe" as compared with the "mild" treatment and they were therefore more anxious to get into the group in order to pursue the discussion of sex. Along similar lines, one could also argue that the girls in the "severe" treatment did not know the meaning of some of the dirty four-letter words and believed that they could find out their meaning by joining the discussion group. This is a variation of the uncertainty-affiliation hypothesis. Still another possibility is that the subjects in the "severe" treatment were intrigued by the obscene material and the dirty words and may have believed that, if not now, sometime in the future these things would be discussed by the group. One could continue to list related interpretations based upon the assumed arousal of one or another motive in the "severe" treatment that might be satisfied by joining the discussion group (thus making the group more attractive).

Another possible interpretation, a "relief" hypothesis, is that the reading of the obscene material built up anxiety which was subsequently reduced by the banal, innocuous material of the group discussion. Since the discussion was responsible for reducing the anxiety, it took on positive value for the subject in the "severe" treatment.

Schopler and Bateson (1962) find partial support for a "dependency" interpretation of the Aronson and Mills findings. Following Thibaut and Kelly (1959), Schopler and Bateson suggest that, as contrasted with the "mild" initiation, the "severe" initiation induced in the subject dependence upon the experimenter. This, according to them, occurred because the experimenter had "moved" the subject in the "severe" treatment through a "wide range of outcomes," consisting of the unpleasant shock and the pleasantness associated with the pride experienced by the "severe" subject upon learning that she had passed the test. Subjects in the "mild" condition had not experienced this range of pleasantness of outcome and hence were less dependent. Also, their argument continues, somehow the subject assumed that the experimenter expected her to like the discussion. Due to the assumed differential dependency induced by the initiation treatments, the subject in the "severe" treatment was more concerned with pleasing the experimenter than was the subject in the "mild" treatment and hence attempted to a greater extent to meet his expectations by indicating to him that she liked the discussion.

Chapanis and Chapanis (1964) suggest an "afterglow" hypothesis to explain the data. All subjects in the experiment were told that they had passed the embarrassment test. Presumably, subjects in the "severe" treatment perceived the test as being more difficult than did subjects in the "mild" treatment and, according to Chapanis and Chapanis, they therefore may have had a greater sense of accomplishment. This self-satisfaction somehow "rubbed off" onto the other aspects of the task situation, including, presumably, the group discussion. This might then account for the "severe" subjects' more positive disposition toward the discussion.

Still another, even more plausible interpretation of quite a different sort, is that any experience following the "severe" initiation, which we assume was unpleasant, would by contrast seem more pleasant than it would following the "mild" initiation. It is important that this rather simple "contrast" hypothesis, which is a compelling explanation of the Aronson and Mills data, be ruled out, if possible.

A problem in the experiment related to the first set of interpretations concerns the nature of the initiation itself. Was the "severe" initiation really more unpleasant than the "mild" one? The authors do not report any check of the success of the experimental manipulation in producing differences in unpleasantness. Without the assurance that this all-important requirement was met, certain other interpretations of the data are quite plausible. It is not unlikely that many of the subjects in the "severe" treatment found the experience pleasant and exciting.

The experiment we shall report here is an attempt to replicate, not so much in fact but in spirit, the Aronson and Mills study, in order to counterpose the dissonance interpretation of the results against the other interpretations discussed above.

METHOD

An Overview of the Design

Two basic treatments were compared, one in which the subject received electrical shocks as part of an initiation procedure and one in which she received shocks as part of a psychological experiment, the "noninitiate" treatment. Within each of these treatments, half of the subjects received strong shocks and half received weak shocks. Half of the "severe" and half of the "mild" initiates were told that they had passed the screening test whereas the other half of each were not told whether they had passed. After the shocks, all subjects heard and then evaluated a boring and worthless group discussion about cheating in college. The "initiates" believed that this was a recording of a previous meeting of the group that they were slated to join, whereas the "noninitiates" evaluated the discussion as just one of a series of stimuli to which they were being exposed.

Procedure

The subjects were 48 female undergraduate volunteers contacted at random from the student body of the University of California at Riverside. All subjects were first contacted by telephone. During the telephone contact a subject selected to be an "initiate" was asked whether or not she would like to volunteer for a discussion club that was to discuss the problem of morals on university campuses. The "noninitiates" were asked, during the telephone contact, whether they would like to volunteer to be a subject in a psychological experiment. Thus, half of the subjects reported to the laboratory believing that they were going to be members of a discussion club whereas the other half believed that they were participating in a psychological experiment. The procedure followed during the experimental session was essentially the same for both "initiates" and "noninitiates." The "noninitiate" condition was introduced in an attempt to rule out the "contrast" and "relief" hypotheses. If the unpleasant experience represented by the initiation was not seen as instrumental to joining the discussion club and the same effect was found as in the Aronson and Mills experiment, both alternative explanations would receive support. If, however, the "initiates" showed the effect and the "noninitiates" did not, both the "contrast" and "relief" hypotheses would have been effectively rule out. We might expect a secondary reinforcement effect in the "noninitiate" condition which would manifest as a negative relationship between the unpleasantness of the shocks and the evaluation of the discussion, the assumption being that the effect produced by the shocks would generalize to the discussion.

When the "initiate" arrived in the laboratory she was seated in an isolation booth and was told:

> In the past we have had considerable difficulty with some of the girls who have joined these discussion clubs. The problem is that some people cannot maintain an attitude of objectivity during the discussion. When this happens, naturally the discussion tends to deteriorate and emotions run very high. In order to avoid this difficulty in the future we have just instituted a screening test to weed out those girls who would tend to let their emotions run away with them during a discussion. You are the first person to whom we will be administering the test which is a very good one that has been used by psychologists for many years. It consists of determining your physiological reaction to a series of stimuli. We do this by hooking you up to these electrodes [the experimenter shows the subject a pair of dummy GSR electrodes] that detect changes in your skin resistance during the test which is done with the aid of this recorder [the experimenter shows the subject a small strip-chart recorder]. By your response on this chart we can tell how objective you are likely to be under conditions represented by the morals discussion.

The subject was told that she was the first one to take the test in order to eliminate the possibility that she would want to be in the group in order to compare her reactions to the test with those of the girls already in the discussion group.

The "noninitiate" was told when she arrived at the laboratory:

> You are going to be a subject in a psychological experiment which involves your being exposed to a variety of different kinds of stimuli. We are going to determine your reaction to these stimuli with the aid of these electrodes [the experimenter shows the subject the GSR electrodes] which are hooked up to this instrument [the experimenter shows the subject the strip chart recorder].

All subjects were hooked up to the electrodes and received exactly the same sequence of stimuli which was designed to be a credible screening test for the "initiate." The sequence consisted of a spray of perfume from an atomizer placed in the ceiling of the subject's booth, a series of slides of paintings projected on the wall in front of the subject's booth (the paintings were: Roualt, *The Apprentice;* Picasso, *Madame Picasso, Portrait of A. Vollard, Figure by the Sea;* La Tour, *Self Portrait;* Matisse, *Landscape;* and Klee, *Girl Possessed*). Each painting was presented for 15 seconds with a 15-second pause between presentations. After all of the paintings were shown, the subject was fitted with headphones and heard the shooting sequence in Copland's ballet, *Billy the Kid*. Finally, the subject received the critical stimuli which were a series of three shocks delivered fifteen seconds apart by a Lafayette inductorium. In the "severe" treatment the shocks were quite strong whereas in the "mild" treatment they were barely supra-liminal. This method of varying suffering would be more likely, on the face of it at least, to produce greater uniformity of psychological state within each of the two suffering levels than the method used by Aronson and Mills. Using electric shock to produce suffering effectively separates the content of the initiation from the content of the discussion. If the Aronson and Mills effect were to be found by using shock this would rule out the family of interpretations that are all based upon the similarity of content of the two phases of the experiment.

Aronson and Mills informed all of their subjects that they had passed the screening test. The subject, thus, had acquired that for which she had suf-fered. It was inappropriate in the present experiment to inform the "non-initiates" as to how they had done in responding to the sequence of stimuli since they had not been told that they were taking a test. In order to control for this difficulty, half of the "initiates" were told, after receiving the shocks, that they had passed the screening test, whereas the other half were treated like the "noninitiates" by not receiving any feed-back concerning their performance on the screening test. This "told" vs. "non-told" factor was counterbalanced across the "severe" and "mild" initiates. More importantly, this treatment also enables us to test the Chapanis and Chapanis "afterglow" hypothesis, the plausibility of which is based on the assumption that the pleasure experienced in passing the severe initiation generalized to the group discussion. If those subjects who were told that they had passed showed the Aronson and Mills effect and those who were not given this information did not show the effect, the "afterglow" explanation would be supported. The Schopler and Bateson "dependence" hypothesis would also be sup-ported if the Aronson and Mills effect replicated in the "told" but not in the "not-told" treatment, since the assumed broader range of outcomes ex-perienced by the "severe" subject depends on the pleasure experienced by the subject upon learning that she had passed the test.

All subjects then listened to a five-minute tape recording of three girls having a discussion of cheating in college. This discussion was absolutely worthless, consisting mostly of hemming, hawing, clearing of throats, and pauses. The "initiate" was told that this was a recording of a previous discussion of the group that she was slated to join. The "noninitiate" was merely asked to listen to the discussion as one of the sequence of stimuli. Aronson and Mills presented the recording as an ongoing discussion. This difference in procedure in our "initiate" treatment did not seem to us to be critical.

In the final phase of the experiment, all subjects evaluated the discussion using semantic differential-type scales similar to those used by Aronson and

Mills. Eight scales dealt with the qualities of the participants and eight with qualities of the discussion itself. Each scale was numbered from 0 to 15, the polarity of the scales being alternated in order to counteract any response bias. After this evaluation sheet was filled out, the subject was administered a post-experimental questionnaire which asked her to rate the pleasantness or unpleasantness of the various stimuli. The subject's evaluation of the shocks on this questionnaire was, of course, the check on the manipulation of suffering.

RESULTS

The two shock levels clearly induced different degrees of pleasantness. The post-questionnaire contained a 7-point scale on which the subject rated the pleasantness of the shocks. The difference between the two shock conditions was extremely large ($p < .001$ by chi-square[1]) with the majority of subjects in the "severe" condition indicating that the shocks were "extremely unpleasant." No subjects in the "mild" treatment found the shocks more than only "mildly unpleasant."

The discussion evaluation data are shown in Table 10.1. The figures in the table represent the means of the pleasantness ratings for both the participant and the discussion evaluation, summed over the eight scales used for each. Tables 10.2 and 10.3 present the analysis of variance for each of the two evaluations. We see a clear main effect of the initiation factor. When the subject anticipated joining the group whose discussion she had heard, she tended to evaluate both the discussion and the participants more highly than she did when there was no such expectation. This shows a general "effort effect" in line with dissonance theory. There was also a main effect of severity that is accounted for by the "initiates." The crucial degree of freedom that concerns us here is the interaction between initiation and severity which also yields a significant F-ratio. A t test applied within the "initiates" and within the "noninitiates" shows that both trends, which are opposite, are significant, the trend in the "initiate" treatment being stronger ($p < .01$) than the trend in the "noninitiate" treatment ($p < .05$). Whether or not the "initiate" received feedback about her performance on the screening test (the "told" vs. "not-told" variations) appears not to have interacted with severity of the shock. We do see, however, that for the participant evaluation there does seem to be a main effect of feedback. Informing the subject that she had passed the test appears to have reduced the evaluation of the participants.

---

[1]Chi-square was used as a test of significance because the distribution in the "severe" treatment was skewed.

TABLE 10.1
The effects of severity of shock, initiation, and feedback on evaluation of the group discussion. (The larger the number, the more favorable the evaluation.)

	Initiate				Noninitiate	
	Mild shock		Severe shock		Mild shock	Severe shock
	Told	Not told	Told	Not told		
Participant rating	11.5	26.1	31.1	41.0	19.8	13.2
Discussion rating	11.0	15.6	27.0	28.2	9.1	5.8

TABLE 10.2
Analysis of variance of the participant evaluation

Source	SS	df	MS	F^b
Initiation (I)	1276	1	1276	8.28
Severity (S)	1045	1	1045	6.78
I × S	1504	1	1504	9.77
Told (T)	1201	1	1201	7.80
S (I) × T^a	45	1	45	
Error	6471	42	159	

^{a}Interation of feedback (Told vs. Not-told within the initiate condition).
$^b F\ .05 = 4.07,\ F\ .01 = 7.27.$

TABLE 10.3
Analysis of variance of the discussion evaluation

Source	SS	df	MS	F
Initiation (I)	1811	1	1811	13.22
Severity (S)	850	1	850	6.20
I × S	835	1	835	6.09
Told (T)	69	1	69	
S (I) × T	23	1	23	
Error	5774	42	137	

Since there was some variation in both the "severe" and "mild" shock conditions in the perception of unpleasantness by the subject, we were in a position to do an internal analysis of the data by examining the correlation between *perceived* severity of the shock and liking for the group discussion. On the basis of dissonance theory we would expect a positive relationship only within the "initiate" condition. The overall correlation with the "initiate" treatment is .52 for the participant rating and .45 for the discussion rating ($p < .01$ for both correlation coefficients). The corresponding correlations in the "noninitiate" treatment are .03 and .07.

DISCUSSION

The data from the experiment strongly support the "suffering-leading-to-liking" hypothesis and effectively rule out a number of other interpretations of the original experiment by Aronson and Mills. Our data for the "initiate" treatment are much stronger than those in the first experiment. This is probably attributable to the shock manipulation which undoubtedly produced more uniform within-treatment levels of suffering. The fact that the content of our suffering manipulation was divorced from the content of the group discussion eliminates the family of interpretations of the Aronson and Mills data that invoke some motive for wanting to affiliate that would be assumed to be greater in the "severe" than in the "mild" initiation treatment. The fact that there was an interaction between the initiate and everity factors eliminates the "contrast" and "relief" hypotheses. Both hypotheses predict the same difference under the "initiate" and the "noninitiate" treatments. We see instead an effect within the "noninitiate" treatment that supports a secondary reinforcement interpretation; the more severe the shock the *less* did the subject like the discussion. The internal correlational analysis adds further support for the "suffering-leading-to-liking" hypothesis and further weakens the "contrast" and "relief" hypotheses, since within the "initiate" treatment the greater was the perceived suffering the greater did the subject like the group discussion, whereas no such relationship was found within the "noninitiate" treatment.

Both the Chapanis and Chapanis "afterglow" and the Schopler and Bateson "dependence" hypotheses depend upon the subject having had a success experience after learning that she had passed the screening test. This success experience is presumed to have been greater in the "severe" than in the "mild" initiation treatment. Greater liking for the discussion under the "severe" initiation should therefore, according to both hypotheses, occur under the "told" but not under the "not-told" treatment. The lack of such an interaction effectively rules out both hypotheses.

Feedback did have a main effect on the evaluation of the participants. The high evaluation of the participants in the "not-told" as compared with the "told" condition may reflect a desire to be in the group. When informed that she had passed the screening test and would be in the group, the subject reduced her evaluation. Objects that a person is not sure he can have may appear more attractive to him under certain circumstance than similar objects that he already possesses. Having suffered or expended effort in order to acquire the object may be just such a circumstance. This effect was not predicted and our interpretation, therefore, must be considered as highly speculative.

References

ARONSON, E., AND MILLS, J. The effect of severity of initiation on liking for a group. *Journal of Abnormal and Social Psychology*, 1959, **59**, 177–181.

CHAPANIS, N. P., AND CHAPANIS, A. Cognitive dissonance: five years later. *Psychological Bulletin*, 1964, **61**, 1–22.

SCHOPLER, J., AND BATESON, N. A dependence interpretation of the effects of a severe initiation. *Journal of Personality*, 1962, **30**, 633–649.

THIBAUT, J., AND KELLEY, H. H. *The social psychology of groups*. New York: Wiley, 1959.

11

Studies in Forced Compliance:

I. The Effect of Pressure for Compliance on Attitude Change Produced by Face-to-Face Role Playing and Anonymous Essay Writing

J. Merrill Carlsmith, Barry E. Collins,
and Robert L. Helmreich

One-half of the experimental Ss (male high school students) were enticed to tell the next S (a female accomplice) that the experimental task was interesting, exciting, fun, and enjoyable (when, in fact, it was quite dull). The other half of the experimental Ss wrote an anonymous essay to the same effect. Experimental Ss were paid an additional $.50, $1.50, or $5 for this counterattitudinal response. Control Ss merely worked on the experimental task and completed the posttest. The data from the face-to-face condition replicates the original Festinger and Carlsmith experiment; small amounts of money were most effective in convincing Ss that the task was really fun and interesting. Data from the essay condition, however, indicated just the opposite. Large amounts of money produce the most attitude change.

An encouragingly large body of literature has appeared in recent years which suggests that inducing a person to adopt a counterattitudinal position causes him to change his attitude in the direction of the position adopted. Unfortunately, there is a growing disagreement concerning the relationship between the size of the incentive which is used to induce the person to adopt a counterattitudinal position and the amount of attitude change. The empirical question is straightforward: Does increasing the amount of incentive offered

Reprinted with permission from the authors and *The Journal of Personality and Social Psychology,* Vol. 4, No. 1, 1966. Copyright 1966 by the American Psychological Association.

This research was supported by funds from National Science Foundation Grant NSF GS 492 to Yale University. The data were collected while J. Merrill Carlsmith was supported by funds from the Office of Naval Research, Contract 4269 (00). Thanks are extended to Juliet Vogel and Katherine Flynn who gave invaluable assistance during data collection.

to a person to engage in counterattitudinal role playing *increase* or *decrease* the amount of attitude change which results from that role playing? Theoretically, there are two opposing predictions which correspond to each of the opposite empirical results.

Dissonance-Theory Prediction

Dissonance theory (Festinger, 1957) predicts that the greater the inducement offered to the subject to adopt a position with which he does not agree, the less the resultant attitude change. The reasoning behind this prediction is spelled out in some detail by Festinger (1957, ch. 4) and by Festinger and Carlsmith (1959, pp. 203–204). Briefly, the argument goes as follows: The two cognitions "I believe X" and "I am publicly stating that I believe not X" are dissonant. However, all pressures, threats, and rewards which induce one to state that he believes "not X" are consonant with the cognition "I am publicly stating that I believe not X." Consequently, the greater the pressures, threats, or rewards, the more consonant cognitions the individual holds, and the lower the magnitude of the dissonance. Since one primary means of dissonance reduction in this situation is to change one's attitude in the direction "not X," it follows that the larger the reward for stating "not X," the *less* the resultant attitude change in that direction should be.

Incentive or Reinforcement Theory Prediction

On the other hand, various forms of "incentive theory" (Janis and Gilmore, 1965), "consistency theory" (Rosenberg, 1965), or "reinforcement theory" argue that the greater the incentives for the counterattitudinal role playing the greater should be the resultant attitude change. Thus, advocates of this position state:

> . . . the significance of a reward received for writing a counterattitudinal essay . . . would be different from that claimed in dissonance theory: such a reward would, in proportion to its magnitude, be likely to have a positive effect both upon the development and the stabilization of the new cognitions. From this it would be predicted that with the removal of the biasing factors the degree of attitude change obtained after the subjects have written counterattitudinal essays will vary directly, rather than inversely, with the amount of reward [Rosenberg, 1965, p. 33].

> . . . two separate kinds of mediation are . . . conceivable: the *expectation* of payment for counterattitudinal advocacy may operate as an incentive and thus affect the quality of the arguments advanced in support of new cognitions; the *receipt* of payment may operate as a reinforcement that further fosters the internalization of the counterattitudinal cognitions . . . [Rosenberg, 1965, p. 39].

[Janis and Gilmore, 1965, make a similar argument:] According to this "incentive" theory, when a person accepts the task of improvising arguments in favor of a point of view at variance with his own personal convictions, he becomes temporarily motivated to think up all the good positive arguments he can, and at the same time suppresses thoughts about the negative arguments which are supposedly irrelevant to the assigned task. This "biased scanning" increases the salience of the positive arguments and therefore increases the chances of acceptance of the new attitude position [pp. 17–18].

Empirical Controversy

Let us briefly review some of the experiments which have dealt with this question. The first such experiment was conducted by Kelman (1953), who asked seventh-grade students to write essays favoring one or another kind of comic book. Different subjects were offered different amounts of incentive to adopt the opposite position of the one they actually held. He found that, among subjects who complied with the request, there was more attitude change among those who were offered a low incentive than among those who were offered a high incentive. Although such a finding is in line with the prediction made by dissonance theory, the fact that many fewer subjects complied with the request in the low-incentive group than in the high-incentive group leaves open the possibility that self-selection may have affected the results. Also, since incentives were offered for compliance and for noncompliance, it is not always easy to identify the "high-incentive" conditions.

In order to check on this possibility, Festinger and Carlsmith (1959) carried out an experiment where the subject was offered varying amounts of money to publicly adopt a counterattitudinal position. Specifically, the subjects were requested to tell a waiting girl (actually a confederate) that an experiment that they had just participated in was interesting and exciting. (In fact, the experiment had been dull and boring.) Subjects were told that the experimenter's assistant, who usually performed this role, had, unexpectedly, failed to show up, and subjects were offered either $1 or $20 to perform this task, and to be on call for a possible similar task in the future. Festinger and Carlsmith found that subjects who had been paid only $1 changed their attitudes more in the direction of the position they had publicly advocated than did $20 subjects.

Although this finding provides good support for the dissonance-theory prediction, several criticisms have been directed toward the experiment. Most of these criticisms argue that the $20 inducement was inordinately large, and would produce guilt, suspicion, or some other reaction which would interfere with the attitude change. To counter this criticism, Cohen (Brehm and Cohen, 1962) carried out a similar experiment using smaller amounts of money. In this experiment, subjects were approached in their rooms by a fellow student who asked them to write an essay in favor of the actions of the New Haven police. (Most students privately disagreed with this position.) Subjects were offered either $.50, $1, $5, or $10 for writing such an essay. After writing the essays the subjects' attitudes toward the police actions were assessed. Cohen's results fit closely with the dissonance-theory predictions; there was decreasing attitude change with increasing amounts of incentive for performing the counterattitudinal behavior. Taken together, the Festinger and Carlsmith and Cohen experiments support the empirical generality of the negative relationship between incentive and attitude change predicted by dissonance theory.

Several more recent experiments, however, have cast some doubt on the generality of the dissonance-theory interpretation of these results. In the first of these experiments (Janis and Gilmore, 1965) subjects were asked to write an essay which argued that all college students should be required to take an extra year of mathematics and of physics. In an attempt to show that the results obtained by Festinger and Carlsmith were due to the use of an "extraordinarily large reward of $20 [which] might have unintentionally generated some degree of suspicion or wariness," they repeated the use of $1 and $20 as rewards. They also added a variation in the sponsor of the project. In one case, the sponsor was described as a new publishing company, in the other as a research organization on the behalf of a number of universities. Unfortunately, they made two major changes in the offering of money, which prevents a direct comparison with the Festinger and Carlsmith experiment. Rather than offering subjects the money as payment *and* as a retainer for possible future work, they made no mention of any possible future work. In addition, whereas in the Festinger and Carlsmith study the money was offered for performing a task for which a sudden, unexpected, and pressing need had arisen, Janis and Gilmore offered this money for a task which was being done by several people, and which many other people might have done just as well. These two factors may have contributed to the fact that Janis and Gilmore report that their subjects perceived the money as a surprising and inappropriate payment.

Janis and Gilmore found that—with their technique of presentation—variations in monetary reward produced no differences in attitude change. Whether this failure to replicate is due to these changed techniques of presentation or due to suspicion and negative feelings is an empirical question.

The one finding that Janis and Gilmore do report is an interaction between role playing and sponsorship conditions. In the role-playing conditions, the public welfare sponsorship produced significantly more attitude change than did the commercial sponsorship; in the control conditions, there was no significant difference. Unfortunately, the role-playing subjects differed from the control subjects not only by virtue of the fact that they wrote an essay against their position, but also because they were given a few "general questions," for example, "Considering the type of career you are likely to be in, how might a background in physics and math enable you to function more adequately?" Such questions might well serve as a persuasive communication, and the difference between the sponsorship conditions would then be attributable to prestige or "demand" effects of the more positive sponsor.

The finding from Janis and Gilmore which is of major interest for our purposes here is the failure to find an effect of incentive on attitude change where the large incentive was designed especially to arouse suspicion. In a more recent experiment, Elms and Janis (1965) were able to detect some effects of incentive under similar circumstances—effects which tended to go in the opposite direction from that predicted by dissonance theory. Varying amount of incentive, nature of sponsorship, and presence or absence of role playing in a $3 \times 2 \times 2$ factorial, Elms and Janis asked subjects to write an anonymous essay advocating that qualified United States students should be sent to study in Russia for four years. The alleged sponsor of the research program was a private firm hired by the Soviet Embassy in one condition (negative sponsorship), while in the other condition the firm had been hired by the United States State Department (positive sponsorship). Subjects were paid either $.50, $1.50, or $5 to write an essay counter to their position. Only 1 of the 10 experimental groups showed significant attitude change. This was the group paid $10 under favorable sponsorship conditions. This group showed more attitude change than those subjects paid $.50. (However, the relationship is not linear. These $.50 subjects showed more—although not significantly—change than those subjects paid $1.50.) Under unfavorable sponsorship conditions, there were no significant effects. The $.50–$10 comparison for favorable sponsorship is the opposite of that predicted by dissonance theory, and is interpreted by Elms and Janis as being in support of "incentive theory."

Stronger evidence for increasing attitude change with increasing incentive is reported by Rosenberg (1965). His study, which is similar to Cohen's (Brehm and Cohen, 1962) study, asked subjects to write essays advocating that the Ohio State football team be banned from playing in the Rose Bowl (a strongly counterattitudinal position). Rosenberg changed Cohen's procedure by separating the "compliance inducer" from the posttester. The person who asked the subject to write the essay was not the same person as the experimenter who gathered the information on the subject's attitudes following the manipulation. In addition to a control condition, in which subjects wrote no counterattitudinal essay, there were three levels of reward for writing the essay—$.50, $1, and $5. The results of the experiment were exactly the opposite of Cohen's—the group paid $5 changed their attitudes much more than did the groups paid $.50 or $1, who in turn changed more than the control condition.

Unfortunately, the interpretation of these results must remain equivocal. As Nuttin (1964) points out:

> Rosenberg's study is, like most replications, not a "duplicate" of Cohen's study, but a very complex chain of interactions which are functionally more or less equivalent or similar to the ones Cohen investigated. Not only the attitude object itself but also the social status of the *E* and the experimental situation as a whole were quite different in both studies . . . . Notwithstanding this, Rosenberg interprets his discrepant findings as due to *his* definition of the difference between the two experiments [pp. 4ff. for other critical discussion of Rosenberg's study].

The most recent study of this problem is a large experiment by Nuttin (1964), for which only preliminary results are available. Nuttin ran twenty experimental conditions in which he essentially attempted to replicate both studies, adding what he felt had been missing control groups in Rosenberg's study. The most clear-cut results he reports are on his replication of the Rosenberg study, where he finds exactly the opposite of what Rosenberg found. Thus, even when some degree of "perceptual separation" is maintained, Nuttin finds identical results to those of Cohen—the larger the incentive, the less the attitude change. However, Nuttin was unable to replicate the Festinger and Carlsmith results.

Since most of the criticisms which are applied to one individual study do not apply to the others, the meaning of all studies, in concert, is not clear. At the very least, these data suggest that the original formulation of the attitude-change process by Festinger and Carlsmith was incomplete. At the most, they suggest that the dissonance results were due to trivial artifacts. Because of the many differences in procedure among these various studies, it would be worthwhile to study differences in procedure which might have produced different results.

There are, of course, many differences, but let us turn our attention to just one. Contrast the Festinger and Carlsmith experiment with, say, that of Elms and Janis. In the study by Festinger and Carlsmith, the subject is asked to make a public statement (at least in front of one other person) which conflicts with his private belief. Furthermore, the person to whom he is making this statement is *unaware* that this is in fact in conflict with the private belief. Such a situation is certainly one in which dissonance would be aroused.

Consider on the other hand the position of the subject in the Elms and Janis experiment. He is being asked to write an essay in favor of a position which he does not agree with. He is assured that his essay will be kept anonymous—no one will ever know that he wrote it except the experimenter. And the experimenter—the only person to read the essay—knows full well that the essay does *not* express the subject's private opinion. The experimenter, in essence, is asking him whether he has the intellectual ability to see some arguments on the opposite side of the issue from that which he holds. It can be argued that writing such an essay will create no dissonance.

Stated in an extreme form, the question is whether the cognition "I am, for good *reasons*, listing some arguments in favor of the position 'not-X' is dissonant with the cognition 'I believe X.'" It is plausible that, especially among college students, the cognition that one is listing such arguments is not at all dissonant with the cognition that one believes the opposite. Rather, the ability intellectually to adopt such a position is the hallmark of the open-minded and intellectual.

The argument in the paragraph above is not altogether different from the emphasis which Brehm and Cohen (1962) have placed on the role of commitment in the arousal of dissonance. A person who is merely writing arguments in favor of a position, but who has not committed himself to that position, would not experience dissonance *about the fact that he was writing arguments.* This is not to say that there may not be dissonance of some other kind, or that there may not be other nondissonance processes operating to produce attitude change as a result of writing these arguments. For example, insofar as the arguments he produces are good ones, there is dissonance aroused between the cognition "This good argument in favor of not X exists" and the cognition "I believe X." This dissonance-theory process sounds quite similar to the incentive-theory process which Janis and Gilmore posit to explain attitude change produced by role playing. The point to be made here is that writing an anonymous essay may not produce dissonance *of the particular kind* studied by Festinger and Carlsmith, and that the predictions from dissonance theory about incentive effects may not be relevant in such situations.

In order to test this post hoc explanation, we attempted to design an experiment which would demonstrate that the results reported by Festinger and Carlsmith could be repeated under appropriate conditions, whereas the opposite kind of results might be expected under different conditions.

One further difference between experiments which have obtained results consistent with the dissonance-theory predictions and those experiments which have not been the theoretical predilection of the experimenters. With the exception of the work of Nuttin, the results in line with dissonance-theory predictions have been obtained by experimenters who were to some extent identified with dissonance theory and who might be expected to "hope for" results consistent with dissonance theory. The converse has been true of experimenters who have obtained results inconsistent with dissonance theory. In light of the increasing interest in subtle effects of so-called "experimenter bias" (Rosenthal, 1963) we carried out the present experiment using two experimenters of different theoretical backgrounds. One of the experimenters (JMC) was presumably identified with a dissonance-theory approach; the other (BEC) was somewhat identified with a more behavioristic or reinforcement theory approach.

The basic design of the experiment to be reported here is a $2 \times 2 \times 4$ factorial. Subjects were asked to adopt a counterattitudinal position in two very different ways. Half of the subjects were asked to lie to a confederate in a fact-to-face confrontation. They were asked to tell a confederate that a decidedly dull task was in fact interesting—a manipulation essentially identical to that of Festinger and Carlsmith. The other half of the subjects were asked to write an anonymous essay in favor of the same position—an essay which would ostensibly be used to help the experimenter prepare another description which would then be presented to future subjects. Half of the subjects were run by each experimenter. Finally, experimental subjects were paid one of three different amounts of money for performing the task, while a control group was paid no additional money and performed no counterattitudinal responses.

METHOD

Subjects

An advertisement was placed in the local paper offering to pay high school age students (14–18) $2.50 for two hours of participation in a psychological experiment. When males called the listed number, they were given appointments for the experiment. Females were put on a "waiting list."

Two hundred and two male subjects participated in the experiment. A total of eleven subjects were eliminated from the reported results. Four subjects (two pairs of brothers) were discarded because, in the judgment of the experimenter administering the posttest, they did not comprehend the 11-point rating scale. Typically they expressed strong approval or disapproval and then chose a number on the opposite end of the scale. The post-tester did not know which condition the subject was in, and, therefore, could not bias the results by selective elimination. Four more subjects (two $.50 role play, one $1.50 role play, and one $.50 essay) were discarded because they did not follow through on the assigned role play or essay. Typically they admitted the task was dull and stated that they had been asked to say it was interesting. Only one subject showed any detectable sign of suspicion, and he was eliminated before he took the posttest. One subject accidentally saw the confederate in conversation with one of the experimenters. Finally, one subject, when he heard from the confederate that her friend "told her it was kind of dull," called in the experimenter and suggested that the accomplice be assigned to a control group since she knew the task was dull.

The subjects were extremely heterogeneous. They ranged from those who could barely master the complexities of an 11-point scale or could produce only 20 or 25 words of essay in 10 minutes to numerous prep-school students and children from professional families. The sample included a substantial number of Negroes.

Setting and Personnel

The study was conducted in six rooms of the Yale Psycho-Educational Clinic over a 3-week period. The five personnel conducting the experiment were the two principal investigators (BEC and JMC, who alternated as "project director" and "posttester"), a graduate assistant who served as experimenter (RLH), a receptionist, and a female high school age accomplice.

Overview of Design

The basic procedure was similar to that used by Festinger and Carlsmith (1959). Experimental subjects were asked either to write an essay or to tell a second, presumably naïve, subject that the experimental task was fun, interesting, exciting, and enjoyable. The subjects knew from their own experience with the task that it was dull and uninteresting. Subjects were paid an *additional* $5, $1.50, or $.50 to role play or write the essay. Control subjects were paid no additional money and were not asked to role play or write an essay. One-half of the subjects were run with BEC as project director and JMC as posttester, and the other half were run with the roles reversed. Attitudes toward the experimental task were then measured in a posttest-only design. The accomplice rated the several dimensions of the role-play performance, and the transcripts of the role plays and the essays were rated on a number of variables by three judges.

Procedure

All subjects. On arriving at the building, each subject was greeted by the receptionist who verified his age and high school status and conducted him to an experimental room furnished with desk, chairs, and writing materials. After the subject had waited alone for several minutes, the experimenter entered the room, introduced himself as Mr. Helmreich, and announced that he was ready to start the experiment. The experimenter then explained that the experiment itself would only take a little over an hour and that since subjects were being paid for two hours' participation, arrangements had been made for every subject to take part in a record survey being conducted in the building by a "man from some consumer research outfit in New York." At this point, the subject was presented with the experimental task—twenty five-page booklets of random numbers. Each booklet had a cover sheet which instructed the subject to strike out each occurrence of two of the digits (e.g., 2s and 6s) contained in the booklet. The subject was told that he should work at a comfortable rate, correct mistakes, and continue working until stopped by the experimenter. The experimenter then explained that he would describe the purpose of the study when he stopped the subject on completion of the task. The subject was then left alone to work for an hour. The supply of booklets left with the subject was many times the number which could be completed in an hour. The task itself was designed to be so dull and repetitious that the subject would leave with a generally negative feeling.

At the end of an hour, the experimenter reentered the room and told the subject that he could stop as the experiment was completed. The experimenter then seated himself next to the subject and said he would explain the purpose of the study. The experimenter described the project as a large-scale study designed to investigate how a person's prior expectation of the nature of a task might affect the amount and accuracy of work performed. The subject was told that the project was investigating the best ways to describe routine tasks so that people would be motivated to work hard and accurately. Each subject was told that he was in a control condition and, therefore, had been given no expectation about how pleasant the task would be. He was told that his group would serve as the standard comparison for other groups which were given positive expectations.

At this point the explanations began to differ according to the experimental condition to which the subject was assigned. Four different procedures were used: role-play control, role-play experimental, essay control, and essay experimental.

Role-play control subjects. Subjects in this condition were told that subjects in the other condition were introduced by the experimenter to a high school boy named Anderson who, presumably, had just finished the experimental task. In fact, continued the experimenter, the boy was paid by the experimenter to say the task was fun, interesting, exciting and enjoyable. The experimenter remarked that after the paid assistant had been with a subject in the other condition two minutes, telling the subject how the experiment was fun, interesting, etc., the experimenter would return to the room, excuse the assistant, and start the subject on the same random-number task. The experimenter pointed out that a high school age assistant was necessary in order to make the description of the task plausible.

At this point, the experimenter asked if the subject had any questions concerning the purpose of the study. After dealing with any questions, the experimenter stated that the project director (BEC or JMC) would like to thank him. The experimenter then left the room and eturned with the project director, who then gave the termination speech.

Role-play experimental subjects. In this condition, as the experimenter was finishing the same description given to role-play control subjects and asking for questions, the project director knocked on the door, entered the room, excused himself, and asked the experimenter if he knew where Anderson was. After the experimenter replied that he had not seen him, the director remarked that a subject was waiting in a condition where he was supposed to be told that the task was fun and interesting. He then asked the experimenter if he knew how to get in touch with Anderson and received a negative reply. After a pause, the director asked the experimenter if the subject with him was finished. The experimenter replied that the subject had completed the task and that he was explaining the purpose of the study. The director then remarked that perhaps the subject could help them; that, as the experimenter had no doubt explained, Anderson had been hired to tell some of the waiting subjects that the task was fun, interesting, exciting, and enjoyable. The subject was told that he could help the director out of a jam by describing the task in those terms to a girl who was waiting to start the experiment. The director said that since he was in a bind, he could pay $.50 ($1.50, $5) for doing this job. After the subject agreed (every subject agreed to undertake the task), the experimenter was sent to obtain the proper amount of money and a receipt form. While the experimenter was gone, the director rehearsed the points (fun, interesting, exciting, enjoyable) that the subject was to make to the waiting confederate. After the experimenter returned, the subject took his money, signed a receipt, and was conducted by the director to another room where the female confederate was waiting, ostensibly to start the experiment.

The director told the confederate that the subject had just finished the experiment and that he would tell her something about it. He then left, saying he would be back in a couple of minutes. The girl said little until the subject made some positive remarks about the task, then remarked that a friend of hers had taken the test and had not said much about it except that it was rather dull. Most subjects attempted to counter this evaluation, and the accomplice listened quietly accepting everything the subject said about the task. The interaction between the subject and the accomplice was recorded on a concealed tape recorder.

After two minutes, the director returned to the room, told the accomplice that the experimenter would be in to get her started on the experiment, and led the subject from the room. The director then gave the termination speech common to all subjects.

Essay control subjects. Procedures in this condition were the same as in the role-play control condition except that subjects were told that subjects in the other condition read a short essay describing the task positively. The experimenter stated that after reading the essay, subjects in this other group were given the same random-number task. After answering any questions concerning the purpose of the study, the experimenter brought in and introduced the project director who gave the termination speech.

Essay experimental subjects. In this condition, subjects were treated in the same manner as essay controls until the project director was introduced. At this point the director seated himself beside the subject, stated that he had a problem and that the subject might be able to help. He remarked that, as the experimenter described, some subjects in other conditions read an essay describing the task as fun, interesting, exciting, and enjoyable. But he further commented that the experimenters were unhappy with this essay. The director felt that the essays were unsatisfactory because they did not sound like they had been written by high school students and that they did not have the perspective of someone who had taken the experiment. The experimenters had decided to write a new description of the task and felt that the best way to proceed would be to ask a few of the subjects to write positive descriptions of the task. He emphasized that no other subjects would read these essays because he would merely use them as sources of phrases and ideas for an essay which he, the director, would write. He then added that since they were "in a bind" he could pay the subject $.50 ($1.50, $5) to write a 5- or 10-minute description of the task. After the subject agreed to do so (all subjects agreed to write the essay), the experimenter was sent to obtain the proper amount of money and a receipt form. While the experimenter was gone, the director rehearsed with the subject the points that he should make in the essay — that the task was fun, interesting, exciting, and enjoyable. After the experimenter returned, the subject took his money, signed a receipt, and followed the director to another office where he was given paper and pen and told to write for 5 or 10 minutes. He was to press a buzzer which would notify the director when he was finished. The subject was then left alone, and an electric timer was started in the adjoining office. The subject stopped the timer when he pressed the buzzer to signify that he had finished the essay. If the subject had not completed the essay by the end of 15 minutes, the director appeared in the room and told him that he had been working about 15 minutes and should finish up in the next couple of minutes. If still working, subjects were told to stop at the end of 17 minutes (1000 seconds). After collecting the essay, the director gave the termination speech.

Termination speech. (Identical for all subjects.) While walking away from the experimental room, the director remarked that, as the experimenter had mentioned, a man from Consumer Research Associates had asked if he could have the subjects rate some records since the experiment did not last the full 2 hours. He stated that he did not know much about what the survey was about, but he would show the subjects where to go. As in the Festinger and Carlsmith (1959) study, the experimenter then stated, "I certainly hope you enjoyed the experiment. Most of our subjects tell us they did." He then directed the subject to the posttest room, thanked him, and made a strong request for secrecy about the experiment. It was clear to the subject that the experiment was over at this point.

Posttest. The subject then arrived at a comfortably appointed office labeled Consumer Research Associates on the door. As the subject entered the office, he was greeted by the posttester (BEC or JMC) who introduced himself as Ted Johnson of Consumer Research Associates. Johnson then ushered the subject into the office and seated him before a desk. Next to the desk was a portable record player equipped with stereo earphones. The desk itself was littered with papers bearing Consumer Research Associates' letterhead and titled "Teen Age Market Survey—Connecticut." Johnson introduced the posttest by saying that his company was interested in the type of music teen-agers listened to and the types of music they liked for specific activities. He added that this was important because teen-agers bought 68 percent of the records sold in this country.

The subject was then asked to listen to a "practice" record for 30 seconds. Johnson then asked the subject to rate the practice record on several questions. He explained the use of an 11-point scale running from −5 to +5 using a graphic illustration of the scale. The subject rated the record as to how much he would like to dance to it, and how much he would like to study by it—each rating on the 11-point scale. After the practice record, Johnson announced that they were ready to start the survey. As he started to hand the earphones to the subject he stated:

> Oh. There is one thing I forgot. As you might imagine, the kind of mood you are in and the kind of experiences you have just had might influence the ratings you give in a situation like this. [The preceding spoken slowly to give the subject opportunity to agree.] If you had a splitting headache, you would not like much of anything we played through those earphones. [Subjects usually laughed—the volume was moderately high.] So I do want to ask you a question or two about that sort of thing. I don't know much about what what they are doing up there, but would you say the test they had you working on was sort of pleasant or unpleasant? [slight pause] As a matter of fact,

why don't we put it in terms of the same scale we used for the records? A minus 5 would be very unpleasant and a plus 5 would be very pleasant.

Since the subject had already used the rating scale for the practice record, the other five questions were covered quickly, and the subject immediately began to listen to the first "survey record." The word "test" was used in each question to make sure that the subjects were reacting to the experimental task only, and not the total experiment.

The six questions asked in the posttest were:

1. How pleasant did you find the test?
2. Was it an interesting test?
3. Did you learn anything from the test?
4. Would you recommend the test to a friend?
5. Would you describe the test as fun?
6. What is your general overall mood at the present time?

In each case a +5 represented a highly positive reaction and a −5 a strongly negative reaction. All subjects seemed convinced about the genuineness of the posttest; several hesitated to discuss the test because the project director had cautioned them to secrecy.

RESULTS

There are fifteen subjects in each of the four control groups, and eleven subjects in all but one of the twelve experimental groups. There are only ten subjects in the $.50, BEC, essay cell. The results can be discussed in three broad categories: the six questions in the posttest, measures evaluating the quality of the role-play performance and of the essays, and experimenter effects.

Posttest Variables

The mean response for each of the six questions in the posttest is shown in Table 11.1. Consider first the questions dealing with words the subject actually used while role playing or essay writing—"How interesting would you say the test was?" and "How much fun would you say the test was?" Table 11.1 shows that both essay and role-play control subjects found that the test, or random-number task, was uninteresting ($M = -1.2$) and not much fun ($M = -1.4$).

Our major hypotheses concerned the differential effects of pressure for compliance in the role-playing and essay-writing situations. Specifically,

TABLE 11.1
Means for posttest variables collapsed over
experimenters

	Control	$.50	$1.50	$5
Interesting				
RP	−1.43	1.23	−0.86	−1.18
E	−1.00	−0.86	1.32	2.41
Fun				
RP	−1.43	0.76	−0.81	−1.10
E	−1.28	−0.80	1.62	1.55
Fun plus interesting				
RP	−2.71	1.81	−1.62	−2.19
E	−2.14	−1.80	3.24	3.95
Pleasant				
RP	0.77	1.18	0.82	1.55
E	0.93	0.86	2.14	2.55
Learn anything				
RP	−0.37	−0.50	−2.00	−0.32
E	−2.27	−0.10	−0.41	−0.64
Recommend				
RP	2.53	2.50	1.59	2.27
E	2.33	2.38	2.50	3.56
Mood				
RP	1.83	2.18	2.27	3.41
E	2.83	2.19	3.32	3.36

Note: Scores from single questions range from −5 (extremely negative toward the task) to +5 (extremely positive). Fun plus interesting can range from −10 to +10. RP = role play; E = essay.

it was anticipated that subjects who engaged in a face-to-face confrontation (role play) would show a *negative* relationship between money offered for the role playing and attitude change. Thus subjects offered $.50 to role play should show maximal change, followed by subjects offered $1.50, and then those offered $5; the control subjects should, of course, be lowest.

Subjects who had written counterattitudinal essays, on the other hand, should show exactly the opposite trend. In this case, those subjects paid $5 should be most positive toward the task, followed in order by subjects paid $1.50, subjects paid $.50, and control subjects. In other words, the hypothesis anticipates a *positive* relationship between attitude change and money for subjects who wrote essays.

Figures 11.1 and 11.2 reveal two facts. First, it can be seen that subjects who adopted a counterattitudinal position, whether this was done by publicly announcing the position or by privately writing an essay adopting the position, changed their attitudes to bring them into line with the counterattitudinal position. That is, they felt that the experiment had been relatively more fun and interesting than did control subjects.

Moreover, both hypotheses are strongly confirmed. The amount of money offered to adopt this counterattitudinal position had sharply different effects

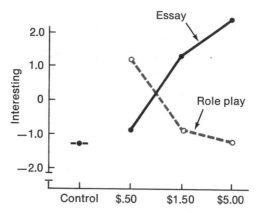

FIGURE 11.1
Responses to posttest question on interesting.
(The value drawn for the control group
represents the average on all control groups.)

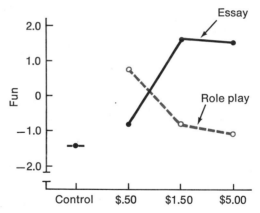

FIGURE 11.2
Responses to posttest question on fun. (The
value drawn for the control group represents the
average of all control groups.)

for role players and essay writers. When a subject is asked to publicly adopt a position which he does not privately believe in a face-to-face confrontation, he changes his attitude less if he is paid large amounts of money to adopt this position. Thus subjects paid $5 thought that the experiment was much less interesting and fun than did subjects paid $.50. An analysis of variance showed that the test for linear trend in the role-playing conditions was significant at the .05 level or better (see Table 11.2).

When a subject is asked to write a private essay which disagrees with his beliefs, however, the effect is exactly the opposite. The more the subject is paid to write this essay, the more his attitude changes in the direction of

TABLE 11.2
A priori hypotheses for posttest variables plus main effect for role play–essay

	Interest-ing	Fun	Fun plus interesting	Pleasant	Learn anything	Recom-mend	General mood
Role play, rank-order linear trend	8.1**	5.4*	7.1*	<1	<1	<1	<1
Essay, rank-order linear trend	18.1†	13.6†	19.3†	8.5†	1.6	1.6	2.0
Role play versus essay (from Table 11.3)	5.0*	4.0*	5.7*	2.7	<1	1.0	2.9
Percentage of between-cell variance contrib-uted by 3 hypotheses	73	73	74	63	23	23	20

Note: Unweighted mean solution. Error term from Experimenter × Role Play–Essay × Money analysis (Table 11.3).
*$p < .05$.
**$p < .01$.
†$p < .005$.

the position he is adopting. Thus, subjects paid $5 thought the experiment was more fun and interesting than did subjects paid $.50. Again an analysis of variance shows a significant linear trend in the hypothesized direction (see Table 11.2).

In general, essay subjects evidenced more attitude change. This finding should be interpreted with some caution, however. A glance at Figures 11.1 and 11.2 suggests that, if the study had used only $.50 incentives, it would have been the role-play subjects who evidenced the most attitude change.

As can be seen from the last line in Table 11.2, the two a priori hypotheses and the role play–essay main effect account for most of the between-cell variance for fun and interesting. The fact that these 3 degrees of freedom (out of a total of 15) account for so much of the variance indicates the unimportance of experimenter main effects and higher order interactions.

As Festinger and Carlsmith found, this effect seems to be quite specific to the particular words used in adopting the counterattitudinal position. When subjects were asked how pleasant the experiment had been, or how much they had learned from it, or whether they would ecommend it to a friend, there were no effects in the role-playing conditions, and only one significant effect in the essay-writing condition (see Tables 11.1 and 11.2). Only the questions asking the subjects how interesting and how much fun the experiment had been seem to show the effects of role playing which are predicted.

Subjects were also asked to rate their general mood, and on this question an interesting trend appears. Although the effect of incentive is not significant for either essay-writing or role-playing subjects taken individually, the

TABLE 11.3
Experimenter, role play–essay, and money standard analyses ($2 \times 2 \times 4$ analysis of variance)

Source	df	Interesting	Fun	Fun plus interesting	Pleasant	Learn anything	Recommend	Mood
Role play vs. essay	1	5.05*	3.98*	5.73*	2.69	<1	1.02	2.90
Money	3	3.05*	2.90*	3.42*	2.60	<1	<1	3.17*
Interaction	3	7.04**	4.74**	7.15**	1.28	1.60	<1	<1
MS_e		9.91	9.75	31.64	5.14	15.67	10.05	4.22
df error		175	167[a]	167[a]	175	175	175	175

Note: Since none of the experimenter main effects and none of the experimenter interactions reached the .05 level (only 1 of 28 reached the .10 level), they have been omitted from the table. The unweighted mean solution was used.
[a]The fun measure was not included in the posttest until 8 subjects (all in different cells) had been run. Consequntly, the N for fun and for fun plus interesting is only 183.
*$p < .05$.
**$p < .01$.

trend is identical in both cases, so that there is a significant main effect of money. As inspection of Table 11.1 shows, the more subjects were paid, the better the mood they were in at the end of the experiment, irrespective of whether they were paid to write essays or to engage in fact-to-face role playing. Such an effect may seem hardly surprising for the subjects who wrote essays. Essay subjects said that they were in a better mood after they had been paid $5; they also said that the experiment had been more fun and more interesting.

However, subjects who had engaged in face-to-face role playing and were paid $5 said that they were in a better mood, but thought that the experiment had benn *less* fun and *less* interesting than subjects paid $.50. Thus, the results for essay-writing subjects might be interpreted as a simple generalization: they had been paid more money, were consequently in a better mood, and consequently rated the experiment as more fun and more interesting. Such a possible effect is, of course, impossible for the role-playing subjects. The more they were paid, the better the mood they were in, but the less they thought the experiment was fun and interesting. Such a finding is especially interesting in view of the interpretation of the results of Festinger and Carlsmith offered by several writers (e.g., Elms and Janis, 1965) which focuses on the hypothesis that subjects paid $20 failed to show attitude change because they felt anxious or guilty. Insofar as this question about mood can tap some of these presumed feelings we find that contrary to this hypothesis, the more subjects are paid for performing a task like this, the better they feel.

Role-Play and Essay Performance

Evidence on the subjects' actual performances was gathered when all three authors independently rated the essays and transcripts of the role plays. Transcriptions of role-play performance were rated on the following six scales:

1. Persuasiveness and emphasis before the accomplice remarks that she has heard the task is dull.
2. Persuasiveness and emphasis after remark.
3. Overall positiveness.
4. Overall persuasiveness and conviction.
5. Percent of time spent on assigned topic.
6. Dissociation of self from content of message.

Ratings by the accomplice are also available on role-play subjects for the first four scales and for:

5. Apparent conflict.
6. Signs of discomfort.

Essays were rated on the following four scales:

1. Emphasis used in making points.
2. The extent to which the subject went beyond the statements given and created reasons in support of his general theme.
3. Overall quality and persuasiveness.
4. Apparent effort (with an attempt to control for ability).

It was anticipated that, if any differences were found at all, high incentives should improve the quality of both role-play and essay performance. (Control groups were, of course, omitted from all analyses, and separate analyses were performed for essay and role-play measures.) The interjudge reliabilities were typically in the 70s and 80s, and the various performance measures were highly correlated among themselves. None of these ratings of role-play transcripts showed even a .10 trend in any analysis of variance. Similarly, evaluations of the content of the essays show no glimmer of a difference among treatment groups. Also, there is no evidence that any of the measures of role-play or essay performance were correlated with posttest attitudes. According to the ratings made by the accomplice, role-play subjects showed highest conflict when they were paid only \$.50 (the $F = 5.58$, $p < .01$, for the 2×3 Experimenter $\times$ Money analysis of variance). But this is the only "quality of performance" accomplice rating which shows any sign of a money effect.

Experimenter Effects

The results from the two experimenters are remarkably similar. The Fs for experimenter main effects and experimenter interactions are, in general, smaller than might be expected by chance. There are two variables, however, which produced significant experimenter effects: the accomplice's ratings of conflict (necessarily for role-play subjects only since it is an accomplice rating) and the "number of words used once" measure. According to the accomplice's ratings of conflict, subjects run by BEC indicated more conflict than those run by JMC ($p < .05$). Since the role play occurred before the subject met the posttester, we can safely assume the effect was created in the experimental manipulations and not in the posttest. Posttest attitudes show no parallel trend.

Subjects were told to use four words: interesting, exciting enjoyable, and fun. Each role play and essay was scored for the number of these words which were used at least once. Both role-play ($p < .05$) and essay ($p < .01$) subjects run by BEC used more words than subjects run by JMC in both conditions. This effect is easily understood in terms of the heavier emphasis placed on the four words by BEC. In contrast to JMC, he asked the subjects to repeat the words back to him after he had stated them to the subjects. For the *role-play subjects only,* subjects run by JMC tended to use more words in high-incentive conditions, while BEC's subjects show no such trend (interaction $p < .05$). The attitude data show no patterns similar to any of those revealed by the number of words measure.

DISCUSSION

As can be seen in Figures 11.1 and 11.2, the major hypotheses from the study have been dramatically confirmed. There is one set of circumstances where increasing pressure for compliance leads to smaller amounts of attitude change. A subject who was enticed to make a patently false statement before a peer who believed the subject was sincere showed less attitude change with increased pressure for compliance. Figures 11.1 and 11.2 clearly indicate that the comparison between the $.50 group and the $1.50 group is the more crucial for role-play subjects. The highly significant difference between these two relatively small rewards represents a very strong replication of the original Festinger and Carlsmith study. These results, taken in conjunction with those of Cohen (Brehm and Cohen, 1962), make it highly unlikely that the original Festinger and Carlsmith result is an artifact of the unusual magnitude of the $20 reward.

It is equally clear, however, that there is another set of circumstances in which increasing pressure for compliance produces more attitude change. A subject who wrote an anonymous essay (to be read only by the experimenter) showed more attitude change with increasing pressure for compliance. This dramatic interaction is quite consistent with the theory outlined in the introduction.

The results for the experimenter manipulation are also encouraging. The two experimenters produced remarkably similar effects. It is clearly the case that the differing theoretical orientations of the experimenters—and their somewhat different expectations about the outcomes—had no effect whatsoever on attitude change.

What remains unspecified, however, is the crucial difference between the role-play and essay-writing conditions. The following list describes just a few of the many components in the complex manipulation used in this study: The essays were written while the role plays were oral; the role-play sessions lasted for a maximum of two minutes while the essay sessions lasted for a maximum of seventeen minutes; as a result of the differing justifications used to entice compliance, role-play subjects performed under somewhat more "hectic" or "crisis" circumstances than essay subjects; finally, if looked at from the subjects' perspective, the social consequences or implications of the compliant act differed greatly between the two conditions. In the essay condition, the only reader of the essays would be the experimenter, who understood why the essay had been written. In the role-play condition, however, the audience—the experimental accomplice—presumably believed that the subject was sincere when he said that the task was fun, interesting, exciting, and enjoyable. It seems quite clear that the latter condition is more dissonance producing.

What is unclear from dissonance theory, however, is why the essay condition should show an *increasing* amount of attitude change with increased incentive. If there is no dissonance at all produced in the essay condition, then the different incentives should have no effect on attitude change—there should, in fact, be no attitude change. If the amount of effort is greater for high-incentive subjects, then dissonance theory can predict a positive relationship between the amount of incentive and attitude change. *If* subjects in the high-incentive conditions exerted more effort, then this greater effort should lead to greater dissonance in the high-incentive conditions, and, consequently, greater attitude change. A long and careful examination of both essays and role-play performance, however, unearthed no evidence whatsoever that the high-incentive essays were in any way superior. The fact that the finished product in the high-incentive condition is not better, of course, does not imply that the students did not try harder. Subjects were given four words to repeat, and there was little else that they could do other than repeat the four words and include them in complete sentences. It is possible that an increased effort in the high-incentive condition would not be reflected in higher quality essays.

It is probably necessary to turn somewhere other than dissonance theory for an explanation of the positive relationship between pressure for compliance and attitude change. One very plausible explanation of our results for the essay-writing subjects is a simple generalization phenomenon. We know that the more subjects were paid the better the mood they were in. It would not be surprising if this good mood generalized to the task they had been doing, so that they would report that the task had been more fun and interesting. This explanation would assume that in the role-playing conditions, this tendency to generalize was overcome by the dissonance produced.

Alternatively, it is possible that the theoretical orientation proposed by Hovland (Hovland, Lumsdaine, and Sheffield, 1949) and Janis (Janis and Gilmore, 1965) is needed in order to explain the attitude change in the essay condition. But, as we understand them, these theories also must predict that the performance in the high-incentive condition will be superior in some way to the performance in low-pressure conditions. Nor do they make clear why the opposite effect should be found in the role-play conditions.

One final point should be made about the sensitivity of the incentive manipulation. A quick glance at Figures 11.1 and 11.2 indicates that the results would have appeared quite different had the $.50 group been omitted. There would have been no incentive effects for either essay or role-play subjects, and there would have remained only the main effect indicating that essay subjects showed more attitude change than role-play subjects.

Finally, it should be noted that our results for the role-playing subjects are consistent with several other experiments using different techniques for varying pressure for compliance. Studies on the use of strong or weak threats to induce counterattitudinal behavior (Aronson and Carlsmith, 1963; Freedman, 1965; Turner and Wright, 1965) have consistently shown more attitude change when weaker pressures are applied for compliance. Another kind of evidence comes from experiments by Freedman (1963) in which he shows more attitude change when little justification is provided for the counterattitudinal behavior than when high justification is provided.

References

Aronson, E., and Carlsmith, J. M. Effect of the severity of threat on the devaluation of forbidden behavior. *Journal of Abnormal and Social Psychology,* 1963, **66,** 584–588.

Brehm, J. W., and Cohen, A. R. *Explorations in cognitive dissonance.* New York: Wiley, 1962.

Elms, A., and Janis, I. Counter-norm attitudes induced by consonant versus dissonant conditions of role-playing. *Journal of Experimental Research in Personality,* 1965, **1,** 50–60.

FESTINGER, L. *A theory of cognitive dissonance.* Stanford: Stanford University Press, 1957.

FESTINGER, L., AND CARLSMITH, J. M. Cognitive consequences of forced compliance. *Journal of Abnormal and Social Psychology,* 1959, **58,** 203–210.

FREEDMAN, J. L. Attitudinal effects of inadequate justification. *Journal of Personality,* 1963, **31,** 371–385.

FREEDMAN, J. L. Long-term behavior effects of cognitive dissonance. *Journal of Experimental Social Psychology,* 1965, **1,** 145–155.

HOVLAND, C. I., LUMSDAINE, A. A., AND SHEFFIELD, F. D. *Experiments on mass communication.* Princeton: Princeton University Press, 1949.

JANIS, I. L., AND GILMORE, J. B. The influence of incentive conditions on the success of role playing in modifying attitudes. *Journal of Personality and Social Psychology,* 1965, **1,** 17–27.

KELMAN, H. C. Attitude change as a function of response restriction. *Human Relations,* 1953, **6,** 185–214.

NUTTIN, J. M., JR. Dissonant evidence about dissonance theory. Paper read at Second Conference of Experimental Social Psychologists in Europe, Frascati, Italy, 1964.

ROSENBERG, M. J. When dissonance fails: On eliminating evaluation apprehension from attitude measurement. *Journal of Personality and Social Psychology,* 1965, **1,** 18–42.

ROSENTHAL, R. On the social psychology of the psychological experiment: The experimenter's hypothesis as unintended determinant of experimental results. *American Scientist,* 1963, **51,** 268–283.

TURNER, E. A., AND WRIGHT J. C. Effects of severity of threat and perceived availability on the attractiveness of objects. *Journal of Personality and Social Psychology,* 1965, **2,** 128–132.

12

Long-Term Behavioral Effects of Cognitive Dissonance

Jonathan L. Freedman

Since the publication of *A Theory of Cognitive Dissonance* (Festinger, 1957), a large number of studies have been conducted to test a variety of deductions from the theory. Although not all of the results have been positive, in general the published research has supported the basic theory (see Brehm and Cohen, 1962, for a review).

There is, however, one quite serious limitation in this research. Virtually all of the results supporting dissonance theory have involved attitudes of one sort or another as measured by paper and pencil questionnaires, and all of the significant effects were found a very short time after the experimental manipulation. The authors of these studies have made the explicit or implicit assumption that the same results would also hold for appropriate

Reprinted with permission from the author and *The Journal of Experimental Social Psychology,* Vol. 1, 1965. Copyright 1965 by Academic Press, Inc.

This study was begun in collaboration with the late Dr. Arthur R. Cohen. The author is grateful for the stimulation and advice he received from Bob Cohen, and considers himself privileged to have known and worked with him. Thanks are also due to Dr. Helen Bee and Mr. Thomas Schweitzer for serving as experimenters, and to the Los Altos School system for generously providing space and time for the running of the experimental sessions. The study was supported in part by grant GS-196 from the National Science Foundation.

behavioral measures and that with sufficiently powerful manipulations the effects would endure for some time. Unfortunately, there is little or no evidence supporting such an assumption.

Only two published studies have aroused dissonance in an attempt to produce behavioral changes. Although both of these (Cohen, Greenbaum, and Mansson, 1963; and Wieck, 1964) report positive results, the experimental situations were quite unusual; and the effects were obtained very soon after the manipulation. The data on long-term effects are less consistent. Aronson and Carlsmith (1963) report that 45 days after an initial manipulation there was still some tendency for a dissonance effect to remain. Opposed to this is the result of a study by Walster (1964). Post-decisional changes in attitudes were taken at various intervals after a choice, and it was found that after ninety minutes attitudes were the same as before the decision was made.

The issue of whether or not dissonance theory applies to important, enduring, behavior is particularly important because of the nature of the theory. It is clearly a cognitive theory, and is stated in terms of thoughts, opinions, beliefs, etc. A person's awareness of his own behavior is a cognitive element and fits into the theoretical framework, but the theory does not deal directly with the behavior itself. It is assumed, of course, that changes in cognitions will tend to produce corresponding changes in relevant behavior and vice versa; but as Festinger has recently pointed out (1964), this remains to be shown. The present study, therefore, was designed primarily to demonstrate that the arousal and subsequent reduction of cognitive dissonance can affect relatively important behavior and that this effect can endure over a reasonably long period of time.

One of the most ubiquitous and important problems in behavior modification is the attempt to shape a child's behavior so that it is in accordance with the moral, legal, and social values of society. It is relatively easy to make the child behave correctly when he is offered a reward or threatened with punishment, but this is far from enough. For the socialization process to be successful, the child must also behave correctly in the absence of any such direct pressure, and this is considerably more difficult to accomplish. It has been suggested (Aronson and Carlsmith, 1963; Festinger and Freedman, 1964; Mills, 1958) that the theory of cognitive dissonance provides one possible framework within which to consider this problem.

Attempts to shape a child's behavior often occur in a type of forced compliance situation. The child is told not to do something[1] and is under varying amounts of pressure to obey. The parent or authority giving this restriction

---

[1]The same arguments would hold for situations in which the child is told to do something, but for purposes of this paper the discussion will refer only to the case in which the authority attempts to prevent certain behavior.

may strengthen it with a promise of a reward if the child obeys, a threat of punishment if he does not obey, or some other justification for obeying such as that the toy is fragile and may break if not used correctly. Any of these justifications may vary in magnitude. The rewards may be large or small, the threats mild or severe, the reasons good or bad, etc. If the child obeys the restriction, he is in a potentially dissonant situation because he wanted to perform the forbidden act but did not. As in other forced compliance situations, the greater the justification for obeying the less dissonance should be aroused (cf. Festinger and Carlsmith, 1959; Freedman, 1963; Rabbie, Brehm, and Cohen, 1959; etc.).

Consider a situation in which a child is told not to play with a very attractive, desirably toy, and is threatened with either mild or severe punishment for disobeying. If he obeys, all those factors which made him want to play with the toy are dissonant with the knowledge that he did not play with it. However, these factors are to some extent balanced by those factors which justified not playing with it. With a severe threat, the child has a very good justification for not playing since if he played, he would have been punished severely. Since there is little or nothing dissonant about refraining from playing even with a desirable toy in order to avoid severe punishment, little or no dissonance should be aroused under a severe threat condition. With a mild threat, on the other hand, the child does not have as good a reason for refraining. If the threat is mild enough elative to the desirability of the toy, a considerable amount of dissonance should be aroused. Regardless of the absolute level of threat, more dissonance should be aroused by obeying under mild than under severe threat.

Any dissonance that is aroused may be reduced either by decreasing the desire to play with the toy or by increasing the justification for not playing with it. The most direct and obvious way of accomplishing the former is to devalue the forbidden toy or increase the value of other, nonforbidden toys or activities. Aronson and Carlsmith (1963) and Turner and Wright (1964) have recently demonstrated in a situation similar to the one described above that a forbidden toy is devalued more under mild than under severe threat. The justification for not transgressing may be increased by magnifying the perceived dangerousness of the act, by enhancing the value of the prohibiting agent, by accepting the adult's evaluation of the act as wrong, or by a variety of similar changes in the perception of the situation.

The important point for our purpose is that any of these modes of dissonance reduction would tend to make the child less likely to play with the toy in the future. A lessening in the value of the toy, an increase in the value of the authority, an acceptance of the moral value that playing with that toy was wrong will all decrease the child's tendency to play with the toy. All these modes of dissonance reduction should be reflected in one specific type of behavior—to the extent that these modes of reduction occur the child should have less inclination to play with the toy, and he should be less likely to play with it even if the original threat were no longer salient or had been removed entirely.

It should be recalled that less dissonance should be aroused by obeying under severe than under mild threat, and correspondingly, less dissonance reduction should occur in the severe threat condition. Thus, if children refrain from playing with the toy under either severe or mild threat and are then given another opportunity to play with the toy with the threats removed, more of the children in the mild threat than in the severe condition should refrain from playing in this second session.

One final point should be made. The arousal of dissonance in this situation depends upon the lack of justification for obeying the restriction. If the child never considers transgressing because he perceives the pressure against this to be too great, no dissonance should be aroused. In other words, the child must face and resist temptation in order for dissonance to be produced. If, for example, the parent made the threat, even a mild threat, but never gave the child a chance to transgress, little or no dissonance would be aroused.

The analysis in terms of cognitive dissonance may now be summarized. A child is told not to play with a toy and is threatened with severe or mild punishment if he transgresses. If he is put into a situation in which he is tempted to play with it and he does not, greater dissonance will be aroused under mild than under severe threat. If there is then another opportunity to play with the toy and the threats are removed, those children who resisted temptation under mild threat will be less likely to play with the toy than those who resisted under severe threat. This difference between mild and severe threat will not occur if the child was not exposed to temptation in the first place. The present experiment was done to test this prediction with the additional specification that the effect could be demonstrated three or more weeks after the initial dissonance manipulation.

METHOD

Design

Children were told not to play with a very desirable toy under either high or low threat for disobeying, and were given a five minute free period during which the toy was present and available. During this period half of Ss in each threat condition were left alone with the toy (experimental groups); half were not left alone (control groups). Ratings of the attractiveness of the forbidden toy and four other toys were taken before the threat instructions were given and after the free period. Several weeks later the threats were nullified by a second *E* and *S*s were again given the opportunity to play with the forbidden toy. There were thus four groups: experimental mild and severe threat (EM and ES), and control mild and severe threat (CM and CS). The mild and severe threats served as high or low justification for obeying in the first session, and the major prediction was that fewer *S*s in the EM than in the ES condition would play with the toy during the second session. The control groups were included to assess the direct effect of the threat instructions. There was presumably little or no temptation during the first session of the control condition because *E* was present. Since only those *S*s who resisted temptation should feel any dissonance, the predicted superiority of the mild threat instructions should appear in the experimental conditions but not in the control conditions.

Procedure

The *S*s were 89 boys in the second to fourth grades in the Carmel and Springer schools in Los Altos, California. They were run individually and randomly assigned to conditions. Four *S*s (two in each of the experimental conditions) violated the prohibition by playing with the toy in the first session and were not included in the analysis, and two more were absent and could not be seen in the second session. The remaining 83 *S*s were divided equally among the four conditions except that the CS had 20 *S*s and the other groups had 21 *S*s.

The procedure in the first session was quite similar to that employed by Aronson and Carlsmith (1963). The *S* was told that the study concerned children's preferences among various toys. He was asked to indicate his liking of each of five toys on a scale ranging from 0 ("very, very bad toy") to 100 ("very, very good toy") by pointing to a place on the scale. The five toys were a cheap plastic submarine, an extremely expensive, battery controlled robot, a child's baseball glove, an unloaded Dick Tracy toy rifle, and a Tonka tractor. The robot was the toy which was forbidden in order to maximize the temptation to transgress. It was placed on the floor with its control handle on a table, and the other toys were laid out neatly on the table. The toys were demonstrated briefly by *E* in the order listed above, and were then rated by *S* in the same order. The *E* recorded the ratings on a separate sheet.

At this point the procedure diverged for the various conditions. For the experimental *S*s, *E* pretended to remember that he had an errand to do and said that he had to leave for about 10 minutes. For the control *S*s, *E* said that he had something to do and would be busy for about 10 minutes working in the room.

In the low threat conditions *E* continued, "While I'm gone (or busy) you can play with the toys if you want. You can play with any of them except the robot (pointing to it). Do not play with the robot. It is wrong to play with the robot." The high threat conditions had these same instructions with the addition of the following: "If you play with the robot I'll be very angry and will have to do something about it." Note that *S*s are told that it is "wrong" to play with the robot, and also that the severe threat condition depends primarily on an ambiguous, vague threat to "do something about it." It was felt that this would probably be more threatening and would be less susceptible to disbelief than any specific threat.

The *E* then left the room in the experimental conditions, or worked at some papers in the room in the control conditions. A concealed electric timer was attached to the control switch on the robot so that it would indicate whether or not the robot was turned on, and if so, for how long. At the end of only five minutes, *E* returned to the room (or finished his work), told *S* that we wanted a second rating of the toys, and said that sometimes ratings change and sometimes they did not change, and that *S* should rate them as he felt about them now. After the second rating *S* was thanked, told not to talk about the study with anyone else, and sent back to his class. This first session was run by a male *E*.

The second session was arranged to make it appear unrelated to the first. The interval between the two sessions ranged from 23 to 64 days (Christmas vacation interrupted the course of the study) with a mean interval of 39.8 days. There were no appreciable differences among the groups in either the range of time intervals or the mean interval. This second session was run by a female *E* who was not described as coming from Stanford, whereas the male *E* who ran the first session was explicitly from Stanford. The same experimental room was used to make the presence of the toys plausible, but the furniture was rearranged somewhat. The toys were in the far corner of the room placed in a disorderly manner. The control switch for the robot was draped carelessly over a music stand, and the other toys were scattered around.

The *E*, who did not know what group *S* was in, asked him to sit at the table and told him that she wanted him to copy some drawings. She then administered five cards of the Bender Gestalt (Bender, 1938) which *S* copied while *E* timed his responses. After the Bender was finished, *E* said that she had to score it and might want to ask *S* some questions about it. She said that while she was doing that, if *S* wanted he could play with any of the toys that someone had left in the room (pointing to the toys). This was delivered rather casually, and she then pretended to begin scoring the test. If, as happened occasionally, S continued to sit at the table, E repeated that S could play with the toys, and finally she said that she would prefer it if S did not watch her. Most Ss played with some of the toys, but as will be discussed later, a few did not play with any. If S asked specifically if he could play with the robot, E responded that as far as she was concerned he could play with any of the toys. As before, the timing apparatus timed if and how long S played with the robot, and E also recorded from the stop-watch how many seconds the toy was running. Unfortunately, part-way through the experiment, the robot broke down and would no longer operate. This, of course, made time scores meaningless since S would immediately discontinue playing with the robot as soon as it was obvious that it was not working. Therefore, the major data are simply whether or not S pressed the control switch.

At the end of four minutes, E said she was finished scoring the drawings and that S had done quite well. She thanked him and urged him not to talk about the study. This concluded the experiment.

RESULTS

Our original basic assumption was that less dissonance would be aroused by resisting temptation under high justification than under low justification, and that this difference would be reflected in subsequent behavior. In particular, it was predicted that the mild threat experimental condition (EM) would produce more dissonance than the severe threat experimental (ES) and that fewer Ss in the EM than in the ES would play with the forbidden toy in the second session. The relevant data are presented in Table 12.1, which shows the number of Ss in each group who played with the robot in the second session. It may be seen that more than twice as many Ss in the ES condition as in the EM condition played with the previously forbidden toy. This difference is in the predicted direction and is significant ($\chi^2 = 6.11$, $p < .02$). In other words, the use of a mild threat in the first session more effectively prevented subsequent transgression than the use of a severe threat.

TABLE 12.1
Number in each condition who played with robot in second session

Group	Low threat		High threat	
	Played	Did not play	Played	Did not play
Experimental	6	15	14	7
Control	14	7	13	7

Since the presence of *E* during the first session should have been sufficient justification by itself to prevent the arousal of dissonance, no difference was expected between the mild and evere threat control conditions. Regardless of the severity of the threat, *S*s should have felt little dissonance; and the two groups should therefore not have differed in amount of transgression during the second session. The results are consistent with this analysis — the amount of transgression in the two control conditions was virtually identical.

No prediction was made regarding differences between the experimental severe threat condition and the control groups, because the exact strength of the threat was undetermined. If the severe threat had by itself been sufficient to preclude the arousal of any dissonance, the additional justification provided by *E*'s presence would not have made any difference. If, however, the severe threat were not this effective, additional justification could have further reduced the amount of dissonance; and the control groups would how greater transgression than the experimental severe threat group. Since the actual results show no differences between the control groups and the experimental severe threat group, it appears that the severe threat provided enough justification for not playing with the toy so that little or no dissonance was aroused.

Included in the data presented in Table 12.1 are some *S*s who did not play with any toys in the second session. It might be argued that these *S*s are not resisting the temptation to play with the robot, but rather are not interested in playing with the toys. In a sense these *S*s should not be included among those who do not play with the forbidden toy since they do not play with any toy. As may be seen in Table 12.2, removing these *S*s from the analysis does not change the main effect appreciably. The difference between EM and ES conditions is still in the predicted direction and significant ($\chi^2 = 5.51$, $p < .02$). There is a slight tendency for the CM *S*s to transgress more than the CS *S*s. Although this difference is not significant, it suggests that the effect in the experimental conditions may have occurred despite some direct effect of the threat which operated in the direction opposite to the effect of the dissonance manipulation.

TABLE 12.2
Number in each condition who played with robot in second session, with *S*s who played with no toys omitted from data

Group	Mild threat		Severe threat	
	Played	Did not play	Played	Did not play
Experimental	6	12	14	4
Control	14	1	13	7

TABLE 12.3
Mean changes in ratings of toys

Group	Condition	Robot	Others	Total change in direction of dissonance reduction[a]
Experimental	Mild threat	−5.48[b]	+7.72	13.20
	Severe threat	−4.28	+5.90	10.18
Control	Mild threat	−4.00	+5.31	9.31
	Severe threat	−4.84	+5.93	10.77

[a]The sum of the decrease in rating of the robot and the mean increase in rating of the other toys.
[b]All changes are significantly different from no change at $p < .05$. None of the differences between experimental groups approaches significance.

The other major data are presented in Table 12.3 which shows the changes in evaluations of the toys from the beginning to the end of the first experimental session. The toys were rated on a scale ranging from 0 ("very, very bad toy") to 100 ("very, very good toy"). If dissonance were aroused by not playing with the forbidden toy, one possible way of reducing it would have been to devalue the forbidden toy or increase the value of the other toys. This would make the forbidden toy relatively less attractive and would decrease the temptation to play with it. As may be seen, all of the groups change their ratings significantly in the direction of dissonance reduction. This change need not, however, have been due to dissonance reduction. In the first place, the initial ratings of the robot were so high (all above 90) that an increase in its rating was highly unlikely. In addition, almost all Ss played with some of the toys but not the robot. The relative increase in the other toys might therefore have been due to greater familiarity with them, or some other factor associated with having used them.

A more meaningful way of considering these data is to compare the various groups in amount of change. Presumably the greater the dissonance that was aroused, the more change in the direction of dissonance reduction that should have occurred. Therefore, the mild threat experimental group should show more dissonance reduction than the other groups. On both individual measures and the overall change measure, the EM group does show the most change in the direction of dissonance reduction; but none of these differences are significant. Thus, although the results are consistent with the dissonance analysis, they do not provide significant support for it.

This lack of significance is in contrast with the results of the study by Aronson and Carlsmith (1963) in which a forbidden toy was devalued significantly more under mild threat than under severe threat conditions. The experimental situations are not, however, exactly comparable. In the present study the forbidden toy, the robot, was intentionally made much more attractive than any of the other toys in order to maximize the temptation to play with it. It was so much more desirable than the other toys (it was rated an average of more than ten points higher than the closest toy) that devaluing it below the other toys must have been extremely difficult and unrealistic. It seems likely that re-evaluating the toys was not an efficient or practical mode of dissonance reduction in the present experiment and was not employed to any great extent.

DISCUSSION

Although the difference in amount of transgression between the high and low threat experimental groups is clearly consistent with the prediction from dissonance theory, other explanations of this difference are possible. A more severe threat might have called more attention to the forbidden toy or made it seem more attractive, and this would tend to make the severe threat Ss play with the toy more than did the mild threat Ss. Or, E may have been liked more or believed more when he made a mild threat than when he made a severe threat, and his original commands would have been obeyed more in the former condition. Any of these explanations sounds plausible, and there are probably a number of other reasonable possibilities that could explain the difference between the high and low threat experimental conditions.

It should be noted, however, that the control Ss received exactly the same threat instructions as the corresponding experimental Ss, and that all Ss went through exactly the same procedure with one crucial difference. In the experimental conditions, E left the room and gave S a chance to play with the forbidden toy without being observed; in the control conditions, E did not leave the room. Any explanation of the results must therefore account for the fact that only when E leaves the room during the first session do the threats have differential effects on subsequent behavior. The explanations offered above clearly would require differences in both experimental and control conditions and may thus be ruled out; and most other explanations based on surmises about the differential meaning, plausibility or direct effect of the threat instructions would probably also be eliminated.

The results do fit the analysis in terms of cognitive dissonance. When Ss are given a mild threat and they resist temptation, more dissonance is produced than when they resist temptation because of a severe threat. This dissonance may be reduced in a number of ways, all of which would tend to make S refrain from playing with the toy in the future even in the absence of any threat. Since more dissonance is aroused in the low threat condition, more dissonance reduction occurs in that condition; and the low threat Ss should refrain from playing to a greater extent than should the high threat Ss.

When E remains in the room, there is no temptation to play with the forbidden toy since S would surely get caught. Therefore, no dissonance is aroused in either high or low threat control conditions; and the two should not differ. The lack of difference between control groups is clearly consistent with the dissonance analysis and would seem to make alternative explanations somewhat difficult.

The results thus strongly support the predictions based on the theory of cognitive dissonance. They provide a clear demonstration that the theory does apply to behavioral as well as attitudinal changes and that the arousal and reduction of differential amounts of dissonance can have a significant effect even after an interval of just under 6 weeks.

Since the data on changes in ratings of the toy indicated that this was not a major mode of dissonance reduction in the present situation, it might be interesting to speculate on what the primary mode of reduction was. One provocative possibility is that at least in part dissonance was reduced by an acceptance of the idea that it was wrong to play with the forbidden toy. In other words, the subject may have provided himself with moral justification for obeying the restriction. This would tend to make him less likely to play with the toy in the second session, even though another E said it was all right to play with it.

As Festinger and Freedman have pointed out (1964), one implication of this is that inculcating moral values will be most successful if a minimal amount of justification of any kind is offered for the relevant behavior. If the goal is to make a child accept the values of society, he should not be given a great many logical reasons supporting the valued behavior, nor threatened with severe punishment or eternal damnation if he transgresses, nor promised great rewards, eternal or otherwise, for obeying. Rather, he should be given just enough justification to cause him to obey in the presence of the justification; and then his acceptance of the value itself will be maximal. This analysis of the development of moral values is, of course, highly speculative, and the present study offers no evidence directly supporting it. The present result and that reported by Mills (1958) are, however, consistent with the analysis, and it is hoped that it will be tested more directly by additional research.

SUMMARY

The study was conducted to investigate whether or not the arousal of cognitive dissonance can produce long-term behavioral effects. Children were told not to play with a very desirable toy under high or low threat, and were left alone with the toy. Those who did not play with it were given a second opportunity to play with the toy several weeks later, with the original threat removed. The prediction was that those subjects who had resisted temptation under mild threat would be less likely to play with the toy in this second session than would those who had resisted under severe threat. The results supported this prediction.

References

ARONSON, E., AND CARLSMITH, J. M. The effect of the severity of threat on the devaluation of forbidden behavior. *J. abnorm. soc. Psychol.*, 1963, **66,** 584–588.

BENDER, LAURETTA. A visual motor gestalt test and its clinical use. Research Mongr. No. 3, *Amer. Orthopsychiat. Assoc.*, 1938.

BREHM, J. W., AND COHEN, A. R. *Explorations in Cognitive Dissonance.* Wiley: New York, 1962.

COHEN, A. R., GREENBAUM, C. W., AND MANSSON, H. H. Commitment to social deprivation and verbal conditioning. *J. abnorm. soc. Psychol.*, 1963, **67,** 410–421.

FESTINGER, A. *A theory of cognitive dissonance.* Stanford, Calif.: Univer. Press, 1957.

FESTINGER, L. Behavioral support for opinion change. *Pub. Opin. Quart.*, 1964, **28,** 404–417.

FESTINGER, L., AND CARLSMITH, J. Cognitive consequences of forced compliance. *J. abnorm. soc. Psychol.*, 1959, **58,** 203–210.

FESTINGER, L., AND FREEDMAN, J. L. Dissonance reduction and moral values. In *Personality Change* (Worchel and Byrne, ed.). New York: Wiley, 1964.

FREEDMAN, J. L. Attitudinal effects of inadequate justification. *J. Pers.*, 1963, **31,** 371–385.

MILLS, J. Changes in moral attitudes following temptation. *J. Pers.*, 1958, **26,** 517–531.

RABBIE, J. M., BREHM, J. W., AND COHEN, A. R. Verbalization and reactions to cognitive dissonance. *J. Pers.*, 1959, **27,** 407–417.

TURNER, ELIZABETH A., AND WRIGHT, J. C. The effects of severity of threat and perceived availability on the attractiveness of objects. *J. Pers. and soc. Psychol.*, 1965, **2,** 128–132.

WALSTER, ELAINE. The temporal sequence of post-decision processes. In *Conflict, decision and dissonance* (L. Festinger, ed.). Stanford, Calif.: Univer. Press, 1964. pp. 112–128.

WIECK, K. E. Reduction of cognitive dissonance through task enhancement and effort expenditure. *J. abnorm. soc. Psychol.*, 1964, **68,** 533–539.

13

Compliance Without Pressure:
The Foot-in-the-Door Technique

Jonathan L. Freedman and Scott C. Fraser

Two experiments were conducted to test the proposition that once someone has agreed to a small request he is more likely to comply with a larger request. The first study demonstrated this effect when the same person made both requests. The second study extended this to the situation in which different people made the two requests. Several experimental groups were run in an effort to explain these results, and possible explanations are discussed.

How can a person be induced to do something he would rather not do? This question is relevant to practically every phase of social life, from stopping at a traffic light to stopping smoking, from buying Brand X to buying savings bonds, from supporting the March of Dimes to supporting the Civil Rights Act.

One common way of attacking the problem is to exert as much pressure as possible on the reluctant individual in an effort to force him to comply. This technique has been the focus of a considerable amount of experimental research. Work on attitude change, conformity, imitation, and obedience has all tended to stress the importance of the degree of external pressure. The prestige of the communicator (Kelman and Hovland, 1953), degree of dis-

Reprinted with permission from the authors and *The Journal of Personality and Social Psychology,* Vol. 4, No. 2, 1966. Copyright 1966 by the American Psychological Association.

The authors are grateful to Evelyn Bless for assisting in the running of the second experiment reported here. These studies were supported in part by Grant GS-196 from the National Science Foundation. The first study was conducted while the junior author was supported by an NSF undergraduate summer fellowship.

crepancy of the communication (Hovland and Pritzker, 1957), size of the group disagreeing with the subject (Asch, 1951), perceived power of the model (Bandura, Ross, and Ross, 1963), etc., are the kinds of variables that have been studied. This impressive body of work, added to the research on rewards and punishments in learning, has produced convincing evidence that greater external pressure generally leads to greater compliance with the wishes of the experimenter. The one exception appears to be situations involving the arousal of cognitive dissonance in which, once discrepant behavior has been elicited from the subject, the greater the pressure that was used to elicit the behavior, the less subsequent change occurs (Festinger and Carlsmith, 1959). But even in this situation one critical element is the amount of external pressure exerted.

Clearly, then, under most circumstances the more pressure that can be applied, the more likely it is that the individual will comply. There are, however, many times when for ethical, moral, or practical reasons it is difficult to apply much pressure when the goal is to produce compliance with a minimum of apparent pressure, as in the forced-compliance studies involving dissonance arousal. And even when a great deal of pressure is possible, it is still important to maximize the compliance it produces. Thus, factors other than external pressure are often quite critical in determining degree of compliance. What are these factors?

Although rigorous research on the problem is rather sparse, the fields of advertising, propaganda, politics, etc., are by no means devoid of techniques designed to produce compliance in the absence of external pressure (or to maximize the effectiveness of the pressure that is used, which is really the same problem). One assumption about compliance that has often been made either explicitly or implicitly is that once a person has been induced to comply with a small request he is more likely to comply with a larger demand. This is the principle that is commonly referred to as the foot-in-the-door or gradation technique and is reflected in the saying that if you "give them an inch, they'll take a mile." It was, for example, supposed to be one of the basic techniques upon which the Korean brainwashing tactics were based (Schein, Schneier, and Barker, 1961), and, in a somewhat different sense, one basis for Nazi propaganda during 1940 (Bruner, 1941). It also appears to be implicit in many advertising campaigns which attempt to induce the consumer to do anything relating to the product involved, even sending back a card saying he does not want the product.

The most relevant piece of experimental evidence comes from a study of conformity done by Deutsch and Gerard (1955). Some subjects were faced with incorrect group judgments first in a series in which the stimuli were not present during the actual judging and then in a series in which they were present, while the order of the memory and visual series was reversed for other subjects. For both groups the memory series produced more conformity, and when the memory series came first there was more total conformity to the group judgments. It seems likely that this order effect occurred because, as the authors suggest, once conformity is elicited at all it is more likely to occur in the future. Although this kind of conformity is probably somewhat different from compliance as described above, this finding certainly lends some support to the foot-in-the-door idea. The present research attempted to provide a rigorous, more direct test of this notion as it applies to compliance and to provide data relevant to several alternative ways of explaining the effect.

EXPERIMENT I

The basic paradigm was to ask some subjects (Performance condition) to comply first with a small request and then three days later with a larger, related request. Other subjects (One-Contact condition) were asked to comply only with the large request. The hypothesis was that more subjects in the Performance condition than in the One-Contact condition would comply with the larger request.

Two additional conditions were included in an attempt to specify the essential difference between these two major conditions. The Performance subjects were asked to perform a small favor, and, if they agreed, they did it. The question arises whether the act of agreeing itself is critical or whether actually carrying it out was necessary. To assess this a third group of subjects (Agree-Only) was asked the first request, but, even if they agreed, they did not carry it out. Thus, they were identical to the Performance group except that they were not given the opportunity of performing the request.

Another difference between the two main conditions was that at the time of the larger request the subjects in the Performance condition were more familiar with the experimenter than were the other subjects. The Performance subjects had been contacted twice, heard his voice more, discovered that the questions were not dangerous, and so on. It is possible that this increased familiarity would serve to decrease the fear and suspicion of a strange voice on the phone and might accordingly increase the likelihood of the subjects agreeing to the larger request. To control for this a fourth condition was run (Familiarization) which attempted to give the subjects as much familiarity with the experimenter as in the Performance and Agree-Only conditions with the only difference being that no request was made.

The major prediction was that more subjects in the Performance condition would agree to the large request than in any of the other conditions, and that the One-Contact condition would produce the least compliance. Since the importance of agreement and familiarity was essentially unknown, the expectation was that the Agree-Only and Familiarization conditions would produce intermediate amounts of compliance.

Method

The prediction stated above was tested in a field experiment in which housewives were asked to allow a survey team of five or six men to come into their homes for two hours to classify the household products they used. This large request was made under four different conditions: after an initial contact in which the subject had been asked to answer a few questions about the kinds of soaps she used, and the questions were actually asked (Performance condition); after an identical contact in which the questions were not actually asked (Agree-Only condition); after an initial contact in which no request was made (Familiarization condition); or after no initial contact (One-Contact condition). The dependent measure was simply whether or not the subject agreed to the large request.

Procedure. The subjects were 156 Palo Alto, California, housewives, 36 in each condition, who were selected at random from the telephone directory. An additional 12 subjects distributed about equally among the three two-contact conditions could not be reached for the second contact and are not included in the data analysis. Subjects were assigned randomly to the various conditions, except that the Familiarization condition was added to the design after the other three conditions had been completed. All contacts were by telephone by the same experimenter who identified himself as the same person each time. Calls were made only in the morning. For the three groups that were contacted twice, the first call was made on either Monday or Tuesday and the second always three days later. All large requests were made on either Thursday or Friday.

At the first contact, the experimenter introduced himself by name and said that he was from the California Consumers' Group. In the Performance condition he then proceeded:

> We are calling you this morning to ask if you would answer a number of questions about what household products you use so that we could have this information for our public service publication, "The Guide." Would you be willing to give us this information for our survey?

If the subject agreed, she was asked a series of eight innocuous questions dealing with household soaps (e.g., "What brand of soap do you use in your kitchen sink?") She was then thanked for her cooperation, and the contact terminated.

Another condition (Agree-Only) was run to assess the importance of actually carrying out the request as opposed to merely agreeing to it. The only difference between this and the Performance condition was that, if the subject agreed to answer the questions, the experimenter thanked her, but said that he was just lining up respondents for the survey and would contact her if needed.

A third condition was included to check on the importance of the subject's greater familiarity with the experimenter in the two-contact conditions. In this condition the experimenter introduced himself, described the organization he worked for and the survey it was conducting, listed the questions he was asking and then said that he was calling merely to acquaint the subject with the existence of his organization. In other words, these subjects were contacted, spent as much time on the phone with the experimenter as the Performance subjects did, heard all the questions, but neither agreed to answer them nor answered them.

In all of these two-contact conditions some subjects did not agree to the requests or even hung up before the requests were made. Every subject who answered the phone was included in the analysis of the results and was contacted for the second request regardless of her extent of cooperativeness during the first contact. In other words, no subject who could be contacted the appropriate number of times was discarded from any of the four conditions.

The large request was essentially identical for all subjects. The experimenter called, identified himself, and said either that his group was expanding its survey (in the case of the two-contact conditions) or that it was conducting a survey (in the One-Contact condition). In all four conditions he then continued:

> The survey will involve five or six men from our staff coming into your home some morning for about two hours to enumerate and classify all the household products that you have. They will have to have full freedom in your house to go through the cupboards and storage places. Then all this information will be used in the writing of the reports for our public service publication, "The Guide."

If the subject agreed to the request, she was thanked and told that at the present time the experimenter was merely collecting names of people who were willing to take part and that she would be contacted if it were decided to use her in the survey. If she did not agree, she was thanked for her time. This terminated the experiment.

Results

Apparently even the small request was not considered trivial by some of the subjects. Only about two-thirds of the subjects in the Performance and Agree-Only conditions agreed to answer the questions about household soaps. It might be noted that none of those who refused the first request later

TABLE 13.1
Percentage of subjects complying
with large request in Experiment I

Condition	%
Performance	52.8
Agree-Only	33.3
Familiarization	27.8*
One-Contact	22.2**

Note: $N = 36$ for each group. Significance
levels represent differences from the Performance condition.
*$p < .07$.
**$p < .02$.

ag eed to the large request, although as stated previously all subjects who
were contacted for the small request are included in the data for those groups.

Our major prediction was that subjects who had agreed to and carried out
a small request (Performance condition) would subsequently be more likely
to comply with a larger request than would subjects who were asked only
the larger request (One-Contact condition). As may be seen in Table 13.1,
the results support the prediction. Over 50 percent of the subjects in the
Performance condition agreed to the larger request, while less than 25 percent of the One-Contact condition agreed to it. Thus it appears that obtaining compliance with a small request does tend to increase subsequent
compliance. The question is what aspect of the initial contact produces this
effect.

One possibility is that the effect was produced merely by increased familiarity with the experimenter. The Familiarization control was included to
assess the effect on compliance of two contacts with the same person. The
group had as much contact with the experimenter as the Performance group,
but no request was made during the first contact. As the table indicates, the
Familiarization group did not differ appreciably in amount of compliance
from the One-Contact group, but was different from the Performance group
($\chi^2 = 3.70$, $p < .07$). Thus, although increased familiarity may well lead to
increased compliance, in the present situation the differences in amount of
familiarity apparently were not great enough to produce any such increase;
the effect that was obtained seems not to be due to this factor.

Another possibility is that the critical factor producing increased compliance is simply agreeing to the small request (i.e., carrying it out may not be
necessary). The Agree-Only condition was identical to the Performance
condition except that in the former the subjects were not asked the questions.
The amount of compliance in this Agree-Only condition fell between the
Performance and One-Contact conditions and was not significantly different from either of them. This leaves the effect of merely agreeing somewhat

ambiguous, but it suggests that the agreement alone may produce part of the effect.

Unfortunately, it must be admitted that neither of these control conditions is an entirely adequate test of the possibility it was designed to assess. Both conditions are in some way quite peculiar and may have made a very different and extraneous impression on the subject than did the Performance condition. In one case, a housewife is asked to answer some questions and then is not asked them; in the other, some man calls to tell her about some organization she has never heard of. Now, by themselves neither of these events might produce very much suspicion. But, several days later, the same man calls and asks a very large favor. At this point it is not at all unlikely that many subjects think they are being manipulated, or in any case that something strange is going on. Any such eaction on the part of the subjects would naturally tend to reduce the amount of compliance in these conditions.

Thus, although this first study demonstrates that an initial contact in which a request is made and carried out increases compliance with a second request, the question of why and how the initial request produces this effect remains unanswered. In an attempt to begin answering this question and to extend the results of the first study, a second experiment was conducted.

There seemed to be several quite plausible ways in which the increase in compliance might have been produced. The first was simply some kind of commitment to or involvement with the particular person making the request. This might work, for example, as follows: The subject has agreed to the first request and perceives that the experimenter therefore expects him also to agree to the second request. The subject thus feels obligated and does not want to disappoint the experimenter; he also feels that he needs a good reason for saying "no"—a better reason than he would need if he had never said "yes." This is just one line of causality—the particular process by which involvement with the experimenter operates might be quite different, but the basic idea would be similar. The commitment is to the particular person. This implies that the increase in compliance due to the first contact should occur primarily when both requests are made by the same person.

Another explanation in terms of involvement centers around the particular issue with which the requests are concerned. Once the subject has taken some action in connection with an area of concern, be it surveys, political activity, or highway safety, there is probably a tendency to become somewhat more concerned with the area. The subject begins thinking about it, considering its importance and relevance to him, and so on. This tends to make him more likely to agree to take further action in the same area when he is later asked to. To the extent that this is the critical factor the initial contact should increase compliance only when both requests are related to the same issue or area of concern.

Another way of looking at the situation is that the subject needs a reason to say "no." In our society it is somewhat difficult to refuse a reasonable request, particularly when it is made by an organization that is not trying to make money. In order to refuse, many people feel that they need a reason—simply not wanting to do it is often not in itself sufficient. The person can say to the requester or simply to himself that he does not believe in giving to charities or tipping or working for political parties or answering questions or posting signs, or whatever he is asked to do. Once he has performed a particular task, however, this excuse is no longer valid for not agreeing to perform a similar task. Even if the first thing he did was trivial compared to the present request, he cannot say he never does this sort of thing, and thus one good eason for refusing is removed. This line of reasoning suggests that the similarity of the first and second requests in terms of the type of action required is an important factor. The more similar they are, the more the "matter of principle" argument is eliminated by agreeing to the first request, and the greater should be the increase in compliance.

There are probably many other mechanisms by which the initial request might produce an increase in compliance. The second experiment was designed in part to test the notions described above, but its major purpose was to demonstrate the effect unequivocally. To this latter end it eliminated one of the important problems with the first study which was that when the experimenter made the second request he was not blind as to which condition the subjects were in. In this study the second request was always made by someone other than the person who made the first request, and the second experimenter was blind as to what condition the subject was in. This eliminates the possibility that the experimenter exerted systematically different amounts of pressure in different experimental conditions. If the effect is due primarily to greater familiarity or involvement with the particular person making the first request.

EXPERIMENT II

The basic paradigm was quite similar to that of the first study. Experimental subjects were asked to comply with a small request and were later asked a considerably larger request, while controls were asked only the larger request. The first request varied along two dimensions. Subjects were asked either to put up a small sign or to sign a petition, and the issue was either safe driving or keeping California beautiful. Thus, there were four first request: a small sign for safe driving or for beauty, and a petition for the two issues. The second request for all subjects was to install in their front lawn a very large sign which said "Drive Carefully." The four experimental conditions may be defined in terms of the similarity of the small and large requests along the dimensions of issue and task. The two requests were similar in both issue and task for the small-sign, safe-driving group, similar only in issue for the safe-driving-petition group, similar only in task for the small "Keep California Beautiful" sign group, and similar in neither issue nor task for the "Keep California Beautiful" petition group.

The major expectation was that the three groups for which either the task or the issue were similar would show more compliance than the controls, and it was also felt that when both were similar there would probably be the most compliance. The fourth condition (Different Issue-Different Task) was included primarily to assess the effect simply of the initial contact which, although it was not identical to the second one on either issue or task, was in many ways quite similar (e.g., a young student asking for co-operation on a noncontroversial issue). There were no clear expectations as to how this condition would compare to the controls.

Method

The subjects were 114 women and 13 men living in Palo Alto, California. Of these, 9 women and 6 men could not be contacted for the second request and are not included in the data analysis. The remaining 112 subjects were divided about equally among the five conditions (see Table 13.2). All subjects were contacted between 1:30 and 4:30 on weekday afternoons.

Two experimenters, one male and one female, were employed, and a different one always made the second contact. Unlike the first study, the experimenters actually went to the homes of the subjects and interviewed them on a face-to-face basis. An effort was made to select subjects from blocks and neighborhoods that were as homogeneous as possible. On each block every third or fourth house was approached, and all subjects on that block were in one experimental condition. This was necessary because of the likelihood that neighbors would talk to each other about the contact. In addition, for every four subjects contacted, a fifth house was chosen as a control but was, of course, not contacted. Throughout this phase of the experiment, and in fact throughout the whole experiment, the two experimenters did not communicate to each other what conditions had been run on a given block nor what condition a particular house was in.

The small-sign, safe-driving group was told that the experimenter was from the Community Committee for Traffic Safety, that he was visiting a number of homes in an attempt to make the citizens more aware of the need to drive carefully all the time, and that he would like the subject to take a small sign and put it in a window or in the car so that it would serve as a reminder of the need to drive carefully. The sign was three inches square, said "Be a safe driver," was on thin paper without a gummed backing, and in general looked rather amateurish and unattractive. If the subject agreed, he was given the sign and thanked; if he disagreed, he was simply thanked for his time.

The three other experimental conditions were quite similar with appropriate changes. The other organization was identified as the Keep California Beautiful Committee and its sign said, appropriately enough, "Keep California Beautiful." Both signs were simply black block letters on a white background. The two petition groups were asked to sign a petition which was being sent to California's United States Senators. The petition advocated support for any legislation which would promote either safer driving or keeping California beautiful. The subject was shown a petition, typed on heavy bond paper, with at least twenty signatures already affixed. If she agreed, she signed and was thanked. If she did not agree, she was merely thanked.

The second contact was made about 2 weeks after the initial one. Each experimenter was armed with a list of houses which had been compiled by the other experimenter. This list contained all four experimental conditions and the controls, and, of course, there was no way for the second experimenter to know which condition the subject had been in. At this second contact, all subjects were asked the same thing: Would they put a large sign concerning safe driving in their front yard? The experimenter identified himself as being from the Citizens for Safe Driving, a different group from the original safe-driving group (although it is likely that most subjects who had been in the safe-driving conditions did not notice the difference). The subject was shown a picture of a very large sign reading "Drive Carefully" placed in front of an attractive house. The picture was taken so that the sign obscured much of the front of the house and completely concealed the doorway. It was rather poorly lettered. The subject was told that: "Our men will come out and install it and later come and remove it. It makes just a small hole in your lawn, but if this is unacceptable to you we have a special mount which will make no hole." She was asked to put the sign up for a week or a week and a half. If the subject agreed, she was told that more names than necessary were being gathered and if her home were to be used she would be contacted in a few weeks. The experimenter recorded the subject's response and this ended the experiment.

Results

First, it should be noted that there were no large differences among the experimental conditions in the percentages of subjects agreeing to the first

TABLE 13.2
Percentage of subjects complying with large request
in Experiment II

Issue[a]	Task[a]			
	Similar	N	Different	N
Similar	76.0**	25	47.8*	23
Different	47.6*	21	47.4*	19
One-Contact 16.7 (N = 24)				

Note: Significance levels represent differences from the One-
Contact condition.
[a]Denotes relationship between first and second requests.
*$p < .08$.
**$p < .01$.

request. Although somewhat more subjects agreed to post the "Keep California Beautiful" sign and somewhat fewer to sign the beauty petition, none
of these differences approach significance.

The important figures are the number of subjects in each group who agreed
to the large request. These are presented in Table 13.2. The figures for the
four experimental groups include all subjects who were approached the
first time, regardless of whether or not they agreed to the small request.
As noted above, a few subjects were lost because they could not be reached
for the second request, and, of course these are not included in the table.

It is immediately apparent that the first request tended to increase the
degree of compliance with the second request. Whereas fewer than 20 percent of the controls agreed to put the large sign on their lawn, over 55 percent of the experimental subjects agreed, with over 45 percent being the
lowest degree of compliance for any experimental condition. As expected,
those conditions in which the two requests were similar in terms of either
issue or task produced significantly more compliance than did the controls
(χ^2's range from 3.67, $p < .07$ to 15.01, $p < .001$). A somewhat unexpected
result is that the fourth condition, in which the first request had relatively
little in common with the second request, also produced more compliance
than the controls ($\chi^2 = 3.40$, $p < .08$). In other words, regardless of whether
or not the two requests are similar in either issue or task, simply having the
first request tends to increase the likelihood that the subject will comply
with a subsequent, larger request. And this holds even when the two requests are made by different people several weeks apart.

A second point of interest is a comparison among the four experimental
conditions. As expected, the Same Issue-Same Task condition produced
more compliance than any of the other two-contact conditions, but the
difference is not significant (χ^2's range from 2.7 to 2.9). If only those subjects who agreed to the first request are considered, the same pattern holds.

DISCUSSION

To summarize the results, the first study indicated that carrying out a small request increased the likelihood that the subject would agree to a similar larger request made by the same person. The second study showed that this effect was quite strong even when a different person made the larger request, and the two requests were quite dissimilar. How may these results be explained?

Two possibilities were outlined previously. The matter-of-principle idea which centered on the particular type of action was not supported by the data, since the similarity of the tasks did not make an appreciable difference in degree of compliance. The notion of involvement, as described previously, also had difficulty accounting for some of the findings. The basic idea was that once someone has agreed to any action, no matter how small, he tends to feel more involved than he did before. This involvement may center around the particular person making the first request or the particular issue. This is quite consistent with the results of the first study (with the exception of the two control groups which as discussed previously were rather ambiguous) and with the Similar-Issue groups in the second experiment. This idea of involvement does not, however, explain the increase in compliance found in the two groups in which the first and second request did not deal with the same issue.

It is possible that in addition to or instead of this process a more general and diffuse mechanism underlies the increase in compliance. What may occur is a change in the person's feelings about getting involved or about taking action. Once he has agreed to a request, his attitude may change. He may become, in his own eyes, the kind of person who does this sort of thing, who agrees to requests made by strangers, who takes action on things he believes in, who cooperates with good causes. The change in attitude could be toward any aspect of the situation or toward the whole business of saying "yes." The basic idea is that the change in attitude need not be toward any particular issue or person or activity, but may be toward activity or compliance in general. This would imply that an increase in compliance would not depend upon the two contacts being made by the same person, or concerning the same issue or involving the same kind of action. The similarity could be much more general, such as both concerning good causes, or requiring a similar kind of action, or being made by pleasant, attractive individuals.

It is not being suggested that this is the only mechanism operating here. The idea of involvement continues to be extremely plausible, and there are probably a number of other possibilities. Unfortunately, the present studies offer no additional data with which to support or refute any of the possible explanations of the effect. These explanations thus remain simply descriptions of mechanisms which might produce an increase in compliance after agreement with a first request. Hopefully, additional research will test these ideas more fully and perhaps also specify other manipulations which produce an increase in compliance without an increase in external pressure.

It should be pointed out that the present studies employed what is perhaps a very special type of situation. In all cases the requests were made by presumably nonprofit service organizations. The issues in the second study were deliberately noncontroversial, and it may be assumed that virtually all subjects initially sympathized with the objectives of safe driving and a beautiful California. This is in strong contrast to campaigns which are desinged to sell a particular product, political candidate, or dogma. Whether the technique employed in this study would be successful in these other situations remains to be shown.

References

ASCH, S. E. Effects of group pressure upon the modification and distortion of judgments. In H. Guetzkow (ed.), *Groups, leadership and men; research in human relations*. Pittsburgh: Carnegie Press, 1951. Pp. 177–190.

BANDURA, A., ROSS, D., AND ROSS, S. A. A comparative test of the status envy, social power, and secondary reinforcement theories of identificatory learning. *Journal of Abnormal and Social Psychology,* 1963, **67,** 527–534.

BRUNER, J. The dimensions of propaganda: German short-wave broadcasts to America. *Journal of Abnormal and Social Psychology,* 1941, **36,** 311–337.

DEUTSCH, M., AND GERARD, H. B. A study of normative and informational social influences upon individual judgment. *Journal of Abnormal and Social Psychology,* 1955, **51,** 629–636.

FESTINGER, L., AND CARLSMITH, J. Cognitive consequences of forced compliance. *Journal of Abnormal and Social Psychology,* 1959, **58,** 203–210.

HOVLAND, C. I., AND PRITZKER, H. A. Extent of opinion change as a function of amount of change advocated. *Journal of Abnormal and Social Psychology,* 1957, **54,** 257–261.

KELMAN, H. C., AND HOVLAND, C. I. "Reinstatement" of the communicator in delayed measurement of opinion change. *Journal of Abnormal and Social Psychology,* 1953, **48,** 327–335.

SCHEIN, E. H., SCHNEIER, I., AND BARKER, C. H. *Coercive pressure.* New York: Norton, 1961.

14

Dishonest Behavior as a Function of Differential Levels of Induced Self-Esteem

Elliot Aronson and David R. Mettee

After taking a personality test, Ss were given false feedback aimed at temporarily inducing either an increase in self-esteem, a decrease in self-esteem, or no change in their self-esteem. They were then allowed to participate in a game of cards, in the course of which they were provided with opportunities to cheat under circumstances which made it appear impossible to be detected. Significantly more people cheated in the low self-esteem condition than in the high self-esteem condition. A chi-square evaluating cheater frequency among the high self-esteem, the no information (no change in self-esteem), and the low self-esteem conditions was significant at the .05 level. The results are discussed in terms of cognitive consistency theory.

Recent theorizing and experimentation have suggested that a person's expectancies may be an important determinant of his behavior. Working within the framework of the theory of cognitive dissonance, Aronson and Carlsmith (1962) conducted an experiment in which subjects were led to develop an expectancy of poor performance on a "social sensitivity" test. The subjects then proceeded to perform beautifully. Aronson and Carlsmith found that these subjects subsequently changed their superior performance to an inferior one when retested over the same material. Similarly, Wilson (1965) found that subjects were significantly more attracted to a negative evaluator

Reprinted with permission from the authors and *The Journal of Personality and Social Psychology,* Vol. 9, No. 2, 1968. Copyright 1968 by the American Psychological Association.

This experiment was supported by a National Science Foundation Graduate Fellowship (NSF-26–1140-3971) to David R. Mettee and by grants from the National Science Foundation (NSF GS 750) and the National Institute of Mental Health (MH 12357-01) to Elliot Aronson. Authors are listed in alphabetical order.

than to a positive evaluator if the negative evaluations were in accord with a strong performance expectancy which had led the subjects to withdraw from a competitive event. Consistency theory thus has received some support in specific expectancies and performance directly related to these expectancies.

But what about more pervasive expectancies such as those about the self? Bramel (1962) showed some evidence for the impact of self-esteem on subsequent behavior. In his study he temporarily raised or lowered the subjects' self-esteem by providing them with positive or negative information about their personalities. He then allowed them to discover irrefutable negative information about themselves. The individuals who held low self-concepts were more willing to accept this information; that is, they were not prone as people who had been induced toward high self-esteem to project this specific negative attribute onto others. These results are consistent with the work of Rogers (1951), who argued that negative or maladaptive responses occur as the result of being consistent with a negative self-concept, and that such responses can be altered only by first changing the self-concept in a direction consistent with adaptive responses.

The prediction being tested in the present experiment is in accord with the experiments cited above. In addition, it carries our interest in the self-concept one step further in the direction Rogers has taken—toward greater generalization. What Aronson and Carlsmith showed is that people try to behave in a highly specific manner which will coincide with a highly specific self-expectancy; that is, people who believe that they are poor in a "social sensitivity" test will take action aimed at performing poorly on that test. But does this generalize? If we feel low and worthless on one or two dimensions do we behave generally in low and worthless ways—even if the behavior is not directly and specifically related to the low aspects of the self-concept? For example, if a person is jilted by his girlfriend (and thus feels unloved), is he more apt to go out and rob a bank, kick a dog, or wear mismatched pajamas?

In the present experimental situation we are predicting just that. Concretely, individuals who are provided with self-relevant information which temporarily causes them to lower their self-esteem (but does *not* specifically make them feel immoral or dishonest) are more apt to cheat than those who are made to raise their self-esteem—or those who are given no self-relevant information at all (control condition). Similarly, people who are induced to raise their self-esteem will be less likely to cheat than the controls. This hypothesis is based upon the assumption that high self-esteem acts as a barrier against dishonest behavior because such behavior is inconsistent. In short, if a person is tempted to cheat, it will be easier for him to yield to this temptation if his self-esteem is low than if it is high. Cheating is not inconsistent with generally low self-esteem; it *is* inconsistent with generally high self-esteem.

METHOD

General Procedure

The subjects were led to believe that they were participating in a study concerned with the correlation between personality test scores and extrasensory perception (ESP). They were told that their personalities would be evaluated with the self-esteem scales of the California Personality Inventory (CPI) and that their ESP ability would be ascertained with the aid of a modified game of blackjack. Before participating in the blackjack game, subjects took the personality test and received false feedback (either positive, negative, or neutral) about their personalities. During the blackjack game subjects were faced with the dilemma of either cheating and winning or not cheating and losing in a situation in which they were led to believe (erroneously) that cheating was impossible to detect. The opportunity to cheat occurred when the subjects were "accidentally" dealt two cards at once instead of one. The rightful card put the subject over 21 and ensured defeat, whereas the mistakenly dealt extra card, if kept, provided the subject with a point total that virtually assured victory. The card which the subject kept constituted the dependent variable.

Subjects

The subjects were 45 females taken from introductory psychology classes at the University of Texas, who were randomly assigned to one of three self-esteem conditions: high, low, and neutral. In actuality, 50 subjects were run; the results of five subjects were discarded because of suspicion. Three of these were in the low self-esteem condition; two were in the high self-esteem condition. The criteria for elimination were determined a priori and were followed rigidly throughout the experiment. It was made explicit that the experimenter had no preconceptions as to how personality traits might be related to ESP ability, but simply wanted to determine whether or not, for example, people who are easily angered have more ESP than calm people.

Personality Test

All subjects came to the first session together and were given the self-esteem scales of the CPI. The CPI was administered by a person who introduced himself as a member of the University Counseling Center staff. Subjects were told at this session that the experiment was concerned with

ESP and personality characteristics. They were informed that this session was to determine the personality traits of the subjects, with ESP ability to be measured in the second session.

A shortened version of the CPI was used to evaluate the personalities of the subjects. This version contained only the six scales related to self-esteem and, for our purposes, constituted a measure of the subjects' chronic self-esteem. However, the *primary* experimental purpose of this test was merely to provide the opportunity and rationale for situationally manipulating the subjects' self-esteem via preprogrammed feedback regarding subjects' personality test results.

In order to separate the experimenter as much as possible from the personality evaluation aspects of the experiment, subjects were told by the experimenter that Miss Jacobs,[1] a member of the University of Texas Counseling Center staff, had kindly consented to administer the personality tests. It was emphasized that she would score the personality inventories and that the experimenter's access to their scores would not be on a name basis but via a complicating coding process. It was indicated that, as a matter of convenience, subjects would be given feedback regarding their personality tests when they came for the second session of the experiment. Following this, the CPI's were distributed, subjects completed them, and before leaving were assigned a time to return for the second session with three subjects assigned to each specific time slot.

Personality Score

In the second session subjects were tested in groups of three. Upon arrival for the second session, subjects were greeted by Miss Jacobs and told to be seated in an outer office which provided access to three adjoining offices. After all three subjects had arrived, Miss Jacobs handed each subject a manila envelope bearing appropriate Counseling Center insignia and assigned each subject to a different office where she was to go to read the results of her personality test. In addition, Miss Jacobs told the subjects that she had been given a sheet of instructions to deliver to them. The sheet of instructions was handed to the subjects along with the manila envelope.

The personality test results consisted of three standard feedbacks unrelated to subjects' performance on the CPI. Each of the three subjects present at any one specific time was randomly assigned feedback of either high self-esteem (HSE = positive), no self-esteem (NSE = neutral), or low self-esteem (LSE = negative) in content.

---

[1]The authors would like to express their appreciation to Sylvia Jacobs for her assistance in running the study.

The HSE and LSE personality reports were parallel in content except, of course, for the nature of the evaluation. For example, a portion of the HSE report stated:

> The subject's profile indicates she has a stable personality and is not given to pronounced mood fluctuations of excitement or depression. Her stableness does not seem to reflect compulsive tendencies, but rather an ability to remain calm and level-headed in almost any circumstance. Her profile does suggest she might be rather impulsive concerning small details and unimportant decisions. This impulsive tendency is probably reflected in a lack of concern with material things. In addition, it appears that material things are important to the subject only insofar as they enable her to express her generosity, good nature, and zest for living. . . . [she] is intellectually very mature for her age.

The corresponding portion of the LSE report stated:

> The subject's profile indicates that she has a rather unstable personality and is given to pronounced mood fluctuations of excitement or depression. Her instability seems to reflect compulsive tendencies and relative inability to remain calm and level-headed in circumstances which involve tension and pressure. Her profile does suggest she might be rather meticulous and careful concerning small details and when making unimportant decisions. In addition, it appears that material things are very important to the subject as an end in themselves. She appears to be a very selfish person who clings to material things as a source of personal gratification and as an emotional crutch.

In the NSE condition the subject was told that her report had not yet been evaluated due to a heavy backlog of work at the Counseling Center. Instead, she was presented with a sample profile which was described as a typical or average CPI profile such as one might find in a psychological textbook. The comments in this NSE report paralleled those of the HSE and LSE reports (e.g., ". . . fairly stable personality . . . occasionally experiences mood fluctuations . . ."). The contents of the rest of the reports was designed to be global in nature and contained comments concerning the person's ability to make friends, general impact of personality, and depth of thought. Since the dependent variable involved honesty, special care was taken to refrain from mentioning anything directly involving honesty. Similarly, nothing whatever was mentioned, either explicitly or implicitly about the person's moral behavior or "goodness" of conduct.

Warm-up Instructions

After reading their personality test results, subjects turned to their page of instructions. The instructions stated:

> The purpose of this experiment is to correlate extrasensory perception ability with personality characteristics. In order to get a true measure of a person's

ESP ability, it is necessary that one's mind be primed for thinking. In order to accomplish this, I am having you engage in a period of cerebral warm-up. It's not important what you think about—anything will do—but the crucial point is that you are to use your mind, warm it up by thinking. You need not concentrate intensely, just keep your mind active and filled with thought. A few minutes of this will suffice to prepare you for the ESP experiment.

The purpose of this "warm-up" period was to provide an opportunity for the impact of our manipulations to sink in. Since the subjects had just received an evaluation of their personalities we were quite confident that they would be thinking about this material.

Following the warm-up period, the subjects were sent, one at a time, at intervals of approximately 30 seconds, from the second floor of the psychology building to a room on the fourth floor. Here they were met by the experimenter who was unaware of which subject had received which type of personality feedback. The subjects were placed in one of three cubicles which isolated them from each other. Thus it was impossible for subjects to converse with one another between the time they received their personality results and the time the dependent measure was collected.

Apparatus

The apparatus consisted of four booths or cubicles; the front panels of three of the cubicles bounded an area 1 foot square. Access to this area was available via the fourth cubicle which had no front panel. The experimenter, when sitting in the fourth cubicle, was thus able to receive and dispense playing cards to the subjects in the other three cubicles via slots in their front panels. Subjects in their cubicles had no means of communicating with their fellow subjects nor could they see the experimenter due to plywood panels on both sides and at the top of their booths.

Inside each booth there were two slots and two toggle switches. One switch was designated to be turned on to indicate a "no" answer and the other to indicate a "yes" answer. One of the slots was horizontal with the base of the booth, and was situated in the middle of the front panel one-half inch above the cubicle base. The other slot was vertical and was the slot through which subjects returned cards to the experimenter.

The experimenter's cubicle contained three inclined sheet-metal slides leading down to the horizontal slots of the subjects' booths, three vertical slots from each subject's booth which were shielded so that subjects could not see into the experimenter's compartment, three scoreboards (one for each subject), six small light bulbs, each connected to one of the subjects' "yes" and "no" switches. The experimenter's booth also contained a small electric motor. The motor was functionless except for sound effects, and was activated periodically during the experimental session.

Experimental Materials

The experimenter had two decks of cards. One deck was used for the general game of cards to be played; the other deck was divided into three stacks of cards (one stack for each subject) with a prearranged sequence. These were the crucial hands which a subject would be dealt on those occasions when she would be given the opportunity to cheat. The prearranged stacks consisted of four hands of blackjack with four cards in each hand. The first two cards in all hands totaled approximately 11–13 points with the third card sending the point total over 21. The fourth card, if substituted for the third, always brought the point total to between 19 and 21 points.

Each subject's cubicle contained, in addition to the two toggle switches, a 15-watt light bulb and 10 fifty-cent pieces (or $5). The half-dollars were used as "chips" and potential reward in the experimental task.

Experimental Instructions

After the subjects were seated, the experimenter recited the instructions. He described the results of some previous experiments concerning ESP. Rhine's conclusion that some persons do indeed possess ESP was presented; however, *no* indication was given that certain types of persons possess ESP while others do not. In order to make the cover story appear more credible, subjects were asked to read a recent newspaper article taped to a side panel of their cubicles, which told of how a young girl had been winning an astonishing number of raffle contests which, according to a research institute at Duke University, was perhaps due to her ESP powers. This article indicated that having ESP could be materially valuable, but no mention was made either in the article or in the instructions that having ESP was an intrinsically positive or valued trait to possess. Following this, subjects were told that their ESP ability was going to be evaluated in the context of a modified game of blackjack. It was clearly explained that the game was to be played among the three subjects and that the experimenter was not participating in the game as a contestant. The subjects were then informed of the presence and necessity of a "card-dealing machine." The experimenter said that the cards were to be dealt by a machine "in order to insure against possible interference with your ESP due to another person handling the cards." In actuality, the machine was used in order to provide an opportunity for the subjects to cheat, and to make it easier for subjects to cheat since the machine apparently removed the experimenter from the situation; this will be described below. According to the experimenter's description, the machine automatically dealt them a card on each round. In order to "stand pat," subjects had to switch on their "no" light so that the experimenter could divert the dealing machine from giving them a card on the next round. The use of light signals rather than verbal ones to inform the experimenter that the subject wanted to stand pat was justified by "the necessity of keeping talking at a minimum in order not to interfere with your ESP." The modifications and rules of the blackjack game were as follows:

Each subject was provided with $5 by the psychology department as a stake with which to play the game. Each subject was to "bet 50¢, no more or no less," on the outcome of each hand. Subjects were informed that at the conclusion of the experiment they would be allowed to keep all winnings over $5, but that subjects having less than $5 at the game's conclusion *would not* be required or obligated to make up the deficit out of their own pockets; this made it impossible for any subject to "lose" any of her own money.

We presented the following cover story regarding how ESP ability would be measured: The subjects were told to "concentrate for approximately 5 to 10 seconds before each hand," that is, to think about whether they would win or not win the upcoming hand. If they thought or felt they were going to win, they were to push the "yes" switch in front of them to the "on" position for 5 seconds, whereas if subjects felt they were not going to win the upcoming hand, they were to push the "no" switch to the "on" position for 5 seconds. The number of correct guesses *above chance* supposedly constituted a subject's ESP score. Prior to each guess, all subjects deposited a fifty-cent piece in the vertical slot, and it was explained to the subjects that on every hand they were trying to win a kitty with $1.50 in it.

A thorough explanation of the objectives of blackjack was given in order to equalize differential card game experience between the subjects. It was emphasized that point totals of 14–15 made the choice of whether or not to take another card especially difficult because of the high probability of going over 21 if another card was taken, and the low probability of winning by standing pat. The point totals of the various cards were also emphasized with the Ace counting only 11 points rather than 1 or 11 points, to simplify the experiment; also, all face cards were worth 10 points, and all numbered cards were worth their face values.

It was explained to subjects that:

> The card-dealing machine is a "home-made" affair. It has not as yet been perfected and at times makes mistakes. So far we've been able to iron out most of the mistakes, but occasionally the machine will deal two cards at a time instead of one. The machine is set up so that it deals from the top of the deck, as in a normal game of cards; when a person receives two cards, the top card is actually the card he should have gotten and the bottom card is the mistaken card. Now, the machine is fairly good, but at times will make this mistake. If it ever happens that you are dealt two cards, pick up the two cards and immediately return the bottom card to me by slipping it through the vertical slot. Remember, the top card is your card, the bottom card should be returned to me through the vertical slot.

Subjects were told that when all "no" switches were turned on, the experimenter would say "Game," which was a signal to subjects that they were to push all their cards through the vertical slot to the experimenter. Again, no talking was allowed under the pretext of not interfering with ESP. The experimenter then examined each player's hand, determined the winner, collected the three fifty-cent pieces and slid them down the slide of the winner. When the experimenter said "Begin," indicating that the next game was to start, the two subjects not having received any money were thus informed of their losing status.

Resumé of Procedural Instructions to the Subjects

The word "begin" was a signal to subjects that the previous hand was finished and that a new hand was to commence immediately. Following the word "begin," subjects deposited their fifty-cent pieces through the vertical slot, concentrated for 5 seconds, made a choice of the "yes" or "no" switches regarding their outcome expectancy on the upcoming hand, and the game began. The hand continued until all subjects had indicated they no longer wanted any more cards, at which time the experimenter said "game" and subjects then pushed all their cards through the vertical slot to the experimenter. This same procedure was repeated 35 times for all subjects. However, subjects were not aware as to exactly how many hands had been played at any given point in the experiment, nor did they know precisely when the game would end.

Dependent Measure

The dependent measure was the number of times during the experimental session that subjects kept the card they should have returned to the experimenter, thus enabling them to win the hand. The experiment was designed so as to present each subject with four opportunities to cheat during a session; thus, as far as each subject was concerned, the machine had mistakenly dealt two cards at once only four times in 35 hands. In reality, the experimenter dealt all cards but synchronized his dealing with the onset and termination of the machine-generated sound effects.

The method for providing subjects with a cheating opportunity was quite simple. However, complications arose in determining precisely *when* this opportunity should present itself. We decided to present a subject with an opportunity to cheat when the following conditions could be satisfied: (*a*) If she (the subject) had guessed "yes"; (*b*) when she possessed the same amount of money as the other subjects; (*c*) if she had not previously received more opportunities to cheat than the other subjects; (*d*) when her ESP hit rate was near chance level.

The separate stacks of "cheating cards" were prearranged so that the first two cards totaled 11–14 points, the third put the total over 21, and the fourth, if substituted for the third, brought the total to 19–21 points. Thus, when subjects received two cards at once they were faced with a dilemma: if they did not cheat, they would lose the hand; if they did cheat, they would almost certainly win. Cheating, therefore, was made relatively safe from exposure by having the cards dealt by a machine and also enabled subjects to net $1. The behavioral measure of cheating was whether or not subjects returned to the experimenter the card that was actually theirs and kept the bottom card which enabled them to win. The remaining two subjects in such a game were dealt cards from the general deck. If the subject had cheated, she was always declared the winner on that hand and was given the three fifty-cent pieces. This subject, of course, lost if she did not cheat. The other two subjects, in this hand, were always dealt a hand less than 21 or at times one of them was dealt a hand exceeding 21. If a subject did *not* cheat, the other subject with the score closest to and under 21 was declared the winner. The experimenter used scoreboards to keep track of how often a subject had won a hand, how often each had been given a cheating opportunity, and whether or not a subject had cheated. The scoreboard also provided for an evaluation of trial effects.

Following the card game, all subjects were asked to be seated at a table in the same room. They then filled out a questionnaire consisting of a check on the experimental manipulations and several filler items. Subjects were then debriefed completely. The purpose of the experiment was explained and subjects were assured that the results of the personality test were preprogrammed and had no relationship to their actual test scores.

RESULTS AND DISCUSSION

Analyses of variance on continuous data were all nonsignificant, although the mean differences were of the order hypothesized (mean cheats: LSE = 1.87, NSE = 1.54, HSE = 1.07). Frequency analyses, however, produced significant chi-squares. Subjects were divided according to whether they never cheated or cheated on at least one occasion. Table 14.1 shows a 2×3 contingency table chi-square with $df = 2$. Note that 13 people who were given negative feedback cheated at least once, while there were only 6 cheaters among the positive-feedback subjects. The chi-square proved to be significant at beyond the .05 level ($\chi^2 = 7.00, p < .05$). Another chi-square

TABLE 14.1
Number of people cheating at least
once as a function of self-esteem

Condition	Cheat	Never cheat
LSE	13	2
NSE	9	6
HSE	6	9

Note: $\chi^2_{LHN} = 7.00$, $df = 2$, $p < .05$. $\chi^2_{LH} = 5.17$, $df = 1$, $p < .03$.

was computed to evaluate the cheating differences between just the high and low self-esteem groups. This chi-square with $df = 1$ also proved to be significant after the correction for continuity had been made $\chi^2 = 5.17, p < .03$).

Taken as a whole, the data indicate that whether or not an individual cheats is influenced by the nature of the self-relevant feedback he received. People who learned uncomplimentary information about themselves showed a far greater tendency to cheat (on at least one occasion) than individuals who received positive information about themselves. This suggests that individuals with low self-esteem are more prone to commit immoral acts than individuals with high self-esteem, at least when the immoral act is instrumental in producing immediate material gain. Moreover, the number of people cheating in each of the above groups fell on either side of the neutral condition. Although neither experimental condition was singificantly different from the control, it is important to note that in the high self-esteem condition there was a greater trend toward honest behavior than in the control, whereas in the low self-esteem condition there was a greater trend toward cheating than in the control.

Our interpretation of the results hinges upon our contention that the manipulation employed in the experiment made subjects feel good about themselves or bad about themselves. In short, we contend that the feedback the subjects received had some impact (however temporary) upon their level of self-esteem. This interpretation is bolstered by our check on the manipulation which indicated that LSE subjects felt worse about themselves than either NSE or HSE subjects. However, since the manipulation check occurred subsequent to the card game, this difference might be due to the cheating behavior rather than the self-esteem manipulation.

There is some additional evidence which is also consistent with our interpretation. This involves the cheating behavior of subjects in terms of their *chronic levels* of self-esteem. Although it was not our intention to measure chronic self-esteem, one can extract a rough measure by looking at the self-concept scores on the CPI, which all subjects filled out as part of the cover story of the experiment. According to these measures, people of high, medium, and low self-esteem had been almost equally distributed among experimental conditions. The following data emerge: In the no feedback (NSE) condition, slightly more "low chronics" cheat than "high chronics." Also, as one might expect, the greatest percentage of cheaters falls among the low chronics who were given negative feedback; the smallest percentage of cheaters falls among the high chronics who were given positive feedback. The small number of subjects in each cell makes statistical analysis of these data unfeasible. The most one can say about these results is that they are consistent with our interpretation of the overall data on the basis of the experimental treatments themselves.

It should be emphasized that one of the unique aspects of this study is the nonspecific nature of the self-concept manipulation. The subjects were not told anything about themselves which would lead them to infer that they were moral-honest or immoral-dishonest people. Rather, they were told things designed to reduce their self-esteem in general. The social implications of these findings may be of some importance. Our results suggest that people who have a high opinion of themselves are less prone to perform any activities which are generally dissonant with their opinion. Similarly, it may be easier for a person with a low self-concept to commit acts of a criminal nature. Moreover, it may be that a common thread running through the complex variables involved in successful socialization (Sears, Maccoby, and Levin, 1957) is that of different development of self-esteem. Granted that most children become aware of what behavior is approved (moral) or disapproved (immoral), the development of high self-esteem in the individual may be crucial in his choosing a moral rather than an immoral mode of behaving.

This discussion is highly speculative to say the least. Further experimentation is necessary before the validity of our reasoning can be determined. One reason for the note of caution is the fact that it is difficult to perform an experiment involving complex human cognitions, emotions, and behavior which leaves us with a single, untarnished explanation for the results. This experiment is no exception. One conceivable alternative interpretation concerns aggressiveness: the subjects in the LSE condition, because they received a negative evaluation, may have been angry at the evaluator and, consequently, may have cheated as a way of punishing him. We attempted to eliminate this possibility in two ways: (a) We separated the experimenter who ran the ESP experiment from the evaluator (a member of the Counseling Center). Toward this end, the experimenter appeared ignorant of and uninterested in these evaluations; it was made to seem to be strictly between the subject and the Counseling Center. (b) The subjects were playing against other subjects rather than against "the house." Thus, when an individual cheated, she was clearly not hurting the experimenter; rather, she was unjustly taking money from a fellow college student.

Perhaps a more compelling explanation involves compensation. The subjects in the low self-esteem situation may, in effect, be saying "Well, I may not have done well on that personality test, but at least I'm going to see to it that I win some money." This explanation is quite different from the one that holds that it is easier to cheat because such behavior is consistent with feelings of low self-esteem. Note, however, that the "compensation" explanation applies only to the subjects in the low self-esteem condition. Thus, this alternative explanation would have been weakened if the subjects in the high self-esteem condition had cheated less than those in the control condition. But as the reader will recall, although these data were in a direction favoring consistency theory, they were not statistically significant. Thus, until further research is performed on this problem, compensation remains a possible explanation.

A final piece of unclarity should be mentioned. We predicted that people in the LSE condition would *cheat* and people in the HSE condition would *not cheat* because we felt that such actions would reflect a consistency between self-esteem and behavior. But *cheating* is merely one of many ways in which a person's behavior could show consistency with low or high self-esteem. For example, in the present situation a LSE subject could try to *lose*; being a loser might be considered as consistent with a low self-esteem. It should be noted that the experimenters took special pains to assure the subjects that they could not lose money. In this situation it seems reasonable to assume that being a loser simply means having bad luck—not being a bad person or even a poor person (financially). We selected cheating as our dependent variable because we felt that it is an unambiguously unethical piece of behavior. Although losing at cards in not pleasant, it does not seem as bad, especially since a loss of money is not involved. The data indicate that our reasoning was correct—that if a sizable number of LSE subjects had sought to lose, our data would have failed to reach significance.

References

Aronson, E., and Carlsmith, J. M. Performance expectancy as a determinant of actual performance. *Journal of Abnormal and Social Psychology,* 1962, **62,** 178–182.

Bramel, D. A dissonance theory approach to defensive projection. *Journal of Abnormal and Social Psychology,* 1962, **64,** 121–129.

Rogers, C. R. *Client-centered therapy.* Boston: Houghton-Mifflin, 1951.

Sears, R. R., Maccoby, E. E., and Levin, H. *Patterns of child rearing.* Evanston, Ill.: Row-Peterson, 1957.

Wilson, D. T. Ability evaluation, postdecision dissonance, and co-worker attractiveness. *Journal of Personality and Social Psychology,* 1965, **1,** 486–489.

15

Effect of Initial Selling Price on Subsequent Sales

Anthony N. Doob, J. Merrill Carlsmith,
Jonathan L. Freedman, Thomas K Landauer,
and Soleng Tom, Jr.

Five field experiments investigated the effect of initial selling price on subsequent sales of common household products. Matched pairs of discount houses sold the same product at either a discounted price or the regular price for a short period of time. The prices were then made the same for all stores. The results were consistent with the prediction from dissonance theory that subsequent sales would be higher where the initial price was high.

The "introductory low price offer" is a common technique used by marketers. A new product is offered at a low price for a short period of time, and the price is subsequently raised to its normal level. Since the goal naturally is to maximize final sales of the product, the assumption behind this technique is that it will accomplish this goal. An economic model based entirely on supply and demand would of course predict that the eventual sales would not be affected by the initial price. The lower price would be expected to attract many marginal buyers and produce greater sales; but as soon as the price is raised, these buyers should drop out of the market. The hope of the marketer, however, is that some of these marginal buyers will learn to like the product enough so that they will continue to purchase it even at the higher price.

Reprinted with permission from the authors and *The Journal of Personality and Social Psychology,* Vol. 11, No. 4, 1969. Copyright 1969 by the American Psychological Association.

This study was supported in part by National Science Foundation grants to Carlsmith and to Freedman. The authors are grateful to management and personnel of the discount chain for their cooperation in this research.

Unfortunately for the marketer, this may be a vain hope. There are various psychological reasons why we might expect the introductory low price to have an opposite effect from that which the marketers intend, such that the introductory low price would reduce rather than increase eventual sales. Since this technique is so widespread, it provides an unusual opportunity to investigate the applicability of social psychology in a natural setting, and to compare the marketer's predictions with that of social psychology.

The most interesting analysis of this situation is based on the theory of cognitive dissonance (Festinger, 1957). One of the clearest deductions from the theory is that the more effort in any form a person exerts to attain a goal, the more dissonance is aroused if the goal is less valuable than expected. The individual reduces this dissonance by increasing his liking for the goal, and therefore the greater the effort, the more he should like the goal. This prediction has received some substantiation in laboratory experimentation (e.g., Aronson and Mills, 1959; Gerard and Mathewson, 1966). Its applicability to the marketing situation is straightforward: the theory predicts that the higher the price a person initially pays for a product, the more he will come to like it. Presumably this greater liking will produce "brand loyalty" in the form of repeat purchases. Thus, when the initial price is high, a higher *proportion* of buyers should continue to purchase the product than when the initial price is low. Accordingly, although the introductory price will initially attract more customers, we may expect the sales curves for the two conditions to cross at some later point, and the higher brand loyalty induced by the dissonance involved in paying a high price to manifest itself in higher final sales in that condition.

Five experiments were performed to demonstrate that introducing a new brand of a product at a low price for a short time and then raising it to the normal selling price leads to lower sales in the long run than introducing the product at its normal selling price. The general design of all the experiments was to introduce the new brand at a low price in one set of stores and, after the price is raised to the normal selling price, compare sales with matched stores where the product was introduced at the normal selling price and held there throughout the course of the experiment.

All of the experiments that are to be reported here were done in a chain of discount houses. All sales figures have been multiplied by a constant in order to maintain confidentiality.

This chain of discount houses differs from most others in a number of important ways. They do not advertise much, and what advertising they do does not include prices on specific items. Price changes occur very seldom in these stores and are usually not advertised. In most cases, prices are lowered because an item is overstocked, and unless the customer remembers the regular selling price, he has no way of knowing that the price is lower than usual. Management in most of these stores is under direct control of the central office. When the manager receives orders from the central office, he has little or no power to change them.

The chain sells a large number of "house brands" at prices lower than the equivalent name brands. These house brands have the same registered trademark, and constitute a brand which customers can easily identify with the store. Generally, the quality of the house brand item is as high as the equivalent name brand, the differences usually being in characteristics which do not directly affect the usefulness of the item (e.g., mouthwash bottles are not as attractive as those of the name brand; the average grain size of powdered detergent is larger than that of the name brand which is chemically equivalent).

The products used in the studies reported here were house brands. All were being introduced into the stores at the time when the study was being run. The particular products used and the price differential were both determined by management.

EXPERIMENT I

Method

Twelve pairs of discount houses, matched on gross sales, were randomly assigned to one of two experimental conditions. In one store of each pair, the house brand of mouthwash was introduced at $.25 per quart bottle. The price was held at this level for 9 days (two weekends and the intervening days), and then the price was brought up to $.39 for all stores. In the other store, it was introduced at its normal selling price of $.39.

None of the managers had any reason to believe that the price of mouthwash at his store was not the same as in all other stores in the chain. No one was given any special instructions beyond the place in the store where the item was to be sold and its selling price. The location was essentially identical for all stores. In stores where mouthwash was introduced at the low price, the manager received a memo at the end of the first week instructing him to change the price to $.39 after that weekend.

Results

Sales were recorded by the sundries buyer as he replenished stock. At the end of each week these figures were sent to the central office and then relayed to the experimenters. Average sales for the 12 matched stores in each con-

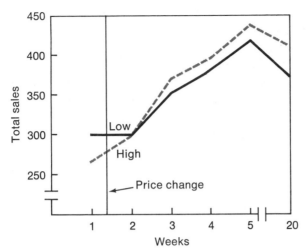

FIGURE 15.1
Mouthwash sales.

dition are shown in Figure 15.1. It is estimated that at least 2 weeks had to
pass before customers would return to buy more mouthwash, and, therefore,
one would not expect there to be any difference between the height of the
curves until the third week. In fact, the curves cross at this point, and after
this point, it is clear that the stores where the initial selling price was high
were selling more mouthwash than stores where the initial price was low.
This is true in spite of the fact that more mouthwash was sold the first week
in stores where the price was low. Unfortunately, for a variety of reasons,
the authors were not able to collect continuous data. They were able, however, to check sales 19 weeks after the price change, and clearly the difference still existed. When sales for Weeks 3, 4, 5, and 20 are combined, sales
of mouthwash were higher in the store where the initial selling price was
high in 10 of the 12 pairs of stores ($p = .02$).

Sales in the two sets of stores during Weeks 3, 4, 5, and 20 (pooled) were
also compared by use of a t test, resulting in a t of 2.11 ($df = 11$, $p < .10$).
Thus, stores where the initial selling price was low sold less mouthwash than
did stores where the initial selling price was the same as the final selling price.

REPLICATIONS

The same experiment was repeated four times, using different products. The
procedures were very similar in all cases. In each experiment, the stores
were rematched and randomly assigned independent of all other replications.

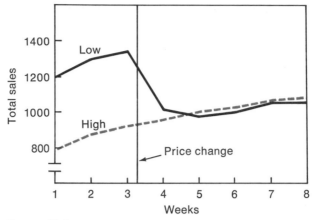

FIGURE 15.2
Toothpaste sales.

Experiment II: Toothpaste

Six pairs of stores were matched on the basis of sundries sales and randomly assigned to conditions in which the selling price for the first 3 weeks was either $.41 or $.49 for a "family size" tube of toothpaste. After 3 weeks, the price in all stores was set at $.49. The results are presented in Figure 15.2. When the sales for the last 4 weeks are combined as in the previous experiment, four of the six pairs show differences in the predicted direction ($p = .34$). When the more sensitive t test is done on the data from these 4 weeks, the t is 2.26 ($df = 5, p < .10$).

Experiment III: Aluminum Foil

Seven pairs of stores were matched on the basis of grocery sales and randomly assigned to conditions in which the selling price for the first 3 weeks was either $.59 or $.64 for a 75-foot roll of foil. After 3 weeks, the price in all stores was set at $.64. The results are presented in Figure 15.3. For Weeks 5–8 combined, all seven pairs ($p = .01$) show differences in the predicted direction ($t = 5.09, df = 6, p < .005$).

Experiment IV: Light Bulbs

Eight pairs of stores were matched on the basis of hardware sales and randomly assigned to conditions in which selling price for the first week was either $.26 or $.32 for a package of light bulbs. After 1 week, the price was brought up to $.32 in all stores. The results are presented in Figure 15.4. For

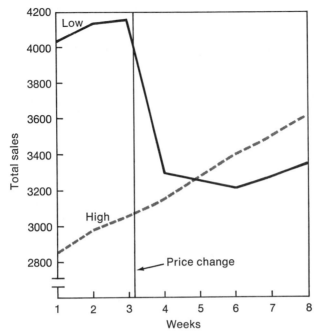

FIGURE 15.3
Aluminum-foil sales.

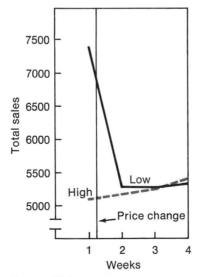

FIGURE 15.4
Light-bulb sales.

Weeks 3 and 4 combined, six of the eight pairs ($p = .15$) show differences in the predicted direction ($t = .837$, $df = 7$). Although this difference is not significant, it might be noted in Figure 15.4 that there was the predicted reversal, even though initial sales were almost 50 percent higher at the low price.

Experiment V: Cookies

Eight pairs of stores were matched on the basis of grocery sales and randomly assigned to conditions in which the selling price for the first 2 weeks was \$.24 or \$.29 for a large bag of cookies. After 2 weeks, the price was at \$.29 for all stores. The results are presented in Figure 15.5. For Weeks 4–6 combined, six of the eight pairs show differences in the predicted direction ($t = .625$, $df = 7$).

RESULTS

When the results of all five experiments are combined into one test of the hypothesis, a z of 3.63 ($p < .0002$) is obtained. Clearly, so far as this has been tested, the practice of introducing a product at a low price is not a good strategy for this chain of stores to use.

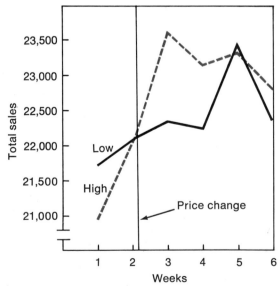

FIGURE 15.5
Cookie sales.

DISCUSSION

These studies indicate that introducing products at a lower than usual price is harmful to final sales. It was earlier argued that one possible reason for this is the lower proportion of buyers who return to a product when the initial price is lower than the normal price. Whether or not this causes eventual sales actually to be lower when the initial price is low is not critical to the argument. If, for example, there is an extremely large difference in initial sales, even a lower proportion of returning buyers may produce an advantage for the initial low price. Similarly, if the product has some special feature which would be expected to produce loyalty merely from exposure, it would be beneficial to maximize initial sales by the use of low introductory offers. In the experiments reported here, neither of these possibilities seems to have been present. For the range of prices studied, even a 50 percent increase in sales due to the lower price was not enough to overcome the increased consumer loyalty engendered by the higher price. Because of the presence of other identical brands, differing only in price, exposure alone was not enough to produce loyalty.

Whether or not eventual sales are actually lower when the initial price is low is not critical to the argument. From a theoretical point of view, the only essential comparison is the relative proportion of repurchases in the two conditions. A stringent method of showing that this proportion is higher when the initial price is high is to demonstrate that the absolute volume of eventual sales is greater for the high-price condition, even though initial sales are lower. For the products and prices studied here, this was true.

There are at least two alternative explanations of this result. The first is that in the low-initial-price stores the market is glutted after the first few weeks, and it takes a long time for there to be any need to repurchase the product. This might be a partial explanation of the difference between the conditions, but seems implausible as a total explanation. For all the products except light bulbs the length of time that the sales curves were followed exceeded by a goodly margin the marketer's estimate of the normal time until repurchase. Indeed, with mouthwash, for which the repurchase period is about 2 weeks, the difference between conditions is still present 19 weeks after the price switch. Customers might have stocked up by buying more than their usual supply of a product, but pricing practices of this chain of stores makes this unlikely. These stores have rarely used low introductory price offers and they were not advertised as such for the products studied. Buyers therefore had no reason to believe that the "low price" was a special price and accordingly had ittle reason to stock up on the product. Thus, although one cannot entirely rule out this "glutting the market" explanation, it is not convincing.

A second and more interesting alternative is in terms of what might be called the customers' adaptation level regarding the particular product. When mouthwash is put on sale at $.25, customers who buy it at that price or notice what the price is may tend to think of the product in terms of $.25. They say to themselves that this is a $.25 bottle of mouthwash. When, in subsequent weeks, the price increases to $.39, these customers will tend to see it as over-priced, and are not inclined to buy it at this much higher price. Therefore, sales drop off considerably. In the $.39 steady condition, initial sales are lower, but there is no reason for them to drop off due to this effect. Therefore, introducing it at the ultimate price results in greater sales in the long run than does introducing it at the low price. This explanation fits the data as nicely as does the one in terms of cognitive dissonance. In many ways, they are quite similar and are difficult to distinguish experimentally.

It should be noted that the adaptation level and dissonance explanations are by no means mutually exclusive. It is entirely possible that both mechanisms are operating to some extent. In any case, the basic esult stands — the introduction of a product at a low price tended to decrease subsequent sales, and this effect lasted for at least 20 weeks.

References

ARONSON, E., AND MILLS, J. The effect of severity of initiation on liking for a group. *Journal of Abnormal and Social Psychology,* 1959, **59,** 177–181.

FESTINGER, L. *A theory of cognitive dissonance.* Stanford, Calif.: Stanford University Press, 1957.

GERARD, H. B., AND MATHEWSON, G. C. The effects of severity of initiation on liking for a group: A replication. *Journal of Experimental Social Psychology,* 1966, **2,** 278–287.

IV

HUMAN AGGRESSION

16

The Effects of Observing Violence

Leonard Berkowitz

Experiments suggest that aggression depicted in television and motion picture dramas, or observed in actuality, can arouse certain members of the audience to violent action.

An ancient view of drama is that the action on the stage provides the spectators with an opportunity to release their own strong emotions harmlessly through identification with the people and events depicted in the play. This idea dates back at least as far as Aristotle, who wrote in *The Art of Poetry* that drama is "a representation . . . in the form of actions directly presented, not narrated; with incidents arousing pity and fear in such a way as to accomplish a purgation of such emotions."

Aristotle's concept of catharsis, a term derived from the Greek word for purgation, has survived in modern times. It can be heard on one side of the running debate over whether or not scenes of violence in motion pictures and television programs can instigate violent deeds, sooner or later, by people who observe such scenes. Eminent authorities contend that filmed violence, far from leading to real violence, can actually have beneficial results in that the viewer may purge himself of hostile impulses by watching other people behave aggressively, even if these people are merely actors appearing on a screen. On the other hand, authorities of equal stature contend that, as one psychiatrist told a Senate subcommittee, filmed violence is a "preparatory school for delinquency." In this view emotionally immature individuals can be seriously affected by fighting or brutality in films, and disturbed young people in particular can be led into the habit of expressing their aggressive energies by socially destructive actions.

Until recently neither of these arguments had the support of data obtained by controlled experimentation; they had to be regarded, therefore, as hypotheses, supported at best by unsystematic observation. Lately, however, several psychologists have undertaken laboratory tests of the effects of filmed aggression. The greater control obtained in these tests, some of which were done in my laboratory at the University of Wisconsin with the support of the National Science Foundation, provides a basis for some statements that have a fair probability of standing up under continued testing.

First, it is possible to suggest that the observation of aggression is more likely to induce hostile behavior than to drain off aggressive inclinations; that, in fact, motion picture or television violence can stimulate aggressive actions by normal people as well as by those who are emotionally disturbed. I would add an important qualification: such actions by normal people will occur only under appropriate conditions. The experiments point to some of the conditions that might result in aggressive actions by people in an audience who had observed filmed violence.

Second, these findings have obvious social significance. Third, the laboratory tests provide some important information about aggressive behavior in general. I shall discuss these three statements in turn.

Catharsis appeared to have occurred in one of the first experiments, conducted by Seymour Feshbach of the University of Colorado. Feshbach deliberately angered a group of college men; then he showed part of the group a filmed prizefight and the other students a more neutral film. He found that the students who saw the prizefight exhibited less hostility than the other students on two tests of aggressiveness administered after the film showings. The findings may indicate that the students who had watched the prizefight had vented their anger vicariously.

FIGURE 16.1
Typical experiment tests reaction of angered man to filmed violence. Experiment begins with introduction of subject (*white shirt*) to a man he believes is a co-worker but who actually is a confederate of the author's. In keeping with pretense that experiment is to test physiological reactions, student conducting the experiment takes blood-pressure readings. He assigns the men a task and leaves; during the task, the confederate insults the subject. Experimenter returns and shows filmed prizefight. Confederate leaves; experimenter tells subject to judge a floor plan drawn by confederate and to record opinion by giving confederate electric shocks. Shocks actually go to recording apparatus. The fight film appeared to stimulate the aggressiveness of angered men. (Photographs by Gordon Coster.)

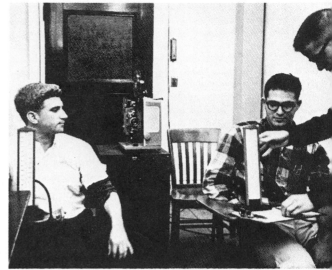
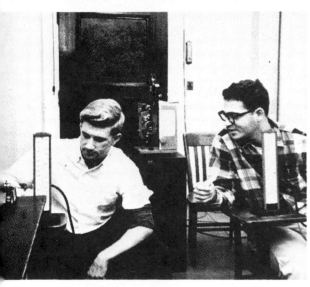

That, of course, is not the only possible explanation of the results. The men who saw the filmed violence could have become uneasy about their own aggressive tendencies. Watching someone being hurt may have made them think that aggressive behavior was wrong; as a result they may have inhibited their hostile responses. Clearly there was scope for further experimentation, particularly studies varying the attitude of the subjects toward the filmed aggression.

Suppose the audience were put in a frame of mind to regard the film violend as justified — for instance because a villain got a beating he deserved. The concept of symbolic catharsis would predict in such a case that an angered person might enter vicariously into the scene and work off his anger by thinking of himself as the winning fighter, who was inflicting injury on the man who had provoked him. Instead of accepting this thesis, my associates and I predicted that justified film aggression would lead to stronger rather than weaker manifestations of hostility. We believed that the rather low volume of open hostility in the Feshbach experiment was attributable to film-induced inhibitions. If this were so, an angered person who saw what appeared to be warranted aggression might well think he was justified in expressing his own hostile desires.

To test this hypothesis we conducted three experiments. Since they resulted in essentially similar findings and employed comparable procedures, I shall describe only the latest. In this experiment we brought together two male college students at a time. One of them was the subject; the other was a confederate of the experimenter and had been coached on how to act, although of course none of this was known to the subject. Sometimes we introduced the confederate to the subject as a college boxer and at other times we identified him as a speech major. After the introduction the experimenter announced that the purpose of the experiment was to study physiological reactions to various tasks. In keeping with that motif he took blood-pressure readings from each man. Then he set the pair to work on the first task: a simple intelligence test.

During this task the confederate either deliberately insulted the subject — for example, by remarks to the effect that "You're certainly taking a long time with that" and references to "cow-college students" at Wisconsin — or, in the conditions where we were not trying to anger the subject, behaved in a netural manner toward him. On the completion of the task the experimenter took more blood-pressure readings (again only to keep up the pretense that the experiment had a physiological purpose) and then informed the men that their next assignment was to watch a brief motion picture scene. He added that he would give them a synopsis of the plot so that they would have a better understanding of the scene. Actually he was equipped with two different synopses.

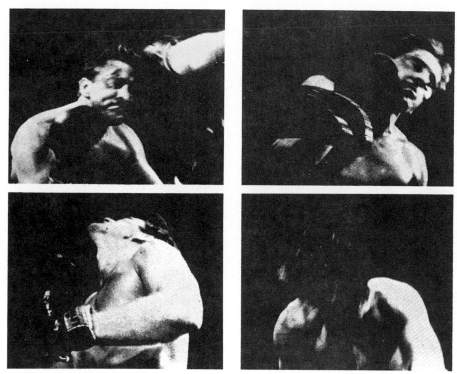

FIGURE 16.2
Filmed aggression shown in author's experiments was from the motion picture *Champion* and included these scenes in which Kirk Douglas receives a bad beating. Watchers had been variously prepared; after showing, they were tested for aggressive tendencies. (Astor Pictures, Inc.)

To half of the subjects he portrayed the protagonist of the film, who was to receive a serious beating, as an unprincipled scoundrel. Our idea was that the subjects told this story would regard the beating as retribution for the protagonist's misdeeds; some tests we administered in connection with the experiment showed that the subjects indeed had little sympathy for the protagonist. We called the situation we had created with this synopsis of the seven-minute fight scene the "justified fantasy aggression."

The other subjects were given a more favorable description of the protagonist. He had behaved badly, they were told, but this was because he had been victimized when he was young; at any rate, he was now about to turn over a new leaf. Our idea was that the men in this group would feel sympathetic toward the protagonist; again tests indicated that they did. We called this situation the "less justified fantasy aggression."

Then we presented the film, which was from the movie *Champion;* the seven-minute section we used showed Kirk Douglas, as the champion, apparently losing his title. Thereafter, in order to measure the effects of the

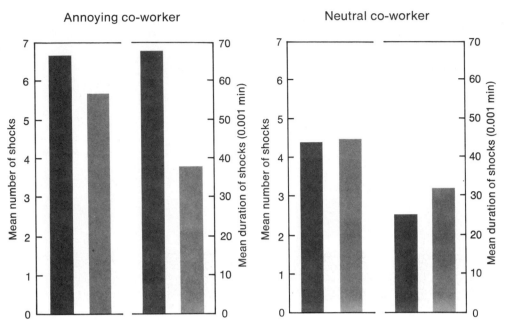

FIGURE 16.3

Responses of subjects invited to commit aggression after seeing prizefight film varied according to synopsis they heard beforehand. One (*dark gray*) called Douglas' beating deserved; the other (*light gray*) said it was undeserved. After the film the subjects were told they could give electric shocks to an annoying or neutral co-worker based on his "creativeness" in doing a task. Seeing a man receive what had been described as a well-deserved beating apparently lowered restraints against aggressive behavior.

film, we provided the subjects with an opportunity to show aggression in circumstances where that would be a socially acceptable response. We separated each subject and accomplice and told the subject that his co-worker (the confederate) was to devise a "creative" floor plan for a dwelling, which the subject would judge. If the subject throught the floor plan was highly creative, he was to give the co-worker one electric shock by depressing a telegraph key. If he thought the floor plan was poor, he was to administer more than one shock; the worse the floor plan, the greater the number of shocks. Actually each subject received the same floor plan.

The results consistently showed a greater volume of aggression directed against the anger-arousing confederate by the men who had seen the "bad guy" take a beating than by the men who had been led to feel sympathy for the protagonist in the film (Fig. 16.3). It was clear that the people who saw the justified movie violence had not discharged their anger through vicarious participation in the aggression but instead had felt freer to attack their tormenter in the next room. The motion picture scene had apparently influenced their judgment of the propriety of aggression. If it was all right for the movie villain to be injured aggressively, they seemed to think, then perhaps it was all right for them to attack the villain in their own lives — the person who had insulted them.

Another of our experiments similarly demonstrated that observed aggression has little if any effectiveness in reducing aggressive tendencies on the part of an observer. In this experiment some angered men were told by another student how many shocks they should give the person, supposedly in the next room, who had provoked them. Another group of angered men, instead of delivering the shocks themselves, watched the other student do it. Later the members of both groups had an opportunity to deliver the shocks personally. Consistently the men who had watched in the first part of the experiment now displayed stronger aggression than did the people who had been able to administer shocks earlier. Witnessed aggression appeared to have been less satisfying than self-performed aggression.

Our experiments thus cast considerable doubt on the possibility of a cathartic purge of anger through the observation of filmed violence. At the very least, the findings indicated that such a catharsis does not occur as readily as many authorities have thought.

Yet what about the undoubted fact that aggressive motion pictures and violent athletic contests provide relaxation and enjoyment for some people? A person who was tense with anger sometimes comes away from them feeling calmer. It seems to me that what happens here is quite simple: He calms down not because he has discharged his anger vicariously but because he was carried away by the events he witnessed. Not thinking of his troubles, he ceased to stir himself up and his anger dissipated. In addition, the enjoyable motion picture or game could have cast a pleasant glow over his whole outlook, at least temporarily.

The social implications of our experiments have to do primarily with the moral usually taught by films. Supervising agencies in the motion picture and television industries generally insist that films convey the idea that "crime does not pay." If there is any consistent principle used by these agencies to regulate how punishment should be administered to the screen villain, it would seem to be the talion law: an eye for an eye, a tooth for a tooth.

Presumably the audience finds this concept of retaliation emotionally satisfying. Indeed, we based our "justified fantasy aggression" situation on the concept that people seem to approve of hurting a scoundrel who has hurt others. But however satisfying the talion principle may be, screenplays based on it can lead to socially harmful consequences. If the criminal or "bad guy" is punished aggressively, so that others do to him what he has done to them, the violence appears justified. Inherent in the likelihood that the audience will regard it as justified is the danger that some angered person in the audience will attack someone who has frustrated *him,* or perhaps even some innocent person he happens to associate with the source of his anger.

Several experiments have lent support to this hypothesis. O. Ivar Lövaas of the University of Washington found in an experiment with nursery school children that the youngsters who had been exposed to an aggressive cartoon film displayed more aggressive responses with a toy immediately afterward than a control group shown a less aggressive film did. In another study Albert Bandura and his colleagues at Stanford University noted that preschool children who witnessed the actions of an aggressive adult in a motion picture tended later, after they had been subjected to mild frustrations, to imitate the kind of hostile behavior they had seen.

This tendency of filmed violence to stimulate aggression is not limited to children. Richard H. Walters of the University of Waterloo in Ontario found experimentally that male hospital attendants who had been shown a movie of a knife fight generally administered more severe punishment to another person soon afterward than did other attendants who had seen a more innocuous movie. The men in this experiment were shown one of the two movie scenes and then served for what was supposedly a study of the effects of punishment. They were to give an electric shock to someone else in the room with them each time the person made a mistake on a learning task. The intensity of the electric shocks could be varied. This other person, who was actually the experimenter's confederate, made a constant number of mistakes, but the people who had seen the knife fight gave him more intense punishment than the men who had witnessed the nonaggressive film. The filmed violence had apparently aroused aggressive tendencies in the men and, since the situation allowed the expression of aggression, their tendencies were readily translated into severe aggressive actions.

These experiments, taken together with our findings, suggest a change in approach to the manner in which screenplays make their moral point. Although it may be socially desirable for a villain to receive his just deserts at the end of a motion picutre, it would seem equally desirable that this retribution should not take the form of physical aggression.

The key point to be made about aggressiveness on the basis of experimentation in this area is that a person's hostile tendencies will persist, in spite of any satisfaction he may derive from filmed violence, to the extent that his frustrations and aggressive habits persist. There is no free-floating aggressive energy that can be released through attemps to master other drives, as Freud proposed or by observing others as they act aggressively.

In fact, there have been studies suggesting that even if the angered person performs the aggression himself, his hostile inclinations are not satisfied unless he believes he has attacked his tormentor and not someone else. J. E. Hokanson of Florida State University has shown that angered subjects permitted to commit aggression against the person who had annoyed them often display a drop in systolic blood pressure. They seem to have experienced a physiological relaxation, as if they had satisfied their aggressive

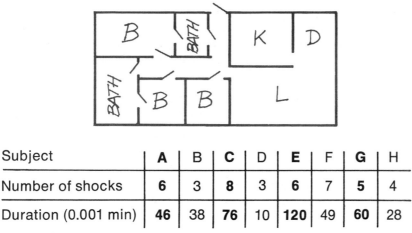

Subject	A	B	C	D	E	F	G	H
Number of shocks	**6**	3	**8**	3	**6**	7	**5**	4
Duration (0.001 min)	**46**	38	**76**	10	**120**	49	**60**	28

FIGURE 16.4
Task by annoying co-worker supposedly was to draw a floor plan. Actually, each
subject saw the floor plan shown here. The subject was asked to judge the
creativeness of the plan and to record his opinion by pressing a telegraph key
that he thought would give electric shocks to the co-worker; one shock for a good
job and more for poor work. Responses of eight subjects who saw prizefight film
are shown; those in boldface type represent men told that Douglas deserved his
beating; those in lightface type, men informed it was undeserved.

urges. Systolic pressure declines less, however, when the angered people
carry out the identical motor activity involved in the aggression but without
believing they have attacked the source of their frustration.

I must now qualify some of the observations I have made. Many aggressive motion pictures and television programs have been presented to the
public, but the number of aggressive incidents demonstrably attributable to
such shows is quite low. One explanation for this is that most social situations, unlike the conditions in the experiments I have described, impose
constraints on aggression. People are usually aware of the social norms
prohibiting attacks on others, consequently they inhibit whatever hostile
inclinations might have been aroused by the violent films they have just
seen.

Another important factor is the attributes of the people encountered by a
person after he has viewed filmed violence. A man who is emotionally
aroused does not necessarily attack just anyone. Rather, his aggression is
directed toward specific objectives. In other words, only certain people are
capable of drawing aggressive responses from him. In my theoretical analyses of the sources of aggressive behavior I have suggested that the arousal
of anger only creates a readiness for aggression. The theory holds that
whether or not this predisposition is translated into actual aggression depends on the presence of appropriate cues: stimuli associated with the present or previous instigators of anger. Thus if someone has been insulted,

the sight or the thought of others who have provoked him, whether then or earlier, may evoke hostile responses from him.

An experiment I conducted in conjunction with a graduate student provides some support for this train of thought. People who had been deliberately provoked by the experimenter were put to work with two other people, one a person who had angered them earlier and the other a neutral person. The subjects showed the greatest hostility, following their frustration by the experimenter, to the co-worker they disliked. He, by having thwarted them previously, had acquired the stimulus quality that caused him to draw aggression from them after they had been aroused by the experimenter.

My general line of resaoning leads me to some predictions about aggressive behavior. In the absence of any strong inhibitions against aggression, people who have recently been angered and have then seen filmed aggression will be more likely to act aggressively than people who have not had those experiences. Moreover, their strongest attacks will be directed at those who are most directly connected with the provocation or at others who either have close associations with the aggressive motion picture or are disliked for any reason.

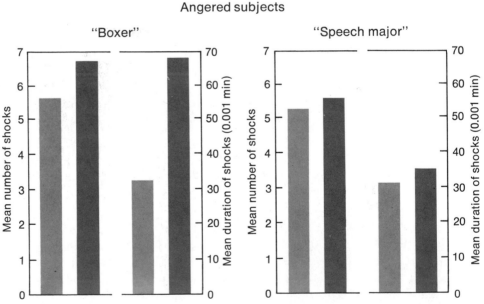

Angered subjects

FIGURE 16.5
Co-worker's introduction also produced variations in aggressiveness of subjects. Co-worker was introduced as boxer or as speech major; reactions shown here are of men who were angered by co-worker and then saw either a fight film (*dark gray*) or neutral film (*light gray*). Co-worker received strongest attacks when subjects presumably associated him with fight film.

One of our experiments showed results consistent with this analysis. In this study male college students, taken separately, were first either angered or not angered by *A*, one of the two graduate students acting as experimenters. *A* had been introduced earlier either as a college boxer or as a speech major. After *A* had had his session with the subject, *B*, the second experimenter, showed the subject a motion picture: either the prizefight scene mentioned earlier or a neutral film. (One that we used was about canal boats in England; the other, about the travels of Marco Polo.)

We hypothesized that the label "college boxer" applied to *A* in some of the cases would produce a strong association in the subject's mind between *A* and the boxing film. In other words, any aggressive tendencies aroused in the subject would be more likely to be directed at *A* the college boxer than at *A* the speech major. The experiment bore out this hypothesis. Using questionnaires at the end of the session as the measures of hostility, we found that the deliberately angered subjects directed more hostility at *A*, the source of their anger, when they had seen the fight film and he had been identified as a boxer. Angered men who had seen the neutral film showed no particular hostility to *A* the boxer. In short, the insulting experimenter received the strongest verbal attacks when he was also associated with the aggressive film. It is also noteworthy that in this study the boxing film did not influence the amount of hostility shown toward *A* when he had not provoked the subjects.

A somewhat inconsistent note was introduced by our experiments, described previously, in "physiological reactions." Here the nonangered groups. regardless of which film they saw, gave the confederate more and longer shocks when they thought he was a boxer than when they understood him to be a speech major (see Fig. 16.6). To explain this finding I assume that our subjects had a negative attitude toward boxers in general. This attitude may have given the confederate playing the role of boxer the stimulus quality that caused him to draw aggression from the angered subjects. But it could only have been partially responsible, since the insulted subjects who saw the neutral film gave fewer shocks to the boxer than did the insulted subjects who saw the prizefight film.

Associations between the screen and the real world are important. People seem to be emotionally affected by a screenplay to the extent that they associate the events of the drama with their own life experiences. Probably adults are less strongly influenced than children because they are aware that the film is make-believe and so can dissociate it from their own lives. Still, it seems clear from the experiments I have described that an aggressive film can induce aggressive actions by anyone in the audience. In most instances I would expect that effect to be short-lived. The emotional reaction produced by filmed violence probably dies away rather rapidly as

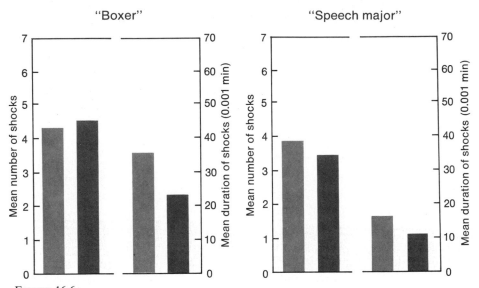

FIGURE 16.6
Similar test, varied by the fact that the co-worker behaved neutrally toward the subjects and therefore presumably did not anger them, produced these reactions. The greater number of shocks given to the coworker introduced as a boxer than to the one introduced as a speech major apparently reflected a tendency to take a generally negative attitude toward persons identified as boxers.

the viewer enters new situations and encounters new stimuli. Subjected to different influences, he becomes less and less ready to attack other people.

Television and motion pictures, however, may also have some persistent effects. If a young child sees repeatedly that screen heroes gain their ends through aggressive actions, he may conclude that aggression is desirable behavior. Fortunately screenplays do not consistently convey that message, and in any event the child is exposed to many other cultural norms that discourage aggression.

As I see it, the major social danger inherent in filmed violence has to do with the temporary effects produced in a fairly short period immediately following the film. For that period, at least, a person—whether an adult or a child—who had just seen filmed violence might conclude that he was warranted in attacking those people in his own life who had recently frustrated him. Further, the film might activate his aggressive habits so that for the period of which I speak he would be primed to act aggressively. Should he then encounter people with appropriate stimulus qualities, people he dislikes or connects psychologically with the film, this predisposition could lead to open aggression.

What, then, of catharsis? I would not deny that it exists. Nor would I reject the argument that a frustrated person can enjoy fantasy aggression because he sees characters doing things he wishes he could do, although in most cases his inhibitions restrain him. I believe, however, that effective catharsis occurs only when an angered person perceives that his frustrater has been aggressively injured. From this I argue that filmed violence is potentially dangerous. The motion picture aggression has increased the chance that an angry person, and possibly other people as well, will attack someone else.

References

BANDURA, ELBERT, ROSS, DOROTHEA, AND ROSS, SHEILA A. Imitation of film-mediated aggressive models. *Journal of Abnormal and Social Psychology,* Vol. 66, No. 1, pp. 3–11; January, 1963.

BERKOWITZ, LEONARD. *Aggression: a social psychological analysis.* McGraw-Hill Book Company, 1962.

BERKOWITZ, LEONARD, AND RAWLINGS, EDNA. Effects of film violence on inhibitions against subsequent aggression. *Journal of Abnormal and Social Psychology,* Vol. 66, No. 5, pp. 405–412; May, 1963.

SCHRAMM, WILBUR, LYLE, JACK, AND PARKER, EDWIN B. *Television in the lives of our children.* Stanford University Press, 1961.

WALTERS, RICHARD H., THOMAS, EDWARD LLEWELLYN, AND ACKER, C. WILLIAM. Enhancement of punitive behavior by audio-visual displays. *Science,* Vol. 1236, No. 3519, pp. 872–873; June 8, 1962.

17

Transmission of Aggression through Imitation of Aggressive Models

Albert Bandura, Dorothea Ross, and Sheila A. Ross

A previous study, designed to account for the phenomenon of identification in terms of incidental learning, demonstrated that children readily imitated behavior exhibited by an adult model in the presence of the model (Bandura and Huston, 1961). A series of experiments by Blake (1958) and others (Grosser, Polansky, and Lippitt, 1951; Rosenblith, 1959; Schachter and Hall, 1952) have likewise shown that mere observation of responses of a model has a facilitating effect on subjects' reactions in the immediate social influence setting.

While these studies provide convincing evidence for the influence and control exerted on others by the behavior of a model, a more crucial test of imitative learning involves the generalization of imitative response patterns to new settings in which the model is absent.

Reprinted with permission from the authors and *The Journal of Abnormal and Social Psychology,* Vol. 63, No. 3, 1961. Copyright 1961 by the American Psychological Association.

This investigation was supported by Research Grant M-4398 from the National Institute of Health, United States Public Health Service.

The authors wish to express their appreciation to Edith Dowley, Director, and Patricia Rowe, Head Teacher, Stanford University Nursery School for their assistance throughout this study.

In the experiment reported in this paper children were exposed to aggressive and nonaggressive adult models and were then tested for amount of imitative learning in a new situation in the absence of the model. According to the prediction, subjects exposed to aggressive models would reproduce aggressive acts resembling those of their models and would differ in this respect both from subjects who observed nonaggressive models and from those who had no prior exposure to any models. This hypothesis assumed that subjects had learned imitative habits as a result of prior reinforcement, and these tendencies would generalize to some extent to adult experimenters (Miller and Dollard, 1941).

It was further predicted that observation of subdued nonaggressive models would have a generalized inhibiting effect on the subjects' subsequent behavior, and this effect would be reflected in a difference between the nonaggressive and the control groups, with subjects in the latter group displaying significantly more aggression.

Hypotheses were also advanced concerning the influence of the sex of model and sex of subjects on imitation. Fauls and Smith (1956) have shown that preschool children perceive their parents as having distinct preferences regarding sex appropriate modes of behavior for their children. Their findings, as well as informal observation, suggest that parents reward imitation of sex appropriate behavior and discourage or punish sex inappropriate imitative responses, e.g., a male child is unlikely to receive much reward for performing female appropriate activities, such as cooking, or for adopting other aspects of the maternal role, but these same behaviors are typically welcomed if performed by females. As a result of differing reinforcement histories, tendencies to imitate male and female models thus acquire differential habit strength. One would expect, on this basis, subjects to imitate the behavior of a same-sex model to a greater degree than a model of the opposite sex.

Since aggression, however, is a highly masculine-typed behavior, boys should be more predisposed than girls toward imitating aggression, the difference being most marked for subjects exposed to the male aggressive model.

METHOD

Subjects

The subjects were 36 boys and 36 girls enrolled in the Stanford University Nursery School. They ranged in age from 37 to 69 months, with a mean age of 52 months.

Two adults, a male and a female, served in the role of model, and one female experimenter conducted the study for all 72 children.

Experimental Design

Subjects were divided into eight experimental groups of six subjects each and a control group consisting of 24 subjects. Half the experimental subjects were exposed to aggressive models and half were exposed to models that were subdued and nonaggressive in their behavior. These groups were further subdivided into male and female subjects. Half the subjects in the aggressive and nonaggressive conditions observed same-sex models, while the remaining subjects in each group viewed models of the opposite sex. The control group had no prior exposure to the adult models and was tested only in the generalization situation.

It seemed reasonable to expect that the subjects' level of aggressiveness would be positively related to the readiness with which they imitated aggressive modes of behavior. Therefore, in order to increase the precision of treatment comparisons, subjects in the experimental and control groups were matched individually on the basis of ratings of their aggressive behavior in social interactions in the nursery school.

The subjects were rated on four five-point rating scales by the experimenter and a nursery school teacher, both of whom were well acquainted with the children. These scales measured the extent to which subjects displayed physical aggression, verbal aggression, aggression toward inanimate objects, and aggressive inhibition. The latter scale, which dealt with the subjects' tendency to inhibit aggressive reactions in the face of high instigation, provided a measure of aggression anxiety.

Fifty-one subjects were rated independently by both judges so as to permit an assessment of interrater agreement. The reliability of the composite aggression score, estimated by means of the Pearson product-moment correlation, was .89.

The composite score was obtained by summing the ratings on the four aggression scales; on the basis of these scores, subjects were arranged in triplets and assigned at random to one of two treatment conditions or to the control group.

Experimental Conditions

In the first step in the procedure subjects were brought individually by the experimenter to the experimental room and the model, who was in the hallway outside the room, was invited by the experimenter to come and join in the game. The experimenter then escorted the subject to one corner of the room, which was structured as the subject's play area. After seating the child at a small table, the experimenter demonstrated how the subject could design pictures with potato prints and picture stickers provided. The potato prints included a variety of geometrical forms; the stickers were attractive multicolor pictures of animals, flowers, and western figures to be pasted on a pastoral scene. These activities were selected since they had been established, by previous studies in the nursery school, as having high interest value for the children.

After having settled the subject in his corner, the experimenter escorted the model to the opposite corner of the room which contained a small table and chair, a tinker toy set, a mallet, and a five-foot inflated Bobo doll. The experimenter explained that these were the materials provided for the model to play with and, after the model was seated, the experimenter left the experimental room.

With subjects in the *nonaggressive condition,* the model assembled the tinker toys in a quiet subdued manner totally ignoring the Bobo doll.

In contrast, with subjects in the *aggressive condition,* the model began by assembling the tinker toys but after approximately a minute had elapsed, the model turned to the Bobo doll and spent the remainder of the period aggressing toward it.

Imitative learning can be clearly demonstrated if a model performs sufficiently novel patterns of responses which are unlikely to occur independently of the observation of the behavior of a model and if a subject reproduces these behaviors in substantially identical form. For this reason, in addition to punching the Bobo doll, a response that is likely to be performed by children independently of a demonstration, the model exhibited distinctive aggressive acts which were to be scored as imitative responses. The model laid Bobo on its side, sat on it and punched it repeatedly in the nose. The model then raised the Bobo doll, picked up the mallet and struck the doll on the head. Following the mallet aggression, the model tossed the doll up in the air aggressively and kicked it about the room. This sequence of physically aggressive acts was repeated approximately three times, interspersed with verbally aggressive responses such as, "Sock him in the nose . . . ," "Hit him down . . . ," "Throw him in the air . . . ," "Kick him . . . ," "Pow . . . ," and two nonaggressive comments, "He keeps coming back for more" and "He sure is a tough fella."

Thus in the exposure situation, subjects were provided with a diverting task which occupied their attention while at the same time insured observation of the model's behavior in the absence of any instructions to observe or to learn the responses in question. Since subjects could not perform the model's aggressive behavior, any learning that occurred was purely on an observational or covert basis.

At the end of 10 minutes, the experimenter entered the room, informed the subject that he would now go to another game room, and bid the model goodbye.

Aggression Arousal

Subjects were tested for the amount of imitative learning in a different experimental room that was set off from the main nursery school building. The two experimental situations were thus clearly differentiated; in fact, many subjects were under the impression that they were no longer on the nursery school grounds.

Prior to the test for imitation, however, all subjects, experimental and control, were subjected to mild aggression arousal to insure that they were under some degree of instigation to aggression. The arousal experience was included for two main reasons. In the first place, observation of aggressive behavior exhibited by others tends to reduce the probability of aggression on the part of the observer (Rosenbaum and deCharms, 1960). Consequently, subjects in the aggressive condition, in relation both to the nonaggressive and control groups, would be under weaker instigation following exposure to the models. Second, if subjects in the nonaggressive condition expressed little aggression in the face of appropriate instigation, the presence of an inhibitory process would seem to be indicated.

Following the exposure experience, therefore, the experimenter brought the subject to an anteroom that contained these relatively attractive toys: a fire engine, a locomotive, a jet fighter plane, a cable car, a colorful spinning top, and a doll set complete with wardrobe, doll carriage, and baby crib. The experimenter explained that the toys were for the subject to play with but, as soon as the subject became sufficiently involved with the play material (usually in about 2 minutes), the experimenter remarked that these were her very best toys, that she did not let just anyone play with them, and that she had decided to reserve these toys for the other children. However, the subject could play with any of the toys that were in the next room. The experimenter and the subject then entered the adjoining experimental room.

It was necessary for the experimenter to remain in the room during the experimental session; otherwise a number of the children would either refuse to remain alone or would leave before the termination of the session. However, in order to minimize any influence her presence might have on the subject's behavior, the experimenter remained as inconspicuous as possible by busying herself with paper work at a desk in the far corner of the room and avoiding any interaction with the child.

Test for Delayed Imitation

The experimental room contained a variety of toys including some that could be used in imitative or nonimitative aggression, and others that tended to elicit predominantly nonaggressive forms of behavior. The aggressive toys included a three-foot Bobo doll, a mallet and peg board, two dart guns, and a tether ball with a face painted on it which hung from the ceiling. The nonaggressive toys, on the other hand, included a tea set, crayons and coloring paper, a ball, two dolls, three bears, cars and trucks, and plastic farm animals.

In order to eliminate any variation in behavior due to mere placement of the toys in the room, the play material was arranged in a fixed order for each of the sessions.

The subject spent 20 minutes in this experimental room during which time his behavior was rated in terms of predetermined response categories by judges who observed the session through a one-way mirror in an adjoining observation room. The 20-minute session was divided into 5-second intervals by means of an electric interval timer, thus yielding a total number of 240 response units for each subject.

The male model scored the experimental sessions for all 72 children. Except for the cases in which he served as model, he did not have knowledge of the subjects' group assignments. In order to provide an estimate of interscorer agreement, the performances of half the subjects were also scored independently by a second observer. Thus one or the other of the two observers usually had no knowledge of the conditions to which the subjects were assigned. Since, however, all but two of the subjects in the aggressive condition performed the models' novel aggressive responses while subjects in the other conditions only rarely exhibited such reactions, subjects who were exposed to the aggressive models could be readily identified through their distinctive behavior.

The responses scored involved highly specific concrete classes of behavior and yielded high interscorer reliabilities, the product-moment coefficients being in the .90s.

Response Measures

Three measures of imitation were obtained:

Imitation of physical aggression: This category included acts of striking the Bobo doll with the mallet, sitting on the doll and punching it in the nose, kicking the doll, and tossing it in the air.

Imitative verbal aggression: Subject repeats the phrases, "Sock him," "Hit him down," "Kick him," "Throw him in the air," or "Pow."

Imitative nonaggressive verbal responses: Subject repeats, "He keeps coming back for more," or "He sure is a tough fella."

During the pretest, a number of the subjects imitated the essential components of the model's behavior but did not perform the complete act, or they directed the imitative aggressive response to some object other than the Bobo doll. Two responses of this type were therefore scored and were interpreted as partially imitative behavior.

Mallet aggression: Subject strikes objects other than the Bobo doll aggressively with the mallet.

Sits on Bobo doll: Subject lays the Bobo doll on its side and sits on it, but does not aggress toward it.

The following additional nonimitative aggressive responses were scored:

Punches Bobo doll: Subject strikes, slaps, or pushes the doll aggressively.

Nonimitative physical and verbal aggression: This category included physically aggressive acts directed toward objects other than the Bobo doll and any hostile remarks except for those in the verbal imitation category; e.g., "Shoot the Bobo," "Cut him," "Stupid ball," "Knock over people," "Horses fighting, biting"

Aggressive gun play: Subject shoots darts or aims the guns and fires imaginary shots at objects in the room.

Ratings were also made of the number of behavior units in which subjects played nonaggressively or sat quietly and did not play with any of the material at all.

RESULTS

Complete Imitation of Models' Behavior

Subjects in the aggression condition reproduced a good deal of physical and verbal aggressive behavior resembling that of the models, and their mean scores differed markedly from those of subjects in the nonaggressive and control groups who exhibited virtually no imitative aggression (see Table 17.1).

Since there were only a few scores for subjects in the nonaggressive and control conditions (approximately 70 percent of the subjects had zero scores), and the assumption of homogeneity of variance could not be made, the Friedman two-way analysis of variance by ranks was employed to test the significance of the obtained differences.

The prediction that exposure of subjects to aggressive models increases the probability of aggressive behavior is clearly confirmed (see Table 17.2). The main effect of treatment conditions is highly significant both for physical and verbal imitative aggression. Comparison of pairs of scores by the sign test shows that the obtained over-all differences were due almost en-

TABLE 17.1
Mean aggression scores for experimental and control subjects

| Response category | Experimental groups | | | | Control groups |
| | Aggressive | | Nonaggressive | | |
	F Model	M Model	F Model	M Model	
Imitative physical aggression					
Female subjects	5.5	7.2	2.5	0.0	1.2
Male subjects	12.4	25.8	0.2	1.5	2.0
Imitative verbal aggression					
Female subjects	13.7	2.0	0.3	0.0	0.7
Male subjects	4.3	12.7	1.1	0.0	1.7
Mallet aggression					
Female subjects	17.2	18.7	0.5	0.5	13.1
Male subjects	15.5	28.8	18.7	6.7	13.5
Punches Bobo doll					
Female subjects	6.3	16.5	5.8	4.3	11.7
Male subjects	18.9	11.9	15.6	14.8	15.7
Nonimitative aggression					
Female subjects	21.3	8.4	7.2	1.4	6.1
Male subjects	16.2	36.7	26.1	22.3	24.6
Aggressive gun play					
Female subjects	1.8	4.5	2.6	2.5	3.7
Male subjects	7.3	15.9	8.9	16.7	14.3

tirely to the aggression displayed ny subjects who had been exposed to the aggressive models. Their scores were significantly higher than those of either the nonaggressive or control groups, which did not differ from each other (Table 17.2).

Imitation was not confined to the model's aggressive responses. Approximately one-third of the subjects in the aggressive condition also repeated the model's nonaggressive verbal responses while none of the subjects in either the nonaggressive or control groups made such remarks. This difference, tested by means of the Cochran Q test, was significant well beyond the .001 level (Table 17.2).

Partial Imitation of Models' Behavior

Differences in the predicted direction were also obtained on the two measures of partial imitation.

Analysis of variance of scores based on the subjects' use of the mallet aggressively toward objects other than the Bobo doll reveals that treatment conditions are a statistically significant source of variation (Table 17.2). In

TABLE 17.2
Significance of the differences between experimental and control groups in the expression of aggression

Response category	$\chi^2{}_r$	Q	p	Comparison of pairs of treatment conditions		
				Aggressive vs. non-aggressive p	Aggressive vs. control p	Non-aggressive vs. control p
Imitative responses						
Physical aggression	27.17		<.001	<.001	<.001	.09
Verbal aggression	9.17		<.02	.004	.048	.09
Nonaggressive verbal responses		17.50	<.001	.004	.004	*ns*
Partial imitation						
Mallet aggression	11.06		<.01	.026	*ns*	.005
Sits on Bobo		13.44	<.01	.018	.059	*ns*
Nonimitative aggression						
Punches Bobo doll	2.87		*ns*			
Physical and verbal	8.96		<.02	.026	*ns*	*ns*
Aggressive gun play	2.75		*ns*			

addition, individual sign tests show that both the aggressive and the control groups, relative to subjects in the nonaggressive condition, produced significantly more mallet aggression, the difference being particularly marked with regard to female subjects. Girls who observed nonaggressive models performed a mean number of 0.5 mallet aggression responses as compared to mean values of 18.0 and 13.1 for girls in the aggressive and control groups, respectively.

Although subjects who observed aggressive models performed more mallet aggression ($M = 20.0$) than their controls ($M = 13.3$), the difference was not statistically significant.

With respect to the partially imitative response of sitting on the Bobo doll, the over-all group differences were significant beyond the .01 level (Table 17.2). Comparison of pairs of scores by the sign test procedure reveals that subjects in the aggressive group reproduced this aspect of the models' behavior to a greater extent than did the nonaggressive ($p = .018$) or the control ($p = .059$) subjects. The latter two groups, on the other hand, did not differ from each other.

Nonimitative Aggression

Analyses of variance of the remaining aggression measures (Table 17.2) show that treatment conditions did not influence the extent to which subjects engaged in aggressive gun play or punched the Bobo doll. The effect of conditions is highly significant ($\chi^2{}_r = 8.96$, $p < .02$), however, in the case of the subjects' expression of nonimitative physical and verbal aggression. Further comparison of treatment pairs reveals that the main source of the overall difference was the aggressive and nonaggressive groups which differed significantly from each other (Table 17.2), with subjects exposed to the aggressive models displaying the greater amount of aggression.

Influence of Sex of Model and Sex of Subjects on Imitation

The hypothesis that boys are more prone than girls to imitate aggression exhibited by a model was only partially confirmed: *t* tests computed for subjects in the aggressive condition reveal that boys reproduced more imitative physical aggression than girls ($t = 2.50$, $p < .01$). The groups do not differ, however, in their imitation of verbal aggression.

The use of nonparametric tests, necessitated by the extremely skewed distributions of scores for subjects in the nonaggressive and control conditions, preclude an over-all test of the influence of sex of model per se, and of the various interactions between the main effects. Inspection of the means presented in Table 17.1 for subjects in the aggression condition, however, clearly suggests the possibility of a Sex × Model interaction. This interaction effect is much more consistent and pronounced for the male model than for the female model. Male subjects, for example, exhibited more physical ($t = 2.07$, $p < .05$) and verbal imitative aggression ($t = 2.51$, $p < .05$), more nonimitative aggression ($t = 3.15$, $p < .025$), and engaged in significantly more aggressive gun play ($t = 2.12$, $p < .05$) following exposure to the aggressive male model than the female subjects. In contrast, girls exposed to the female model performed considerably more imitative verbal aggression and more nonimitative aggression than did the boys (Table 17.1). The variances, however, were equally large and with only a small *N* in each cell the mean differences did not reach statistical significance.

Data for the nonaggressive and control subjects provide additional suggestive evidence that the behavior of the male model exerted a greater influence than the female model on the subjects' behavior in the generalization situation.

It will be recalled that, except for the greater amount of mallet aggression exhibited by the control subjects, no significant differences were obtained between the nonaggressive and control groups. The data indicate, however, that the absence of significant differences between these two groups was due primarily to the fact that subjects exposed to the nonaggressive female model did not differ from the control on any of the measures of aggression.

With respect to the male model, on the other hand, the differences between the groups are striking. Comparison of the sets of scores by means of the sign test reveals that, in relation to the control group, subjects exposed to the nonaggressive male model performed significantly less imitative physical aggression ($p = .06$), less imitative verbal aggression ($p = .002$), less mallet aggression ($p = .003$), less nonimitative physical and verbal aggression ($p = .03$), and they were less inclined to punch the Bobo doll ($p = .07$).

While the comparison of subgroups, when some of the over-all tests do not reach statistical significance, is likely to capitalize on chance differences, nevertheless the consistency of the findings adds support to the interpretation in terms of influence by the model.

Nonaggressive Behavior

With the exception of expected sex differences, Lindquist (1956) Type III analyses of variance of the nonaggressive response scores yielded few significant differences.

Female subjects spent more time than boys playing with dolls ($p < .001$), with the tea set ($p < .001$), and coloring ($p < .05$). The boys, on the other hand, devoted significantly more time than the girls to exploratory play with guns ($p < .01$). No sex differences were found in respect to the subjects use of the other stimulus objects, i.e., farm animals, cars, or tether ball.

Treatment conditions did produce significant differences on two measures of nonaggressive behavior that are worth mentioning. Subjects in the nonaggressive condition engaged in significantly more nonaggressive play with dolls than either subjects in the aggressive group ($t = 2.67, p < .02$), or in the control group ($t = 2.57, p < .02$).

Even more noteworthy is the finding that subjects who observed nonaggressive models spent more than twice as much time as subjects in aggressive condition ($t = 3.07, p < .01$) in simply sitting quietly without handling any of the play material.

DISCUSSION

Much current research on social learning is focused on the shaping of new behavior through rewarding and punishing consequences. Unless responses are emitted, however, they cannot be influenced. The results of this study provide strong evidence that observation of cues produced by the behavior of others is one effective means of eliciting certain forms of responses for which the original probability is very low or zero. Indeed, social imitation may hasten or short-cut the acquisition of new behaviors without the necessity of reinforcing successive approximations as suggested by Skinner (1953).

Thus subjects given an opportunity to observe aggressive models later reproduced a good deal of physical and verbal aggression (as well as nonaggressive responses) substantially identical with that of the model. In contrast, subjects who were exposed to nonaggressive models and those who had no previous exposure to any models only rarely performed such responses.

To the extent that observation of adult models displaying aggression communicates permissiveness for aggressive behavior, such exposure may serve to weaken inhibitory responses and thereby to increase the probability of aggressive reactions to subsequent frustrations. The fact, however, that subjects expressed their aggression in ways that clearly resembled the novel patterns exhibited by the models provides striking evidence for the occurrence of learning by imitation.

In the procedure employed by Miller and Dollard (1941) for establishing imitative behavior, adult or peer models performed discrimination responses following which they were consistently rewarded, and the subjects were similarly reinforced whenever they matched the leaders' choice responses. While these experiments have been widely accepted as demonstrations of learning by means of imitation, in fact, they simply involve a special case of discrimination learning in which the behavior of others serves as discriminative stimuli for responses that are already part of the subject's repertoire. Auditory or visual environmental cues could easily have been substituted for the social stimuli to facilitate the discrimination learning. In contrast, the process of imitation studied in the present experiment differed in several important respects from the one investigated by Miller and Dollard in that subjects learned to combine fractional responses into relatively complex novel patterns solely by observing the performance of social models without any opportunity to perform the models' behavior in the exposure setting and without any reinforcers delivered either to the models or to the observers.

An adequate theory of the mechanisms underlying imitative learning is lacking. The explanations that have been offered (Logan, Olmsted, Rosner, Schwartz, and Stevens, 1955; Maccoby, 1959) assume that the imitator performs the model's responses covertly. If it can be assumed additionally that rewards and punishments are self-administered in conjunction with the covert responses, the process of imitative learning could be accounted for in terms of the same principles that govern instrumental trial-and-error learning. In the early stages of the developmental process, however, the range of component responses in the organism's repertoire is probably increased through a process of classical conditioning (Bandura and Huston, 1961; Mowrer, 1950).

The data provide some evidence that the male model influenced the subjects' behavior outside the exposure setting to a greater extent than was true for the female model. In the analyses of the Sex × Model interactions, for example, only the comparisons involving the male model yielded significant differences. Similarly, subjects exposed to the nonaggressive male model performed less aggressive behavior than the controls, whereas comparisons involving the female model were consistently nonsignificant.

In a study of learning by imitation, Rosenblith (1959) has likewise found male experimenters more effective than females in influencing childrens' behavior. Rosenblith advanced the tentative explanation that the school setting may involve some social deprivation in respect to adult males which, in turn, enhances the male's reward value.

The trends in the data yielded by the present study suggest an alternative explanation. In the case of a highly masculine-typed behavior such as physical aggression, there is a tendency for both male and female subjects to imitate the male model to a greater degree than the female model. On the other hand, in the case of verbal aggression, which is less clearly sex linked, the greatest amount of imitation occurs in relation to the same-sex model. These trends together with the finding that boys in relation to girls are in general more imitative of physical aggression but do not differ in imitation of verbal aggression, suggest that subjects may be differentially affected by the sex of the model but that predictions must take into account the degree to which the behavior in question is sex-typed.

The preceding discussion has assumed that maleness-femaleness rather than some other personal characteristics of the particular models involved, is the significant variable — an assumption that cannot be tested directly with the data at hand. It was clearly evident, however, particularly from boys' spontaneous remarks about the display of aggression by the female model, that some subjects at least were responding in terms of a sex discrimination and their prior learning about what is sex appropriate behavior (e.g., "Who is that lady. That's not the way for a lady to behave. Ladies are supposed to act like ladies . . ." "You should have seen what that girl did in there. She was just acting like a man. I never saw a girl act like that before. She was punching and fighting but no swearing."). Aggression by the male model, on the other hand, was more likely to be seen as appropriate and approved by both the boys ("Al's a good socker, he beat up Bobo. I want to sock like Al.") and the girls ("That man is a strong fighter, he punched and punched and he could hit Bobo right down to the floor and if Bobo got up he said, 'Punch your nose.' He's a good fighter like Daddy.").

The finding that subjects exposed to the quiet models were more inhibited and unresponsive than subjects in the aggressive condition, together with the obtained difference on the aggression measures, suggests the exposure to inhibited models not only decreases the probability of occurrence of aggressive behavior but also generally restricts the range of behavior emitted by the subjects.

"Identification with aggressor" (Freud, 1946) or "defensive identification" (Mowrer, 1950), whereby a person presumably transforms himself from object to agent of aggression by adopting the attributes of an aggressive threatening model so as to allay anxiety, is widely accepted as an explanation of the imitative learning of aggression.

The development of aggressive modes of response by children of aggressively punitive adults, however, may simply reflect object displacement without involving any such mechanism of defensive identification. In studies of child training antecedents of aggressively antisocial adolescents (Bandura and Walters, 1959) and of young hyperaggressive boys (Bandura, 1960), the parents were found to be nonpermissive and punitive of aggression directed toward themselves. On the other hand, they actively encouraged and reinforced their sons' aggression toward persons outside the home. This pattern of differential reinforcement of aggressive behavior served to inhibit the boys' aggression toward the original instigators and fostered the displacement of aggression toward objects and situations eliciting much weaker inhibitory responses.

Moreover, the findings from an earlier study (Bandura and Huston, 1961), in which children imitated to an equal degree aggression exhibited by a nurturant and a nonnurturant model, together with the results of the present experiment in which subjects readily imitated aggressive models who were more or less neutral figures suggest that mere observation of aggression, regardless of the quality of the model-subject relationship, is a sufficient condition for producing imitative aggression in children. A comparative study of the subjects' imitation of aggressive models who are feared, who are linked and esteemed, or who are essentially neutral figures would throw some light on whether or not a more parsimonious theory than the one involved in "identification with the aggressor" can explain the modeling process.

SUMMARY

Twenty-four preschool children were assigned to each of three conditions. One experimental group observed aggressive adult models; a second observed inhibited nonaggressive models; while subjects in a control groups had no prior exposure to the models. Half the subjects in the experimental conditions observed same-sex models and half viewed models of the opposite sex. Subjects were then tested for the amount of imitative as well as nonimitative aggression performed in a new situation in the absence of the models.

Comparison of the subjects' behavior in the generalization situation revealed that subjects exposed to aggressive models reproduced a good deal of aggression resembling that of the models, and that their mean scores differed markedly from those of subjects in the nonaggressive and control groups. Subjects in the aggressive condition also exhibited significantly more partially imitative and nonimitative aggressive behavior and were generally less inhibited in their behavior than subjects in the nonaggressive condition.

Imitation was found to be differentially influenced by the sex of the model with boys showing more aggression than girls following exposure to the male model, the difference being particularly marked on highly masculine-typed behavior.

Subjects who observed the nonaggressive models, especially the subdued male model, were generally less aggressive than their controls.

The implications of the findings based on this experiment and related studies for the psychoanalytic theory of identification with the aggressor were discussed.

References

BANDURA, A. Relationship of family patterns to child behavior disorders. Progress Report, 1960, Stanford University, Project No. M-1734, United States Public Health Service.

BANDURA, A., AND HUSTON, ALETHA C. Identification as a process of incidental learning. *J. abnorm. soc. Psychol.*, 1961, **63**, 311–318.

BANDURA, A., AND WALTERS, R. H. *Adolescent aggression.* New York: Ronald, 1959.

BLAKE, R. R. The other person in the situation. In R. Tagiuri and L. Petrullo (eds.), *Person perception and interpersonal behavior.* Stanford, Calif: Stanford Univer. Press, 1958. Pp. 229–242.

FAULS, LYDIA B., AND SMITH, W. D. Sex-role learning of five-year olds. *J. genet. Psychol.*, 1956, **89**, 105–117.

FREUD, ANNA. *The ego and the mechanisms of defense.* New York: International Univer. Press, 1946.

GROSSER, D., POLANSKY, N., AND LIPPITT, R. A laboratory study of behavior contagion. *Hum. Relat.*, 1951, **4**, 115–142.

LINDQUIST. E. F. *Design and analysis of experiments.* Boston: Houghton Mifflin, 1956.

LOGAN, F., OLMSTED, O. L., ROSNER, B. S., SCHWARTZ, R. D., AND STEVENS, C. M. *Behavior theory and social science.* New Haven: Yale Univer. Press, 1955.

MACCOBY, ELEANOR E. Role-taking in childhood and its consequences for social learning. *Child Develpm.,* 1959, **30,** 239–252.

MILLER, N. E., AND DOLLARD, J. *Social learning and imitation.* New Haven: Yale Univer Press, 1941.

MOWRER, O. H. Identification: A link between learning theory and psychotherapy. In O. H. Mowrer (ed.), *Learning theory and personality dynamics.* New York: Ronald, 1950. Pp. 69–94.

ROSENBAUM, M. E., AND DECHARMS, R. Direct and vicarious reduction of hostility. *J. abnorm. soc. Psychol.,* 1960, **60,** 105–111.

ROSENBLITH, JUDY F. Learning by imitation in kindergarten children. *Child Develpm.,* 1959, **30,** 69–80.

SCHACHTER, S., AND HALL, R. Group-derived restraints and audience persuasion. *Hum. Relat.,* 1952, **5,** 397–406.

SKINNER, B. F. *Science and human behavior.* New York: Macmillan, 1953.

18

Some Immediate Effects of Televised Violence on Children's Behavior

Robert M. Liebert and Robert A. Baron

The hypothesis that exposure to televised violence would increase the willingness of children to hurt another child was investigated. Boys and girls of two age groups (5–6 and 8–9 years) first viewed excerpts from actual television programs depicting either aggressive or nonaggressive scenes, and were then provided with an opportunity to aggress against a peer. All subjects were subsequently placed in a free play situation and the frequency of their aggressive responses observed. Results indicated that children exposed to the aggressive program engaged in longer attacks against an ostensible child victim than subjects exposed to the nonaggressive program. The aggressive program also elicited a higher level of aggressive play than the nonaggressive one, particularly among the younger boys.

In his review of the social and scientific issues surrounding the portrayal of violence in the mass media, Larsen (1968) noted that we may begin with two facts: "(1) Mass media content is heavily saturated with violence, and (2) people are spending more and more time in exposure to such content [p. 115]." This state of affairs has been used by both laymen and professionals as the basis for appeals to modify the entertainment fare to which viewers, particularly children and adolescents, are exposed (Merriam, 1964; Walters, 1966; Walters and Thomas, 1963; Wertham, 1966). Other writers, however, have argued that the kind of violence found on television or in

Reprinted with permission from the authors and copyrighted as part of *Developmental Psychology*, Vol. 6, No. 3, 1972. American Psychological Association.

This study was supported, in part, by National Institute of Mental Health Contract HSM–42–70–38 and was conducted while both authors were affiliated with the Fels Research Institute. Grateful acknowledgement is due to Robert Devine, Joan Kleban, Diane E. Liebert, Carol Lyons, Charyl Russell, and Sharon Swenson for their many contributions. The contributions of the co-authors to the project were approximately equal.

movies does not necessarily influence observers' "real-life" social behavior (Halloran, 1964; Klapper, 1968). A few have even characterized the portrayal of violence as potentially preventing the overt expression of aggression, at least under some circumstances (Feshbach, 1961; Feshbach and Singer, 1971).

In view of the controversy, it is hardly surprising that recent years have seen a substantial increase in the number of experimental studies directed to this issue. An effort has been made to determine whether children will learn and/or be disinhibited in their performance of aggressive acts as a function of exposure to symbolic aggressive models (e.g., in cartoons, movies, stories, and simulated television programs). This research has indicated consistently that children may indeed *acquire,* from even a very brief period of observation, certain motoric and verbal behaviors which are associated with aggression in life situations. More specifically, it has been repeatedly shown that after viewing a film which depicts novel forms of hitting, kicking, and verbal abuse, children can, when asked to do so, demonstrate this learning by reproducing these previously unfamiliar behaviors with a remarkable degree of fidelity (Bandura, 1965; Hicks, 1965). Taken together with the large body of research on the observational learning of other behaviors (Flanders, 1968), the available evidence appears to leave little doubt that the learning of at least some aggressive responses can and does result from television or movie viewing.

Equally important, however, is the question of whether the observation of violence will influence children's performance of aggressive acts when they have *not* been specifically asked to show what they have seen or learned. Several experiments appear to provide evidence relating to this issue (Bandura, Ross, and Ross, 1961, 1963a, 1963b; Rosekrans and Hartup, 1967). In these studies, subjects have typically been exposed to live or filmed aggressive scenes, then placed in a free play situation with a variety of toys or other play materials. Results obtained with these procedures have shown repeatedly that the exposure of young children to aggression produces increments in such play activities as punching inflated plastic clowns, popping balloons, striking stuffed animals, and operating mechanized "hitting dolls."

It has been argued by critics (Klapper, 1968) that findings such as those reviewed above are not directly relevant to the question of whether exposure to televised aggression will increase children's willingness to engage in behavior which might actually harm another person. Since this criticism was advanced, a human victim has replaced the inanimate target in at least four more recent investigations (Hanratty, 1969; Hanratty, Liebert, Morris, and Fernandez, 1969; Hanratty, O'Neal, and Sulzer, 1972; Savitsky, Rogers, Izard, and Liebert, 1971). These later studies have demonstrated clearly that exposure to the behavior of filmed aggressive models may lead young children to directly imitate aggression against a human, as well as a "toy," victim.

Despite the newer evidence, critics may still question whether exposure to the type of violence generally depicted on regularly broadcast television shows will produce similar effects. Likewise, it is important to consider the possible *disinhibitory* effects (cf. Lovaas, 1961; Siegel, 1956) rather than only the direct *imitative* effects of observing aggressive models. Although such effects have previously been observed with adult subjects and violent scenes taken from motion pictures (e.g., Berkowitz, 1965; Berkowitz and Rawlings, 1963; Walters and Thomas, 1963), in no previous investigation known to the authors has the influence of televised violence on interpersonal aggression been examined for young children. It was with these latter questions that the present research was primarily concerned. We sought to determine whether exposure to violent scenes taken directly from nationally telecast programs increases the willingness of young children to engage in aggressive acts directed toward another child.

METHOD

Participants

Population sampled. The sample was drawn both from Yellow Springs, Ohio, a small college town, and from a larger and more conservative neighboring community, Xenia. The participants were brought to Fels Research Institute in Yellow Springs by one of their parents, in response to a newspaper advertisement and/or a letter distributed in local public elementary schools asking for volunteers to participate in a study of the effects of television on children. To assure that no potential participants were turned away because of scheduling inconveniences, parents were invited to select their own appointment times (including evenings or weekends), and transportation was offered to those who could not provide it for themselves.

Subjects. The subjects were 136 children, 68 boys and 68 girls. Sixty-five of the participants were 5 or 6 years of age at the time of the study; the remaining 71 subjects were 8 or 9 years of age. Within each age group and sex the children were assigned randomly to the treatment conditions. Approximately 20 percent of the children in this study were black; virtually all of the remainder were white. The economic backgrounds from which these participants came was widely varied. Although economic characteristics were not used as a basis for assignment to treatments, inspection suggested that the procedure of random assignment had adequately distributed them among the experimental groups.

Experimental personnel. One of the investigators greeted the parent and child at the outset, served as the interviewer, and obtained informed parental consent for the child's participation. A 28-year-old white female served as experimenter for all the children, and two other adult females served as unseen observers throughout the experiment.

Design

A $2 \times 2 \times 2$ factorial design was employed. The three factors were sex, age (5–6 or 8–9 years old), and treatment (observation of aggressive or nonaggressive television sequences).

Procedure

Introduction to the situation. Upon the arrival of parent and child at the institute, the child was escorted to a waiting room containing nonaggressive magazines and other play materials while the parent was interviewed in a separate room. During the interview, the nature of the experiment was disclosed to the parent, questions were invited and answered, and a written consent to the child's participation was obtained.[1]

Experimental and control treatment. After the interview, but without permitting the parent and the child to interact, the experimenter escorted each subject individually to a second waiting room containing children's furniture and a television video-tape monitor. The television was then turned on by the experimenter, who suggested that the child watch for a few minutes until she was ready for him. The experimenter left the child to watch television alone for approximately 6½ minutes; the subjects were in fact continuously observed through a concealed camera and video monitor. For all groups, the first 120 seconds of viewing consisted of two 1-minute commercials video-taped during early 1970. The first of these depicted the effectiveness of a certain paper towel, and the second advertised a humorous movie (rated G). The commercials were selected for their humor and attention-getting characteristics.

Thereafter, children in the experimental group observed the first 3½ minutes of a program from a popular television series, "The Untouchables."

---

[1]Since no specific information could be provided in public announcements or over the telephone, it appeared necessary to have parents accompany their children to the institute in order to assure that no child participated without the informed consent of his parents. In order to defray the costs of transportation, baby sitters for siblings who remained at home, and the like, and to eliminate economic biases which might otherwise have appeared in the sample, a $10 stipend was given the parent of each participant. No parent who appeared for the interview declined to allow his or her child to participate.

The sequence, which preserved a simple story line, contained a chase, two fist-fighting scenes, two shootings, and a knifing. In contrast, children in the control group viewed a highly active 3½-minute video-taped sports sequence in which athletes competed in hurdle races, high jumps, and the like. For all subjects, the final 60 seconds of the program contained a commercial for automobile tires. Before the end of this last commercial, the experimenter reentered the room and announced that she was ready to begin.

Assessment of willingness to hurt another child. The subject was next escorted by the experimenter from the television room to a second room and seated at a response box apparatus modeled after the one employed by Mallick and McCandless (1966). The gray metal response box, which measured approximately 17 × 6 inches, displayed a red button on the left, a green button on the right, and a white light centered above these two manipulanda. The word "hurt" appeared beneath the red button, while the word "help" appeared beneath the green button. Several plastic wires led from the response box to a vent in the wall. The experimenter explained to the subject that these wires were connected to a game in an adjacent room and that "one of the other children is in the next room right now and will start to play the game in just a minute." She further explained that the game required the player in the other room to turn a handle and that the white light would come on each time the other child in the next room started to turn the handle, thus activating the red and green buttons.

The experimenter continued:

> When this white light comes on, you have to push one of these two buttons. If you push this green button, that will make the handle next door easier to turn and will help the child to win the game. If you push this red button, that will make the handle next door feel hot. That will hurt the child, and he will have to let go of the handle. Remember, this is the *help* button, and this is the *hurt* botton [indicating]. See, it says *help* and *hurt*. . . . You have to push one of these two buttons each time the light goes on, but you can push whichever one you want to. You can always push the same button or you can change from one button to the other whenever you want to, but just remember, each time the light goes on, you can push only one. So if you push this green button then you help the other child and if you push this red button then you hurt the other child. Now if you push this green button for *just a second*, then you *help the other child just a little*, and if you push this red button down for *just a second*, then you *hurt the other child just a little*. But if you push this green button down a little longer, then you help the other child a little more, and if you push this red button down a little longer, then you hurt the other child a little more. *The longer you push the green button, the more you help the other child* and *the longer you push the red button, the more you hurt the other child.*

This explanation, with slightly varied wording was repeated a second time if the child did not indicate comprehension of the instructions. After being assured that the subject understood the task, the experimenter left the room.[2]

Although all the subjects were led to believe that other children were participating, there was, in fact, no other child; the entire procedure was controlled in the next room so as to produce 20 trials, with an intertrial interval of approximately 15 seconds. Each child's response to each trial (appearance of the white light) and the duration of the response, recorded to the hundredth of a second, was automatically registered. When the subject had completed 20 trials, the experimenter reentered the room and announced that the game was over.

Assessment of aggressive play. The influence of televised violence on the children's subsequent play activities was also explored, although this issue was of secondary interest in the present research (the study being primarily concerned with interpersonal aggression rather than aggression aimed at inanimate objects). After completing the button-pushing task, the child was escorted to a third room (designated the "play room") across the hallway. The room contained two large tables, on each of which appeared three attractive nonaggressive toys (e.g., a slinky, a cookset, a space station) and one aggressive toy (a gun or a knife). Two inflated plastic dolls, 36 inches and 42 inches in height, also stood in the room. The child was told that he would be left alone for a few minutes and that he could play freely with any of the toys.

All the children were observed through a one-way vision mirror, and their aggressive behavior was recorded using a time-sampling procedure. One point was scored for the occurrence of each of three predetermined categories of aggressive play (playing with the knife, playing with the gun, assaulting either of the dolls) during the first 10 seconds of each of ten $1/2$-minute periods. In order to assess interobserver reliability for this measure, 10 subjects were observed independently by the two observers. Their agreement using the scoring procedures was virtually perfect ($r = .99$).

At the end of the play period, the experimenter reentered the room and asked the child to recall both the television program which he had seen and

---

[2]Nine children, all in the 5–6-year-old age group, were terminated prior to the collection of data because they refused to remain alone, cried, or left the experimental situation. Twenty-three other children participated in the entire experiment but were not included in the sample. Of these, 14 (5 in the younger age group and 9 in the older group) did not understand or follow instructions for the response box; 7 (3 younger and 4 older children) played or explored the room instead of watching television. The data for the remaining 2 children were not recorded properly due to the technical difficulties. All potential participants brought to the institute by their parents who were not eliminated for the reasons listed above were included in the experimental sample.

the nature of the game he had played. (All children included in the analyses were able to recall correctly the operation of the red and green buttons and the essential content of the television programs to which they had been exposed.) The child was then escorted to the lounge where the parent was waiting, thanked for his or her participation, rewarded with a small prize, and asked not to discuss the experiment with his or her friends.

RESULTS

Willingness to Hurt Another Child

The single overall measure which appears to capture the greatest amount of information in this situation is the total duration in seconds of each subject's aggressive responses during the 20 trials. Since marked heterogeneity of variance was apparent among the groups on this measure, the overall $2 \times 2 \times 2$ analysis of variance was performed on square-root transformed scores (i.e., $x' = \sqrt{x} + \sqrt{x + 1}$, Winer, 1962). The means for all groups on this measure are presented in Table 18.1. The analysis itself reveals only one significant effect: that for treatment conditions ($F = 4.16, p < .05$). Children who had observed the aggressive program later showed reliably more willingness to engage in interpersonal aggression than those who had observed the neutral program.

Several supplementary analyses, which may serve to clarify the nature of this overall effect, were also computed. For example, a subject's total duration score may be viewed as the product of the number of times he aggresses and the average duration of each of these aggressive responses. Moreover, these two measures are only moderately, although reliably, related in the overall sample ($r = +.30, p < .05$). Analysis of variance for the average duration of the hurt responses reveals only a significant program effect that directly parallels the effects for total duration ($F = 3.95, p < .05$). The means

TABLE 18.1
Mean total duration (transformed) of
agressive responses in all groups

Program shown	5–6-year-olds		8–9-year-olds	
	Boys	Girls	Boys	Girls
Aggressive	9.65	8.98	12.50	8.53
N	15	18	20	17
Nonaggressive	6.86	6.50	8.50	6.27
N	15	17	18	16

TABLE 18.2
Mean average durations (total duration/number of
hurt responses) of aggressive responses in all groups

Program shown	5–6-year-olds		9–8-year-olds	
	Boys	Girls	Boys	Girls
Aggressive	3.42	2.64	5.18	3.07
Nonaggressive	2.55	2.09	2.07	1.57

Note: The number of subjects for each cell in this analysis is
the same as that shown in Table 18.1.

for all groups on this measure are presented in Table 18.2. In contrast, analysis of the of the frequency measure fails to show any significant effects, although the tendency for the younger children is in the same direction.

Helping Responses

One possible explanation of the higher total aggression scores shown by the aggressive program group is that these children were simply more aroused than their nonaggressive treatment counterparts. To check on this interpretation, an overall analysis of variance was performed on the total duration of the help responses, employing the same square-root transformation described above. Presumably, if general arousal accounted for the effects of the hurt measure, the aggressive program groups should also show larger help scores than the nonaggressive program groups. However, contrary to the general arousal hypothesis, the effect of the treatments on this measure was not significant; the overall F comparing the aggressive program subjects' prosocial responses with those of the nonaggressive program observers was only 1.17. The one effect of borderline significance which did appear in this analysis was a Program $\times$ Sex $\times$ Age interaction ($F = 3.91$, $p \cong .05$). As can be seen in Table 18.3, in which these data are presented, the interaction results from the very large helping responses shown by older girls who saw the aggressive program and the relatively large helping responses shown by younger girls who saw the nonaggressive one.

As a second check on the possibility that the longer durations in the aggressive program groups simply reflected a general arousal, a similar analysis was performed on the average duration scores of the help responses. In contrast to the comparable measure for aggressive responses, no significant differences for any of the main effects or interactions appeared on this measure (main effect for treatments, $F = 1.24$) although paralleling the total duration measure. The older girls who saw the aggressive program

TABLE 18.3
Mean total duration (transformed) of helping
responses in all groups

Program shown	5–6-year-olds		8–9-year-olds	
	Boys	Girls	Boys	Girls
Aggressive	10.81	11.66	11.32	19.97
Nonaggressive	10.76	14.12	11.59	10.69

Note: The number of subjects for each cell in this analysis is
the same as that shown in Table 18.1.

showed particularly long average durations. Finally, to show from a correlational approach that the overall help and hurt scores were not merely
alternate measures of the same phenomenon, the product-moment correlation between the two sets of scores was computed. The resulting r of $-.24$
reflects a weak but significant ($p < .05$, two-tailed) negative relationship.
Thus, overall, it appears clear that a specific disinhibition regarding *aggressive* behavior was produced by observing the televised aggression. This
cannot be explained as a general arousal effect.

Aggression in the Play Situation

The mean aggressive play scores for all subjects are presented in Table
18.4. A $2 \times 2 \times 2$ analysis of variance of these data revealed significant
main effects for treatment ($F = 8.01$, $df = 1/128$, $p < .01$) and sex ($F =
37.87$, $df = 1/128$, $p < .001$). In addition, the Treatment $\times$ Sex ($F = 4.11$,
$df = 1/128$, $p < .05$), Treatment $\times$ Age ($F = 4.28$, $df = 1/128$, $p < .05$), and
Treatment $\times$ Sex $\times$ Age ($F = 4.68$, $df = 1/128$, $p < .05$) interactions were all
significant. As is apparent from inspection of Table 18.4, these interactions
arose from the fact that, although children exposed to the aggressive program tended to show a higher level of aggressive play than children exposed
to the nonaggressive one in all simple comparisons, the effect was much
greater for the younger boys than for any of the remaining groups.

TABLE 18.4
Mean number of time-sampled aggressive
play responses in all groups

Program shown	5–6-year olds		8–9-year-olds	
	Boys	Girls	Boys	Girls
Aggressive	7.13	2.94	5.65	3.00
Nonaggressive	3.33	2.65	5.39	2.63

Note: The number of subjects for each cell in this analysis
is the same as that shown in Table 18.1.

DISCUSSION

The overall results of the present experiment provide relatively consistent evidence for the view that certain aspects of a child's willingness to aggress may be at least temporarily increased by merely witnessing aggressive television episodes. These findings confirm and extend many earlier reports regarding the effects of symbolically modeled aggression on the subsequent imitative aggressive behavior of young observers toward inanimate objects (e.g., Bandura, Ross, and Ross, 1963a; Hicks, 1965; Rosekrans and Hartup, 1967). Likewise, the present data are in accord with other studies which have shown disinhibition of both young children's aggressive play and older viewers' willingness to shock another person after observing filmed aggressive modeling. As in many earlier studies, subjects exposed to symbolic aggressive models regularly tended to behave more aggressively than control group subjects tested under identical circumstances. Further, the present results emerged despite the brevity of the aggressive sequences (less than 4 minutes), the absence of a strong prior instigation to aggression, the clear availability of an alternative helping response, and the use of nationally broadcast materials rather than specially prepared laboratory films.

The various measures employed, considered together, provide some clarification of the nature of the effects obtained in the overall analysis. The significant effect for the total duration measure appears to stem predominantly from the average duration of the subjects' aggressive responses. In fact, as seen in Table 18.2, the group means on this measure did not overlap; the *lowest* individual cell mean among those who observed the aggressive program was higher than the *highest* mean among those groups who observed the nonaggressive program.

It should also be recalled that the instructions given to all children emphasized that a brief depression of the hurt button would cause only minimal distress to the other child, while longer depressions would cause increasingly greater discomfort. This fact, coupled with the finding that the overall average duration of such responses was more than 75 percent longer in the aggressive program group than in the control group, suggests clearly that the primary effect of exposure to the aggressive program was that of reducing subjects' restraints against inflicting severe discomfort on the ostensible peer victim, that is, of increasing the *magnitude* of the hurting response. With the exception of the older girls, this effect was not paralleled by an increment in the corresponding measures of helping; thus it cannot be attributed to simple arousal effects.

It should be noted that the measure of aggressive play responses was obtained after all the subjects had been given an opportunity to help or hurt another child. Thus the observed effects might reflect an interaction between the programs and some aspect of the hurting/helping opportunity rather than the simple influence of the programs themselves. While the present data do not permit us to address the possibility of such interactions directly, it is clear that the obtained results are consistent with earlier studies in which other types of aggressive scenes were used and where there were no such intervening measures.

The present experiment was designed primarily to determine whether children's willingness to engage in interpersonal aggression would be affected by the viewing of violent televised material. Within the context of the experimental situation and dependent measures employed, it appeared that this was indeed the case. However, it is clear that the occurrence and magnitude of such effects will be influenced by a number of situational and personality variables. It is thus important to examine the antecedents and correlates of such reactions to violence in greater detail. In view of the fact that a child born today will, by the age of 18, have spent more of his life watching television than in any other single activity except sleep (Lesser, 1970), few problems seem more deserving of attention.

References

BANDURA, A. Influence of models' reinforcement contingencies on the acquisition of imitative responses. *Journal of Personality and Social Psychology,* 1965, **1,** 589–595.

BANDURA, A. ROSS, D., AND ROSS, S. A. Transmission of aggression through imitation of aggressive models. *Journal of Abnormal and Social Psychology,* 1961, **63,** 575–582.

BANDURA, A., ROSS, D., AND ROSS, S. A. Imitation of film-mediated aggressive models. *Journal of Abnormal and Social Psychology,* 1963, **66,** 3–11. (a)

BANDURA, A., ROSS, D., AND ROSS, S. A. Vicarious reinforcement and imitative learning. *Journal of Abnormal and Social Psychology,* 1963, **67,** 601–607. (b)

BERKOWITZ, L. Some aspects of observed aggression. *Journal of Personality and Social Psychology,* 1965, **2,** 359–369.

BERKOWITZ, L., AND RAWLINGS, E. Effects of film violence on inhibitions against subsequent aggression. *Journal of Abnormal and Social Psychology,* 1963, **66,** 405–412.

FESHBACH, S. The stimulating versus cathartic effects of a vicarious aggressive activity. *Journal of Abnormal and Social Psychology,* 1961, **63,** 381–385.

FESHBACH, S., AND SINGER, R. D. *Television and aggression.* San Francisco: Jossey-Bass, 1971.

FLANDERS, J. P. A review of research on imitative behavior. *Psychological Bulletin,* 1968, **69,** 316–337.

HALLORAN, J. D. Television and violence. *The Twentieth Century,* 1964, **174,** 61–72.

HANRATTY, M. A., LIEBERT, R. M., MORRIS, L. W., AND FERNANDEZ, L. E. Imitation of film-mediated aggression against live and inanimate victims. *Proceedings of the 77th Annual Convention of the American Psychological Association,* 1969, **4,** 457–458. (Summary)

HANRATTY, M. A., O'NEAL, E., AND SULZER, J. L. The effect of frustration upon imitation of aggression. *Journal of Personality and Social Psychology,* 1972, **21,** 30–34.

HICKS, D. J. Imitation and retention of film-mediated aggressive peer and adult models. *Journal of Personality and Social Psychology,* 1965, **2,** 97–100.

KLAPPER, J. T. The impact of viewing "aggression": Studies and problems of extrapolation. In O. N. Larsen (ed.), *Violence and the mass media.* New York: Harper and Row, 1968.

LARSEN, O. N. *Violence and the mass media.* New York: Harper and Row, 1968.

LESSER, G. S. Designing a program for broadcast television. In F. F. Korten, S. W. Cook, and J. I. Lacey (eds.), *Psychology and the problems of society.* Washington, D.C.: American Psychological Association, 1970.

LOVAAS, O. I. Effect of exposure to symbolic aggression on aggressive behavior. *Child Development,* 1961, **32,** 37–44.

MALLICK, S. K., AND MCCANDLESS, B. R. A study of catharsis of aggression. *Journal of Personality and Social Psychology,* 1966, **4,** 591–596.

MERRIAM, E. We're teaching our children that violence is fun. *The Ladies' Home Journal,* 1964, **52,** 44, 49, 52.

ROSEKRANS, M. A., AND HARTUP, W. W. Imitative influences of consistent and inconsistent responses consequences to a model on aggressive behavior in children. *Journal of Personality and Social Psychology,* 1967, **7,** 429–434.

SAVITSKY, J. C., ROGERS, R. W., IZARD, C. E., AND LIEBERT, R. M. The role of frustration and anger in the imitation of filmed aggression against a human victim. *Psychological Reports,* 1971, **29,** 807–810.

SIEGEL, A. E. Film-mediated fantasy aggression and strength of aggressive drive. *Child Development,* 1956, **27,** 365–378.

WALTERS, R. H. Implications of laboratory studies for the control and regulation of violence. *The Annals of the American Academy of Political and Social Science,* 1966, **364,** 60–72.

WALTERS, R. H., AND THOMAS, E. L. Enhancement of punitiveness by visual and audiovisual displays. *Canadian Journal of Psychology,* 1963, **16,** 244–255.

WERTHAM, F. Is T.V. hardening us to the war in Vietnam? *New York Times,* December 4, 1966.

WINER, B. J. *Statistical principles in experimental design.* New York: McGraw-Hill, 1962.

19

Retaliation as a Means of Restoring Equity

Ellen Berscheid, David Boye, and Elaine Walster

Previous research has shown that when a harm-doer is faced with the suffering of his victim he will attempt to eliminate the inequity he has created by compensating the victim. When this is not possible, he will restore psychological equity by justifying the victim's suffering. It was suggested that equity can be restored by still another method: the victim can "get even" with the harm-doer by retaliating against him. It was proposed that when compensation is impossible, a harm-doer will derogate a victim who is powerless to retaliate but will not derogate a victim from who he anticipates retaliation. *S*s who had not harmed the victim were not expected to respond in the same way. This hypothesis was confirmed.

Some recent interest in social psychology has focused on the reactions of a harm-doer to his deed. It is known that if a harm-doer is given the opportunity, he will often exert considerable effort to compensate his victim (i.e., Berkowitz, 1962; Berscheid and Walster, 1967; Berscheid, Walster, and Barclay, in preparation; Freedman, Wallington, and Bless, 1967; Walster and Prestholdt, 1966). Recent evidence, however, indicates that certain conditions may attenuate the harm-doer's tendency to compensate his victim. For example, if the perpetrator is publicly committed to the harmful act, he tends to avoid compensating his victim (Walster and Prestholdt, 1966). If available compensation cannot completely restore equity, the perpetrator will tend not to compensate (Berscheid and Walster, 1967). And, finally, if a

Reprinted with permission from the authors and *The Journal of Personality and Social Psychology*, Vol. 10, No. 4, 1968. Copyright 1968 by the American Psychological Association.

This study was supported by National Science Foundation Grants GS-1577 and GS-1588 to Ellen Berscheid and Elaine Walster and by the Student Activities Bureau, University of Minnesota. The authors would also like to express their appreciation to Robert Fisher, who served as the experimental assistant.

delay is enforced before the perpetrator is allowed to compensate, his reluctance to make a less than totally adequate compensation increases (Berscheid et al., preparation).

Laboratory experiments indicate that if the harm-doer doesn't compensate his victim, either because proper channels are not open (Davidson, 1964; Davis and Jones, 1956; Glass, 1964) or because he chooses to withhold compensation (Walster and Prestholdt, 1966), he will then distort his perceptions in such a way as to justify his actions. Usually one justifies the harm he has done by derogating his victim, but one may also justify his behavior in other ways. He may minimize the harm he has done or he may deny responsibility for the harm (Brock and Buss, 1962, 1964; Sykes and Matza, 1957). It appears that the harm-doer will attempt to eliminate, at least in his own mind, the inequity that he has created, either by compensating his victim or by justifying his act.

Removal of inequity through justification rather than compensation is potentially dangerous. Not only does the harm-doer end up with a distorted and unreal assessment of his actions, but he may commit further acts based on these distortions (Berscheid, Boye, and Darley, 1967). When the harm-doer's response to his act is justification, the victim is likely to be left in sad straits. Not only has he been hurt, but as a result of justification of the harmful act the probability that the harm-doer will hurt him again has increased.

Obviously, from the victim's point of view, it is desirable to have equity restored before the perpetrator is forced to justify what he has done. Unfortunately for the victim, compensation — the most desirable and constructive means of equity restoration — is entirely under the control of the harm-doer. And, it is often the case that the harm-doer is either unwilling or unable to compensate. Under such circumstances, is there a means of restoring equity which is under the victim's control? The phrase "getting even" suggests that, in our culture at least, there may be. It is possible that the victim's immediate retaliation against the harm-doer may "even up" the inequity of the harm-doing situation and thus arrest the harm-doer's tendency to justify his harmful act.

The idea that retaliation restores equity to an inequitable relationship is a common one: retaliation far antedates compensation as a technique for establishing just relations between individuals. According to legal theorists (See Fry et al., 1959; Schafer, 1960), Hammurabi's Code (approximately 2250 B.C.) relied entirely on retaliation to establish justice. Not until Republican Roman Law (450–449 B.C.) was compensation conceived as a suitable means for restoring equitable relations between individuals.

At the present time, Negro militants often stress the importance of actual retaliation and the fear of anticipated retaliation, in producing equitable relationships between racial groups. Some militants have argued that widespread actual violence is necessary to restore the Negro to full citizenship.

They talk of the "white devil," his guilt and subsequent denial of racial injustices, and the equity-establishing potential of actual violence. Other spokesmen for this position, for example James Baldwin, have argued that it is important for individuals to *anticipate* retaliation for their wrong doing. Baldwin (1963) stated:

> Neither civilized reason nor Christian love would cause any of those people to treat you as they presumably wanted to be treated; only the *fear* of your power to retaliate would cause them to do that, or to seem to do it, which was (and is) good enough [p. 35].

The experiment reported in this paper was designed to investigate the effect that the *anticipation* of the victim's retaliation has on a harm-doer's tendency to justify his act through derogation of the victim. It was hypothesized that if the harm-doer believes that his victim will retaliate against him in kind, he will expect that his relationship with the victim will shortly be an equitable one and, thus, the harm-doer will have no need to restore psychological equity to the relationship by derogating the victim.

Overview

In order to test this hypothesis, it was necessary that half of the subjects harm another individual (by administering electric shock) and half simply observe the harm-doing. Secondly, it was necessary to lead half of the harm-doers and half of the observers to expect that the victim would be able to shock them at the conclusion of the experiment, and to lead the remainder to believe that he would be shocking someone else.

In accord with previous studies, harm-doers who did not expect retaliation were expected to derogate the victim. Harm-doers who expected retaliation were not expected to derogate the victim. Subjects who did not themselves harm the victim served as a control group. It was not anticipated that control subjects would feel more positively toward someone who would soon shock them than toward someone who would not. In brief, subjects' responsibility for harm-doing and subjects' expectations of being punished by the victim were expected to interact in affecting the subjects' liking for the victim.

METHOD

Forty-eight male students from nine Minnesota high schools participated in the experiment. Subjects were paid $4 for their participation.

When the five boys (four subjects and one confederate) who were scheduled for each session arrived, the experimenter provided a rationale for the experiment. At length he explained the three "purposes" of the research: (*a*) to study the effects of stress of verbal performance; *b*) to try out the new research technique, designed to remove experimental bias, of having subjects run the experiment themselves; (*c*) to compare physiological and observational measures of stress. (Machines were said to provide the physiological measures; subjects were asked to provide the observational evaluations.) The experimenter elaborated on the importance of his research until he felt the subjects were interested and engrossed in it.

The experimenter then suggested that a "reader" (the victim) be chosen. Though selection of a reader was said to be random, in actuality the confederate was always chosen to read experimental material while being subjected to stress.

While the subjects watched and listened, the confederate was given his instructions. He was told that his task was to read, as clearly and distinctly as possible, ten paragraphs from an article. He was instructed to pause at the beginning of each paragraph so that one of the subjects (the "trainer") could induce stress by administering one of five levels of electric shock to him. The others would observe him through a one-way mirror and would evaluate his reading performance. The confederate was told that he would never know which of the four boys was administering the electric shock.

All subjects, with the exception of the confederate, were then led into an adjoining room. This room contained a four-cubicle conformity apparatus with opaque screens between each cubicle. This arrangement made it impossible for the boys to know what the other boys were doing. The apparatus faced a one-way mirror, through which one could look into the room where the confederate was seated. Since the subjects' room was dimly lit, it was clear that although the subjects could clearly see the confederate, he could not see them.

Each cubicle was equipped with a five-choice response panel. The five levers were labeled "moderate," "somewhat strong " "strong," "very strong," and "severe." With this equipment it was possible for any of the harm-doers to choose any of five shock levels, for the experimenter to monitor these choices from a control room to make sure the subjects were administering the chosen shock levels, and for the experimenter to give feedback to control subjects as to the choice the harm-doer had made. Subjects were also provided with headphones over which they could hear either the experimenter or the victim.

The subjects then observed the confederate being seated in the adjoining room. The victim's room contained an array of electrical devices, including an Esterline Ampmeter, a large GSR indicator, several shock generators, timers, and so on. As soon as the victim was seated, an experimental assistant dressed in a white coat strapped some "physiological measuring devices" to the victim's head and arms. A microphone was put around his neck. A headpiece with a number of wires and electrodes dangling from it and with a small light bulb protruding from the front was attached to his head. (The light bulb lit up when the victim was receiving electric shock.) After the equipment was attached, the experimental assistant checked the victim's heart rate and pulse, and obtained other physiological information.

The experimenter told the subjects that *one* of them would be randomly chosen as the "trainer" (the harm-doer). The trainer's task was to map out a schedule of ten shock intensities and then to deliver these shocks to the reader. While the victim was receiving shock, the subjects were to observe the level of shock the reader received (this level would be indicated on their control panels) and to observe its effect on his performance. No one (including the confederate) would know who had been the trainer and who had been observers.

Actually, *two* subjects, one on either end of the apparatus, were led to believe that they had been randomly chosen as the sole trainer. The two subjects in the center of the apparatus were led to believe that they were one of three observers. (Thus, one subject was run in each of the four experimental conditions during each experimental session.)

At this point, the experimenter went into an adjoining room where he remained for the rest of the experiment. Through their headphones, subjects then heard the experimenter instruct the harm-doer to map out a schedule of shocks. The experimenter emphasized that unless a wide variety of shocks was used it would be difficult to see much change in the reader's performance. Harm-doers were asked to write down the shocks that they would deliver and the order in which they would deliver them on a piece of paper.

After the harm-doers had devised their shock schedules, subjects were told that there would be a second session.[1] They were informed that in the second session the current reader would devise and administer the shock schedule, and one of the current subjects would be the reader. The reader during the second session was presumably also to be chosen by random processes. In actuality, one harm-doer and one observer were led to believe that they would be the second reader (and the second victim). The experimenter then indicated that the first session could begin.

It will be recalled that two subjects believed that they, and they alone, were administering shock to the reader. This posed some problems. It was inevitable that the harm-doers would administer their shocks at slightly

---

[1] The reader will note that at this point each subject knew whether he was the harm-doer or simply an observer. Subjects did not yet know, however, that there was a possibility that the victim would be able to shock them. The authors wanted all harm-doers to decide which shock levels to administer *before* they were exposed to the retaliation information, so that their choice of shock levels would not be affected by the retaliation manipulation.

different times, even though they were both administering them "when the victim paused for a paragraph." To forestall the suspicion that would have arisen had the victim responded at an inappropriate time to the harm-doer's shock, an explanation for any possible delay in response was provided. The experimenter explained that because of the electrical wiring it would take a moment for the shock to get to the reader. Everyone would know when the reader was being shocked, however, because the light bulb attached to the band on the reader's head would light up. During the shock trials, then, the experimenter would simply wait until both harm-doers had administered shock to the reader before lighting the bulb on the reader's head which indicated that the shock had finally arrived. The light also served a second purpose in that it gave the confederate the clue to respond as if he had received electric shock. When the bulb was lit, the confederate breathed heavily, moved around in an agitated way in his chair, and his reading appeared markedly disrupted.

Subjects could check on how much shock was being administered by looking at a light on their panel board which indicated the amount the victim was currently receiving. The particular shock magnitude indicated on a subject's panel was determined in the following way: Each observed was assigned as a partner to the harm-doer next to him. Whatever shock level the harm-doer administered to the confederate was flashed on the harm-doer's and the yoked observer's board immediately before the confederate's headlight flashed on. The stress procedure continued for ten trials.

At the end of the first session the experimenter reminded the subjects that one of them, the subject who had been randomly chosen previously, would be the second reader. Before that second session began, however, all subjects were asked to rate the first reader's performance. This rating questionnaire included eight questions, ostensibly designed to give the experimenter some idea of how the victim had responded to stress. Actually three of these questions constituted the dependent measure and were designed to determine how much subjects in various conditions liked the reader. Subjects were asked: "Was your impression of the speaker favorable or unfavorable?" "Did the speaker have a likable personality?" "From what you have seen of him so far, how much do you like the speaker personally?" Subjects could respond on an 18-point scale which varied from 0, indicating that the subject liked the confederate very much, to 17, indicating that the subject disliked him very much.

As is typically done in experiments dealing with the psychology of justification, the authors tried to block off all modes of justification save one — derogation (cf. Berscheid et al., 1968). They also attempted to make it easy for subjects to utilize the derogation mode of justification. The victim was made to appear overweight and unattractive; unlike the other boys, he was not at all friendly with the others while they waited together before the experiment; he appeared to be somewhat unintelligent when reading the paragraphs.

Despite these efforts, it was possible, of course, for subjects to use justifications other than derogation. To assess whether or not subjects were in fact engaging in other types of justification, several additional items were included on the questionnaire: (*a*) "How much discomfort did shock cause the speaker?" It is possible that the subjects could restore equity by minimizing the victim's suffering. The authors attempted to make this type of distortion difficult by labeling the degree of the victim's discomfort and having subjects actually observe his reactions. (*b*) "How important was the experiment?" It is probably easier to defend hurting another in the interest of an important scientific experiment than in connection with a trivial one. The authors attempted to make this type of distortion difficult by having the experimenter emphasize the experiment's importance in his introduction. (*c*) "Do you feel there is anything wrong with participating in experiments in which people are shocked?" Harm-doers could deny that they had done anything to feel guilty about. The authors attempted to make this type of distortion difficult by stressing in the preliminary instructions the subject's sole responsibility for his decision to harm the other and for his choice of the magnitude of shocks to be delivered, and by giving him repeated opportunities to leave during the experiment.[2]

Filler questions asked if the experiment had been conducted in a manner fair to the subject himself and how intelligent the speaker appeared to be. Immediately after all subjects had completed their questionnaires, the experimenter asked who was to be shocked next. All subjects in the retaliation conditions anticipated being the next reader. At this point subjects were debriefed.

RESULTS AND DISCUSSION

It was predicted that the subject's responsibility for harming the victim and his anticipation of being punished would interact in affecting liking for the victim: it was expected that a harm-doer would derogate his victim more when the victim was powerless to retaliate than when retaliation was likely; and that control subjects, who had done no harm, would not react to the anticipation of retaliation in the same way.

Since all four conditions were run in each of 11 different groups, analysis of the data required that each group be treated as one observation and the

---

[2]One group of four subjects was discarded from the analysis because one subject refused to continue shocking the speaker. (This group yielded results similar to the other 11 groups.)

TABLE 19.1
Liking for the confederate and other justification measures for subjects in the various conditions

| Condition | Derogation of victim[a] | Additional justifications[b] | | | Fairness of this experiment to you[c] |
		Minimization of suffering	Aggrandizement of project	Denial of wrongdoing	
Harm-doer – retaliation expected	6.1	2.1	11.8	11.2	13.09
Harm-doer – no retaliation expected	6.8	1.3	8.9	6.9	14.68
Observer – retaliation expected	7.3	2.1	11.9	10.6	8.73
Observer – no retaliation expected	6.1	3.6	11.4	8.9	13.82
F tests					
Harm-doer vs. observer	.79	1.59	3.24	.24	2.68
Retaliation vs. no retaliation	.26	.38	3.04	4.59	9.22*
Interaction	5.19*	4.39	.70	.45	1.67

[a]The higher the number, the less the subject likes the victim.
[b]The higher the number, the more the subject is justifying having harmed the victim (minimizing his aggrandizing the importance of the project, and denying that there is anything wrong with administering shock in an experiment).
[c]The higher the number, the fairer the subject feels the experiment was.
*$p < .05$, $df = 1/10$.

responses of each member of the group as a separate dependent variable. Thus, the design for the analysis is one cell with 11 observations and four dependent measures on each observation. To test whether various linear combinations of the four dependent measures were equal to 0, a multivariate analysis of variance was conducted. The particular linear combinations chosen for analysis were identical to those which would test hypotheses conventionally tested by main effects or interactions in univariate analysis of variance.[3]

Looking at the data (see Table 19.1), it can be seen that the hypothesis appears to be confirmed. When one has himself harmed the victim, he likes the victim more (or derogates him less) when he expects retaliation than when he does not. The relationship between retaliation and liking is reversed for control subjects: those who expect to be hurt by the victim in the future like him less than those who do not expect to be hurt. The predicted interaction is significant at the .05 level of confidence ($F = 5.19$, $df = 1/10$).

The reader will recall the authors attempted to maximize the probability that all subjects would use only the derogation mode of justification. It is possible, however, that subjects used other justification techniques despite efforts to block these other modes and to enhance the probability that the

---

[3]The authors would like to thank G. William Walster for his help in analyzing the data.

derogation mode be used. If the data revealed between-conditions differences in the use of justification techniques other than derogation, an alternative explanation of the results would be possible. It could be argued that retaliation, instead of eliminating the harm-doer's need to restore equity to his relationship through the use of a justification technique, may have had (for some unspecified reason) a different effect: anticipated retaliation may have made the harm-doer less likely to derogate the victim but more likely to restore equity by utilizing some other justification technique.

The data, however, provide little support for such an alternative. If the correct explanation for this data is that harm-doers who expect retaliation (H-R subjects) still experience dissonance but reduce it by use of some mode of justification other than derogation, one would expect H-R subjects to be especially predisposed to score high on these alternative modes when compared to control subjects. There is no evidence for this. In no case is a significant interaction secured for alternative measures of justification ($Fs = 4.39, .70$, and $.45, df = 1/10$).[4]

The additional justification data are puzzling in one respect: Presumably harm-doers who do not anticipate retaliation (H-NR subjects) should have a more inequitable relationship with the victim (and have more dissonance to reduce) than do other subjects. Since the authors attempted to make it easy for subjects to reduce dissonance by derogating the victim and difficult for them to justify their behavior by utilizing other distortions, one would expect H-NR subjects to derogate the victim more than do O-NR subjects (which they do) and to score at least as high on the additional justification measures as do O-NR subjects (which they do not). On all three of the additional justification measures H-NR subjects receive lower justification scores than do other subjects. However, H-NR subjects do not score significantly lower than do other subjects. The interaction Fs for the three additional justification measures are nonsignificant, regardless of whether they are examined singly or combined into a total index. However, the fact that H-NR subjects consistently tend to secure lower scores on these three measures is puzzling and decreases the confidence that all of the variance to be accounted for in this experiment can be explained.

Main Effects

The authors' hypothesis concerned the possible interaction of two variables: (*a*) whether or not the subject shocked the victim, and (*b*) whether or

---

[4]In the case of "Minimization of harm," which almost reaches significance, the interaction is not produced by the propensity of H-R subjects to justify the victim's suffering by minimizing it; H-R subjects estimate his suffering exactly as do the comparable observers (O-R subjects). The obtained interaction is due to the fact that, more than any other group, O-NR subjects estimate that the victim has suffered little.

not the subject expected to be shocked by the victim. In the previous section the data and the interaction *F*s which could confirm or disconfirm the hypothesis were considered. In addition to interacting with each other it is also possible that the two independent variables, in and of themselves, might have had a strong impact on the dependent variable. For example, one might expect that Anticipation of Punishment would have a strong impact on an individual's ratings. The subject who anticipates being shocked is probably frightened. (Since the victim does not know who shocked him, both the observer and the harm-doer who anticipated shock have equal reason to be afraid, and so their possible reactions will be considered jointly.) Fear, regardless of whether or not the anticipated punishment will restore equity, might affect a subject's ratings.

Two different types of reactions sound possible:

1. *Self-deceptive reactions.* The subject who anticipates being shocked might wish to assure himself (at least until the shock comes) that he has little to fear. Several distortions would help to maintain an optimistic outlook: He could convince himself that the victim is a good person, who has no reason to be angry, and who will shock him only mildly. Such a desire to perceive coming events as pleasant could produce main effects of the following type: H-R and O-R subjects may rate the victim more highly, his suffering as less intense, the project as more important, and deny that they have done anything wrong, to a greater extent than do H-NR and O-NR subjects.

2. *Angry, resentful reactions.* One might make a plausible argument for predicting a main effect in the opposite direction. The frightening discovery that they are going to be shocked might make subjects angry and resentful. H-R and O-R subjects thus may react aggressively to everyone and everything they are asked to rate. If anger does breed aggressive reactions, one might expect the following main effects: H-R and O-R subjects might dislike the victim for what he is about to do to them and might express hostility toward the experiment by rating it as worthless and unfair. In addition, once they realize that they will be shocked, the victim's experiences might become more salient, and the amount of discomfort caused by the shocks might thus be magnified.

Examining the data on main effects: In no case did harm-doing have a significant effect on the subjects' ratings. Anticipation of punishment had one effect that approached significance and one significant effect on subjects' ratings: (*a*) Subjects who anticipated punishment tended to deny that they had done wrong to a greater extent than did subjects who did not expect shock. The difference was not significant, however; (*b*) subjects who were about to be punished felt the experimental procedure which had singled them out for shock was more unfair to them than did subjects who had escaped punishment. From an examination of the means, it appears that it is the O-R subjects who felt the experiment was most unjust. The O-R subjects rate the experiment as much less fair than do O-NR subjects ($D_M = 5.09$). H-R subjects rate the procedure as only slightly less fair than do H-NR subjects. ($D_M = 1.59$.) The O-R subjects are not significantly more critical of the experiment than are other subjects, however. The interaction F is definitely nonsignificant.

References

BALDWIN, J. *The fire next time.* New York: Dial, 1963.

BERKOWITZ, L. *Aggression: A social psychological analysis.* New York: McGraw-Hill, 1962.

BERSCHEID, E., BOYE, D., AND DARLEY, J. M. Effects of forced association on voluntary choice to associate. *Journal of Personality and Social Psychology,* 1968, **7,** 13–19.

BERSCHEID, E., AND WALSTER, E. When does a harm-doer compensate a victim? *Journal of Personality and Social Psychology,* 1967, **6,** 435–441.

BROCK, T. C., AND BUSS, A. H. Dissonance, aggression, and evaluation of pain. *Journal of Abnormal and Social Psychology,* 1962, **65,** 192–202.

BROCK, T. C., AND BUSS, A. H. Effects of justification for aggression in communication with the victim on postaggression dissonance. *Journal of Abnormal and Social Psychology,* 1964, **68,** 403–412.

DAVIDSON, J. Cognitive familiarity and dissonance reduction. In L. Festinger (ed.), *Conflict, decision, and dissonance.* Stanford, Calif.: Stanford University Press, 1964.

DAVIS, K. E., AND JONES, E. E. Changes in interpersonal perception as a means of reducing cognitive dissonance. *Journal of Abnormal and Social Psychology,* 1960, **61,** 402–410.

FREEDMAN, J. L., WALLINGTON, S. A., AND BLESS, E. Compliance without pressure: The effect of guilt. *Journal of Personality and Social Psychology,* 1967, **7,** 117–124.

FRY, M., ET AL. Compensation for victims of criminal violence: A round table. *Journal of Public Law,* 1959, **8,** 155–253.

GLASS, D. C. Changes in liking as a means of reducing cognitive discrepancies between self-esteem and aggression. *Journal of Personality,* 1964, **32,** 520–549.

SCHAFER, S. *Restitution to victims of crime.* London: Stevens, 1960.

SYKES, G. M., AND MATZA, D. Techniques of neutralization: A theory of delinquency. *American Sociological Reveiw,* 1957, **22,** 664–670.

WALSTER, E., AND PRESTHOLDT, P. The effect of misjudging another: Over-compensation or dissonance reduction? *Journal of Experimental Social Psychology,* 1966, **2,** 85–97.

V

PREJUDICE

20

Current Stereotypes:
A Little Fading, a Little Faking

Harold Sigall and Richard Page

The possibility that social-desirability-tainted responses emerge in the study of stereotypes is suggested and examined. Sixty white American subjects were randomly assigned to one of four experimental conditions. Subjects were asked to indicate how characteristic each of 22 adjective traits was of either "Americans" or "Negroes." This was cross-cut by a measurement variable: Half of the subjects responded in a rating situation in which they were presumably free to distort their responses. Remaining subjects responded under "bogus pipeline" conditions; that is, they were led to believe that the experimenter had an accurate, distortion-free physiological measure of their attitudes, and they were asked to predict that measure. The results supported our expectation that the stereotype ascribed to Negroes would be more favorable under rating than under bogus pipeline conditions. Americans were more favorably stereotyped under bogus pipeline than under rating conditions. A number of explanations for these results are discussed, and consideration is given to the relationship between verbally expressed attitudes and other, overt, behavior.

Ethnic stereotypes have been subject to examination for quite some time. The first empirical investigation of such stereotypes was the now well-known study by Katz and Braly (1933). They looked at the stereotypes held by Princeton undergraduates toward 10 ethnic groups and thereby established a paradigm and a tradition. The tradition has been followed by Gilbert (1951) and more recently by Karlins, Coffman, and Walters (1969), who also examined the stereotypes held by Princeton students. The paradigm was a simple one: subjects were presented with a list of traits and asked to indicate which of them were necessary to adequately characterize each

Reprinted with permission from the authors and *The Journal of Personality and Social Psychology,* Vol. 18, No. 2, 1971. Copyright 1971 by the American Psychological Association.

This research was supported by Research Grant MH 17180–01 from the National Institute of Mental Health. The authors would like to thank Robert Strahan for helpful suggestions.

ethnic group. They also were asked to choose from among the assigned traits the five traits most typical of each group. Katz and Braly were then able to look at the qualitative descriptions ascribed to each group and to calculate the degree of uniformity associated with each stereotype. The smaller the number of traits needed to account for at least 50 percent of the ascriptions, the greater the uniformity of the stereotype.

Katz and Braly's (1933) results were quite striking. Their subjects manifested strong stereotyping, that is, high uniformity; they also demonstrated a powerful tendency to describe certain ethnic groups quite favorably, while viewing others rather unfavorably. Gilbert (1951) reported some fading of such stereotypes, finding that there was a considerable decrease in the uniformity of traits assigned to the groups. However, Karlins et al. (1969) reported a return to high uniformity in the stereotypes held by Princeton students. On the other hand, they did find "fading," but of another type. Certain groups who were viewed earlier as either extremely positive or extremely negative took on more moderate stereotypes. Perhaps most noteworthy for contemporary America was the sharp decrease in American chauvinism and the sharp increase in favorability ascribed to Negroes.

These latter findings represent the point of departure for the experiment reported here. While such findings may in fact reflect basic attitude change over time, it seems intuitively that social desirability (Crowne and Marlowe, 1964) or other demand-characteristic-related variables could affect responses in a study of stereotypes. For example, self-criticism by Americans and concern about Negroes currently are active phenomena on many college campuses. It certainly seems "modish" to be favorable when describing Negroes, and it may be fashionable to be less than favorable when describing Americans. The fact that many subjects in the research conducted by Karlins et al. and by Gilbert objected to participating in the studies documents the sensitive nature of the research situation.

In the present study we departed from the Katz and Braly paradigm and used a relatively new technique in an attempt to reduce socially desirable responses in the assessment of Negro and American stereotypes. The full rationale underlying this technique, a version of the "bogus pipeline," is described elsewhere (Jones and Sigall, 1971). As used by Jones and Sigall, the term bogus pipeline refers to a paradigm in which an experimenter claims to have access (a pipeline) to his subject's covert reactions. Briefly, the procedure is designed to encourage the subject to respond honestly, by leading him to believe that the experimenter can assess precisely the direction and intensity of his attitudes, via a machine that provides a direct physiological measure of those attitudes. The subject is then asked to *predict* what the machine is saying about him. We assume that the subject will be motivated to predict the machine reading accurately—that he will not want to be second-guessed by it. Once the subject believes that the experimenter will know his real attitude anyway, distortion serves little purpose: at best, the experimenter would regard him as insensitive to his own feelings; at worst, he might be viewed as actively deceptive.

We expected that using this technique would lead subjects to present less socially desirable stereotypes than would result in a more typical rating-scale situation, where subjects are relatively free to distort. Half of our subjects responded under bogus pipeline conditions, while the remainder responded in a rating situation in which the experimenter did not claim to have independent evidence concerning attitudes.

METHOD

Subjects and Design

Sixty white male undergraduates were recruited from an introductory psychology course at the University of Rochester. Half of the subjects indicated how characteristic they felt each of a series of 22 traits was of "Americans." The other half did the same with respect to "Negroes." Within each of these groups, half of the subjects were led to believe that an independent and distortion-free physiological measure of their attitudes was being obtained. This design resulted in a 2×2 factorial, and subjects were randomly assigned to one of the four experimental conditions. Subjects were tested individually.

Apparatus

Subjects sat before a console. A semicircular 7-point scale ranging from -3 to $+3$ was drawn on the console, and a slot in which a label could be placed was located at each end of the scale. A steering wheel, mounted on a shaft which extended from the console, turned a pointer along the scale.

Alongside the console sat a hammertone gray metal box labeled "EMG." Dials, lights, and cable connections adorned the box. The box also contained a meter with a 7-point scale geometrically similar to one drawn on the console. This meter was labeled "EMG Output." Two skin electrodes were connected to the box by cable, and cables also extended from the box to an array of impressive-looking electrical junk, described as a small computer.

In an adjacent room a rheostat could be manipulated to control EMG-output meter readings.

Procedure

The subject reported to an experiment entitled "Perception." Upon arriving at a waiting room, the subject was greeted by the experimenter and presented with a five-item attitude inventory. The purpose of administering this inventory was to obtain information which later would be used to convince the subject that the EMG did provide an accurate measure of his attitudes. Since it was important that responses to these items would not be distorted, the attitude statements dealt with relatively innocuous issues. Subjects indicated agreement or disagreement, along a 7-point scale, with statements on movies, music, sports, automobiles, and record clubs. The experimenter left the waiting room, allowing the subject to fill out the questionnaire in private. A few minutes later the experimenter returned, escorted the subject to the experimental room, and seated the subject, such that he was facing the console with his back to the door of the room. The experimenter took the completed inventory and casually placed it on a table near the door, which was left slightly ajar so that an accomplice secretly could copy the responses from the corridor. The foregoing events took place in all conditions in order to maximize procedural similarity. Actually, they were necessitated only by the bogus pipeline or EMG conditions, which are described below.

EMG Conditions

The experimenter told the subject that using questionnaires in psychological research involved a variety of problems. He then informed him that the elaborate device before him was a recently developed "adapted electromyograph, or EMG," which made possible direct, accurate physiological measurement of attitudes, thereby eliminating some problems, including response distortion. The experimenter explained that EMG devices measured electrical potentials in muscle groups. He further explained that when a subject held the steering wheel, which was locked in place with its pointer at zero, and focused on the scale on the console, electrodes attached to his forearm would record his "first reaction tendency to turn the wheel — his undistorted response" to attitude statements read to him. The experimenter pointed out that the EMG recorded the potentials generated by implicit muscle movements, and that therefore no overt response was required for measurement. "In fact," the experimenter said, "the EMG is unaffected by gross muscle movements." The electrical junk was identified as a small computer which analyzed the electrophysiological input, and then presented the resultant information on the EMG output meter. Thus, the subject was led to believe that the EMG would indicate where he would turn the wheel, if the wheel was not locked, and if he was not distorting responses. The experimenter noted similarities between the EMG and the lie detector, and pointed out that the EMG had considerable advantages over the lie detector, the major one being that it was sensitive to both direction and intensity of responses, while the lie detector did not assess direction.

The experimenter placed the electrodes on the subject's forearms, and then "validated" the EMG. The validation was intended to convince the subject that the EMG did indeed possess its alleged powers. The experimenter explained that occasionally the EMG needed adjustment because of individual differences in base-line response levels. The experimenter told the subject that to check on whether much adjustment was necessary, EMG readings would be obtained on the same five sample items that the subject had responded to upon his arrival. "Agree" and "Disagree" labels were inserted in the slots on the console, and the subject was told to hold the wheel and concentrate on the scale. He was asked to remain silent. The experimenter read the first item and then threw a switch on the computer. The computer buzzed for a few moments, and then it seemingly turned itself off as the needle on the EMG output meter swung to a number. The second, third, and fifth items were handled in the same way. Prior to administering the fourth item, the subject was encouraged to try to "fool" the EMG. The experimenter, again emphasizing that the EMG was sensitive only to the implicit muscle movements generated by the first reaction tendency, suggested to the subject that he consciously think in opposition to his true feeling and that he exert pressure on the steering wheel in a similarly opposite direction. The experimenter pointed out that EMG readings should not be affected by either behavior. EMG readings were noted after each item. Actually, of course, both the buzzing by the computer and output meter readings were controlled from the adjacent room by the accomplice who had copied the subject's questionnaire answers. After the fifth item, the questionnaire was retrieved and compared with the EMG readings. Clearly, the EMG did not need adjustment; its readings were in perfect correspondence with the questionnaire for each item.

The subject was then told that the main purpose of the study was to assess perceptions of various groups. The labels "Characteristic" (+3) and "Uncharacteristic" (−3) were inserted in the console, and the subject was told that he would be presented with one group, Americans (Negroes), and that a series of traits would be read to him. The EMG would indicate how characteristic the subject felt each trait was of the group. The experimenter then informed the subject that he was also interested in seeing "to what extent people are in touch with their real feelings." He explained that in order to test how sensitive the subject was to his feelings, he would ask the subject to predict the EMG readings. The subject's view of the EMG meter was shielded, he was encouraged to present his undistorted reactions, and he was told that he would be permitted to see how well he had predicted upon completion of the list.

The experimenter proceeded to read twenty-two traits, one at a time. After each item he recorded the subject's prediction (the dependent measure) and also pretended to obtain and note the EMG reading.

Rating Conditions

In these conditions the electrodes were hidden, the computer was turned off, and the wheel was free to be turned. The apparatus was casually dismissed as a small computer used to analyze data. The experimenter informed the subject that there were certain problems inherent in paper-and-pencil measures, and that the steering wheel device was being employed because it produced greater attention and concentration from subjects than did questionnaires.[1] The subject was asked to turn the pointer to the appropriate place on the scale and to state the corresponding number aloud. The five-item questionnaire was used as illustration. The "purpose" of the experiment was described, and, as in the EMG conditions, the subject was asked to present his undistorted first reaction. The experimenter stressed the importance of honest responses. The experimenter read the 22 traits, 1 at a time, and recorded the subject's responses. All subjects were thoroughly debriefed.

RESULTS AND DISCUSSION

All subjects in the EMG conditions were successfully convinced that the EMG accurately measured attitudes. A few subjects, distributed throughout the four experimental conditions, did express some reluctance over attributing traits to groups. In these cases the experimenter acknowledged that he understood such reluctance and encouraged subjects to do their best anyway. Without exception, the subjects performed as requested.

Responses to specific traits could range from -3 (uncharacteristic) to $+3$ (characteristic). The mean trait assignments are presented in Table 20.1. The traits are listed in the order in which they were presented to the subjects. Table 20.1 also includes the F ratios resulting from the twenty-two separate analyses of variance, one for each trait. While we acknowledge

[1]We do not view this rating situation as substantially different from other typical rating situations (e.g., those using paper-and-pencil measures). Support for this view comes from Byrne (1969), who has reported that responses indicated by simple physical manipulations do not differ from responses indicated with paper and pencil. We used the steering wheel as part of our attempt to keep the rating and EMG conditions as similar as possible.

TABLE 20.1
Mean assignment of traits and *F* ratios

| Trait | Condition | | | | *F* ratios | | |
| | Americans | | Negroes | | Ethnic group (A) | Measurement (B) | A × B |
	EMG	Rating	EMG	Rating			
Talkative	1.40	1.60	.67	.47	14.004††	<1	<1
Happy-go-lucky	.53	.53	.93	−.13	<1	2.841*	2.841*
Honest	.60	−.27	−.33	.67	<1	<1	14.866††
Musical	−.20	.53	1.53	2.00	31.683††	4.455**	<1
Conventional	.87	1.33	−.60	−.73	29.261††	<1	<1
Ostentatious	1.07	1.27	1.13	.33	1.627	<1	2.166
Progressive	1.47	1.33	.47	.40	12.991††	<1	<1
Ignorant	−.53	−.07	.60	.20	4.349**	<1	1.667
Practical	1.20	1.33	−.40	−.27	25.515††	<1	<1
Superstitious	−.40	−.13	.20	.00	<1	<1	<1
Intelligent	1.73	1.00	.00	.47	20.497††	<1	5.745**
Pleasure loving	1.93	2.07	1.80	1.07	4.267**	1.196	2.495
Imitative	.80	.33	.33	.20	<1	<1	<1
Stupid	−1.07	−.20	.13	−1.00	<1	<1	6.824**
Industrious	2.33	2.20	.07	.00	64.777††	<1	<1
Physically dirty	−1.67	−1.53	.20	−1.33	11.989†	5.501**	7.797†
Ambitious	2.07	2.13	−.07	.33	55.149††	<1	<1
Aggressive	1.73	1.60	1.20	.67	4.895**	1.012	<1
Unreliable	−.73	−.40	.27	−.67	1.244	<1	3.712*
Materialistic	2.42	2.20	.60	.87	33.892††	<1	<1
Sensitive	1.47	.07	.87	1.60	1.726	<1	9.016†
Lazy	−.80	−.40	.60	−.73	2.424	1.856	6.402**

*$p < .10$.   **$p < .05$.   †$p < .01$.   ††$p < .001$.

that by performing so many analyses we run the risk of obtaining some statistically significant *F* ratios by chance, the large number of significant *F* ratios strongly suggests that on the whole we have tapped some very real differences. Let us consider the ethnic group's main effects first. Thirteen of the twenty-two traits were differentially assigned to Americans and Negroes at statistically significant levels. Americans were rated as characteristically more talkative, conventional, progressive, practical, intelligent, pleasure loving, industrious, ambitious, aggressive, and materialistic. Negroes were rated as more musical, ignorant, and physically dirty. Considering the data collected in the three previous Princeton studies, these main effects are not particularly surprising. In one or more of those studies, conventional, progressive, practical, intelligent, industrious, ambitious, aggressive, and materialistic were among the 10 most frequently selected traits for Americans, but not for Negroes; musical, ignorant, and physically dirty never were assigned to Americans with sufficient frequency to make the "top ten," but have been assigned with such sufficient frequency with respect to Negroes. "Pleasure loving" was assigned with approximately equal frequency to Americans and Negroes in the Karlins et al.

(1969) study, and it is unclear why Americans were seen as significantly more pleasure loving than were Negroes in the present investigation. Our finding that Americans were rated as more talkative seems to run against earlier data: Karlins et al. reported that 13 percent of their subjects included that trait in their description of Negroes, while it was not among those frequently assigned to Americans. Our subjects suggested a possible explanation during the postexperimental interviews. They commented that the black students at the university seemed to "stay quietly to themselves." To the extent, then, that subject responses were influenced by exposure to black students on campus, it is understandable that Negroes received lower ratings on talkativeness.

It is appropriate at this point to comment on the relationship between the present experiment and the Princeton studies. While major inconsistencies in the substance of results require attempts at explication, it must be stressed that vast differences in approach and procedure preclude placing extraordinary emphasis on direct comparisons. Beyond differences in time of testing, subject population, the introduction of a measurement variable, and a myriad of other minor variations, it is extremely important to note that subjects in the present study responded to only one ethnic group, whereas in the Katz and Braly paradigm subjects assigned traits to all ethnic groups considered. In addition, our subjects indicated *how* characteristic each trait was, while in the Katz and Braly procedure subjects simply indicated whether or not a trait applied. Thus, it is conceivable, though unlikely, that any particular trait could produce differences of great magnitude in the present study, say +2.80 for Negroes and +1.10 for Americans, but not show up as differentially assigned to the two groups in the Princeton studies. There are numerous other possible implications resulting from the difference in approaches; we just wish to caution against ignoring such differences and their implications. At the same time it is clear that we are interested in looking at the pattern and overall trends in our results in the context of the general findings and trends in the Princeton studies.

We will turn now to those traits which yielded Measurement × Ethnic Group interactions. It is these traits that illuminate most clearly the contrasting effects of using the bogus pipeline versus the more typical rating approach. Six traits yielded interactions, the statistical significance of which easily surpassed conventional standards: "honest," "intelligent," "stupid," "physically dirty," "sensitive," and "lazy." Two other traits, "happy-go-lucky" and "unreliable," produced F ratios significant at less than .10. Finally, directional interactions, with significance levels between .10 and .20, resulted from the analyses of "ostentatious," "ignorant," and "pleasure loving." The interaction F ratios for the remaining 11 traits were all less than one.

TABLE 20.2
Trait favorability of the 22 adjectives

Traits yielding A × B interaction	Favorability	Traits not yielding A × B interaction	Favorability
Intelligent	1.61	Industrious	1.32
Honest	1.56	Ambitious	1.06
Sensitive	.99	Progressive	.99
Pleasure loving	.46	Musical	.90
Happy-go-lucky	.45	Practical	.82
Ostentatious	−.89	Aggressive	.18
Lazy	−1.12	Talkative	−.13
Ignorant	−1.37	Conventional	−.30
Physically dirty	−1.45	Materialistic	−.45
Stupid	−1.59	Imitative	−.63
Unreliable	−1.64	Superstitious	−.84

Is this pattern haphazard, or does it make sense? To answer this question, a variety of considerations must be entertained. Karlins et al. (1969) had their subjects rate the favorableness of all of the trait adjectives used by Katz and Braly. These ratings were made on a 5-point scale, ranging from +2 (very favorable) to −2 (Very unfavorable). In our attempt to account for the present data, we made use of these ratings. Again, caution needs to be exercised. As Karlins et at. pointed out, ratings of adjectives out of context may not reflect the connotation of those adjectives when part of a stereotype. In addition the favorability assigned to a trait may change over time (Karlins et al. sampled in 1967, while our subjects were tested in 1969). Finally, it is possible that different subject populations value traits differentially. Nevertheless, it is useful to consider those trait-favorability values in attempting to conceptually organize the present results.

Table 20.2 presents the trait favorability according to Karlins et al. of the twenty-two traits employed here. We have organized the traits in the table so that one can easily see the favorability assigned to traits yielding interactions juxtaposed with traits that did not.

One way to compare the two lists is in terms of the *absolute values* of trait favorability. The mean absolute value of traits yielding Ethnic Group × Measurement interactions was 1.19; the mean absolute value of the remaining traits was .69. Moreover, if we ignore those traits (ostentatious, ignorant, pleasure loving) which manifested the weakest interactions, the mean absolute value of interaction traits increases from 1.19 to 1.30. Unfortunately, due to the nature of these data—traits are not subjects and are not independent of one another—inferential statistics are not readily applicable. Therefore, we are left with the descriptive fact that the two means are quite different, and we are unable to assign probability values to the difference. Nevertheless, given the bogus pipeline concept, these data are very meaningful. Examining absolute values helps us to focus on the fact that interactions tended to result when a particular trait carried a relatively large amount of affective loading. If subjects' responses in stereotyping investigations are influenced by social desirability, then we would expect that such influences would be most marked when the adjectives were value laden. This, of course, is consistent with our procedure in which we deliberately used innocuous items when validating the EMG, precisely because we expected little distortion on items with bland content.

Further evidence for the notion that the EMG is affecting the social desirability of responses emerges when the direction of the interactions is examined. Looking at intelligent, honest, and sensitive, all highly favorable, it can be seen that in each instance the trait was reported as more characteristic of Americans in the EMG than in the rating condition, while these same adjectives were seen as more characteristic of Negroes in the rating than in the EMG condition. This effect was most pronounced in the case of honest, where the zero point was crossed. Taking the unfavorable traits, ostentatious, lazy, ignorant, physically dirty, stupid, and unrealiable, we find a complementary pattern: these adjectives were reported as more characteristic of Americans in the rating than in the EMG condition, and more characteristic of Negroes in the EMG than in the rating condition. Pleasure loving and happy-go-lucky did not result in interactions consistent with the others. With both of these "favorable" traits, Americans were *not* more favorably viewed in the EMG condition, and Negroes were more favorably evaluated in the EMG condition. It is our feeling that the note of caution expressed previously, that traits rated out of stereotype contexts do not necessarily reflect their connotations in such contexts, is relevant here. While we may want our spouses and friends to be pleasure loving and happy-go-lucky, these traits can have negative connotations when they form part of a stereotype. The happy-go-lucky Negro dancing through his woe in Hollywood productions of the 1930s hardly represents a favorable image.

In analyzing our results we made one further use of the trait-favorability values reported by Karlins et al. (1969). We computed a "favorability" score for each subject by multiplying the trait value of each adjective by the score assigned by the subject to that adjective. For example, if the subject's response to stupid was +1, the favorability of that response was (-1.59) $(+1)$ or -1.59; if the subject indicated that stupid was uncharacteristic, say -2, the favorability score would be $+3.18$. We simply obtained a mean favorability score for each subject by averaging his twenty-two individual favorability scores. Given the trait values and the response range of -3 to $+3$, the possible range of mean favorability scores could extend from -2.83 (unfavorable) to $+2.83$ (favorable). Analyzing the data in this way allows an overview of the results to emerge, and also avoids some of

TABLE 20.3
Mean favorability of
assigned stereotypes

Ethnic group	EMG	Rating
Americans	.84	.53
Negroes	−.03	.49

TABLE 20.4
Analysis of variance of favorability scores

Source	df	MS	F
Ethnic group (A)	1	3.11	14.14**
Measurement (B)	1	.17	<1
A × B	1	2.56	11.64*
Within groups	56	.22	

*$p < .005$.   **$p < .001$.

the objections to conducting a large number of separate analyses. The mean favorability scores are presented in Table 20.3, and the analysis of variance for these scores appears in Table 20.4. It can be seen that Americans were assigned more favorable stereotypes than were Negroes. Moreover, the Ethnic Group × Measurement interaction again points to the utility of the bogus pipeline. Americans received more favorable evaluations in the EMG than the rating condition, while Negroes were more favorably evaluated in the rating than in the EMG condition. If one were to examine only the EMG condition, a large difference in favorability would emerge. On the other hand, the difference in favorability within the rating condition was virtually nonexistent.

We would suggest that "demands" for social-desirability-related responses in the Katz and Braly paradigm fall somewhere in between the demands for such responses in our rating and EMG conditions. The EMG conditions clearly are designed to inhibit socially desirable responses. However, in the rating conditions social desirability may manifest itself at an especially high level. Despite the encouragement given to rating-condition subjects to emit undistorted responses, they responded in a one to one, face-to-face situation. In contrast, the subjects in the Katz and Braly paradigm, although free to distort, may have less need to do so by virtue of the fact that they were relatively anonymous, and were tested in large groups.

Earlier we pointed out that our data cannot be compared directly with the data collected in the Princeton studies. Similarly, the evidence we have gathered, which suggested that social desirability needs affected our rating-condition subjects, does not in any way prove that such demand characteristics were operative in any of the Princeton studies. Casual observation tells us that college students in the late 1960s were not as negative when talking about Negroes as they seem to have been thirty-five years earlier. In that respect the Karlins et al. study mirrors an intuitively ascertainable reality. The present experiment is not based on that research. That is, the present experiment would have been performed even if the Karlins et al. study had not been conducted. On the other hand, the existence of the work by Karlins et al. made our research easier in at least three direct ways. In the first place, as a well-conducted study of stereotyping, it provides hard data which strongly supports casual observation, and the latter is rarely, if ever, an adequate substitute for the former. One tends to stand on much sturdier ground when dealing with data than when dealing with intuition. Second, because of our approach, we had to select a relatively limited number of adjective traits. The Karlins et al. study was helpful in this regard because by examining their results, we were able to choose adjectives that would be likely to yield interesting response patterns. Finally, we are indebted to Karlins et al. (1969) for providing quantitative favorableness values for adjectives. As they noted: "the ratings are especially useful for present and future investigations, and they provide us with an overall index of the direction and intensity of stereotype composition [p. 11]."

In sum, we should state explicitly that we make no claims to have demonstrated the Karlins et al. findings to be artifactual. However, to the extent that our results indicate that subjects' responses in investigations of stereotypes are influenced by social-desirability needs, it does not seem unreasonable to speculate that while some of the neutralization found by Karlins et al. is real, some of it may reflect the social desirability needs of the respondents.

It will be obvious by this point that we have elected to interpret the results of the EMG condition as relatively distortion free, as more honest, and as "truer" than rating-condition responses. Thus, the EMG may be viewed as a lie detection device which facilitates truthful reporting. While we tend to *favor* this interpretation—indeed, it underlies the development of the bogus pipeline—it is not the only one possible. Rival, equally plausible, alternatives are available. They are more fully discussed by Jones and Sigall (1971). Here we will consider them briefly.

Perhaps the subjects in the EMG condition, uncertain about their ability to designate a number which describes precisely their feeling, prefer "negative" to "positive" errors. Aware of current norms and that they may be influenced by them in complex ways, subjects may decide to "predict" in a manner such that any errors in prediction would be on the negative side. As Jones and Sigall (1971) stated, "it may be better to admit being a bigot and have it shown that you are fairly liberal than to claim tolerance while being revealed as a bigot." The same could be said regarding chauvinism.

Another alternative involves the conceptualization of attitude as com posed of an affective and a cognitive component. Perhaps the EMG, due to its purported sensitivity to physiological responses, places emphasis on the affective component. If EMG subjects are trying to report affective autonomic nervous system responses, while rating-condition subjects are reporting attitudinal or cognitive responses, we may well expect a difference between conditions. However, explaining the difference does not have to involve a consideration of distortion. Subjects in both conditions may be responding honestly. We may believe that most people, including ourselves, have hidden stereotyped negative feelings about certain ethnic groups—feelings which we are unaware of. As Jones and Sigall (1971) pointed out: "When asked to estimate the affective component of their racial attitudes, therefore, it is not altogether surprising that they would accede to some extent to the implications of this stereotype."

Some Final Considerations

The enormous amount of work invested by students of attitudes and attitude change most likely reflects more than an interest in attitudes and attitude structure, per se. As other writers (e.g., Cohen, 1964; Wicker, 1969) have suggested, many investigators make the assumption that verbally expressed attitudes are indicators of other, overt, social behaviors. Certainly, many social psychologists interested in overt social behavior consider verbally stated attitudes as indicators of behavior, if for no other reason than because it is easy and economical to do so (cf. Aronson and Carlsmith, 1968).

Wicker (1969) has examined the relationship between verbally expressed attitudes and overt actions. After reviewing a sizable portion of the literature, he concluded that there is little evidence to support the assumption that verbally expressed attitudes correlate highly with the overt behaviors implied by those attitudes. One possible reason for this is that verbally expressed attitudes may frequently be distorted because the subject wants to appear socially desirable (see Wicker, 1969, for a discussion of many other considerations). One potentially fruitful line of research which hopefully will be stimulated by the bogus pipeline involves investigating the relationship between attitudes assessed with the bogus pipeline and overt behavior, and comparing that relationship with one between typical ratings and identical overt behavior.

At the same time we must remain cognizant of the fact that although laboratory behavior may differ in many respects from real-world behavior, the latter is not unaffected by those forces which influence the former. That is, real-world behavior is also susceptible to effects accruing from social desirability needs. Even if it turns out that we can safely assume that the EMG gives low-distortion responses, we will still have to be extremely careful to scrutinize any particular overt behavior before deciding which type of attitudinal measure would be most likely to correspond highly with it.

References

ARONSON, E., AND CARLSMITH, J. M. Experimentation in social psychology. In G. Lindzey and E. Aronson (eds.), *Handbook of social psychology.* Vol. 2. (2nd ed.) Reading, Mass.: Addison-Wesley, 1969.

BYRNE, D. Attitudes and attraction. In L. Berkowitz (ed.), *Advances in experimental social psychology.* Vol. 4. New York: Academic Press, 1969.

COHEN, A. R. *Attitude change and social influence.* New York: Basic Books, 1964.

CROWNE, D. P., AND MARLOWE, D. *The approval motive.* New York: Wiley, 1964.

GILBERT, G. M. Stereotype persistence and change among college students. *Journal of Abnormal and Social Psychology,* 1951, **46,** 245–254.

JONES, E. E., AND SIGALL, H. The bogus pipeline: A new paradigm for measuring affect and attitude. *Psychological Bulletin,* 1971, **76,** 349–364.

KARLINS, M., COFFMAN, T. L., AND WALTERS, G. On the fading of social stereotypes: Studies in three generations of college students. *Journal of Personality and Social Psychology,* 1969, **13,** 1–16.

KATZ, D., AND BRALY, K. W. Racial stereotypes of one-hundred college students. *Journal of Abnormal and Social Psychology,* 1933, **28,** 282–290.

WICKER, A. W. Attitudes versus actions: The relationship of verbal and overt behavioral responses to attitude objects. *Journal of Social Issues,* 1969, **25,** 41–78.

21

Variables in Interracial Aggression: Anonymity, Expected Retaliation, and a Riot

Edward Donnerstein, Marcia Donnerstein,
Seymore Simon, and Raymond Ditrichs

Two experiments employing white subjects examined the effects of anonymity, expected retaliation, race of target, and a campus racial disturbance on delivered and anticipated aggression (electric shock). Prior to statistical treatment, the data were subjected to principal components analyses, with three aggression components being identified: general direct aggression, extremes in direct aggression, and indirect aggression. In Experiment I, it was found that less direct and more indirect forms of aggression were delivered to black than to white targets when there was opportunity for the target to retaliate. When retaliation was unlikely, the subjects delivered more direct forms of aggression to black than to white targets. Following a campus racial disturbance, there were increases in direct forms of aggression toward black targets, with such aggression now being less dependent on the opportunity for retaliation (Experiment II). In both experiments more direct aggression was anticipated from black than from white targets. The results support the conclusion that white persons have learned to fear black retaliation, but that this fear acts only to inhibit direct forms of aggression in certain defined situations.

Among the most salient characteristics of the current black movement is the use of violence or the threat of violence to produce equality between black and white people. Black authors (e.g., Baldwin, 1963), as well as certain black militant leaders, have emphasized that the black man is determined to get equal rights and that white society must change or face reprisals. It is not surprising then to find some anecdotal evidence which

Reprinted with permission from the authors and *The Journal of Personality and Social Psychology,* Vol. 22, No. 2, 1972. Copyright 1972 by the American Psychological Association.

This study is based on a thesis presented by the first author to the Department of Psychology at Northern Illinois University in partial fulfillment of the requirements for the MA degree. It was reported at the annual meeting of the Midwestern Psychological Association, Cincinnati, April 1970.

suggests that white people have learned to fear black retaliation. A good example is an excerpt from a letter to the editor published by the Northern Illinois University student newspaper, *The Northern Star*:

> We are going to ask that our names be withheld from this letter. Don't bother writing in to sneer, 'what'sa matter whitey, you scared?' Yeah, we are. You militants may feel free to gloat. Those of us, both black and white, who want peace: sorry but once again we must hang our heads in shame. It's a sad time when one cannot stand and say, "I wrote that" without fear of attack [March 22, 1969].

Another is an account by a Chicago 7 Conspiracy juror, Kay S. Richards, as reported by the *Chicago Sun-Times*:

> The point is, I was very much afraid of Bobby Seale . . . I am afraid of Black Panthers. And all through the first part of the trial I had a fear that when I got out of there my life wouldn't be my own if I convicted Bobby Seale. I would be very much afraid to convict Bobby Seale [February 24, 1970].

Given that white people have acquired a fear of black retaliation, it is interesting to speculate about the effect this fear might have on interracial relations, and particularly on interracial aggression. Berkowitz (1962) has suggested that the level of aggression which an individual administers to a target varies directly with both the strength of the instigation to aggress and the aggressive cue value of the target, and inversely with the intensity of inhibitions against aggression. A number of studies bearing on this conceptualization have found that one variable that functions as an effective inhibitor of aggressive acts is the expectation of punishment (e.g., Bandura, 1965; Bandura, Ross, and Ross, 1963; Edwards, 1967). In the present context, the results of these studies suggest that fear of black retaliation by white subjects should generally act to reduce aggression toward black targets. More specifically, the level of aggression directed toward black targets should be low under situational conditions designed to maximize this fear and high under those conditions designed to reduce it.

Some support for this notion comes from a preliminary study conducted by the present authors. White male subjects were provided with an opportunity to aggress against either a black or white target using electric shocks of differential intensities. Each subject in the first experimental group was introduced to his target openly, the target being brought into the experimental room to meet the subject. At this time, the experimenter clearly indicated that the subject would be the person delivering the shocks. For these subjects then, the target could potentially retaliate, and any fear of such action by blacks was presumably high. Each subject in a second group viewed the target over what was purported to be a one-way closed-circuit television system. Since no camera was present in the experimental room and the experimenter made no mention of a subsequent meeting between the subject and the target, a subject in this condition could reasonably believe that the target could not identify him as the aggressor. For these subjects, the opportunity for retaliation was thus minimized, and fear of such action by blacks was presumably lower than for subjects in the first group. Consistent with expectation, an analysis of the high-intensity shocks revealed that subjects paired with black targets administered reliably more intense shocks when they were led to believe that they were aggressing anonymously than when they were known to their targets. The subjects shocking white targets showed no differences in aggressiveness as a function of the same situational conditions, their performances being essentially the same under the anonymous and face-to-face conditions and comparable to those subjects shocking black targets under anonymous conditions. Unfortunately, since the subjects in the two experimental groups differed with respect to both target anonymity and proximity, a completely unambiguous interpretation of the results was precluded.

Under improved design conditions, it was of interest in the current study (*a*) to establish experimentally that white persons have learned to fear black retaliation and (*b*) to examine some of the variables related to this fear and how they might operate to facilitate or inhibit aggression toward blacks. As in the initial experiment, white subjects were provided with an opportunity to aggress against either a black or a white target under conditions designed to either maximize or reduce the subject's expectancy for counteraggression. This expectancy was manipulated in two independent ways. First, as in the preliminary study, the anonymity of the aggressor relative to the target was varied. The subjects in one experimental group were led to believe that the target against whom they were to aggress could identify them, while the subjects in a second group were assured that this individual would never become aware of their identities. However, since the anonymity variable could only be related to the opportunity to retaliate outside of the experimental situation, a variable having more immediate consequences was also introduced. Half of the subjects under each anonymity condition were told prior to aggressing that they would subsequently switch roles with the target, while the other half of the subjects were given these instructions after they had aggressed. Finally, to obtain a direct measure of perceived differences in counteraggressive intent, and hence presumed fear of such action, all subjects were asked to indicate the levels of shock they anticipated receiving from the target.

On the assumption that fear of retaliation would be relatively high when aggressing against a black target, it was predicted that lower levels of aggression would be delivered to black targets under conditions favoring the opportunity for retaliation than under conditions minimizing such opportunity. Moreover, since fear of retaliation was assumed to be higher for black than for white targets, the same situational conditions were expected to have a lesser effect in differentially influencing aggression toward white targets. It was also expected that, independent of delivered aggression, subjects would anticipate higher levels of counteraggression from black than from white targets.

EXPERIMENT I

Method

Subjects. The subjects were 80 white male introductory psychology students at Northern Illinois University who volunteered to participate for extra course credit for "an experiment in learning."

Apparatus. A modified Buss (1961) "aggression machine" was used. The front panel consisted of eight buttons numbered in consecutive order. Under Buttons 1, 2, and 3 was the word LOW; under 4 and 5, the word MEDIUM; and under 6, 7, and 8, the word HIGH. At the side of the machine was a single reward button. A compatible unit in a control room, including a Hunter Klockounter, enabled the experimenter to monitor which one of the buttons was pressed as well as the duration of pressing. A Sony videorecorder, monitor, and camera were used for preparing and showing the target tapes.

Procedure. The experimental procedure comprised four phases: (*a*) general introduction, (*b*) anonymity instructions, (*c*) role-switch instructions and administration of aggression to the target, and (*d*) anticipation of aggression from the target.

General introduction. The subject was ushered into a room that was arranged to appear as though various behavioral and physiological measures could be monitored. An effort was made to assure the subject that the experimenter would be busy recording a number of these measures while the subject was occupied with his task. The subject was then told that the experiment was concerned with the effects of reward and punishment on paired-associate learning, and the study–test method of learning paired associates was described. It was further explained that the experimenter was concerned not only with the rate of learning, but also with the various physiological correlates of reward and punishment, and that since numerous instrument readings had to be taken during testing, additional assistance was needed in carrying out the experiment. Introductory psychology students were therefore being asked to operate some of the apparatus. It was noted that the other student who would be learning the paired associates had arrived earlier and was in another room and that the subject's role would be to operate the reward and punishment equipment by delivering a light (reward) each time the learner made a correct response and an electrical shock (punishment) each time he made an error.

Anonymity instructions. Under the pretext of checking to see if the learner was ready to begin, the videomonitor was turned on, and the subject was led to believe that he was viewing the other student over closed-circuit television. At this point the subject was placed into one of two experimental conditions. In the nonanonymous condition a camera was placed facing both the experimenter and the subject, and a tape of either a black or white male college student (target) was shown. The target was shown wearing earphones and having an electrode attached to the palm of his right hand. The tapes were made so that the experimenter appeared to be communicating with the target. The subject was introduced by the experimenter to the target, who responded and noted that he could see both the experimenter and the subject very clearly. The target was then told by the experimenter that the subject would be delivering the shock and controlling the light during the experiment. The videotape was then turned off, and an explanation was made that "the other person" might be distracted from learning if it were left on.

Instructions and procedures in the anonymous condition were similar to those in the nonanonymous condition. However, there was no videocamera in the room, the experimenter did not introduce the subject to the target, and the experimenter explicitly told the target that he would not know who was delivering the shock and light to him either during or after the experiment. The reason given to the subject for this latter precaution was that nonanonymity distracted the other student from learning. It was further emphasized that since the target would be returning to participate in another, but related, phase of the experiment, it would be necessary for the subject to leave several minutes before the target.

Role-switching instructions. The subject was then taken to another room in which the aggression machine was located, and its use was explained. He was told that when the learner made an incorrect response, he could deliver any one of eight different intensities of shock, and that shock increased from low shocks of 1, 2, and 3 to high shocks of 6, 7, and 8. He was further told that when the other student made a correct response, he was to push a reward button which lit a bulb on the learner's panel. A list of 48 CVC (consonant-vowel-consonant) nonsense syllables of medium meaningfulness value (Noble, 1961), presumably representing the order of correct nonsense syllable responses on the test list, was then handed to the subject. Following an explanation of this list, the subject was placed in one of two role-switching conditions. In the prior-role-switch condition, he was told that after completing the present phase of the experiment, he and the other student would be switching positions such that he would then be learning some paired associates and the other student would be controlling the light and delivering shocks. In the subsequent-role-switch condition, the subject was not informed that he and the target would switch positions until after he had completed the light and shock trials. For all subjects, the experimenter then left the room and played an audiotape of the target attempting to recall the correct paired-associate responses. The tape was constructed so that there were exactly 6 correct responses and 10 incorrect responses (all intralist intrusions) in each of three blocks of 16 words, a total of 30 shock measures being obtained from each subject.

Anticipation of aggression. After the subject had delivered shock to the target and was aware that he would be switching roles, it was explained that before proceeding, the experimenter was interested in knowing what levels of shock the subject expected to receive from the other student. The subject was told that each time a light flashed, he was to imagine he had made an error and indicate the shock level he expected to receive by pushing one of the eight shock buttons. The experimenter then returned to the control room and signaled a total of 30 consecutive simulated errors. Following the last error, the experimenter waited 3 minutes and returned to explain that since the other student had asked to leave, the subject was to leave immediately.

The final design reflected a $2 \times 2 \times 2 \times 2$ factorial, with race of target (black and white), anonymity (nonanonymous and anonymous), role-switching instructions (prior and subsequent), and target replication (two targets nested within each race) treated as factors. There were five subjects randomly assigned to each of the 16 cells, with assignment being made prior to a subject's appearance for the experiment.

Results

The major dependent measures were mean shock intensity, mean shock duration, and the sum of high-intensity shocks (Response Buttons 6, 7, and 8). Since a multivariate response system was of primary interest, the total correlation matrices of both the delivered and anticipated aggression data were first subjected to separate principal-components analyses. Since the principal components obtained in this experiment were highly comparable to those found in an independent analysis of Experiment II, the data from both experiments were pooled in defining the new variates. Analyses of variance were then conducted on the three (orthogonal) principal-component variables. (A rationale for such an approach can be found in Demp-

TABLE 21.1
Coefficients and variances of the three principal components for all subjects on
delivered and anticipated aggression scores (Experiments I and II)

Measure	Component					
	1		2		3	
	Delivered	Anticipated	Delivered	Anticipated	Delivered	Anticipated
Mean intensity	.6881	.7023	−.1281	−.0647	−.7142	−.7089
Mean duration	.2756	.1450	.9567	.9880	.0939	.0534
Sum high shocks	.6712	.6969	−.2614	−.1403	.6936	.7033
% total variance	62	61	31	33	7	6

ster, 1963). To eliminate negative values, a constant of 5 was added to all transformed scores.[1]

The principal components of both the anticipated and delivered shock data are presented in Table 21.1. Since the structures are very similar, the corresponding components may be interpreted together. The first principal component accounts for approximately 62 percent of the total variance and is dominated by intensity-related measures. Since differences in intensity are associated with easily discriminable buttons which ostensibly produce differentiable shocks, it seems reasonable to label this component *general direct aggression.* The second principal component represents an alternative measure of aggression, with duration contributing heavily to this factor. Inasmuch as differences in duration are likely to be less discriminable by the subject than differences in intensity, this component may be thought of as reflecting a type of aggression that is somewhat less direct than that measured by the first component. Approximately 32 percent of the total variance is accounted for by this component, which may be labeled *indirect aggression.* The third component provides a contrast between the values of the standardized high-shock and mean intensity measures. High scorers on this component tended to deliver either very high-level or very low-level shocks, or a combination of these. Low scorers tended to use predominately buttons within the intermediate range. Approximately 6 percent of the total variance is accounted for by this component, which may be characterized as a measure of *extremes in direct aggression.*

Analyses of variance, with race of target, anonymity, role-switch instructions, and target replication treated as factors were first performed on the delivered aggression components.[2] The analysis on the first component

---

[1]For interested readers, analyses of variance results on the raw scores can be found in an appendix of Donnerstein's (1969) thesis.

[2]The targets were obtained without any attempt to sample randomly from populations of black and white targets. A fixed-effects model was therefore employed in all data analyses since inferences are limited to the particular targets chosen.

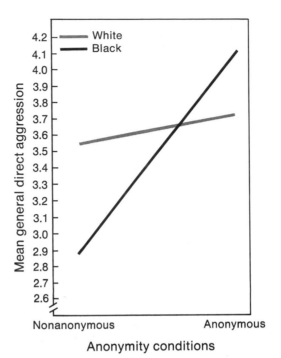

FIGURE 21.1
Mean general direct aggression delivered to
black and white targets as a function of
aggressor anonymity (Experiment I).

revealed significant effects for anonymity ($F = 8.00$, $df = 1/64$, $p < .01$), Race × Anonymity ($F = 4.65$, $df = 1/64$, $p < .05$), and Race × Instructions ($F = 7.96$, $df = 1/64$, $p < .01$). The interactions are presented in Figures 21.1 and 21.2. As is clear, the subjects shocking a black target delivered significantly lower levels of general direct aggression when they were not anonymous than when they were anonymous, and when they received prior-role-switch instructions as contrasted with subsequent-role-switch instructions. The subjects shocking a white target showed no reliable tendency to administer differential levels of general direct aggression as a function of the same situational conditions. In both figures the differences between black and white targets under comparable treatment conditions were statistically reliable. It should also be noted that the tendency for subjects paired with black targets to deliver the lowest levels of aggression under conditions of both nonanonymity and prior-role-switching and the highest levels under anonymous and subsequent-role-switch conditions is contained in the non-significant Race × Anonymity × Instructions interaction ($p < .20$).

The analysis on the second principal component revealed significant effects for race ($F = 4.18$, $df = 1/64$, $p < .05$), anonymity ($F = 4.09$, $df =$

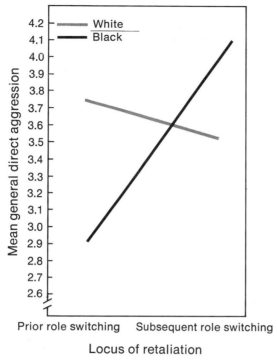

FIGURE 21.2
Mean general direct aggression delivered to black
and white targets as a function of locus of retaliation
instructions (Experiment I).

1/64, $p < .05$), and Race $\times$ Anonymity ($F = 4.02$, $df = 1/64$, $p < .05$). The interaction is presented in Figure 21.3. As can be seen, the subjects paired with a black target delivered a higher level of *indirect aggression* under nonanonymous than anonymous conditions, while the subjects shocking a white target did not exhibit differential levels of this kind of aggression over anonymity conditions. The analysis on the third principal component did not reveal any significant sources of variance.

Separate analyses of covariance were next conducted on the first and second principal components of the anticipated aggression data. Due to marked heterogeneity of regression, an analysis of variance was performed on the third component. In the covariance analyses, delivered scores were used as the covariate, and the reported means are correspondingly adjusted. The analysis on the first component revealed only a significant effect for race ($F = 35.77$, $df = 1/63$, $p < .001$), with subjects shocking a black target anticipating a higher level of general direct aggression than subjects shocking a white target. Respectively, the transformed means were 4.76 and 3.13; the within-groups regression coefficients were .74 and .66.

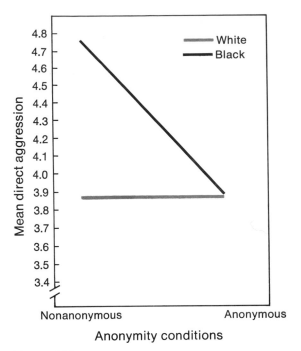

FIGURE 21.3
Mean indirect aggression delivered to black and
white targets as a function of aggressor anonymity
(Experiment I).

The same analysis on the second component yielded a significant main
effect for race ($F = 5.57$, $df = 1/63$, $p < .05$), and a reliable Anonymity $\times$
Target Replication interaction ($F = 3.21$, $df = 2/63$, $p < .05$). The interaction is primarily due to subjects anticipating a higher level of indirect
aggression from one of the white targets ($M = 4.87$) than from one of the
black targets ($M = 3.21$) under nonanonymous conditions. All other means
were comparable and averaged 4.09. The regression coefficients for black
and white targets were .98 and .67, respectively.

The analysis of variance on the third component revealed a marginally
significant effect for race ($F = 3.60$, $df = 1/64$, $p < .10$) and a significant
Race $\times$ Anonymity interaction ($F = 4.58$, $df = 1/64$, $p < .05$). The interaction
is attributable to the fact that subjects expected lower levels of *extremes
in direct aggression* from white ($M = 3.75$) than from black ($M = 4.12$)
targets under anonymous conditions; under nonanonymous conditions,
the means were comparable and averaged 3.95. It was of additional interest
to demonstrate that the foregoing difference was independent of delivered
aggression and primarily due to changes over anonymity conditions in anticipated aggression from white but not black targets. Accordingly, analyses of

covariance were also conducted on the third component scores for black and white targets separately. For white targets, there was only a significant main effect for anonymity ($F = 9.71$, $df = 1/31$, $p < .01$), the adjusted means being 4.11 and 3.74 for nonanonymous and anonymous conditions, respectively. There were no reliable effects for black targets, the corresponding means being 4.10 and 4.12. The regression coefficients were .04 and .87 for black and white targets, respectively.

EXPERIMENT II

Approximately two weeks after Experiment I had been completed, a racial disturbance occurred on the Northern Illinois University campus. An estimated 200 black students were reported to have participated in what resulted in minor injury to a number of whites and damage to university property. Rumors were also spread of possible open conflict between black and white students. This type of disorder had never occurred on the campus before.

The purpose of Experiment II was to examine the effects that these events might have had on interracial aggression. Since the violence associated with such a disturbance could be considered analogous to those events initially producing fear of black retaliation, one hypothesis might be that an increase in this fear followed the disturbance. If so, then under conditions favoring the opportunity for retaliation, for example, nonanonymity, the subjects paired with black targets should be expected to deliver lower levels of more direct kinds of aggression after the disturbance than before it. Based solely on increases in fear, no change in aggression would be predicted when the subjects aggressed anonymously, however, since fear of retaliation is assumed to be minimal under these conditions. It would also be expected that anticipated aggression from black targets would increase over time.

An alternative hypothesis might be that generalized anger and hostility were aroused by the disturbance, and that this had the effect of strengthening the tendency to aggress against black targets. Under this assumption, the anonymity variable should be less effective in controlling behavioral aggression toward blacks, with the result that higher levels of direct aggression would be delivered to black targets after the disturbance than before it.

Method

Subjects. The subjects were 28 white male introductory psychology students at Northern Illinois University. None of these subjects had served in Experiment I. All subjects participated between 2 and 5 days after the disturbance.

Procedure. Since it was important to conduct the study as soon after the disturbance as possible, the experimental design constituted only a partial replication of Experiment I. Twenty subjects were randomly assigned to one of two black targets, with 10 subjects each aggressing under either anonymous or nonanonymous conditions. As a control for general rather than specific increases in arousal or fear, the remaining 8 subjects were randomly assigned to one of two white targets, with 4 subjects under each of the two anonymity conditions. All subjects were without prior knowledge that they would switch roles with the target after they aggressed. In all other respects, the general procedure was identical to that employed in Experiment I.

Results

Unweighted-means analyses of variance with time (before or after the disturbance), race of target, anonymity, and target replication treated as factors were first performed on the principal components of the delivered aggression data. The before-level data was taken from those subjects under subsequent-role-switch instructions in Experiment I. The analysis on the first component revealed only a significant effect for race ($F = 7.99$, $df = 1/52$, $p < .01$), with subjects shocking a black target ($M = 4.62$) delivering higher levels of general direct aggression than subjects shocking a white target ($M = 3.57$). While the Time × Race ($p = .22$) and Time × Race × Anonymity ($p = .24$) interactions were not found to be significant, it should be noted that these tests would be sensitive only to relatively large interaction effects because of the small number of white targets employed in the replication. A more powerful procedure for assessing the effects of the riot on possible changes in aggression toward blacks would be to conduct a Time × Anonymity × Target Replication analysis of variance for those subjects aggressing against black targets alone. The results of this analysis indicated significant effects for time ($F = 5.56$, $df = 1/32$, $p < .05$) and anonymity ($F = 5.68$, $df = 1/32$, $p < .05$), with subjects delivering more general direct aggression to black targets after ($M = 5.16$) than before ($M = 4.09$) the riot, and under anonymous ($M = 5.17$) than nonanonymous ($M = 4.08$) conditions. Also, the Time × Anonymity interaction was marginally significant ($p = .11$), with differences in aggressivess between anonymous and nonanonymous conditions tending to be smaller after the riot ($D_M = .34$) than before it ($D_M = 1.82$). Contrary to the changes noted for black targets, the mean general direct aggression scores for white targets before and after the riot were virtually identical.

The unweighted analysis on the second component revealed significant effects for anonymity ($F = 7.71$, $df = 1/52$, $p < .01$) and target replication ($F = 4.32$, $df = 1/52$, $p < .05$). The subjects delivered a lower level of indirect aggression under anonymous ($M = 3.63$) than under nonanonymous conditions ($M = 4.22$). Additionally, a higher level of indirect aggression was administered to one of the black targets ($M = 4.46$) than to both white targets ($\bar{M} = 3.80$), the difference between the other black target ($M = 3.63$) and the white targets not being reliable. While the Time × Race × Anonymity interaction in the unweighted analysis was not significant ($p = .15$), the Time × Anonymity interaction was reliable in the analysis conducted for black targets alone ($F = 4.20$, $df = 1/32$, $p < .05$), with subjects aggressing under nonanonymous conditions delivering lower levels of indirect aggression to black targets after the riot ($M = 4.16$) than before it ($M = 4.76$); under anonymous conditions, the subjects showed little change in this kind of aggression toward black targets over time ($\bar{M} = 3.67$). For white targets, the means before and after the riot were similar and averaged 3.81.

The unweighted analysis on the third component indicated a significant Time × Race interaction ($F = 6.01$, $df = 1/52$, $p < .05$), which was due to increases in *extremes in direct aggression* toward white targets after the riot. The before and after means for black targets were 3.93 and 4.23, respectively; for white targets, they were 4.10 and 3.83.

Unweighted-means analyses of covariance were also conducted on the anticipation data. The analysis on general direct aggression yielded only a significant effect for race ($p < .05$), this again reflecting the fact that subjects paired with a black target ($M = 4.50$) anticipated a higher level of aggression than subjects paired with a white target ($M = 3.24$). The regression coefficients for black and white targets were comparable and averaged .60. The analyses on the second and third components did not reveal any significant or marginally significant sources of variance.

DISCUSSION

The present results are generally consistent with the hypothesis that white people have learned to fear black retaliation. Evidence supporting this conclusion was provided by the anticipation data which indicated that independent of delivered aggression, the subjects paired with black targets expected higher levels of more direct kinds of aggression than the subjects paired with white targets. Given the component interpretations, the finding that aggressive intent of a relatively direct nature was attributed to blacks would seem to be in accordance with the aims of black militant leaders who have argued that widespread violence and the fear of its occurrence is the only means of achieving racial equality. Whether such perceptions with respect to aggressive behavior might generally influence interracial relationships, such as by providing a basis for lessened prejudicial attitudes toward blacks, is of course a critical question which remains to be answered.

The anticipation data of Experiment I also revealed that subjects expected higher levels of indirect aggression from one of the white targets, and more *extremes in direct aggression* from both white targets, under nonanonymous than anonymous conditions. A possible explanation of these results may be found in Berkowitz's (1962) formulation that persons associated with aggressive behavior are likely to take on aggressive cue value. Thus, white subjects openly (nonanonymously) aggressing against their particular (white) targets might have perceived themselves as becoming more specific and justifiable targets for counteraggression than the subjects aggressing under anonymous conditions. Since it is unclear why the same results were not obtained for either of the white targets on the first component, however, this (post hoc) interpretation should be accepted with caution pending replication.

Additional evidence that blacks have succeeded in instilling fear of retaliation in whites was provided by the delivered aggression data in Experiment I. It was found that white subjects delivered significantly less general direct aggression to black targets under conditions favoring the opportunity for either immediate (prior-role-switching instructions) or future (nonanonymity) counteraggression than under conditions minimizing such opportunity. Moreover, the level of aggression administered to black targets under prior-role-switch and nonanonymous conditions was reliably lower than that delivered to white targets, to whom no differential aggression was given as a function of the same situational conditions. These results are consonant with a large number of studies showing that fear of punishment generally serves to inhibit aggressive behavior, and they agree well with a recent report that subjects who believe that their targets will counteraggress with a painful shock select lower shock levels themselves than do subjects who expect counteraggression to be unpleasant but not painful (Shortell, Epstein, and Taylor, 1970). In the same study, a significant negative correlation was found between ratings of an opponent's aggressiveness and a subject's shock settings ($r = -.67$).

In discussing conceptions of equity in human interaction, Walster, Berscheid, and Walster (1970) cite research which indicates that anticipated contact (namely, nonanonymity) with a (white) victim generally serves to discourage the use of justification techniques for aggressive actions by harmdoers. Specifically, subjects expecting to see their victims again tend to derogate them less than when no further contact is expected. Derogation is also minimized when subjects anticipate retaliation from their victims. In the latter instance, the results are attributed to the equity-establishing effects of anticipated counteraggression, while in the former, to the decreased likelihood of the harm-doer being able to provide a credible basis for his actions when publicly confronted by his victim. On the assumption that the same pattern of results would be obtained with black subjects as targets, this research, together with the present findings, suggests that the variables of nonanonymity and expected retaliation might act to promote racial equality by minimizing aggressive behavior by white persons initially and/or by arresting justification techniques after aggressive action has terminated.

The present data also indicate, however, that subjects exhibit a less direct form of aggression when there is opportunity for the target to retaliate. It was found that subjects paired with black targets delivered higher levels of indirect aggression under nonanonymous than anonymous conditions, and more of this kind of aggression to black than to white targets. As restated by Berkowitz (1962), the notion of response substitution in frustration-aggression theory would appear to account for this finding reasonably well. According to this formulation, the net strength of an aggressive response is taken as the difference between the levels of instigation and inhibition, with direct aggression being greater than indirect aggression when inhibition is low, for example, anonymity. However, where inhibition is high, relative to instigation, as under conditions of nonanonymity in the current study, a heightened form of indirect aggression is likely to be displayed.

That alternate forms of hostility were resorted to with black but not with white targets obviously implies differences in the predispositions of white college students to aggress against the two racial groups. A large body of research on the displacement of aggression toward outgroups (Harding, Proshansky, Kutner, and Chein, 1969), as well as several additional findings in the present study, would appear to support this conclusion. The marked increases in general direct aggression from nonanonymous to anonymous and from prior-role-switch to subsequent-role-switch conditions for black but not white targets can be taken as supporting evidence in the current data. Also pertinent is the fact that the latter results were independent of black target replication even though the particular targets represented on the videotapes were quite unalike. While one depicted a well-dressed college student with short hair who seemed a bit exuberant at times, the other portrayed a student with a more natural Afro-American look. The latter target spoke in a very low and deep voice and could be characterized as being somewhat "militant" in appearance. That subjects showed higher levels of aggression to both of these targets than to both white targets under anonymous and subsequent-role-switch conditions, as well as lower levels under nonanonymous and prior-role-switch conditions, provides evidence for a generalized negative stereotype of black persons as constituting a particular group against which to display hostility on the one hand and as being highly aggressive or militant on the other.

Experiment II constituted a partial replication of Experiment I and was conducted immediately following a campus racial disturbance. It was of interest to determine *(a)* whether anticipated and delivered scores after the disturbance would be comparable to the levels observed in Experiment I and *(b)* whether any observed changes would be confined to black targets. Consistent with notions relating generalized aggression to a particular target's association with observed violence (Berkowitz, 1965), the results showed significant changes in delivered aggression for black but not white targets, with no reliable changes in anticipated aggression being found for either target race. Specifically, higher levels of direct aggression and reduced levels of indirect aggression were delivered to black targets after the disturbance than before it. Although contrary to the hypothesis that increases in fear of black retaliation would follow the disturbance, the findings agree well with a joint disinhibition and elicitation interpretation based on the vicarious instigation of anger.[3] Thus, while still anticipating more counteraggression from black targets, the subjects now displayed comparable degrees of hostility toward blacks under anonymous and nonanonymous conditions, with the overall levels of direct kinds of aggression being higher than that delivered to the same targets under anonymous conditions in Experiment I.

Baldwin (1963) has suggested that the fear of black power to retaliate is the only means of achieving racial equality. While suggesting that white persons have indeed learned to fear black retaliation, the present data reveal that this fear influences only the form of aggressiveness toward blacks and not simply its occurrence. It was also found that direct forms of aggression were instigated by generalized violence. Although the short-term effects of such violence therefore seem not to have been salutary, it may well be true that the very occurrence of conflict and the need for its resolution can, in the long run, provide an important impetus for producing acceptable social change.

References

BALDWIN, J. *The fire next time.* New York: Dial, 1963.

BANDURA, A. Influence of models' reinforcement contingencies on the acquisition of imitative responses. *Journal of Personality and Social Psychology,* 1965, **1,** 589–595.

BANDURA, A., ROSS, D., AND ROSS, S. A. Vicarious reinforcement and imitative learning. *Journal of Abnormal and Social Psychology,* 1963, **67,** 601–607.

BERKOWITZ, L. *Aggression: A social psychological analysis.* New York: McGraw-Hill, 1962.

[3]An alternative interpretation might be that the results of Experiment I were unreliable. However, the findings of both the preliminary study and other research in our laboratory discount this possibility.

BERKOWITZ, L. The concept of aggressive drive: Some additional considerations. In L. Berkowitz (ed.), *Advances in experimental social psychology.* Vol. 2. New York: Academic Press, 1965.

BUSS, A. H. *The psychology of aggression.* New York: Wiley, 1961.

DEMPSTER, A. P. Stepwise multivariate analysis of variance based on principal variables. *Biometrics,* 1963, **19,** 478–490.

DONNERSTEIN, E. I. Variables in interracial aggression: Anonymity, expected retaliation, and a riot. Unpublished master's thesis, Northern Illinois University, 1969.

EDWARDS, N. L. Aggressive expression under threat of retaliation. Unpublished doctoral dissertation, University of Iowa, 1967. *Dissertation Abstracts,* 1968, **28,** 3470.

HARDING, J., PROSHANSKY, H., KUTNER, B., AND CHEIN, I. Prejudice and ethnic relations. In G. Lindzey and E. Aronson (eds.), *The handbook of social psychology.* Vol. 5. (2nd ed.) Reading, Mass.: Addison-Wesley, 1969.

NOBLE, C. E. Measurement of association value (a), rated associations (a'), and scaled meaningfulness (m') for the 2100 CVC combinations of the English alphabet. *Psychological Reports,* 1961, **8,** 487–521.

SHORTELL, J., EPSTEIN, S., AND TAYLOR, S. P. Instigation to aggression as a function of degree of defeat and the capacity for massive retaliation. *Journal of Personality,* 1970, **38,** 313–328.

WALSTER, E., BERSCHEID, E., AND WALSTER, G. W. The exploited: Justice or justification? In J. E. Macaulay and L. Berkowitz (eds.), *Altruism and helping behavior: Social psychological studies of some antecedents and consequences.* New York: Academic Press, 1970.

22

Racial Preference and
Social Comparison Processes

Steven R. Asher and Vernon L. Allen

A number of studies have demonstrated that children negatively evaluate Negroes and positively evaluate whites. The original work by Clark and Clark (1947) found that Negro children preferred a white doll and rejected a black doll when asked to choose which was nice, which looked bad, which they would like to play with and which was the nice color.

This basic result has been found repeatedly in studies using a variety of testing materials, and within various geographical and social settings. The findings hold for Northern Negro children (Clark and Clark, 1947; Goodman, 1952; Greenwald and Oppenheim, 1968; Helgerson, 1943; Radke et al., 1950; Radke and Trager, 1950) as well as for Southern (Clark and Clark, 1947; Morland, 1962; Stevenson and Stewart, 1958), and for integrated as well as segregated children (Goodman, 1952; Stevenson and Stewart, 1958).

Studies of white children have their similar consistency demonstrated the same pattern of white preference and black rejection (Greenwald and Oppen-

Reprinted with permission from the authors and *The Journal of Social Issues,* Vol. 25, No. 1, 1969.

This research was supported in part by a grant from the Institute for Research on Poverty. The authors wish to thank Marvin Phinazee and Bess Norman for their assistance.

heim, 1968; Horowitz, 1936; Helgerson, 1943; Morland, 1962; Stevenson and Stewart, 1958). As with Negro children, the same basic finding of white preference has been repeatedly noted over a range of materials, locations and settings.

Despite this rather sizable literature on racial preference, important variables have been neglected, and unfortunately no well-controlled direct comparisons have been made with the original Clark and Clark (1947) data. The present study was a partial replication and extension of the Clarks' work. Previously neglected social class and sex variables as well as age were investigated. Both white and Negro children were studied to assess the relative amount of preference and to determine whether variables influenced both groups in a similar fashion. Present data on Negro children's responses were compared with Clark and Clark's data to determine whether the past three decades of change in status has resulted in a change in skin color preference.[1]

In addition, past studies have given little attention to theoretical issues. Rather than making direct predictions the present study tests two competing theoretical models. One model posits that social and economic progress, as success experiences and extensions of control over the environment, create enhanced feelings of competence and racial pride. This view follows from the thinking of White (1959), Erikson (1950), and others. It can be seen as a fundamental assumption of the poverty program. Coleman et al. (1966) have recently articulated a similar view regarding the effects of integration. Specifically, this model predicts that Negro children today will show more black color preference than children tested earlier by the Clarks, and furthermore, that middle-class Negroes will respond more favorably to their own race than lower-class Negroes.

Social comparison theory (Festinger, 1954) offers opposite predictions. Economic progress and social mobility should lead to more frequent comparison with whites (Pettigrew, 1967). The result of such comparisons would be greater feelings of inferiority, since whites still are generally more advantaged. This model predicts, then, that white preference will be greater among Negro children today. It also predicts that lower-class Negro children will respond more favorably to their own race than middle-class Negro children.

Social class differences in white children's preferences are not predicted, since the extent to which whites of different classes engage in social comparison with Negroes is unknown. Intuitively, it seems reasonable to believe that both middle- and lower-class whites use middle-class whites as a comparison group. It could be argued, however, that the lower-class whites'

---

[1]The Clark and Clark (1947) data were collected in 1939–1940.

closer social position and more frequent contact with Negro people will make for greater comparison with them. Given this ambiguity, straightforward predictions about white children's responses do not follow. Thus the two competing models discussed above are relevant only to data of Negro children.

METHOD USED

Subjects

A total of 341 white and Negro children from Newark, New Jersey and surrounding areas were tested. Of this number 186 were Negro and 155 were white. Children ranged in age from three to eight and were divided into middle and lower class according to parents' occupation (Strodtbeck, 1958). Falling into the middle-class category were 167 children; lower-class children totaled 174. Children were grouped into age categories of 3–4, 5–6, 7–8 to maximize number of Ss per cell.

Materials

Three pairs of puppets, manufactured by Creative Playthings, were used to match as closely as possible the sex and age of the subject. Within each pair, puppets were identical except for skin and hair color. The "Negro" puppet had medium brown facial color and black hair; the "white" puppet had light skin and light hair. Puppets were chosen rather than dolls so that the testing situation would be appropriate to both girls and boys.

Procedure

Children were tested in fifteen different settings which included private nursery schools, neighborhood centers, pre-school programs, play streets run by the city, and nurseries receiving support through the poverty program. The majority of settings were de facto segregated by virtue of neighborhood, costs of the program or social class criteria for selection. Only one setting was completely segregated, and only two were fairly well-integrated. Most settings, then, had an overwhelming number of children from either one race or the other.

Two puppets, one brown and one white, were placed in a prone position before each child. Younger children (ages three, four, and five) were shown the baby puppets (two boys of about two years old). Older children (ages six, seven, and eight) were shown puppets which were the same sex of the

TABLE 22.1
Racial preferences of Negro and white children (%)

Item	Negro children ($N = 186$)				White children ($N = 155$)			
	White puppet	Brown puppet	χ^2	p	White puppet	Brown puppet	χ^2	p
Nice puppet	76	23	26.0	<.001	76	20	24.9	<.001
Plays with	69	30	14.5	<.001	75	22	22.4	<.001
Looks bad	24	73	22.8	<.001	18	77	28.1	<.001
Nice color	69	29	15.5	<.001	74	20	24.1	<.001

subject (these puppets appear to be about eleven years old). Each child was tested individually in a room apart from the other children.

Two experimenters, one Negro and one white, were employed to control for race. Each experimenter tested children of his own race. Both were male and within one year of age of each other. In this way response bias due to effects of the experimenter's race, age and sex were minimized.

After asking the child his name and generally helping the child to feel comfortable, the experimenter asked the following questions adapted from Clark and Clark (1947):

    (a) Which puppet is the nice puppet?
    (b) Which puppet would you like to play with?
    (c) Which puppet looks bad?
    (d) Which puppet is the nice color?

Questions were asked randomly to prevent any possible order effect. Children responded by pointing to one of the two puppets. Following the child's response, he and the experimenter briefly played with the puppets and the child was returned to the general play area.

OVERALL PREFERENCES

Presented in Table 22.1 are overall preferences of Negro and white children. Included in the table are the response categories "brown puppet" and "white puppet."[2] It is clear from Table 22.1 that the large majority of both Negro and white children preferred the white puppet and rejected the brown puppet. All of these percentages were significant at the .001 level by chi-square tests. Furthermore, Negro and white children did not significantly differ in their preference for the white puppet and rejection of the brown puppet.

---

[2]The small number of "no preference" responses were excluded from the analysis, which accounts for the failure of some percentages to sum to 100 percent.

Only on "nice color" was there a large Negro-white discrepancy in response ($\chi^2 = 2.72$, $p < .10$). In general, then, there was remarkable consistency between Negro and white children in their preference for the white puppet and rejection of the brown puppet.

SOCIAL CLASS DIFFERENCES

Social class did not produce a substantial difference on any item for Negro children; however, on all four questions middle-class children responded with a slight higher proportion of white puppet preference. This tendency was strongest on the item "nice puppet," with 82 percent of the middle-class Negro children choosing the white puppet and 71 percent of the lower-class Negro children giving this response. Class difference on the items "play with," "looks bad," and "nice color" was less sharp, but on each there was somewhat greater white preference by the middle class (average of about 8 percent).

For white children, there was little meaningful social class difference in racial preference. On three of the items lower-class whites more frequently chose the white puppet, while on one of the items ("play with") direction of results were reversed. All of the differences were small and did not approach significance.

Social class data were analyzed another way. Children were categorized according to whether they consistently preferred the white puppet across the four items, consistently favored the brown puppet, or were inconsistent in their preference. Results showed a strong tendency for middle-class Negro children consistently to prefer the white puppet, while lower-class children showed inconsistent responses ($\chi^2 = 6.30$, $p < .05$). White children showed no difference in consistency of response across items as a function of social class.

SEX DIFFERENCES

Table 22.2 presents male-female differences in racial preference among Negro children. On all four items boys favored the white puppet more than girls. The sex difference reached significance on the items "nice puppet," "looks bad," and "nice color," Smallest sex difference was found on the item "play with," though here also there was greater white preference among boys.

The same direction on sex difference was found for white children, as shown in Table 22.3. Again, on all items males showed greater white preference than females. The items "nice puppet" and "looks bad" reached significance at the .10 level.

TABLE 22.2
Sex comparisons for Negro children

Item	Males %	Females %	χ^2	p
Nice puppet				
White puppet	83	68		
Brown puppet	16	31	5.41	<.05
Play with				
White puppet	73	64		
Brown puppet	27	33	1.25	ns
Looks bad				
White puppet	19	30		
Brown puppet	79	67	2.81	<.10
Nice color				
White puppet	74	63		
Brown puppet	24	34	2.80	<.10

Note: Male $N = 96$; female $N = 85$.

TABLE 22.3
Sex comparisons for white children

Item	Males %	Females %	χ^2	p
Nice puppet				
White puppet	80	72		
Brown puppet	15	26	3.08	<.10
Play with				
White puppet	78	72		
Brown puppet	17	27	2.06	ns
Looks bad				
White puppet	12	25		
Brown puppet	81	73	3.54	<.10
Nice color				
White puppet	77	72		
Brown puppet	16	25	1.40	ns

Note: Male $N = 77$; female $N = 71$.

AGE TRENDS

Age trends were quite complex, and less consistent across items than social class and sex findings. Among Negro children only the item "play with" yielded a significant change with age, as white preference increased from 73 percent at age 3–4 to 80 percent at age 5–6, and then decreased to 51 percent at 7–8 ($\chi^2 = 12.25$, $p < .01$). Among whites, only one item ("nice color") approached significance: from 77 percent at age 3–4 there was an increase to 84 percent at 5–6, then a decrease to 59 percent at 7–8 ($\chi^2 = 5.37$, $p < .10$).

No significance interactions emerged from the Sex by Age analyses. However, among Negro children there was a tendency for male-female differences in racial preference to widen with age, as males increased somewhat

TABLE 22.4
Comparison of present results with Clark and Clark's data

Item	1939 %	1967 %	χ^2	*p*
Nice puppet				
White puppet	68	76	2.02	ns
Brown puppet	30	23		
Play with				
White puppet	72	69	0.19	ns
Brown puppet	28	27		
Looks bad				
White puppet	17	24	1.19	ns
Brown puppet	71	73		
Nice color				
White puppet	63	69	1.94	ns
Brown puppet	37	29		

in white puppet preference while females decreased. Results for white children disclosed a general tendency for both males and females to follow a curvilinear relationship between age and racial preference.

HISTORICAL COMPARISON

Table 22.4 compares present findings with those of Clark and Clark (1947). (Data are presented under the year in which the study was conducted, 1939.) The Clarks' Northern data are used to maximize comparability with the present sample.[3]

While degree of consistency between the 1939 and 1967 data is perhaps most striking, there is some evidence of an increase in white color preference among Negro children. On three of the four items there was greater white preference today than 28 years ago: only one item ("play with") showed decreased white preference. On none of the items did differences reach statistical significance.

enhanced status will not necessarily lead to greater racial pride, but may

SOCIAL COMPARISON MODEL FINDS SOME SUPPORT

Results of the present study are more consistent with a social comparison model than an individual competence model. Social class data for Negro children and the historical comparison with the Clarks' results suggest that

---

[3]The Clarks' Northern sample was an integrated one while the present sample was largely segregated. From a social comparison viewpoint integration would lead to greater white preference among Negroes, thus it is possible that the comparison presented in Table 22.3 underestimates the amount of change from 1939 to 1967.

instead contribute, through more frequent comparison with whites, to increased feelings of inferiority.

Caution is advisable in appraising the social class data and historical differences in view of the lack of statistical support; however, these data are consistent with other findings. Clark and Clark (1947) found significant differences on two items between their Northern integrated and Southern segregated samples. The Northern sample showed greater white preference, a finding congruent with the social comparison model. Similarly, the "Coleman report" noted lower "academic self-concept" for Negro children in integrated schools despite the fact that they showed higher achievement than Negro children attending segregated schools. Integration is probably an important variable leading to increased comparison with whites. Finally, the relatively high proportion of seven and eight year old Negro children in the present study who chose the brown puppet to "play with," is a finding consistent with social comparison theory. Festinger (1954) has postulated a tendency to avoid the presence of those who remind one of a large discrepancy in attitude and ability. Perhaps Negro children, as they grow older, chose increasingly to play with members of their own race to avoid threatening social comparisons.[4]

The greater white preference of males is one of the most interesting results of the present study. That both races yielded a sex difference suggests that the greater white preference of males is not the result of personal attacks on one's competence but of a general awareness of the relatively inferior position of Negroes, an awareness made more salient for those enacting the male role. It is the male who suffers the greatest consequences of prejudice and oppression.

The hypothesis of differential sensitivity to Negro-white status differences as a function of the child's own sex role must be offered cautiously. Nonetheless, there is evidence of considerable awareness of social reality in young children. A majority of three year olds showed a strong preference for white skin color. Small children have also been found to assign poorer houses and stereotyped social roles to brown dolls (Radke and Trager, 1950; Stevenson and Stewart, 1958).

SOME OF THE MANY QUESTIONS

Results of the present study suggest questions for future research. First there is a need to determine the relationship between racial preference and behavior. Are black people who express white preference less assertive,

---

[4]These children are, of course, avoiding more than threatening social comparisons. They are avoiding, as well, the insults and disparagement likely to be given by white children. Coles (1967) notes that Negro mothers are likely to caution their children at an early age against playing with whites.

more likely to do well in school, less likely to participate in a civil rights demonstration? Racial preference can be conceptualized as an attitude; unfortunately we know little about the relationship between attitudes and behavior (Deutscher, 1966; Festinger, 1964).

Second, present results suggest that the variables usually believed to be crucial in effecting a positive change in black peoples' identity may be less important than previously thought. As long as a large discrepancy exists between the living conditions and skills of blacks and whites a small closing of the gap may only psychologically magnify the difference. If integration and small socio-economic gains are insufficient to the development of racial pride, then other potential sources of change should be investigated. The relationship between involvement in social and political movements and change in self and race evaluation is worthy of scrutiny.

Possibly such movements contribute to increased feelings of competence not only through victories in social struggles but also by encouraging participants to select new social comparison groups. For example, black people are urged by militant leaders to develop their own values and goals and to cease striving toward middle-class ideals (Carmichael and Hamilton, 1967). Rejection of social comparison with whites may result in a more positive racial and self conception. It is interesting, though only suggestive, that in the present study two children from Black Muslim homes chose the brown puppet. Hopefully, the examination of the effect on self of black peoples' participation in a wide range of social and political movements will allow for more optimism than can be generated from the present study.

References

CARMICHAEL, F. F., AND HAMILTON, C. V. *Black power: politics of liberation in America.* New York: Random House, 1967.

CLARK, K. B., AND CLARK, M. P. Racial identification and racial preference in Negro children. In T. M. Newcomb and E. L. Hartley (eds.), *Readings in social psychology.* New York: Holt, 1947, 169–178.

COLEMAN, J. S., CAMPBELL, E. Q., HOBSON, C. J., MCFARLAND, J., MOOD, A. M., WEINFELD, F. D., AND YORK, R. L. *Equality of opportunity.* Washington, D.C.: United States Government Printing Office, 1966.

COLES, R. *Children of crisis: a study of courage and fear.* Boston: Little, Brown and Co., 1967.

DEUTSCHER, I. Words and deeds: social science and social policy. *Social Problems,* 1966, **13,** 235–254.

ERIKSON, E. H. *Childhood and society.* New York: Norton, 1950.

FESTINGER, L. A theory of social comparison processes. *Human Relations,* 1954, **7,** 117–140.

FESTINGER, L. Behavioral support for opinion change. *Public Opinion Quarterly,* 1964, **28,** 404–417.

GREENWALD, H. J., AND OPPENHEIM, D. B. Reported magnitude of self-misidentification among Negro children—artifact? *Journal of Personality and Social Psychology,* 1968, **8,** 49–52.

GOODMAN, M. E. *Race awareness in young children.* Cambridge, Mass.: Addison-Wesley, 1952.

HELGERSON, E. The relative significance of race, sex and facial expression in choice of playmate by the preschool child. *Journal of Negro Education,* 1943, **12,** 617–622.

HOROWITZ, E. L. The development of attitude toward the Negro. *Archives of Psychology,* N.Y., 1936, (194).

MORLAND, J. K. Racial acceptance and preference of nursery school children in a southern city. *Merrill-Palmer Quarterly,* 1962, **8,** 217–280.

PETTIGREW, T. F. Social evaluation theory: convergences and application. *Nebraska Symposium on Motivation,* 1967, **15,** 241–311.

RADKE, M., SUTHERLAND, J., AND ROSENBERG, P. Racial attitudes of children. *Sociometry,* 1950, **13,** 154–171.

RADKE, M. J., AND TRAGER, H. G. Children's perceptions of the social roles of Negroes and whites. *Journal of Psychology,* 1950, **29,** 3–33.

STEVENSON, H. W., AND STEWART, E. C. A developmental study of race awareness in young children. *Child Development,* 1958, **29,** 399–410.

STRODTBECK, F. L. Family interaction values and achievement. In D. C. McClelland, A. L. Baldwin, U. Bronferbrenner, and F. L. Strodtbeck (eds.), *Talent and society: new perspectives in the identification of talent.* New York: Van Nostrand, 1958.

WHITE, R. W. Motivation reconsidered: the concept of competence. *Psychological Review,* 1959, **66,** 297–333.

23

Experiments in Group Conflict

Muzafer Sherif

What are the conditions which lead to harmony or friction between groups of people? Here the question is approached by means of controlled situations in a boys' summer camp.

Conflict between groups—whether between boys' gangs, social classes, "races" or nations—has no simple cause, nor is mankind yet in sight of a cure. It is often rooted deep in personal, social, economic, religious and historical forces. Nevertheless, it is possible to identify certain general factors which have a crucial influence on the attitude of any group toward others. Social scientists have long sought to bring these factors to light by studying what might be called the "natural history" of groups and group relations. Intergroup conflict and harmony is not a subject that lends itself easily to laboratory experiments. But in recent years there has been a beginning of attempts to investigate the problem under controlled yet lifelike conditions, and I shall report here the results of a program of experimental studies of groups which I started in 1948. Among the persons working with me were Marvin B. Sussman, Robert Huntington, O. J. Harvey, B. Jack White, William R. Hood and Carolyn W. Sherif. The experiments were conducted in 1949, 1953 and 1954; this article gives a composite of the findings.

We wanted to conduct our study with groups of the informal type, where group organization and attitudes would evolve naturally and spontaneously, without formal direction or external pressures. For this purpose we conceived that an isolated summer camp would make a good experimental setting, and that decision led us to choose as subjects boys about eleven or twelve years old, who would find camping natural and fascinating. Since our aim was to study the development of group relations among these boys under carefully controlled conditions, with as little interference as possible from personal neuroses, background influences or prior experiences, we selected normal boys of homogeneous background who did not know one another before they came to the camp.

They were picked by a long and thorough procedure. We interviewed each boy's family, teachers and school officials, studied his school and medical records, obtained his scores on personality tests and observed him in his classes and at play with his schoolmates. With all this information we were able to assure ourselves that the boys chosen were of like kind and background: all were healthy, socially well-adjusted, somewhat above average in intelligence and from stable, white, Protestant, middle-class homes.

None of the boys was aware that he was part of an experiment on group relations. The investigators appeared as a regular camp staff—camp directors, counselors and so on. The boys met one another for the first time in

FIGURE 23.1
Members of one group of boys raid the bunkhouse of another group during the first experiment of the author and his associates, performed at a summer camp in Connecticut. The rivalry of the groups was intensified by the artifical separation of their goals. (Photograph by Muzafer Sherif.)

buses that took them to the camp, and so far as they knew it was a normal summer of camping. To keep the situation as lifelike as possible, we conducted all our experiments within the framework of regular camp activities and games. We set up projects which were so interesting and attractive that the boys plunged into them enthusiastically without suspecting that they might be test situations. Unobtrusively we made records of their behavior, even using "candid" cameras and microphones when feasible.

We began by observing how the boys became a coherent group. The first of our camps was conducted in the hills of northern Connecticut in the summer of 1949. When the boys arrived, they were all housed at first in one large bunkhouse. As was to be expected, they quickly formed particular friendships and chose buddies. We had deliberately put all the boys together in this expectation, because we wanted to see what would happen later after the boys were separated into different groups. Our object was to reduce the factor of personal attraction in the formation of groups. In a few days we divided the boys into two groups and put them in different cabins. Before doing so, we asked each boy informally who his best friends were, and then took pains to place the "best friends" in different groups so far as possible. (The pain of separation was assuaged by allowing each group to go at once on a hike and camp-out.)

As everyone knows, a group of strangers brought together in some common activity soon acquires an informal and spontaneous kind of organization. It comes to look upon some members as leaders, divides up duties, adopts unwritten norms of behavior, develops an *esprit de corps*. Our boys followed this pattern as they shared a series of experiences. In each group the boys pooled their efforts, organized duties and divided up tasks in work and play. Different individuals assumed different responsibilities. One boy excelled in cooking. Another led in athletics. Others, though not outstanding in any one skill, could be counted on to pitch in and do their level best in anything the group attempted. One or two seemed to disrupt activities, to start teasing at the wrong moment or offer useless suggestions. A few boys consistently had good suggestions and showed ability to coordinate the efforts of others in carrying them through. Within a few days one person had proved himself more resourceful and skillful than the rest. Thus, rather quickly, a leader and lieutenants emerged. Some boys sifted toward the bottom of the heap, while others jockeyed for higher positions.

FIGURE 23.2
Members of both groups collaborate in common enterprises during the second experiment, performed at a summer camp in Oklahoma. At the top, the boys of the two groups prepare a meal. In the middle, the two groups surround a water tank while trying to solve a water-shortage problem. At the bottom, the members of one group entertain the other. (Photographs by Muzafer Sherif.)

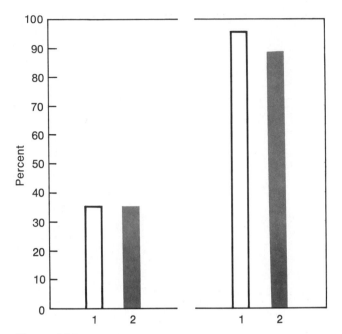

FIGURE 23.3
Friendship choices of campers for others in their own cabin
are shown for Red Devils (*white*) and Bulldogs (*gray*). At
first, a low percentage of friendships were in the cabin group
(*left*). After five days, most friendship choices were within the
group (*right*).

We watched these developments closely and rated the boys' relative positions in the group, not only on the basis of our own observations but also
by informal sounding of the boys' opinions as to who got things started, who
got things done, who could be counted on to support group activities.

As the group became an organization, the boys coined nicknames. The
big, blond, hardy leader of one group was dubbed "Baby Face" by his ad-
miring followers. A boy with a rather long head became "Lemon Head."
Each group developed its own jargon, special jokes, secrets and special
ways of performing tasks. One group, after killing a snake near a place where
it had gone to swim, named the place "Moccasin Creek" and thereafter preferred this swimming hole to any other, though there were better ones nearby.

Wayward members who failed to do things "right" or who did not contribute their bit to the common effort found themselves receiving the "silent
treatment," ridicule or even threats. Each group selected symbols and a
name, and they had these put on their caps and T-shirts. The 1954 camp was
conducted in Oklahoma, near a famous hideaway of Jesse James called Robber's Cave. The two groups of boys at this camp named themselves the
Rattlers and the Eagles.

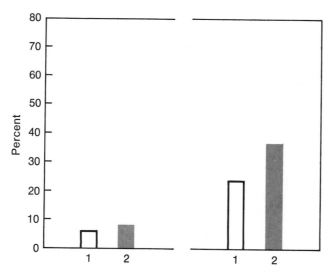

FIGURE 23.4
During conflict between the two groups in the Robber's Cave experiment, there were few friendships between cabins (*left*). After cooperation toward common goals had restored good feelings, the number of friendships between groups rose significantly (*right*).

Our conclusions on every phase of the study were based on a variety of observations, rather than on any single method. For example, we devised a game to test the boys' evaluations of one another. Before an important baseball game, we set up a target board for the boys to throw at, on the pretense of making practice for the game more interesting. There were no marks on the front of the board for the boys to judge objectively how close the ball came to a bull's-eye, but, unknown to them, the board was wired to flashing lights behind so that an observer could see exactly where the ball hit. We found that the boys consistently overestimated the performances by the most highly regarded members of their group and underestimated the scores of those of low social standing.

The attitudes of group members were even more dramatically illustrated during a cook-out in the woods. The staff supplied the boys with unprepared food and let them cook it themselves. One boy promptly started to build a fire, asking for help in getting wood. Another attacked the raw hamburger to make patties. Others prepared a place to put buns, relishes and the like. Two mixed soft drinks from flavoring and sugar. One boy who stood around without helping was told by the others to "get to it." Shortly the fire was blazing and the cook had hamburgers sizzling. Two boys distributed them as rapidly as they became edible. Soon it was time for the watermelon. A low-ranking member of the group took a knife and started toward the melon.

Some of the boys protested. The most highly regarded boy in the group took over the knife, saying, "You guys who yell the loudest get yours last."

When the two groups in the camp had developed group organization and spirit, we proceeded to the experimental studies of intergroup relations. The groups had had no previous encounters; indeed, in the 1954 camp at Robber's Cave the two groups came in separate buses and were kept apart while each acquired a group feeling.

Our working hypothesis was that when two groups have conflicting aims — i.e., when one can achieve its ends only at the expense of the other — their members will become hostile to each other even though the groups are composed of normal well-adjusted individuals. There is a corollary to this assumption which we shall consider later. To produce friction between the groups of boys we arranged a tournament of games: baseball, touch football, a tug-of-war, a treasure hunt and so on. The tournament started in a spirit of good sportsmanship. But as it progressed good feeling soon evaporated. The members of each group began to call their rivals "stinkers," "sneaks" and "cheater." They refused to have anything more to do with individuals in the opposing group. The boys in the 1949 camp turned against buddies whom they had chosen as "best friends" when they first arrived at the camp. A large proportion of the boys in each group gave negative ratings to all the boys in the other. The rival groups made threatening posters and planned raids, collecting secret hoards of green apples for ammunition. In the Robber's Cave camp the Eagles, after a defeat in a tournament game, burned a banner left behind by the Rattlers; the next morning the Rattlers seized the Eagles' flag when they arrived on the athletic field. From that time on name-calling scuffles and raids were the rule of the day.

Within each group, of course, solidarity increased. There were changes: one group deposed its leader because he could not "take it" in the contests with the adversary; another group overnight made something of a hero of a big boy who had previously been regarded as a bully. But morale and co-operativeness within the group became stronger. It is noteworthy that this heightening of cooperativeness and generally democratic behavior did not carry over to the group's relations with other groups.

We now turned to the other side of the problem: How can two groups in conflict be brought into harmony? We first undertook to test the theory that pleasant social contacts between members of conflicting groups will reduce friction between them. In the 1954 camp we brought the hostile Rattlers and Eagles together for social events: going to the movies, eating in the same dining room and so on. But far from reducing conflict, these situations only served as opportunities for the rival groups to berate and attack each other. In the dining-hall line they shoved each other aside, and the group that lost the contest for the head of the line shouted "Ladies first!" at the winner.

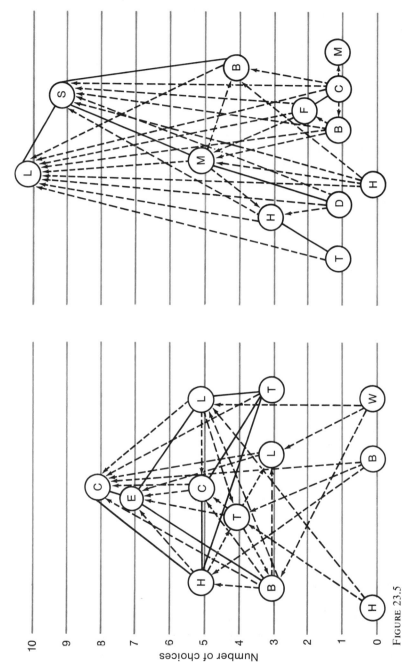

Number of choices

FIGURE 23.5

Sociograms represent patterns of friendship choices within the fully developed groups. One-way friendships are indicated by broken arrows; reciprocated friendships, by solid lines. Leaders were among those highest in the popularity scale. Bulldogs (*left*) had a close-knit organization with good group spirit. Low-ranking members participated less in the life of the group but were not rejected. Red Devils (*right*) lost the tournament of games between the groups. They had less group unity and were sharply stratified.

They threw paper, food and vile names at each other at the tables. An Eagle bumped by a Rattler was admonished by his fellow Eagles to brush "the dirt" off his clothes.

We then returned to the corollary of our assumption about the creation of conflict. Just as competition generates friction, working in a common endeavor should promote harmony. It seemed to us, considering group relations in the everyday world, that where harmony between groups is established, the most decisive factor is the existence of "superordinate" goals which have a compelling appeal for both but which neither could achieve without the other. To test this hypothesis experimentally, we created a series of urgent, and natural, situations which challenged our boys.

One was a breakdown in the water supply. Water came to our camp in pipes from a tank about a mile away. We arranged to interrupt it and then called the boys together to inform them of the crisis. Both groups promptly volunteered to search the water line for the trouble. They worked together harmoniously, and before the end of the afternoon they had located and corrected the difficulty.

A similar opportunity offered itself when the boys requested a movie. We told them that the camp could not afford to rent one. The two groups then got together, figured out how much each group would have to contribute, chose the film by a vote and enjoyed the showing together.

One day the two groups went on an outing at a lake some distance away. A large truck was to go to town for food. But when everyone was hungry and ready to eat, it developed that the truck would not start (we had taken care of that). The boys got a rope—the same rope they had used in their acrimonious tug-of-war—and all pulled together to start the truck.

These joint efforts did not immediately dispel hostility. At first the groups returned to the old bickering and name-calling as soon as the job in hand was finished. But gradually the series of cooperative acts reduced friction and conflict. The members of the two groups began to feel more friendly to each other. For example, a Rattler whom the Eagles disliked for his sharp tongue and skill in defeating them became a "good egg." The boys stopped shoving in the meal line. They no longer called each other names, and sat together at the table. New friendships developed between individuals in the two groups.

In the end the groups were actively seeking opportunities to mingle, to entertain and "treat" each other. They decided to hold a joint campfire. They took turns presenting skits and songs. Members of both groups requested that they go home together on the same bus, rather than on the separate buses in which they had come. On the way the bus stopped for refreshments. One group still had five dollars which they had won as a prize in a contest. They decided to spend this sum on refreshments. On their own initiative they invited their former rivals to be their guests for malted milks.

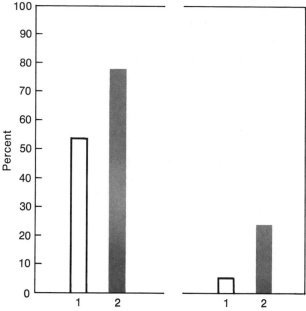

FIGURE 23.6
Negative ratings of each group by the other were common
during the period of conflict (*left*) but decreased when
harmony was restored (*right*). The graphs show percentage
who thought *all* (rather than *some* or *none*) of the other
group were cheaters, sneaks, and so forth.

Our interviews with the boys confirmed this change. From choosing their
"best friends" almost exclusively in their own group, many of them shifted
to listing boys in the other group as best friends (see Fig. 23.4). They were
glad to have a second chance to rate boys in the other group, some of them
remarking that they had changed their minds since the first rating made after
the tournament. Indeed they had. The new ratings were largely favorable
(see Fig. 23.6).

Efforts to reduce friction and prejudice between groups in our society have
usually followed rather different methods. Much attention has been given to
bringing members of hostile groups together socially, to communicating
accurate and favorable information about one group to the other, and to
bringing the leaders of groups together to enlist their influence. But as everyone knows, such measures sometimes reduce intergroup tensions and sometimes do not. Social contacts, as our experiments demonstrated, may only
serve as occasions for intensifying conflict. Favorable information about a
disliked group may be ignored or reinterpreted to fit stereotyped notions
about the group. Leaders cannot act without regard for the prevailing tem-
per in their own groups.

What our limited experiments have shown is that the possibilities for achieving harmony are greatly enhanced when groups are brought together to work toward common ends. Then favorable information about a disliked group is seen in a new light, and leaders are in a position to take bolder steps toward cooperation. In short, hostility gives way when groups pull together to achieve overriding goals which are real and compelling to all concerned.

Reference

SHERIF, MUZAFER, AND SHERIF, CAROLYN W. *Groups in harmony and tension.* Harper & Brothers, 1953.

24

Social Psychology and Desegregation Research

Thomas F. Pettigrew

What one hears and what one sees of southern race relations today are sharply divergent. Consider some of the things that occur in interviews with white Southerners.

"As much as my family likes TV," confided a friendly North Carolina farmer, "we always turn the set off when they put them colored people on." But as the two of us were completing the interview, a series of famous Negro entertainers performed on the bright, twenty-one-inch screen in the adjoining room. No one interrupted them.

A rotund banker in Charleston, South Carolina, was equally candid in his remarks: "Son, under no conditions will the white man and the black man

Reprinted with permission from the author and *The American Psychologist,* Vol. 16, 1961. Copyright by the American Psychological Association.

This paper was given as an invited address at the Annual Meeting of the Southeastern Psychological Association, Atlanta, Georgia, March 31, 1960. The author wishes to express his appreciation to Gordon W. Allport of Harvard University, E. Earl Baughman of the University of North Carolina, and Cooper C. Clements of Emory University for their suggestions.

every get together in this state." He apparently preferred to ignore the government sponsored integration at his city's naval installation, just a short distance from his office.

Another respondent, this time a highly educated Chattanooga businessman, patiently explained to me for over an hour how race relations had not changed at all in his city during the past generation. As I left his office building, I saw a Negro policeman directing downtown traffic. It was the first Negro traffic cop I had ever seen in the South.

The South today is rife with such contradictions; social change has simply been too rapid for many Southerners to recognize it. Such a situation commands the attention of psychologists — particularly those in the South.

There are many other aspects of this sweeping process that should command our professional attention. To name just two, both the pending violence and the stultifying conformity attendant with desegregation are uniquely psychological problems. We might ask, for instance, what leads to violence in some desegregating communities, like Little Rock and Clinton, and not in others, like Norfolk and Winston-Salem? A multiplicity of factors must be relevant and further research is desperately needed to delineate them; but tentative early work seems to indicate that desegregation violence so far has been surprisingly "rational." That is, violence has generally resulted in localities where at least some of the authorities give prior hints that they would gladly return to segregation if disturbances occurred; peaceful integration has generally followed firm and forceful leadership.[1]

Research concerning conformity in the present situation is even more important. Many psychologists know from personal experience how intense the pressures to conform in racial attitudes have become in the present-day South; indeed, it appears that the first amendment guaranteeing free speech is in as much peril as the fourteenth amendment. Those who dare to break consistently this conformity taboo must do so in many parts of the South under the intimidation of slanderous letters and phone calls, burned crosses, and even bomb threats. Moreover, this paper will contend that conformity is the social psychological key to analyzing desegregation.

It is imperative that psychologists study these phenomena for two reasons: first, our psychological insights and methods are needed in understanding and solving this, our nation's primary internal problem; second, this process happening before our eyes offers us a rare opportunity to test in the field the psychological concomitants of cultural stress and social change. Thus, I would like in this paper to assess some of the prospects and directions of these potential psychological contributions.

---

[1]Clark (1953) predicted this from early border-state integration, and a variety of field reports have since documented the point in specific instances.

ROLE OF SOCIAL SCIENCE IN THE DESEGREGATION PROCESS TO DATE

The role of social science, particularly sociology and psychology, in the desegregation process has been much publicized and criticized by southern segregationists.[2] Many of these critics apparently think that sociology is synonymous with socialism and psychology with brainwashing. In any event, their argument that we have been crucially important in the Supreme Court desegregation cases of the fifties is based largely on the reference to seven social science documents in footnote 11 of the famous 1954 *Brown vs. Board of Education* decision. It would be flattering for us to think that our research has had such a dramatic effect on the course of history as segregationists claim, but in all truth we do not deserve such high praise.

In making their claim that the 1954 decision was psychological and not legal, the segregationists choose to overlook several things. The 1954 ruling did not come suddenly "out of the blue"; it was a logical continuation of a forty-four-year Supreme Court trend that began in 1910 when a former private in the Confederate Army, the liberal Edward White, became Chief Justice (Logan, 1956). When compared to this backdrop, our influence on the 1954 ruling was actually of only footnote importance. Furthermore, the language and spirit of the 1896 *Plessy vs. Ferguson,* separate-but-equal decision, so dear to the hearts of segregationists, were as immersed in the jargon and thinking of the social science of that era as the 1954 decision was of our era. Its 1896, Sumnerian argument that laws cannot change "social prejudices" (Allport, 1954, pp. 469–473) and its use of such social Darwinism terms as "racial instincts" and "natural affinities" lacked only a footnote to make it as obviously influenced by the then current social science as the 1954 ruling.

A final reason why we do not deserve the flattering praise of the segregationists is our failure to make substantial contributions to the process since 1954. The lack of penetrating psychological research in this area can be traced directly to three things: the lack of extensive foundation support, conformity pressures applied in many places in the South that deter desegregation research, and the inadequacy of traditional psychological thinking to cope with the present process. Let us discuss each of these matters in turn.

---

[2]For instance, once-liberal Virginius Dabney (1957, p. 14), editor of the *Richmond Times-Dispatch,* charged that "the violence at Little Rock . . . never would have happened if nine justices had not consulted sociologists and psychologists, instead of lawyers, in 1954, and attempted to legislate through judicial decrees."

A few years ago Stuart Cook (1957) drew attention to the failure of foundations to support desegregation research; the situation today is only slightly improved. It appears that a combination of foundation fears has produced this situation. One set of fears, as Cook noted, may stem from concern over attacks by southern Congressmen on their tax free status; the other set may stem from boycotts carried out by some segregationists against products identified with the foundations. In any case, this curtailment of funds is undoubtedly one reason why social scientists have so far left this crucial process relatively unstudied. Recently, however, a few moderate sized grants have been made for work in this area; hopefully, this is the beginning of a reappraisal by foundations of their previous policies. And it is up to us to submit competent research proposals to them to test continually for any change of these policies.

It is difficult to assess just how much damage has been done to desegregation research in the South by segregationist pressures. Probably the number of direct refusals to allow such research by southern institutions outside of the Black Belt has actually been small. More likely, the greatest harm has been rendered indirectly by the stifling atmosphere which prevents us from actually testing the limits of research opportunities. Interested as we may be in the racial realm, we decide to work in a less controversial area. Perhaps it is less a matter of courage than it is of resignation in the face of what are thought to be impossible barriers. If these suspicions are correct, there is real hope for overcoming in part this second obstacle to desegregation research.

In some situations, there should be little resistance. In racially integrated veterans' hospitals, for instance, much needed personality studies comparing Negro and white patients should be possible. In other situations, the amount of resistance to race research may be less than we anticipate. Since Little Rock, many so-called "moderates" in the South, particularly businessmen, have become more interested in the dynamics of desegregation. This is not to say that they are more in favor of racial equality than they were; it is only to suggest that the bad publicity, the closing of schools, and the economic losses suffered by Little Rock have made these influential Southerners more receptive to objective and constructive research on the process. It is for this reason that it is imperative the limits for the southern study of desegregation be tested at this time.

Finally, psychological contributions to desegregation research have been restricted by the inadequacy of traditional thinking in our discipline. More specifically, the relative neglect of situational variables in interracial behavior and a restricted interpretation and use of the attitude concept hinder psychological work in this area.

The importance of the situation for racial interaction has been demonstrated in a wide variety of settings. All-pervasive racial attitudes are often not involved; many individuals seem fully capable of immediate behavioral change as situations change. Thus in Panama there is a divided street, the Canal Zone side of which is racially segregated and the Panamanian side of which is racially integrated. Biesanz and Smith (1951) report that most Panamanians and Americans appear to accommodate without difficulty as they go first on one side of the street and then on the other. Likewise, in the coal mining county of McDowell, West Virginia, Minard (1952) relates that the majority of Negro and white miners follow easily a traditional pattern of integration below the ground and almost complete segregation above the ground. The literature abounds with further examples: southern white migrants readily adjusting to integrated situations in the North (Killian, 1949), northern whites approving of employment and public facility integration but resisting residential integration (Reitzes, 1953), etc. Indeed, at the present time in the South there are many white Southerners who are simultaneously adjusting to bus and public golf course integration and opposing public school integration. Or, as in Nashville, they may have accepted school integration but are opposing lunch counter integration.

This is not to imply that generalized attitudes on race are never invoked. There are some Panamanians and some Americans who act about the same on both sides of the Panamanian street. Minard (1952) estimated about two-fifths of the West Virginian miners he observed behave consistently in either a tolerant or an intolerant fashion both below and above ground. And some whites either approve or disapprove of all desegregation. But these people are easily explained by traditional theory. They probably consist of the extremes in authoritarianism; their attitudes on race are so generalized and so salient that their consistent behavior in racial situations is sometimes in defiance of the prevailing social norms.

On the other hand, the "other directed" individuals who shift their behavior to keep in line with shifting expectations present the real problem for psychologists. Their racial attitudes appear less salient, more specific, and more tied to particular situations. Conformity needs are predominantly important for these people, and we shall return shortly to a further discussion of these conformists.

One complication introduced by a situational analysis is that interracial contact itself frequently leads to the modification of attitudes. A number of studies of racially integrated situations have noted dramatic attitude changes, but in most cases the changes involved specific, situation linked attitudes. For example, white department store employees become more accepting of Negroes in the work situation after equal status, integrated contact but not necessarily more accepting in other situations (Harding and Hogrefe, 1952). And *The American Soldier* studies (Stouffer, Suchman, DeVinney, Star, and Williams, 1949) found that the attitudes of white army personnel toward the Negro as a fighting man improve after equal status, integrated contact in combat, but their attitudes toward the Negro as a social companion do not necessarily change. In other words, experience in a novel situation of equal status leads to acceptance of that specific situation for many persons. Situations, then, not only structure specific racial behavior, but they may change specific attitudes in the process.

One final feature of a situational analysis deserves mention. Typically in psychology we have tested racial attitudes in isolation, apart from conflicting attitudes and values. Yet this is not realistic. As the desegregation process slowly unfolds in such resistant states as Virginia and Georgia, we see clearly that many segregationist Southerners value law and order, public education, and a prosperous economy above their racial views. Once such a situation pits race against other entrenched values, we need to know the public's hierarchy of these values. Thus a rounded situational analysis requires the measures of racial attitudes in the full context of countervalues.[3]

A second and related weakness in our psychological approach is the failure to exploit fully the broad and dynamic implications of the attitude concept. Most social psychologcial research has dealt with attitudes as if they were serving only an expressive function; but racial attitudes in the South require a more complex treatment.

In their volume, *Opinion and Personality,* Smith, Bruner, and White (1956) urge a more expansive interpretation of attitudes. They note three attitude functions. First, there is the *object appraisal* function; attitudes aid in understanding "reality" as it is defined by the culture. Second, attitudes can play a *social adjustment* role by contributing to the individual's identification with, or differentiation from, various reference groups. Finally, attitudes may reduce anxiety by serving an expressive or *externalization* function.

> Externalization occurs when an individual . . . senses an analogy between a perceived environmental event and some unresolved inner problem . . . [and] adopts an attitude . . . which is a transformed version of his way of dealing with his inner difficulty (pp. 41–44).

At present the most fashionable psychological theories of prejudice— frustration-aggression, psychoanalytic, and authoritarianism—all deal chiefly with the externalization process. Valuable as these theories have been, this exclusive attention to the expressive component of attitudes has

---

[3]A popular treatment of this point has been made by Zinn (1959).

been at the expense of the object appraisal and social adjustment components. Moreover, it is the contention of this paper that these neglected and more socially relevant functions, particularly social adjustment, offer the key to further psychological advances in desegregation research.[4]

The extent to which this psychological concentration on externalization has influenced the general public was illustrated recently in the popular reaction to the swastika desecrations of Jewish temples. The perpetrators, all agreed, must be juvenile hoodlums, or "sick," or both. In other words, externalization explanations were predominantly offered.[5] Valid though these explanations may be in many cases, is it not also evident that the perpetrators were accurately reflecting the anti-Semitic norms of their subcultures? Thus their acts and the attitudes behind their acts are socially adjusting for these persons, given the circles in which they move.

Much less the public, some sociologists, too, have been understandably misled by our overemphasis on externalization into underestimating the psychological analysis of prejudice. One sociologist (Rose, 1956) categorically concludes:

> There is no evidence that . . . any known source of "prejudice" in the psychological sense is any more prevalent in the South than in the North (p. 174).

Two others (Rabb and Lipset, 1959) maintain firmly:

> the psychological approach, as valuable as it is, does not explain the preponderance of people who engage in prejudiced behavior, but do *not* have special emotional problems (p. 26).

Both of these statements assume, as some psychologists have assumed, that externalization is the only possible psychological explanation of prejudice. These writers employ cultural and situational norms as explanatory concepts for racial prejudice and discrimination, but fail to see that conformity needs are the personality reflections of these norms and offer an equally valid concept on the psychological level. To answer the first assertion, recent evidence indicates that conformity to racial norms, one "known source of prejudice," is "more prevalent in the South than in the North." To answer the second assertion, strong needs to conform to racial norms in a sternly sanctioning South, for instance, are *not* "special emotional problems." Psychology is not just a science of mental illness nor must psychological theories of prejudice be limited to the mentally ill.

---

[4]Though this paper emphasizes the social adjustment aspect of southern attitudes toward Negroes, the equally neglected object appraisal function is also of major importance. Most southern whites know only lower class Negroes; consequently their unfavorable stereotype of Negroes serves a definite reality function.

[5]Such explanations also serve for many anti-Semitic observers as an ego-alien defense against guilt.

CONFORMITY AND SOCIAL ADJUSTMENT IN
SOUTHERN RACIAL ATTITUDES

Evidence of the importance of conformity in southern attitudes on race has been steadily accumulating in recent years. The relevant data come from several different research approaches; one of these is the study of anti-Semitism. Roper's (1946, 1947) opinion polls have twice shown the South, together with the Far West, to be one of the least anti-Semitic regions in the United States. Knapp's (1944) study of over 1000 war rumors from all parts of the country in 1942 lends additional weight to this finding. He noted that anti-Semitic stories constituted 9 percent of the nation's rumors but only 3 percent of the South's rumors. By contrast, 8.5 percent of the southern rumors concerned the Negro as opposed to only 3 percent for the nation as a whole. Consistent with these data, too, is Prothro's (1952) discovery that two-fifths of his white adult sample in Louisiana was quite favorable in its attitudes toward Jews but at the same time quite unfavorable in its attitudes toward Negroes. But if the externalization function were predominant in southern anti-Negro attitudes, the South should also be highly anti-Semitic. Externalizing bigots do not select out just the Negro; they typically reject all out-groups, even, as Hartley (1946) has demonstrated, out-groups that do not exist.

Further evidence comes from research employing the famous F Scale measure of authoritarianism (Adorno, Frenkel-Brunswik, Levinson, and Sanford, 1950). Several studies, employing both student and adult samples, have reported southern F Scale means that fall well within the range of means of comparable nonsouthern groups (Milton, 1952; Pettigrew, 1959; Smith and Prothro, 1957). Moreover, there is no evidence that the family pattern associated with authoritarianism is any more prevalent in the South than in other parts of the country (Davis, Gardner, and Gardner, 1941; Dollard, 1937). It seems clear, then, that the South's heightened prejudice against the Negro cannot be explained in terms of any regional difference in authoritarianism. This is not to deny, however, the importance of the F Scale in predicting individual differences; it appears to correlate with prejudice in southern samples at approximately the same levels as in northern samples (Pettigrew, 1959).

The third line of evidence relates conformity measures directly to racial attitudes. For lack of a standardized, nonlaboratory measure, one study defined conformity and deviance in terms of the respondents' social characteristics (Pettigrew, 1959). For a southern white sample with age and education held constant, potentially conforming respondents (i.e., females or church attenders) were *more* anti-Negro than their counterparts (i.e., males or nonattenders of church), and potentially deviant respondents (i.e., armed service veterans or political independents) were *less* anti-Negro than their counterparts (i.e., nonveterans or political party identifiers). None of these differences were noted in a comparable northern sample. Furthermore, Southerners living in communities with relatively small percentages of Negroes were less anti-Negro than Southerners living in communities with relatively large percentages of Negroes, though they were *not* less authoritarian. In short, respondents most likely to be conforming to cultural pressures are more prejudiced against Negroes in the South but not in the North. And the percentage of Negroes in the community appears to be a fairly accurate index of the strength of these southern cultural pressures concerning race.

Thus all three types of research agree that conformity to the stern racial norms of southern culture is unusually crucial in the South's heightened hostility toward the Negro.[6] Or, in plain language, it is the path of least resistance in most southern circles to favor white supremacy. When an individual's parents and peers are racially prejudiced, when his limited world accepts racial discrimination as a given of life, when his deviance means certain ostracism, then his anti-Negro attitudes are not so much expressive as they are socially adjusting.

This being the case, it is fortunate that a number of significant laboratory and theoretical advances in the conformity realm have been made recently in our discipline. Solomon Asch's (1951) pioneer research on conformity, followed up by Crutchfield (1955) and others, has provided us with a wealth of laboratory findings, many of them suggestive for desegregation research. And theoretical analyses of conformity have been introduced by Kelman (1958, 1961), Festinger (1953, 1957), and Thibaut and Kelley (1959); these, too, are directly applicable for desegregation research. Indeed, research in southern race relations offers a rare opportunity to test these empirical and theoretical formulations in the field on an issue of maximum salience.

Consider the relevance of one of Asch's (1951) intriguing findings. Asch's standard situation, you will recall, employed seven pre-instructed assistants and a genuine subject in a line judgment task. On two-thirds of the judgment, the seven assistants purposely reported aloud an obviously incorrect estimate; thus the subject, seated eighth, faced unanimous pressure to conform by making a similarly incorrect response. On approximately one-third of such judgments, he yielded to the group; like the others, he would estimate a 5-inch line as 4 inches. But when Asch disturbed the unanimity by having one of his seven assistants give the correct response, the subjects

---

[6]Similar analyses of South African student data indicate that the social adjustment function may also be of unusual importance in the anti-African attitudes of the English in the Union (Pettigrew, 1958, 1960).

yielded only a tenth, rather than a third, of the time. Once unanimity no longer existed, even when there was only one supporting colleague, the subject could better withstand the pressure of the majority to conform. To carry through the analogy to today's crisis in the South, obvious 5-inch lines are being widely described as 4 inches. Many Southerners, faced with what appears to be solid unanimity, submit to the distortion. But when even one respected source—a minister, a newspaper editor, even a college professor—conspicuously breaks the unanimity, *perhaps* a dramatic modification is achieved in the private opinions of many conforming Southerners. Only an empirical test can learn if such a direct analogy is warranted.

Consider, too, the relevance of recent theoretical distinctions. Kelman (1958, 1961), for example, has clarified the concept of conformity by pointing out that three separate processes are involved: *compliance, identification,* and *internalization.* Compliance exists when an individual accepts influence not because he believes in it, but because he hopes to achieve a favorable reaction from an agent who maintains surveillance over him. Identification exists when an individual accepts influence because he wants to establish or maintain a satisfying relationship with another person or group. The third process, internalization, exists when an individual accepts influence because the content of the behavior itself is satisfying; unlike the other types of conformity, internalized behavior will be performed without the surveillance of the agent or a salient relationship with the agent. It is with this third process that Kelman's ideas overlap with authoritarian theory.

We have all witnessed illustrations of each of these processes in the acceptance by Southerners of the region's racial norms. The "Uncle Tom" Negro is an example of a compliant Southerner; another example is furnished by the white man who treats Negroes as equals only when not under the surveillance of other whites. Identification is best seen in white Southerners whose resistance to racial integration enables them to be a part of what they erroneously imagine to be Confederate tradition. Such identifiers are frequently upwardly mobile people who are still assimilating to urban society; they strive for social status by identifying with the hallowed symbols and shibboleths of the South's past. Southerners who have internalized the white supremacy dictates of the culture are the real racists who use the issue to gain political office, to attract resistance group membership fees, or to meet personality needs. Southerners with such contrasting bases for their racial attitudes should react very differently toward desegregation. For instance, compliant whites can be expected to accept desegregation more readily than those who have internalized segregationist norms.

On the basis of this discussion of conformity, I would like to propose a new concept: *the latent liberal.* This is not to be confused with the cherished southern notion of the "moderate"; the ambiguous term "moderate" is presently used to describe everything from an integrationist who wants to be socially accepted to a racist who wants to be polite. Rather, the latent liberal refers to the Southerner who is neither anti-Semitic nor authoritarian but whose conformity habits and needs cause him to be strongly anti-Negro. Through the processes of compliance and identification, the latent liberal continues to behave in a discriminatory fashion toward Negroes even though such behavior conflicts with his basically tolerant personality. He is at the present time *il*liberal on race, but he has the personality potentiality of becoming liberal once the norms of the culture change. Indeed, as the already unleased economic, legal, political, and social forces restructure the South's racial norms, the latent liberal's attitudes about Negroes will continue to change. Previously cited research suggests that there are today an abundance of white Southerners who meet this latent liberal description; collectively, they will reflect on the individual level the vast societal changes now taking place in the South.

SOME SUGGESTED DIRECTIONS FOR FUTURE PSYCHOLOGICAL RESEARCH ON DESEGREGATION[7]

We are in serious need of research on the Negro, both in the North and in the South. Most psychological research in this area was conducted during the 1930s and directed at testing racists' claims of Negro inferiority. But the most sweeping advances in American Negro history have been made in the past generation, requiring a fresh new look — particularly at the Negro personality.

Two aspects of this research make it complex and difficult. In the first place, the race of the interviewer is a complicating and not as yet fully understood factor. Further methodological study is needed on this point. Moreover, special problems of control are inherent in this research. Not only are there some relatively unique variables that must be considered (e.g., migration history, differential experience with the white community, etc.), but such simple factors as education are not easy to control. For instance, has the average graduate of a southern rural high school for Negroes received an education equal to the average graduate of such a school for whites? No, in spite of the South's belated efforts to live up to separate-but-equal education, available school data indicate that the graduates have

---

[7]For other suggestions, see the important analysis of desegregation by Cook (1957).

probably not received equivalent educations. Yet some recent research on Negro personality has been based on the assumption that Negro and white education in the South are equivalent (e.g., Smith and Prothro, 1957).

Fortunately, the Institute for Research in the Social Sciences at the University of North Carolina has embarked on a large study of many of these content and methodological problems. It is to be hoped that their work will stimulate other efforts.

Some of the most valuable psychological data now available on desegregation have been collected by public opinion polls. But typically these data have been gathered without any conceptual framework to guide their coverage and direction.

For example, one of the more interesting poll findings is that a majority of white Southerners realize that racial desegregation of public facilities is inevitable even though about six out of seven strongly oppose the process (Hyman and Sheatsley, 1956). The psychological implications of this result are so extensive that we would like to know more. Do the respondents who oppose desegregation but accept its inevitability have other characteristics of latent liberals? Are these respondents more often found outside of the Black Belt? Typically, we cannot answer such questions from present poll data; we need to build into the desegregation polls broader coverage and more theoretical direction.

The third direction that psychological research in desegregation could usefully take concerns measurement. Save for the partly standardized F Scale, we still lack widely used, standardized field measures of the chief variables in this realm. Such instruments are necessary both for comparability of results and for stimulation of research; witness the invigorating effects on research of the F Scale, the Minnesota Multiphasic Inventory, and the need achievement scoring scheme. Mention of McClelland's need achievement scoring scheme should remind us, too, that projective and other indirect techniques might answer many of these measurement requirements—especially for such sensitive and subtle variables as conformity needs.

Finally, the definitive interdisciplinary case study of desegregation has yet to be started. Properly buttressed by the necessary foundation aid, such a study should involve comparisons before, during, and after desegregation of a wide variety of communities. The interdisciplinary nature of such an undertaking is stressed because desegregation is a peculiarly complex process demanding a broad range of complementary approaches.

Any extensive case project must sample three separate time periods: before a legal ruling or similar happening has alerted the community to imminent desegregation, during the height of the desegregating process, and after several years of accommodation. Without this longitudinal view, desegregation as a dynamic, ongoing process cannot be understood. This time perspective, for instance, would enable us to interpret the fact that an overwhelming majority of Oklahoma whites in a 1954 poll sternly objected to mixed schools, but within a few years has accepted without serious incident integrated education throughout most of the state (Jones, 1957).

A carefully selected range of communities is required to test for differences in the process according to the characteristics of the area. Recent demographic analyses and predictions of the South's school desegregation pattern (Ogburn and Grigg, 1956; Pettigrew, 1957; Pettigrew and Campbell, 1960) could help in making this selection of communities. Comparable data gathered in such a selected variety of locations would allow us to pinpoint precisely the aspects of desegregation unique to, say, a Piedmont city, as opposed to a Black Belt town.

Compare the potential value of such a broad research effort with the limited case studies that have been possible so far. Low budget reports of only one community are the rule; many of them are theses or seminar projects, some remain on the descriptive level, all but a few sample only one time period, and there is almost no comparability of instruments and approach. A comprehensive case project is obviously long overdue.

This has been an appeal for a vigorous empirical look at southern race relations. Despite segregationists' claims to the contrary, social psychological contributions to desegregation research have been relatively meager. There are, however, grounds for hoping that this situation will be partly corrected in the near future—particularly if psychologists get busy.

Foundations appear to be re-evaluating their previous reluctance to support such research. And we can re-evaluate our own resignation in the face of barriers to conduct investigations in this area; the tragedy of Little Rock has had a salutary effect on many influential Southerners in this respect.

Recognition of the importance of the situation in interracial behavior and the full exploitation of the attitude concept can remove inadequacies in the traditional psychological approach to the study of race. In this connection, an extended case for considering conformity as crucial in the Negro attitudes of white Southerners was presented and a new concept—the latent liberal—introduced. One final implication of this latent liberal concept should be mentioned. Some cynics have argued that successful racial desegregation in the South will require an importation of tens of thousands of psychotherapists and therapy for millions of bigoted Southerners. Fortunately for desegregation, psychotherapists, and Southerners, this will not be necessary; a thorough repatterning of southern interracial behavior will be sufficient therapy in itself.

References

ADORNO, T. W., FRENKEL-BRUNSWIK, ELSE, LEVINSON, D. J., AND SANFORD, N. *The authoritarian personality.* New York: Harper, 1950.

ALLPORT, G. W. *The nature of prejudice.* Cambridge, Mass.: Addison-Wesley, 1954.

ASCH, S. E. Effects of group pressure upon the modification and distortion of judgments. In H. Guetzkow (ed.), *Groups, leadership and men.* Pittsburgh: Carnegie, 1951.

BIESANZ, J., AND SMITH, L. M. Race relations of Panama and the Canal Zone. *Amer. J. Sociol.,* 1951, **57,** 7–14.

CLARK, K. B. Desegregation: An appraisal of the evidence. *J. soc. Issues,* 1953, **9,** 1–76.

COOK, S. W. Desegregation: A psychological analysis. *Amer. Psychologist,* 1957, **12,** 1–13.

CRUTCHFIELD, R. S. Conformity and character. *Amer. Psychologist,* 1955, **10,** 191–198.

DABNEY, V. The violence at Little Rock. *Richmond Times-Dispatch,* 1957, **105,** September 24, 14.

DAVIS, A., GARDNER, B., AND GARDNER, MARY. *Deep South.* Chicago: Univer. Chicago Press, 1941.

DOLLARD, J. *Caste and class in a southern town.* New Haven: Yale Univer. Press, 1937.

FESTINGER, L. An analysis of compliant behavior. In M. Sherif and M. O. Wilson (eds.), *Group relations at the crossroads.* New York: Harper, 1953.

FESTINGER, L. *A theory of cognitive dissonance.* Evanston, Ill.: Row, Peterson, 1957.

HARDING, J., AND HOGREFE, R. Attitudes of white department store employees toward Negro co-workers. *J. soc. Issues,* 1952, **8,** 18–28.

HARTLEY, E. L. *Problems in prejudice.* New York: King's Crown, 1946.

HYMAN, H. H., AND SHEATSLEY, P. B. Attitudes toward desegregation. *Scient. Amer.,* 1956, **195,** 35–39.

JONES, E. City limits. In D. Shoemaker (ed.), *With all deliberate speed.* New York: Harper, 1957.

KELMAN, H. C. Compliance, identification, and internalization: Three process of attitude change. *J. conflict Resolut.,* 1958, **2,** 51–60.

KELMAN, H. C. *Social influence and personal belief.* New York: Wiley, 1961.

KILLIAN, L. W. Southern white laborers in Chicago's West Side. Unpublished doctoral dissertation, University of Chicago, 1949.

KNAPP, R. H. A psychology of rumor. *Publ. opin. Quart.,* 1944, **8,** 22–37.

LOGAN, R. W. The United States Supreme Court and the segregation issue. *Ann. Amer. Acad. Pol. Soc. Sci.,* 1956, **304,** 10–16.

MILTON, O. Presidential choice and performance on a scale of authoritarianism. *Amer. Psychologist,* 1952, **7,** 597–598.

MINARD, R. D. Race relations in the Pocahontas coal field. *J. soc. Issues,* 1952, **8,** 29–44.

OGBURN, W. F., AND GRIGG, C. M. Factors related to the Virginia vote on segregation. *Soc. Forces,* 1956, **34,** 301–308.

PETTIGREW, T. F. Demographic correlates of border-state desegregation. *Amer. sociol. Rev.,* 1957, **22,** 683–689.

PETTIGREW, T. F. Personality and sociocultural factors in intergroup attitudes: A cross-national comparison. *J. conflict Resolut.,* 1958, **2,** 29–42.

PETTIGREW, T. F. Regional differences in anti-Negro prejudice. *J. abnorm. soc. Psychol.,* 1959, **59,** 28–36.

PETTIGREW, T. F. Social distance attitudes of South African students. *Soc. Forces,* 1960, **38,** 246–253.

PETTIGREW, T. F., AND CAMPBELL, E. Q. Faubus and segregation: An analysis of Arkansas voting. *Publ. opin. Quart.,* 1960, **24,** 436–447.

PROTHRO, E. T. Ethnocentrism and anti-Negro attitudes in the deep South. *J. abnorm. soc. Psychol.,* 1952, **47,** 105–108.

RABB, E., AND LIPSET, S. M. *Prejudice and society.* New York: Anti-Defamation League of B'nai B'rith, 1959.

REITZES, D. C. The role of organizational structures: Union versus neighborhood in a tension situation. *J. soc. Issues,* 1953, **9,** 37–44.

ROPER, E. United States anti-Semites. *Fortune,* 1946, **33,** 257–260.

ROPER, E. United States anti-Semites. *Fortune,* 1947, **36,** 5–10.

ROSE, A. M. Intergroup relations vs. prejudice: Pertinent theory for the study of social change. *Soc. Probl.,* 1956, **4,** 173–176.

SMITH, C. U., AND PROTHRO, J. W. Ethnic differences in authoritarian personality. *Soc. Forces,* 1957, **35,** 334–338.

SMITH, M. B., BRUNER, J. S., AND WHITE, R. W. *Opinion and personality.* New York: Wiley, 1956.

STOUFFER, S. A., SUCHMAN, E. A., DeVINNEY, L. C., STAR, SHIRLEY A., AND WILLIAMS, R. M., JR. *Studies in social psychology in World War II.* Vol. 1. *The American soldier: Adjustment during army life.* Princeton: Princeton Univer. Press, 1949.

THIBAUT, J. W., AND KELLEY, H. H. *The social psychology of groups.* New York: Wiley, 1959.

ZINN, H. A fate worse than integration. *Harper's,* 1959, **219,** August, 53–56.

VI

ATTRACTION: WHY PEOPLE LIKE EACH OTHER

25

Flattery Will Get You Somewhere: Styles and Uses of Ingratiation

Edward E. Jones

Dale Carnegie, author of *How to Win Friends and Influence People,* was enraged at the implication that he would advocate using compliments just to get something out of people: "Great God Almighty!!! If we are so contemptibly selfish that we can't radiate a little happiness and pass on a bit of honest appreciation without trying to screw something out of the other person in return—if our souls are no bigger than sour crab apples, we shall meet with the failure we so richly deserve." The chapter containing this observation (entitled "How to Make People Like You Instantly") is composed of anecdotes describing precisely how complimenters *do* gain advantages. The message is clearly stated in other chapters as well: success in one's chosen line of work may be dramatically furthered by practicing the arts of ingratiation along the way.

Carnegie is not the only advocate of "applied human relations" who has had trouble distinguishing between the legitimate and illegitimate in social behavior. In certain business and political circles, for example, "sincere" is used as a synonym for agreeable. Self-serving flattery is usually deplored — but when does "honest appreciation" become flattery? Everyone likes a cooperative, agreeable attitude, but where is the line between manipulative conformity and self-effacing compromise? Many see great evil in ingratiation; Milton considered it hypocrisy, which he called "the only evil that walks invisible, except to God alone." Norman Vincent Peale, on the other hand, is much more tolerant; he considers pleasantness a mark of Christian virtue, from which peace of mind and prosperity flow naturally — and rightly.

Between these two extremes we find the charmingly honest Lord Chesterfield:

> Vanity . . . is, perhaps, the most universal principle of human actions . . . if a man has a mind to be thought wiser, and a woman handsomer than they really are, their error is a comfortable one for themselves, and an innocent one with regard to other people; and I would rather make them my friends, by indulging them, than my enemies by endeavoring (in that to no purpose) to undeceive them.

Adlai Stevenson was also willing to counsel moderation with the remark, after being given a glowing introduction, "I have sometimes said that flattery is all right if you don't inhale."

What is custom and what is manipulation depends on time, place, the society, and often the individual. In those cultures where fulsome compliments are the norm, like the more traditional groups in Japan, anything less may be considered insulting. On the other hand, in many masculine circles in our own society praise is considered an affectation — a man who pays compliments easily will be thought untrustworthy or effeminate.

Most theories of social structure make the strong assumption that persons adjust their actions to what is generally accepted and expected. Ingratiation can be defined as impression-management which stretches or exploits these expectations or norms. Acts of ingratiation are designed to increase an individual's attractiveness beyond the value of what he really can offer to his target. Ingratiation is the illegitimate — the seamy — side of interpersonal communication.

BREAKING THE SOCIAL CONTRACT

But how do we determine when behavior is "legitimate"? Relationships and associations involve, in normal circumstances, an unstated contract between the actors. Different authorities describe this contract in different ways. Sociologist Erving Goffman, in his book *The Presentation of Self in Everyday Life,* emphasizes what he calls "ritual elements" in social interaction. Goffman believes that not only does communication take place in its usual sense but the communicators also engage in a "performance"—each transmits and receives clues about his definition of the situation, his view of himself, and his evaluation of the other. Mutual adjustment occurs. *Perhaps most important, the actors enter into a silent compact to help each other save face.* Each becomes involved in "face-work"—give-and-take actions that smooth over potentially embarrassing threats, lend mutual support, and make for coherent and consistent performances. Each person has a "defensive orientation toward saving his own face and a protective orientation toward saving the other's face."

Within this frame of reference, the ingratiator may be seen as exploiting this contract while seeming to support it. He neither violates the contract openly, nor merely fulfills it. Rather, he keeps sending out reassuring signals that he accepts the terms of the contract; but all the while he is actually working toward other goals.

To put it in slightly different terms: while relying on his target to stick to the rule that each should get out of a relationship what he brings to it, the ingratiator deliberately violates the rule himself in hopes of gaining a one-sided advantage. By definition, ingratiation occurs when a person cannot or does not want to offer as much as he hopes to get from the other, so he tries to make his "offer" appear more valuable by fancy packaging, misrepresenting how much he brings to the relationship, or advertising the effort or cost involved in his contribution. For instance, the worker may apply himself with greatest industry when he expects the supervisor to appear momentarily, he may try to convince others that his job is more difficult than it really is, or attempt to convince his boss that it requires considerable experience or specialized education.

While the dependent member of a relationship has more to gain from successful ingratiation than the more powerful member, the latter may be also quite concerned about his image. It has often been noted that men rising in organizations tend to lose the spontaneity of old relationships and certainty about the loyalty and reliability of old colleagues. In spite of their increasing power, they are dependent on subordinates for signs of their own effectiveness and—perhaps as a way of hedging their bets—they will use ingratiating tactics to increase morale and performance.

Ingratiation raises important problems in human relations and self-knowledge. Much of our understanding of the world around us, and of ourselves, comes to us indirectly through the impressions we get from others. In particular, self-evaluation is to a large extent determined by how others judge us—personal qualities like friendliness, respectability, or moral worth can only be assessed by social means or mirrored in the reactions of others. Since ingratiation subverts this response, it is a threat to normal interaction and to reliable information. Like the traditional Hollywood producer and his yes-men, the executive surrounded by ingratiators may find himself adrift in a sea of uncertainties in which the only markers are the selfish interests of his advisers.

Ingratiation takes three general tactical forms.

Other-enhancement. The ingratiator may try to elicit favorable reactions to himself by building up his target. At the extreme this involves obvious flattery; but there are also more subtle and indirect ways. The ingratiator may, for instance, concentrate on playing up the real strong points of the target, passing over or playing down the weak ones.

The ultimate design is to convince the target that the ingratiator thinks highly of him. We tend to like those who like us. Sometimes, however, the tactics are not simple or direct. The higher the target's regard for himself, the less he needs the ingratiator's praise, and the more he accepts it as obvious and routine. Targets may prefer praise, as Lord Chesterfield puts it, "upon those points where they wish to excel, and yet are doubtful whether they do or not. . . . The late Sir Robert Walpole, who was certainly an able man, was little open to flattery upon that head . . . but his prevailing weakness was, to be thought to have a polite and happy turn of gallantry; of which he had undoubtedly less than any man living . . . (and) those who had any penetration—applied to it with success."

Conformity. People tend to like those whose values and beliefs appear similar to their own. Again, however, the relationship is not always direct. The ingratiator must seem sincere. His agreement must seem to be arrived at independently, for no ulterior purpose. The tactical conformer might be wise to disagree on non-essentials in order to underline the "independence" and value of his agreement on essentials. Agreement may be more valued if it seems to result from a *change* in opinion, made at some psychological cost, seeming to reflect a sincere change of conviction.

Self-presentation is the explicit description or presentation of oneself in such a way as to become attractive to the target. This includes avoiding those characteristics the target might consider unpleasant, and subtly emphasizing those he might approve. The ingratiator walks a tightrope: he must boast without seeming to, since open boasting is frowned on in our society; he must "be" those things his target considers ideal for his situation, and yet appear sincere; he must seem admirable to the target and yet not a threat. He may have to ride a paradox—to be both self-enhancing and self-depre-cating at the same time. This may not be difficult for someone with strong and obvious credentials—someone widely acknowledged to be the best in his field may gain by not mentioning it, and instead acknowledging his all-too-human failings. But those with dubious credentials must be more blatant in advertising their strengths.

In sum, in each of these classes the main problem of the ingratiator is to seem sincere and yet impressive and engaging. It is also better if his tactics and stated opinions support some pet but not universally admired or accepted ideas of the target.

Little research has been done on ingratiation. To carry the inspection of the subject beyond anecdote and intuition, we conducted a number of experiments in which college student subjects were given strong or weak incentives to make themselves attractive to a particular target. Sometimes targets knew that the ingratiators were dependent on them for benefits and therefore had selfish reasons to be attractive; sometimes they did not know. In other experiments, subjects were exposed to ingratiating overtures by others and their impressions of these others were assessed.

One experiment, designed to test ingratiation tactics in an organizational hierarchy, used as subjects seventy-nine male volunteers from the Naval ROTC unit at Duke University. Pairs of freshmen (low-status) and pairs of upper-classmen (high-status) were brought together in units of four. Each subject in the experimental condition (designed to promote ingratiation) was told that the purpose of the study was to find out if "compatible groups provide a better setting in which to test leadership potential than do incompatible groups." The experimenter's instructions continued: "For this reason I hope that you will make a special effort to gain (the other's) liking and respect, always remembering your position as commander (or subordinate)." With the remaining subjects, in the control condition, emphasis was on the importance of obtaining *valid* information: "We are not especially concerned with whether you end up liking each other or not. . . . We are interested only in how well you can do in reaching a clear impression of the other person."

Another experiment used fifty male volunteers from the introductory psychology course at the University of North Carolina in what was supposed to be a game designed to simulate a business situation. An experimental accomplice, presented as a graduate student from the School of Business Administration, was introduced as the "supervisor," conducting and scoring the games. Actually, the "business games" were used to discover and measure ingratiation tactics which might be used to gain advantage in comparable professional or business contexts.

From the results of the experiments thus far completed *there is no doubt that the average undergraduate behaves differently when he wants to be liked than when he wants only to be accurate in presenting himself socially.*

Specifically, let us break down the results in terms of the three major types of ingratiation tactics.

Self-presentation. Generally, when instructed to try to make a good impression, our subjects played up their strong points and played down their weaknesses. (These varied according to the situation.) However, there were a few significant exceptions:

In a status hierarchy, tactics vary according to the ingratiator's position. In the ROTC experiment, the lower-classmen usually inflated only those qualities they considered unimportant. Apparently they felt that to inflate the important qualities might make them seem pushy, and perhaps even threatening. Upper-classmen became more modest about all qualities. They felt secure, and their high status was obvious because of age and rank — therefore they did not feel it necessary to assert superiority. Modesty, we infer, helped them build up the impression of friendliness toward the lower ranks, which they considered desirable.

Who and what the target is influences how the ingratiator describes himself. In the business games, those trying to impress the supervisor favorably emphasized their competence and respectability rather than their geniality. "Attractiveness" can, therefore, be sought by emphasizing what is more desired in a given situation — perhaps efficiency, perhaps compatibility, perhaps trustworthiness or integrity. If the ingratiator knows that the target is aware of his dependence, his tactics are apt to be subtle or devious. He may very well deprecate himself in those areas he does not consider important in order to build up his credibility in areas he *does* consider important. If, however, the ingratiator believes the target is innocent enough to accept him at face value, he will be tempted to pull out all stops.

Conformity. Perhaps the clearest research finding was that to be successful, ingratiation must result in greater public agreement with the target's stated opinions. (Hamlet asked Polonius, "Do you see yonder cloud that's almost in the shape of a camel?" "By the mass, and 'tis like a camel, indeed." "Methinks it is like a weasel." "It is backed like a weasel." "Or like a whale?" "Very like a whale.")

Such conformity was true of both high-status and low-status students — with some significant differences. The low-status freshmen conformed more on relevant than irrelevant items. Upper-classmen conformed more on the irrelevant than the relevant — presumably they were eager to appear good fellows, but not at the price of compromising any essential source of power or responsibility.

Further, as the business games showed, an ingratiator will cut the cloth of his agreement to fit the back of what is important to his target. If the target clearly values tact, cooperation, and getting along with others, the ingratiator will understand that the strategic use of agreement will probably result in personal advantage. Subjects were quick to reach this conclusion and to act on it, in contrast to their show of independence when the target appeared to be austerely concerned with the productivity of subordinates rather than the congeniality of their views.

When the ingratiator happens to agree closely with the target anyway, there is some evidence that too much agreement is deliberately avoided. Actually, agreement is almost never total. In most of the experimental cases of conformity, the ingratiator's final stated views were a compromise between his original opinion and that of his target. He might be described as avoiding extreme disagreement rather than seeking close agreement; nevertheless, the evidence is clear that expressed opinions are influenced by a desire to create a good impression.

Other-enhancement. In this tactical area the results were quite inconclusive. There was some evidence that low-status subjects, after being instructed concerning the importance of compatibility with their superiors, were more complimentary than when operating under instructions to be accurate. High-status subjects did not show this same tendency to flatter more under conditions stressing compatibility. On the other hand, they were more inclined to view the low-status complimenter as insincere in a final private judgment, when the instructions stressed compatibility. The low-status subjects showed no such suspicions of their superiors.

THE BOUNDS OF VANITY

Our experiments have answered a few questions and posed many more which may be profitably studied. Among the more important questions raised:

Given the ethical barriers to deceit and social manipulation, what *are* the modes of rationalization or self-justification in ingratiation? How does the ingratiator keep his self-respect? Though our data consistently revealed differences between experimental (compatibility) and control (accuracy) conditions, we were unable to detect any intent to win favor, or the *conscious* adoption of attraction-gaining strategies.

How are power differences affected by ingratiation tactics? Does ingratiation by the follower subvert or augment the power of the leader?

How precisely do the distortions of ingratiation affect our perceptions of ourselves and others?

What of the psychology of favor-giving as part of ingratiation? When does it help and when does it hurt the ingratiator? Is it possible that sometimes targets will like us more if we let *them* do favors for *us*? Why might this be so?

There remains the problem of defining ingratiation. Microscopic examination of ingratiating behavior keeps revealing an evanescent "something" that in any given case can be identified under more familiar headings such as: social conformity, deference to status, establishing credibility. It is my contention, however, that the concept of ingratiation links together various kinds of communicative acts that would otherwise be separately viewed and studied. By recognizing that there is a strategic side to social interaction, we open to examination the forms in which one person presents his "face" to another, when that other occupies an important position in his scheme of things.

Perhaps by acknowledging that ingratiation is part of the human condition, we may bring its facets into the light of day. As psychologists, if not as moralists, we may, in this vein, admire Lord Chesterfield's candor:

> Vanity is, perhaps, the most universal principle of human actions. . . . If my insatiable thirst for popularity, applause, and admiration made me do some silly things on the one hand, it made me, on the other hand, do almost all the right things that I did. . . . With the men I was a Proteus, and assumed every shape to please them all: among the gay, I was the gayest; among the grave, the gravest; and I never omitted the least attention to good breeding, to the least offices of friendship, that could either please or attach them to me. . . .

26

Observer's Reaction to the "Innocent Victim": Compassion or Rejection?

Melvin J. Lerner and Carolyn H. Simmons[1]

Under the guise of an experiment on the perception of emotional cues, seventy-two under-graduate female Ss observed a peer (victim) participating in a paired-associate learning task. The victim, as a result of making the usual errors, appeared to receive severe and painful electric shocks (negative reinforcement). In describing the suffering victim after these observations, Ss rejected and devalued her when they believed that they would continue to see her suffer in a 2nd session, and when they were powerless to alter the victim's fate. Rejection and devaluation were strongest when the victim was viewed as suffering for the sake of Ss ("martyr" condition). These results offer support for the hypothesis that rejection and devaluation of a suffering victim are primarily based on the observer's need to believe in a just world.

Recent experiments by Milgram (1963, 1964) provide important insights into the manner in which a social order can employ relatively normal people to commit cruel acts. A related problem is how societies which produce cruelty and suffering maintain even minimal popular support. What must occur is that the people come to accept the misery and suffering as well as the norms and laws which produce these conditions. There is evidence already available to account for how this acceptance might occur in those

[1]The authors wish to express their great appreciation to Joan Logsdon and Gail Matthews as well as Michael Romano, Coordinator of Medical Center Television at the University of Kentucky, and his staff whose cooperation and support enabled the experiment to be done in its present form.

This research was supported by Grant Gs-957 from the National Science Foundation administered by the senior author.

who feel responsible for the suffering of others. Davis and Jones (1960), Glass (1964), and Lerner (1965a) have shown that when a person has harmed someone, he may devalue his victim. Apparently the persecutor justifies his behavior by persuading himself that the victim deserved what happened to him.

These experiments, however, do not tell us how the average citizen— the observer or bystander who has not harmed the victim—comes to terms with the suffering he sees around him. Heider (1958) and others have noted that in some cases people reject, or at least blame, those who are unfortunate. However, they have also pointed out that compassion or sympathy for the suffering person may also occur. As yet no one has spelled out the conditions under which these various reactions occur or the processes underlying them.

It was proposed in an earlier paper (Lerner, 1965b) that people must believe there is an appropriate fit between what they do and what happens to them—their outcomes. It was reasoned that if people did not believe they could get what they want and avoid what they abhor by performing certain appropriate acts, they would be virtually incapacitated. It seems obvious that most people cannot afford, for the sake of their own sanity, to believe in a world governed by a schedule of random reinforcements. To maintain the belief that there is an appropriate fit between effort and outcome, the person must construe this as a relatively "objective" belief—one that applies to everyone (Festinger, 1954). If this is true, then the person who sees suffering or misfortune will be motivated to believe that the unfortunate victim in some sense merited his fate.

There are some data relevant to this assertion. Lerner (1965b) found that observers persuaded themselves that a fortuitously rewarded worker had performed better than his partner who was deprived, also by chance. In the same vein, Walster (1966), replicating the finding of Shaw and Sulzer (1964), illustrated that the more serious the outcome of a person's acts the more an observer will want to find the person responsible for the outcome. A more general interpretation of these findings is that people will arrange their cognitions so as to maintain the belief that people get what they deserve or, conversely, deserve what they get.

The key to the relation between these studies and the rejection of a victim is the realization that there seem to be two senses in which people are considered to be deserving. They are seen as deserving if they have behaved in an appropriate or commendable fashion, and, in another sense, are considered deserving if they are personally good and desirable. If the person is motivated to believe he lives in a world where he can obtain the things he wants and avoid threatening events, then it seems likely that these two paths to reward (performance versus personal worth) can be ordered in terms of preference for the individual. It would be preferable for a person to believe that desired goals come as a result of appropriate acts rather than of personal characteristics, since he is more able to change and control his behavior than his intrinsic personal worth. Some support for this assertion is found in the previously mentioned experiments. Lerner found that the fortuitous reward had no effect on the perceived attractiveness of the two workers, but merely on the judged worth of their performance. Walster also found this variable unaffected by her experimental conditions.

One interpretation of these findings is that the experimental situations provided by Lerner and Walster enabled their subjects to modify their cognitions of the behavior of the person judged, and therefore the subjects had no need to alter, to any significant degree, their evaluations of the other's personal worth. Although this is mostly conjecture, these notions do provide some hypotheses about when the bystander will reject or repudiate a suffering victim. The main hypothesis is that rejection is the result of the observer's attempt to maintain his belief in a just world. Also, this rejection will occur primarily when this need is not satisfied by the assignment of misdeeds to the victim.

Obviously, then, the clearest test of the hypothesis requires that the victim be perceived as virtually innocent—his behavior did not merit the suffering. Two other factors are required to reproduce the situation of the deprived or persecuted victim in society. One of these is that the observer believes the suffering he sees will probably continue in one form or another —the suffering is not a single, relatively isolated event in the victim's life. The other required element is that the observer is powerless to help the victim—given that he acts within the rules of the system in which the event takes place.

To approximate these conditions in a laboratory setting, groups of students who volunteered to participate in an experiment on the perception of emotional cues found themselves observing another experiment in which a subject was receiving extremely painful electric shocks. After seeing the victim suffer for ten minutes, there was an intermission. Before observing the next ten-minute session the observers were given an opportunity to rate the attractiveness of the victim. It was expected that in this condition (midpoint) the observers, faced with the prospect of seeing an innocent victim continue to suffer, would be compelled to devalue the personal characteristics of the victim.

On the other hand, if the observer believes the suffering is at an end and no permanent harm was done, he would have less need to reject the victim. Accordingly, the ratings of the victim in the previously described condition (midpoint) were compared with ratings made by subjects in two other conditions. In one condition the subjects believed the ten-minute session they had observed constituted all the suffering the victim would undergo in that experiment—the experiment was over except for the ratings (end-point condition). In the other condition the subjects believed they were watching a video tape of a victim who was now fine and in good spirits (past-event condition).

A third condition, in which rejection should be eliminated or reduced, would be one in which the observer is convinced he can alleviate the victim's suffering and/or provide him with compensatory rewards. Again, the victim's suffering would not threaten the observer's belief in a just world, and the observer can then afford, at least, to be objective in his appraisal of the victim. To test this prediction some subjects in this experiment were given an opportunity to vote after seeing the victim suffer during the initial session. Before making their ratings of the victim the observers learned that their votes were successful in placing the victim in a positive-reinforcement condition for the next session in which she would be certain to be paid a considerable amount of money (reward condition).

Actually there are two different processes which would predict less rejection in this "reward condition." The theoretical notions presented in this paper require that the observer be convinced that the victim's fate will actually be altered in order to prevent rejection of the victim. A prediction derived from the theory of cognitive dissonance (Festinger, 1957) would be that the observer's cognition that he has acted on behalf of the victim is sufficient to prevent rejection. To test this latter prediction, some additional subjects participated in a condition quite similar to the reward condition, except that they were not told of the outcome of their votes before they made their ratings of the victim (reward-decision condition).

The final hypothesis tested in this experiment provides the severest test of the ideas presented in this paper. Although it is commonly believed that people will admire and feel compassion for a person who has suffered for the sake of others, the suffering of someone who has acted out of altruistic motives should be most threatening to the belief in a just world. If this is true, then the observer should reject the willing martyr even more than the innocent victim. The hypothesis was tested in this experiment by having the innocent victim reluctantly agree to undergo the negative reinforcement so that the observers could observe her and thereby satisfy a course requirement to participate in an experiment (martyr condition).

The underlying hypothesis of this experiment is that observers, in order to maintain their belief in a just world, will devalue the personal characteristics of an innocent victim. To test this hypothesis specific predictions were made concerning the way in which observers will describe the personal characteristics of someone they have just seen suffering. The predictions are: If observers believe the victim's suffering will continue, they will describe her as a less attractive person than when they believe her suffering is ended (Hypothesis 1), when they see the victim after the event as apparently un-affected by the experience (Hypothesis 2), or when they have successfully arranged for her suffering to be changed to reward (Hypothesis 3). The observers will describe the victim as less attractive when they have merely decided to reward her than when they receive confirmation that she will be rewarded (Hypothesis 4). Finally, a victim who reluctantly agrees to con-tinue suffering for the sake of the observers will be judged less attractive than a victim whose suffering is ended (Hypothesis 5).

METHOD

Subjects

The subjects were seventy-five female students who volunteered to par-ticipate in this experiment as part of the requirements for a course in introductory psychology.[2] They were exposed to the experimental situation in small groups of four to ten subjects, preassigned on a nonsystematic basis to one of the various conditions. No subjects doubted the experimental ruse; however, three subjects were not included in the analysis because they had learned in advance of the true nature of the experiment.

Procedure

The subjects gathered in a waiting room a few minutes before the sche-duled experiment and were joined by a confederate (the "victim"), who was a girl of their own age dressed as another student. The subjects and the victim then accompanied the experimenter to the observation side of a one-way-mirror testing room, where it was established that the subjects were to take part in a study on the perception of emotional cues, while the victim, identified as another student, was to take part in a study on human learn-ing with another experimenter. At this point, all subjects were asked to complete a set of bipolar adjective scales designed to describe their "per-sonality traits," and a "personal attribute inventory" consisting of forced-choice pairs of personal characteristics equated for social desirability.

---

[2]The selection of female students was determined by a number of considerations. One was the desire to keep the subjects the same sex as the victim and the experimenters. The main consideration in the choice of females was based on the generally accepted stereotype as well as some data from Schopler and Bateson (1965) indicating that females would be more likely than males to exhibit compassion—thus providing the clearest test of the hypotheses.

When the forms had been completed, the experimenter gave, as a rationale for the experiment, the following explanation:

> Military officers, as well as business administrators, are presently very interested in studying the effects of emotional situations on learning and performance. I'm sure you all know people who, when they are faced with stressful or exciting situations, are able to continue working well in spite of their emotional state and other people who seem to fall apart and are unable to perform well when faced with the same emotional situation. Now obviously it is very important to leaders in a war situation or on an industrial assembly line, for example, to be able to make quick, accurate decisions as to which of the people working under them will be able to continue work under conditions of elation or stress, and which workers should be pulled off the job before their work is seriously affected by their emotional state. Often, these decisions must be made on the basis of only a few minutes' observation. As yet, we do not have any reliable cues which these people could use to make their important decisions. So today, we are taking advantage of a human learning study which Dr. Stewart is conducting to observe someone performing in an emotion-arousing situation. Your job will be to observe closely the emotional state of the worker and to watch for cues which indicate her state of arousal. Dr. Stewart is running her subjects under three different conditions: some subjects are rewarded for making correct responses, and these subjects usually earn between $2.00 and $8.00 for their work; other subjects receive electrical shocks for incorrect responses made to the learning task; and a third group of subjects is neither rewarded nor punished during the learning task, but is used as a control group.

At this point, the curtains covering the one-way mirror were opened to show the test room, where a memory drum was seen on a table with two chairs drawn up to it. Dr. Stewart was observed "adjusting" the shock equipment and electrode leads next to the memory drum. A technician was also adjusting the television camera. The experimenter explained that previous observers had relied most heavily on changes in skin color of the subject as an indication of her emotional state, and that in order to see what other possible cues could be used the observers today would watch the task over a television monitor. The curtains were then closed, and the subjects were directed to watch the monitor. At this point, Dr. Stewart entered the observation room and asked her subject (the victim) to accompany her. Before leaving the room, Dr. Stewart informed the experimenter that she was "running subjects in the shock condition today."

The subjects then watched what was actually a ten-minute video tape in which the victim was seen entering the next room with Dr. Stewart and, after being strapped to the "shock apparatus," attempted to learn pairs of nonsense syllables. During the task, the victim received several apparently painful electric "shocks" for incorrect responses, and reacted to them with both exclamations and expressions of pain and suffering. Of course, the victim was not actually shocked, but merely gave a very effective performance.

Following the tape, the subjects received one of the following sets of instructions, depending on the experimental condition to which they had been assigned:[3]

1. Midpoint ($N = 14$): The subjects were told they were at the midpoint in the experiment, and there would be another session of equal length after they made their first ratings of the victim.

2. Reward ($N = 14$): After being told that they had just seen the first session in the experiment, the subjects were asked to vote, by private ballot, as to what condition (negative reinforcement, positive reinforcement, or control) they would like to see the same person (victim) perform in for the second session. Ostensibly this choice was to enable them to select the condition which would provide the best opportunity to test out their hunches about what cues indicated the victim's state of arousal. Actually, it was designed to allow the subjects to alter the victim's fate and provide her with some rewards. After the vote the experimenter announced that the group had elected to observe the positive-reinforcement condition. One of the subjects in this condition voted for the control rather than the reward condition.

3. Reward decision ($N = 11$): The instructions were the same as the reward condition, but the subjects were not told of the outcome of the vote prior to making their ratings. One subject in this condition voted for the neutral rather than the positive-reinforcement condition.

4. End point ($N = 14$): The subjects were told the experiment was over, and they were asked to make their ratings of the victim.

5. Past event ($N = 10$): This condition was similar to the end point, except that the subjects were told that they would see a video tape of someone who had been shocked in the past. They were given an opportunity to meet the victim and see that she was fine and had in fact been paid a sum of money.

---

[3]Some of the important considerations in designing the basic situation were that the subjects should have a legitimate reason for seeing the suffering but in no way feel responsible for the victim's fate. Second, it should appear to be clearly inappropriate for the observer to interfere in any way with what was happening. Also, the victim should appear to have arrived at her fate through the normal channels of activity. In this experiment the victim had merely signed up for an experiment in human learning, of which there were a number being conducted at that time. It would also appear conceivable in terms of what the subjects had learned in their course work that someone could be administered "negative reinforcement" (shock) in that kind of experiment. Additionally, it was important to choose a task (paired-associate learning) in which it was obvious to the subjects that anyone would, especially in the early stages, make a number of errors. The first two considerations were intended to allow the subject to feel that she was not responsible for the victim's fate. The latter two were designed to make it extremely difficult for the subject to perceive the victim's behavior as responsible for her suffering. In addition to these factors the victim's suffering was portrayed as so intense that the subjects would be unlikely to be satisfied by merely deciding the victim had acted unwisely or lacked an inordinate amount of foresight.

6. Martyr ($N = 9$): The subjects were given the same instructions as the end point with these exceptions. When Dr. Stewart entered the room to get her subject and announced that they were running only negative-reinforcement conditions that day, the victim protested that she would not take part in an experiment in which she would be shocked. Dr. Stewart then urged her to continue for the sake of the observers (subjects) who would not be able to obtain lab credits for participating in an experiment if she (the victim) refused to do her part so they could observe her. It was also pointed out to her that her refusal would create a great deal of inconvenience and trouble for the observers (subjects), but, of course, the decision to participate or not was up to her. After a few moments of persuasion, based on the elicitation of altruistic motives, the victim agreed to participate "if it is necessary for all of them [subjects] to get credit." Three psychologists who observed this scene in rehearsal agreed with no reluctance whatever that the victim created the impression of acting generously from altruistic motives when she agreed to go on with her part in the experiment.

Measures

Following the exposure to the video tape and the experimental instructions, the subjects filled out a number of scales in order to describe the "impression which the person you saw [victim] gives others of what she is like." These scales, including those the subject had initially filled out to describe herself, were designed to allow the observer to describe the attractiveness of the victim as well as to create any desired degree of similarity. There were also some questions and scales designed to lend validity to the experimental ruse.

Two different measures of the attractiveness of the victim were employed: (*a*) The ratings on the fifteen highly evaluative bipolar scales (e.g., likable-unlikable and mature-immature) were combined to yield an overall index of attractiveness. The range of possible scores was from 15 to 135 (the higher the score the more positive the rating). On the basis of previous work with these scales, the attractiveness rating the subject ascribed to herself, initially, was subtracted from that ascribed to the victim to yield the final measure used in the analysis. (*b*) The subjects rated the victim in response to five questions about her "Social Stimulus Value": "How would people in general react to this person after a brief acquaintance, in terms of getting to know him (her) better?" (Would prefer not to become further acquainted = 1, would be intensely interested = 6). "How easily would this person fit in with your friends?" (Probably not easily = 1, would be eagerly sought out = 6). "Some people are able to gain admiration and respect from others very easily and other people are not. How easily can this person gain admiration from others?" (Very easily = 1, very difficult = 6). Similar to the preceding but the terms "affection and liking" were substituted for "admiration." "From the impression this person gives, how likely is he (she) to be able to get the things he (she) wants out of life?" (Will have to struggle for what she wants = 1, the things he (she) wants will come very naturally and easily = 6). The responses to each of these questions were combined to yield a second index of the victim's attractiveness.

To measure similarity the subject's description of herself on a twenty-item, forced-choice scale was compared with her postexperimental description of the victim. (Some examples are: Item 6, good sense of humor, good sense of fairness; Item 17, tend to be insecure, tend to be selfish). The number of similar choices was used as the measure of ascribed similarity.

In order to learn more about the subjects' general reaction to the experiment, they were asked to respond freely to three general questions. "Were the instructions given clearly . . . etc.?" "How did you feel about cooperating in this experiment?" "What . . . in your words . . . was the experiment about?" The subjects were also given an opportunity to express any other reactions: "Additional comments and constructive criticism." Besides testing the effectiveness of the experimental ruse, these questions were intended to allow the subject to react to all aspects of the experimental situation.

RESULTS

An examination of Table 26.1 reveals that there was a clear difference between the attractiveness (bipolar scales) of the victim in the midpoint and the reward conditions ($t = 2.95$, $p < .01$, Hypothesis 3). Also, it appears that the reward-decision condition elicited as much rejection[4] as the midpoint condition, and considerably more than the reward ($t = 2.68$, $p < .01$, Hypothesis 4). The means of the past-event and end-point conditions are virtually identical and lie between reward and midpoint. Although closer to reward, they are not reliably different from either reward or midpoint (Hypotheses 1 and 2). The end-point condition provided the most appropriate control and test for the martyr conditions. A comparison of the

---

[4]The use of the term "rejection" here is based on findings of previous research using this instrument. In an earlier experiment with similarly obtained female subjects, it was found that there was a tendency for them to rate others slightly higher than themselves with the two scores being highly correlated. Even after an experience with another person who had harmed the subjects somewhat, the lowest mean rating was not lower than -10. Obviously, then, the mean in the midpoint condition is considerably lower than those found with a number of different subjects rating a number of other people.

TABLE 26.1
Ratings of the victim

	Past event ($N = 10$)	Reward ($N = 14$)	Reward decision ($N = 11$)	Midpoint ($N = 14$)	End point ($N = 14$)	Martyr ($N = 9$)
Attractiveness[a] (bipolar scales)	−11.10	−5.07	−25.18	−25.78	−12.85	−34.00
Social stimulus value[a]	18.70	19.21	15.27	14.71	17.00	14.11
Similarity[b]	11.60	9.42	9.36	9.36	9.82	8.78

		Analyses of variance				
	df	Attractiveness		Social stimulus value		Similarity	
		MS	F	MS	F	MS	F
Conditions	5	1381.0	4.00*	53.38	3.86*	9.57	1.08
Error	66	344.9		13.82		8.83	

[a]The more positive (less negative) the rating the more attractive the victim.
[b]The higher the rating the greater the perceived similarity.
*$p < .005$.

means in these two conditions yields a t of 2.66 ($p < .01$, Hypothesis 5). Apparently, the martyr condition elicited the lowest ratings of attractiveness.

The responses to the Social Stimulus Value index of attractiveness present a pattern similar to the one described above. When the subjects believed they successfully assigned the victim to the reward condition, they rated her as considerably less negative than when they were uncertain as to whether they were successful (reward decision versus reward $t = 2.64$, $p < .02$, Hypothesis 4) or when they were powerless to alter her fate (reward versus midpoint $t = 3.19$, $p < .005$, Hypothesis 3). Again the means in the past-event and end-point conditions fell between those in the reward and midpoint (Hypotheses 1 and 2). However, with this measure the past-event mean was significantly higher than the midpoint ($t = 2.59$, $p < .02$). The martyr condition again elicited the greatest amount of rejection, but the difference between the ratings in this condition in comparison with those in the end point was not significant ($t = 1.81$, $p < .08$, Hypothesis 5).

There were no reliable differences in the similarity attributed to the victim among the experimental conditions. The most likely interpretation of this is that the measure of similarity which was constructed for this experiment was not adequate to pick up what differences may actually have been elicited. A more sensitive measure or one that measured other aspects of similarity might have yielded significant results.

Some of the most interesting data in this experiment were found in the written comments. Although a complete analysis of the contents of these comments is not within the scope of this paper, some of the preliminary findings can be reported. It should be remembered in interpreting these comments that they were written before the subjects were disabused of the experimental ruse. As one might expect, the comments varied from extremely positive (e.g., "I think it is about the most interesting experiment I have been able to participate in. I enjoyed it very much.") to extremely negative (e.g., "I thought there was no sense in the experiment and it was very cruel.").

Also, the comments tended to be either predominantly positive or negative, rather than equivocal or ambivalent. Sixty-five of the 72 subjects provided responses easily codable into either positive or negative, and the majority, 40 of the 65, responded positively.

By using these comments, coded as either positive or negative, it was possible to test an important prediction from the theoretical ideas presented in this paper. It was stated earlier that when a person is confronted with the sight of someone suffering the observer will be compelled to decide that either he lives in a cruel, unjust world where innocent people can suffer or that he lives in a just and good world and the victim deserves his suffering. If this reasoning is true, then those subjects who rejected the situation should rate the victim much more positively (or rather, less negatively) than did those who wrote something positive about the experiment. This hypothesis was confirmed by the data. The subjects who responded negatively to the situation rated the victim -5.16 (the bipolar adjective scales), and those who responded positively gave a mean rating of -24.35. A comparison of these two means yields a t of 3.73, $df = 63$, $p < .001$.

This clear negative relation between the reaction to the experimental situation and the reaction to the victim also indicates that the rejection of the victim observed in this experiment did not merely reflect a global negative response to everything in the environment caused by the subject being forced to undergo the stress of seeing someone else suffer.

DISCUSSION

In general, the data provide good support for the hypotheses. As expected, the least rejection occurred when the observer has actually altered the fate of the victim and allowed her to obtain a reward. When the observer was unable to stop the suffering, other than by an act of open rebellion against the experimenter, she chose to devalue and reject the victim. Also supported was the hypothesis that acting to benefit a suffering victim is not sufficient to insure that the law-abiding observer will not reject the victim. The crucial element seems to lie in the observer's becoming aware that the victim will be compensated or at least that his suffering is at an end.

The amount of rejection which appeared in the martyr condition was somewhat surprising, but theoretically important. Although all safeguards were taken to insure that the impression which the victim created truly represented someone acting out of altruistic motives, there is no way of insuring that this was the case—other than by an elaborate set of control conditions. However, given that the data do represent a real finding, and there is every reason to believe this is true, then they provide strong support for the assertion that people have a great need to believe in a good and just world. Apparently the martyr's suffering threatens this need more than suffering of less nobly motivated people.

The written comments provided equally important support for the assertion that the observer is faced with a conflict when he sees someone suffering. The subjects who verbally condemned the experiment exhibited much less rejection of the victim. Why some observers rejected the experiment and other rejected the victim is an important, but as yet uninvestigated, question. The usual, but untested, answer provided for this question centers around the concept of identification. But certainly to say that those observers who identify with the victim will show compassion, and not reject him, merely substitutes another concept for an answer. In this vein, it is important to note that one of the most frequently used indexes of identification, perceived similarity, did not reveal any systematic differences among the conditions. However, as stated earlier this may well have resulted from employing an inadequate instrument to measure similarity.

There are a number of important questions and related hypotheses raised by the findings of this experiment.

A note of caution in generalizing these results may be appropriate. In the strictest sense, the findings of this experiment were obtained from female subjects only, and some reservations about extending the conclusions to men may be in order.

One untested, but extremely interesting, hypothesis which follows from the earlier discussion is that if observers can attribute the victim's suffering to something the victim did or failed to do they will have less need to devalue his personal characteristics (other things being equal). The observers' belief in a just and predictable world will not be threatened.

Another question is, When does the actual rejection occur? A reasonable hypothesis is that some, if not all, of the rejection will occur merely with the cognition that the observer will see the victim suffer. It may not be necessary actually to observe the suffering to elicit rejection. Some support for this notion is found in the fact that subjects in the reward condition did not actually have to see the victim being paid, in order for the condition to be effective. They merely had to be sure that the subject would get a good deal of money and the suffering would be at an end.

The most compelling question raised by these data is, Under what conditions will a person whose suffering derives from altruistic motives be reacted to with compassion and admiration rather than rejection?

References

DAVIS, K. E., AND JONES, E. E. Changes in interpersonal perception as a means of reducing cognitive dissonance. *Journal of Abnormal and Social Psychology,* 1960, **61,** 402–410.

FESTINGER, L. A theory of social comparison processes. *Human Relations,* 1954, **7,** 117–140.

FESTINGER, L. *A theory of cognitive dissonance.* Stanford: Stanford University Press, 1957.

GLASS, D. C. Changes in liking as a means of reducing cognitive discrepancies between self-esteem and aggression. *Journal of Personality,* 1964, **32,** 531–549.

HEIDER, F. *The psychology of interpersonal relations.* New York: Wiley, 1958.

LERNER, M. J. The effect of responsibility and choice on a partner's attractiveness following failure. *Journal of Personality,* 1965, **33,** 178–187. (a)

LERNER, M. J. Evaluation of performance as a function of performer's reward and attractiveness. *Journal of Personality and Social Psychology,* 1965, **1,** 355–360. (b)

MILGRAM, S. Behavioral study of obedience. *Journal of Abnormal and Social Psychology,* 1963, **67,** 371–378.

MILGRAM, S. Group pressure and action against a person. *Journal of Abnormal and Social Psychology,* 1964, **69,** 137–143.

SCHOPLER, J., AND BATESON, N. The power of dependence. *Journal of Personality and Social Psychology,* 1965, **2,** 247–254.

SHAW, M. E., AND SULZER, J. L. An empirical test of Heider's levels in attribution of responsibility. *Journal of Abnormal and Social Psychology,* 1964, **69,** 39–47.

WALSTER, E. Assignment of responsibility for an accident. *Journal of Personality and Social Psychology,* 1966, **3,** 73–79.

27

Gain and Loss of Esteem as Determinants of Interpersonal Attractiveness

Elliot Aronson and Darwyn Linder

One of the major determinants of whether or not one person (*P*) will like another (*O*) is the nature of the other's behavior in relation to the person. Several investigators have predicted and found that if *P* finds *O*'s behavior "rewarding," he will tend to like *O* (Newcomb, 1956, 1961; Thibaut and Kelley, 1959; Homans, 1961; Byrne, 1961; Byrne and Wong, 1962). One obvious source of reward for *P* is *O*'s attitude regarding him. Thus, if *O* expresses invariably positive feelings and opinions about *P*, this constitutes a reward and will tend to increase *P*'s liking for *O*.

Although this has been demonstrated to be true (Newcomb, 1956, 1961), it may be that a more complex relationship exists between being liked and liking others. It is conceivable that the sequence of *O*'s behavior toward *P* might have more impact on *P*'s liking for *O* than the total number of rewarding acts emitted by *O* toward *P*. Stated briefly, it is our contention that

Reprinted with permission from *The Journal of Experimental Social Psychology*, Vol. 1, 1965. Copyright 1965 by Academic Press, Inc.

This research was supported by a grant from the National Science Foundation (NSF GS 202) to Elliot Aronson. The authors wish to thank Mrs. Ellen Berscheid who served as the experimenter during a pilot study, and Miss Darcy Oman, who served as the confederate during the experiment.

the feeling of gain or loss is extremely important — specifically, that a gain in esteem is a more potent reward than invariant esteem, and similarly, the loss of esteem is a more potent "punishment" than invariant negative esteem. Thus, if O's behavior toward P was initially negative but gradually became more positive, P would like O more than he would had O's behavior been uniformly positive. This would follow even if, in the second case, the sum total of rewarding acts emitted by O was less than in the first case.

This "gain-loss" effect may have two entirely different causes. One is largely affective, the other cognitive. First, when O expresses negative feelings toward P, P probably experiences some negative affect, e.g., anxiety, hurt, self-doubt, anger, etc. If O's behavior gradually becomes more positive, his behavior is not only rewarding for P in and of itself, but it also serves to reduce the existing negative drive state previously aroused by O. The total reward value of O's positive behavior is, therefore, greater. Thus, paradoxically, P will subsequently like O better *because* of O's early negative, punitive behavior.

This reasoning is similar to that of Gerard and Greenbaum (1962). Their experiment involved an Asch-type situation in which they varied the behavior of the stooge whose judgments followed those of the subject. In one condition the investigators varied the trial on which the stooge switched from disagreeing with the judgment of the subject (and agreeing with that of the majority) to agreeing with the judgment of the subject. The results showed a curvilinear relationship between the point at which the stooge switched and his attractiveness for the subjects — the subjects liked him best if he switched either very early or very late in the sequence of judgments. The investigators predicted and explained the high degree of liking for the "late-switcher" as being due to the fact that he was reducing a greater degree of uncertainty. Our reasoning is also consistent with that of Walters and Ray (1960) who, in elaborating on an experiment by Gewirtz and Baer (1958), demonstrated that prior anxiety arousal increases the effectiveness of social reinforcement on children's performance. In their experiment social approval had a greater effect on performance in the anxiety conditions because it was reducing a greater drive.

We are carrying this one step further. What we are suggesting is that the existence of a prior negative drive state will increase the attractiveness of an individual who has both created and reduced this drive state. The kind of relationship we have in mind was perhaps best expressed by Spinoza (1955) in proposition 44 of *The Ethics:* "Hatred which is completely vanquished by love passes into love: and love is thereupon greater than if hatred had not preceded it. For he who begins to love a thing, which he has wont to hate or regard with pain, from the very fact of loving feels pleasure. To this pleasure involved in love is added the pleasure arising from aid given to the endeavour to remove the pain involved in hatred, accompanied by the idea of the former object of hatred as cause."

The same kind of reasoning (in reverse) underlies the "loss" part of our notion. Here, P will like O better if O's behavior toward P is invariably negative than if O's initial behavior had been positive and gradually became more negative. Although in the former case O's behavior may consist of a greater number of negative acts, the latter case constitutes a distinct loss of esteem and, therefore, would have a greater effect upon reducing P's liking for O. When negative behavior follows positive behavior, it is not only punishing in its own right but also eradicates the positive affect associated with the rewarding nature of O's earlier behavior. Therefore, P dislikes the positive-negative O more than the entirely negative O precisely because of the fact that, in the first case, O had previously rewarded him.

The predicted gain-loss effect may also have a more cognitive cause. By changing his opinion about P, O forces P to take his evaluation more seriously. If O expresses uniformly positive or uniformly negative feelings about P, P can dismiss this behavior as being a function of O's style of response, i.e., that O likes everybody or dislikes everybody, and that is *his* problem. But if O begins by evaluating P negatively and then becomes more positive, P must consider the possibility that O's evaluations are a function of O's perception of him and not merely a style of responding. Because of this he is more apt to be impressed by O than if O's evaluation had been invariably positive. It is probably not very meaningful to be liked by a person with no discernment or discrimination. O's early negative evaluation proves that he has discernment and that he's paying attention to P—that he's neither blind nor bland. This renders his subsequent positive evaluation all the more meaningful and valuable.

By the same token, if O's evaluation of P is entirely negative, P may be able to write O off as a misanthrope or a fool. But if O's initial evaluation is positive and then becomes negative, P is forced to conclude that O can discriminate among people. This adds meaning (and sting) to O's negative evaluation of P and, consequently, will decrease P's liking for O.

The present experiment was designed to test the major prediction of our gain-loss notion, that is, the primary intent of this experiment was to determine whether or not *changes* in the feelings of O toward P have a greater effect on P's liking for O than the total number of rewarding acts emitted by O. A secondary purpose was to shed some light on the possible reasons for this relationship. The specific hypotheses are (1) P will like O better if O's initial attitude toward P is negative but gradually becomes more positive, than if his attitude is uniformly positive; (2) P will like O better if his attitude is uniformly negative than if his initial attitude toward P is positive and becomes increasingly negative.

METHOD

Subjects and Design

In order to provide a test of the hypotheses, it was necessary to design an experiment in which a subject interacts with a confederate over a series of discrete meetings. During these meetings the confederate should express either a uniformly positive attitude toward the subject, a uniformly negative attitude toward the subject, a negative attitude which gradually becomes positive, or a positive attitude which gradually becomes negative. It was essential that the interactions between subject and confederate be constant throughout experimental conditions except for the expression of attitude. At the close of the experiment, the subject's liking for the confederate could be assessed.

The subjects were eighty female students[1] at the University of Minnesota. Virtually all of them were sophomores; they were volunteers from introductory classes in psychology, sociology, and child development. All subjects were randomly assigned to one of the four experimental conditions.

Procedure

The experimenter greeted the subject and led her to an observation room which was connected to the main experimental room by a one-way window and an audio-amplification system. The experimenter told the subject that two students were scheduled for this hour, one would be the subject and the other would help the experimenter perform the experiment. He said that since she arrived first, she would be the helper. He asked her to wait while he left the room to see if the other girl had arrived yet. A few minutes later, through the one-way window, the subject was able to see the experimenter enter the experimental room with another female student (the paid confederate). The experimenter told the confederate to be seated for a moment and that he would return shortly to explain the experiment to her. The experimenter then returned to the observation room and began the instructions to the subject. The experimenter told the subject that she was going to assist him in performing a verbal conditioning experiment on the other student. The experimenter explained verbal conditioning briefly and told the subject that his particular interest was in the possible generalization of conditioned verbal responses from the person giving the reward to

---

[1] Actually, 84 subjects were run in these four conditions. Four of the subjects were unusable because they were able to guess the real purpose of the experiment.

a person who did not reward the operant response. The experimenter explained that he would condition the other girl to say plural nouns to him by rewarding her with an "mmm hmmm" every time she said a plural noun. The experimenter told the subject that his procedure should increase the rate of plural nouns employed by the other girl. The subject was then told that her tasks were: (1) to listen in and record the number of plural nouns used by the other girl, and (2) to engage her in a series of conversations (not rewarding plural nouns) so that the experimenter could listen and determine whether generalization occurred. The experimenter told the subject that they would alternate in talking to the girl (first the subject, then the experimenter, then the subject) until each had spent seven sessions with her.

The experimenter made it clear to the subject that the other girl must not know the purpose of the experiment lest the results be contaminated. He explained that, in order to accomplish this, some deception must be used. The experimenter said that he was going to tell the girl that the purpose of the experiment was to determine how people form impressions of other people. He said that the other girl would be told that she was to carry on a series of seven short conversations with the subject, and that between each of these conversations both she and the subject would be interviewed, the other girl by the experimenter and the subject by an assistant in another room, to find out what impressions they had formed. The experimenter told the subject that this "cover story" would enable the experimenter and the subject to perform their experiment on verbal behavior since it provided the other girl with a credible explanation for the procedure they would follow. In actuality, this entire explanation was, in itself, a cover story which enabled the experimenter and his confederate to perform their experiment on the formation of impressions.

The independent variable was manipulated during the seven meetings that the experimenter had with the confederate. During their meetings the subject was in the observation room, listening to the conversation and dutifully counting the number of plural nouns used by the confederate. Since the subject had been led to believe that the confederate thought that the experiment involved impressions of people, it was quite natural for the experimenter to ask the confederate to express her feelings about the subject. Thus, without intending to, the subject heard herself evaluated by a fellow student on seven successive occasions.

There were four experimental conditions: (1) Negative-Positive, (2) Positive-Negative, (3) Negative-Negative, and (4) Positive-Positive. In the Negative-Positive condition the confederate expressed a negative impression of the subject during the first three interviews with the experimenter. Specifically, she described her as being a dull conversationalist, a rather ordinary person, not very intelligent, as probably not having many friends, etc. During the fourth session she began to change her opinion about her. The confederate's attitude became more favorable with each successive meeting until, in the seventh interview, it was entirely positive. In the Positive-Positive condition the confederate's stated opinions were invariably positive. During the seventh interview her statements were precisely the same as those in the seventh meeting of the Negative-Positive condition. In the Negative-Negative condition the confederate expressed invariably negative feelings about the subject throughout the seven interviews. The Positive-Negative condition was the mirror image of the Negative-Positive condition. The confederate began by stating that the subject seemed interesting, intelligent, and likeable, but by the seventh session she described the subject as being dull, ordinary, etc.

In the Positive-Positive condition the confederate made 28 favorable statements about the subject and zero unfavorable statements. In the Negative-Negative condition the confederate made 24 unfavorable statements about the subject and zero favorable ones. In both the Negative-Positive and Positive-Negative conditions the confederate made 14 favorable and 8 unfavorable statements about the subject.

At the opening of the first interview, the experimenter informed the confederate that she should be perfectly frank and honest and that the subject would never be told anything about her evaluation. This was done so that the subject, upon hearing favorable statements, could not readily believe that the confederate might be trying to flatter her.

Interactions Between Subjects and Confederate

Prior to each interview with the experimenter, the confederate and the subject engaged in a three-minute conversation. This provided a credible basis upon which the confederate might form and change her impression of the subject. During these sessions it was essential that the confederate's conversations with the subject be as uniform as possible throughout the four experimental conditions. This was accomplished by informing the subject, prior to the first session, of the kind of topics she should lead the confederate into. These included movies, teachers, courses, life goals, personal background information, etc. Once the subject brought up one of these topics, the confederate spewed forth a prepared set of facts, opinions, and anecdotes which were identical for all experimental subjects. Of course, since a social interaction was involved, it was impossible for the confederate's conversations to be entirely uniform for all of the subjects. Occasionally the confederate was forced to respond to a direct question which was idiosyncratic to a particular subject. However, any variations in the statements made by the confederate were minor and nonsystematic.

The subject and confederate met in the same room but they were separated at all times by a cardboard screen which prevented visual communication. This was done for two reasons. First, it made it easier for the confederate to play the role of the naive subject. We feared that the confederate, after saying negative things about the subject, might be reluctant to look her squarely in the eye and engage in casual conversation. In addition, the use of the screen allowed for a more precise control of the conversation of the confederate by enabling her to read her lines from a prepared script which was tacked to the screen. The use of the screen was easily explained to the subject (in terms of the verbal reinforcement cover story) as a necessary device for eliminating inadvertent nonverbal reinforcement, like nods and smiles.

The confederate carried on her end of the conversation in a rather bland, neutral tone of voice, expressing neither great enthusiasm nor monumental boredom. The same girl (an attractive twenty-year-old senior) was used as the confederate throughout the experiment. In order to further convince the subject of the validity of the cover story, the confederate used increasingly more plural nouns throughout the course of the experiment.

The Dependent Variable

At the close of the experiment the experimenter told the subject that there was some additional information he needed from her, but that it was also necessary for him to see the other girl to explain the true nature of the experiment to her. He said that, since he was pressed for time, the subject would be interviewed by his research supervisor while he, the experimenter, explained the experiment to the other girl. The experimenter then led the subject into the interviewer's office, introduced them, and left.

A separate interviewer[2] was used in order to avoid bias, the interviewer being ignorant of the subject's experimental condition. The purpose of the interview was to measure the subject's liking for the confederate; but this could not be done in any simple manner because the bare outlines of this experiment were extremely transparent: the confederate evaluated the subject, then the subject evaluated the confederate. Unless the interviewer

---

[2]It should be reported that in an earlier attempt to test this hypothesis, a questionnaire was administered instead of an interview. This was a more economical procedure, but it proved to be less effective. Although the results in the four experimental conditions were in the predicted order, the variance was extremely large. Postexperimental discussions with the subjects led us to suspect that one reason for the large variance might be due to the fact that the subjects were treating the questionnaires in a rather casual manner, believing that this aspect of the experiment was of little importance. It was primarily for this reason that we decided to use a high-status interviewer, whose earnest presence forced the subjects to treat the interview seriously and to respond in an honest and thoughtful manner.

could provide the subject with a credible rationale (consistent with the cover story) for asking her to evaluate the other girl, even the most naive of our subjects might have guessed the real purpose of the experiment. Therefore, the interviewer took a great deal of time and trouble to convince the subject that these data were essential for an understanding of the other girl's verbal behavior. The essence of his story was that the attitudes and feelings that the "helpers" in the experiment had for the "subjects" in the experiment often found expression in such subtle ways as tone of voice, enthusiasm, etc. "For example, if you thought a lot of the other girl you might unwittingly talk with warmth and enthusiasm. If you didn't like her you might unwittingly sound aloof and distant." The interviewer went on to explain that, much to his chagrin, he noticed that these subtle differences in inflection had a marked effect upon the gross verbal output of the other girls, that is, they talked more when they were conversing with people who seemed to like them than when they were conversing with people who seemed not to like them. The interviewer said that this source of variance was impossible to control but must be accounted for in the statistical analysis of the data. He explained that if he could get a precise indication of the "helpers" feelings toward the "subjects," he could then "plug this into a mathematical formula as a correction term and thereby get a more or less unbiased estimate of what her gross verbal output would have been if your attitude toward her had been neutral."

The interviewer told the subject that, in order to accomplish this, he was going to ask her a number of questions aimed at getting at her feelings about the other girl. He emphasized that he wanted her *feeling,* her "gut response"; i.e., that it was essential that she give her frank impression of the other girl regardless of whether or not she had solid, rational reasons for it.

After the subject indicated that she understood, the interviewer asked her whether she liked the other girl or not. After she answered, the interviewer showed her a card on which was printed a 21-point scale, from -10 to $+10$. The interviewer asked her to indicate the magnitude of her feeling as precisely as possible. He verbally labeled the scale: "$+10$ would mean you like her extremely, -10 that you dislike her extremely. Zero means that you are completely indifferent. If you liked her a little, you'd answer $+1, +2$, or $+3$; if you liked her moderately well, you'd answer $+4, +5$, or $+6$; if you liked her quite a bit, you'd answer with a higher number. What point on the scale do you feel reflects your feeling toward the girl most accurately?"

This was the dependent measure. In addition, the interviewer asked the subjects to rate the confederate on 14 evaluative scales including intelligence, friendliness, warmth, frankness, etc. Most of these were asked in order to ascertain whether or not general liking would manifest itself in terms of higher ratings on specific attributes; a few were asked as possible checks on the manipulations.

Finally, the interviewer asked the subject if it bothered, embarrassed, annoyed, or upset her to hear the other girl evaluate her to the experimenter. After recording her answer, the interviewer probed to find out whether or not the subject suspected the real purpose of the experiment. He then explained, in full, the true nature of the experiment and the necessity for the deception. The subjects, especially those who had been negatively evaluated, were relieved to learn that it was not "for real." Although several of the girls admitted to having been quite shaken during the experiment, they felt that it was a worthwhile experience, inasmuch as they learned the extent to which a negative evaluation (even by a stranger) can affect them. They left the interview room in good spirits.

In most cases the interviewer remained ignorant of which of the four experimental conditions the subject was in until the conclusion of the interview. On a few occasions, however, a subject said something casually, in the midst of the interview, from which the interviewer could infer her experimental condition. It should be emphasized, however, that the dependent variable was the first question asked; in no case was the interviewer aware of a subject's experimental condition before she responded to that question.

RESULTS AND DISCUSSION

Our hypotheses were that the confederate would be liked better in the Negative-Positive condition than in the Positive-Positive condition and that she would be liked better in the Negative-Negative condition than in the Positive-Negative condition. To test these hypotheses we compared the subjects' ratings of their liking for the confederate across experimental conditions. The significance of the differences were determined by t-test.[3] Table 27.1 shows the means, SDs, t-values, and significance levels. An examination of the table reveals that the means are ordered in the predicted direction. Moreover, it is clear that the confederate was liked significantly more in the Negative-Positive condition than in the Positive-Positive condition ($p < .02$, two-tailed). The difference between the Negative-Negative

---

[3]A t-test was used because it is the most direct statistical technique and it also allowed us to perform an internal analysis to be described later. However, it is not the most powerful method of analyzing the data. An analysis of variance was also performed, and the results were slightly more significant than those of the t-test. The difference between Negative-Positive and Positive-Positive conditions reached the .02 level of significance; the difference between the Negative-Negative and the Positive-Negative conditions reached the .07 level of significance. The over-all treatment effect was highly significant ($p < .0005$).

TABLE 27.1
Means and standard deviations for liking of the Confederate

Experimental condition	Mean	*SD*	*t*-values	
1. Negative-Positive	+7.67	1.51	1 vs. 2	2.71**
2. Positive-Positive	+6.42	1.42	2 vs. 3	7.12†
3. Negative-Negative	+2.52	3.16	3 vs. 4	1.42*
4. Positive-Negative	+0.87	3.32		

*$p < .15$. **$p < .02$. †$p < .001$ (all p levels are two-tailed).

condition and the Positive-Negative condition showed a strong trend in the predicted direction, although it did not reach an acceptable level of significance ($p < .15$, two-tailed). There is a great deal of variability in these two conditions. This large variability may be partly a function of the well-known reluctance of college students to express negative feelings about their fellow students, even when the behavior of the latter is objectively negative (e.g., Aronson and Mills, 1959). Typically, in social psychological experiments, regardless of how obnoxiously a stooge behaves toward a subject, many subjects find it difficult to verbalize negative evaluations of the stooge. In these two conditions the behavior of the stimulus person would seem to have brought forth a negative evaluation; although most of the subjects were able to do this, several came out with highly positive evaluations. Thus, the range for the Negative-Negative and Positive-Negative conditions was 15 scale units (from +7 to −7). In the other two conditions negative evaluations were *not* in order; thus, this difficulty was not encountered. The range for these two conditions was only seven scale units (from +9 to +3). Therefore, although the mean difference between the Positive-Negative and Negative-Negative conditions was actually larger than the mean difference between the Positive-Positive and Negative-Positive conditions, it fell short of statistical significance.

Table 27.1 also indicates that there is a very large difference between those conditions in which the confederate ended by expressing a positive feeling for the subject and those in which she ended with a negative feeling for the subject. For example, a comparison of the Positive-Positive condition with the Negative-Negative condition yields a *t* of 7.12, significant at far less than the .001 level. As predicted, the widest mean difference occurs between the Negative-Positive condition (M = +7.67) and the Positive-Negative condition (M = +0.87). This is interesting in view of the fact that the confederate made the same number of positive and negative statements in these two conditions; only the sequence was different.

It will be recalled that the subjects were asked to rate the confederate on 14 evaluative scales in order to ascertain whether or not greater liking would manifest itself in terms of higher ratings on specific attributes. No evidence for this was found; e.g., although the subjects liked the confederate better in the Negative-Positive condition than in the Positive-Positive condition, they did not find her significantly more intelligent or less conceited. In fact, the only ratings that reached an acceptable level of significance showed a reverse effect: In the Positive-Positive condition the confederate was rated more friendly ($p < .01$), nicer ($p < .01$), and warmer ($p < .01$) than in the Negative-Positive condition. Our failure to predict this effect may be attributable to a naive belief in generalization which served to blind us to more obvious factors. Thus, although we did not predict this result, it is not startling if one considers the simple fact that in the Positive-Positive condition the confederate's evaluations of the subject, because they were entirely positive, *did* reflect greater friendliness, niceness, and warmth. That is, when forced to consider such things as friendliness, niceness, and warmth, the subjects in the Negative-Positive condition could not give the confederate a very high rating. The confederate, here, is not the kind of person who exudes niceness; by definition she is capable of saying negative things. Nevertheless, when asked for their "gut-response" regarding how much they liked the confederate, the subjects in the Negative-Positive condition tended to give her a high rating. To speculate, we might suggest the following: When one is asked to rate a person on a particular attribute, one tends to sum the person's relevant behavior in a rather cognitive, rational manner. On the other hand, when one is asked how much one likes a person, one tends to state a current feeling rather than to add and subtract various components of the person's past behavior.

Degree of Liking as a Function of "Upset"

The major results are consistent with the hypotheses derived from the gain-loss notion. Although, in this experiment, it was not our intention to test the underlying assumptions of this notion, there are some data which may be of relevance. Recall that one of the suggested causes of the gain-loss effect is that, in the negative conditions, the subjects experienced negative feelings such as anxiety, anger, self-doubt, etc. That is, it was predicted that the subjects in the Negative-Positive condition would like the confederate better than would the subjects in the Positive-Positive condition because in the Negative-Positive condition the confederate's behavior was reducing a negative drive state. If this assumption is correct, the effect should not occur if, for some reason, the confederate's negative behavior did not produce a negative drive state in the subjects. For example, in the Negative-Positive condition, if the subjects did not take the negative evaluation personally there would be no negative drive state to be reduced.

Similarly, in the Positive-Negative condition, loss would not be experienced if the confederate's negative behavior, for some reason, were not taken personally by the subject. As mentioned earlier, near the end of the experiment the interviewer asked the subject if it bothered, embarrassed, or upset her to listen to herself being evaluated by the other girl. As one might expect, in the Positive-Positive condition none of the subjects were at all bothered, upset, or embarrassed by the situation. In the Negative-Positive condition, however, eleven subjects admitted to having been somewhat upset when the other girl was evaluating them negatively; similarly, nine girls in the Negative-Negative condition and nine in the Positive-Negative condition admitted that they were upset by the negative evaluation. In these latter conditions the subjects who claimed that they were not upset by the negative evaluation tended to explain this by saying that the situation was so restricted that they lacked the freedom and relaxation to "be themselves" and "make a good impression" on the other girl. Typically, they felt that it was reasonable for the other girl to think of them as dull and stupid — the situation *forced* them to appear dull. Thus, many of the girls refused to take a negative evaluation personally; instead, they felt that the confederate would have liked them better if the situation had been freer, allowing them to express their usual, loveable personalities.

For what it is worth, let us compare those who were upset by a negative evaluation with those who were not in terms of how much they liked the confederate. Within the Negative-Positive condition those subjects who were upset by the negative evaluation liked the confederate *more* than those who were not upset ($t = 3.36$, $p < .01$, two-tailed). Similarly, within the Positive-Negative condition those who were upset by the negative evaluation liked the confederate *less* than those who were not upset ($t = 4.44$, $p < .01$). In the Negative-Negative condition, as might be expected, there was a tendency for those who were not upset to like the confederate better than those who were upset ($t = 1.26$, N.S.). We can also compare degree of liking across experimental conditions, eliminating those subjects who were not upset by a negative evaluation. The difference between the Negative-Positive and Positive-Positive conditions is highly significant ($t = 4.57$, $p < .005$, two-tailed). When the "upset" subjects only are compared, the difference between the Negative-Negative and Positive-Negative conditions approaches significance ($t = 1.91$, $p < .08$, two-tailed).

These data are consistent with the affective assumption of the gain-loss notion inasmuch as they suggest that a feeling of upset is a necessary precondition for the great liking in the Negative-Positive condition and the great dislike in the Positive-Negative condition. However, since these data are based on an internal analysis, they are not unequivocal; those subjects who were upset (strictly speaking, those who admitted to being upset) by a negative evaluation may be different kinds of animals from those who did not admit to being upset. The differences in their liking for the stimulus person may be a reflection of some unknown individual differences rather than of the manipulated differences in the independent variable. For example, considering the explanations given by those subjects who were not upset, it is conceivable that these individuals may be extreme on "ego-defensiveness"; or, conversely, those subjects who *were* upset may be extremely "hypersensitive." From our data it is impossible to judge whether or not such individual differences could be correlated with the dependent variable. In sum, although the results from the internal analysis are suggestive, they are equivocal because they do not represent a systematic experimental manipulation.

A Neutral-Positive Condition

If, for the moment, one ignores the internal analysis, the possibility exists that *any* increase in the confederate's positive evaluation of the subject would have produced an increase in the subject's liking for the confederate, even if pain had not been involved. For example, suppose the confederate's initial evaluation of the subject had been neutral rather than negative, and then had become increasingly positive; would the subject like the confederate as much in this condition as in the Negative-Positive condition? If so, then, clearly, pain and suffering are not necessary factors. To test this possibility, 15 additional subjects were run in a Neutral-Positive condition.[4] This condition is identical to the Negative-Positive condition except that during the first three meetings, instead of expressing negative evaluations of the subject, the confederate was noncommital, saying such things as "She seems to be pretty intelligent, but perhaps just a little on the dull side. . . ." "I'm not sure; she kind of strikes me both ways. . . ." "I just can't make up my mind about her. My feelings are rather neutral." The subjects were randomly assigned to this condition, although assignment did not commence until after two or three subjects had been run in each of the other four conditions. In this condition the mean liking score was 6.66. This is almost identical with the mean in the Positive-Positive condition. The difference between the Neutral-Positive and Negative-Positive conditions approaches statistical significance ($t = 1.96$, $p < .07$, two-tailed).

These data, coupled with the data from the internal analysis, suggest that some upset on the subjects part increased her liking for the stimulus person. However, other factors may contribute to the effect. One such contributing

---

[4]We wish to thank Ellen Berscheid, who first suggested this condition.

factor has already been discussed as the cognitive assumption underlying the gain-loss notion. Specifically, when *O* changes his evaluation of *P*, it is indicative of the fact that he (*O*) has some discernment and that his evaluation is a considered judgment. Consequently, his evaluation of *P* should have greater impact on *P* than an invariably positive or invariably negative evaluation. This would lead to greater liking in the Negative-Positive condition and less liking in the Positive-Negative condition. We made no great attempt to investigate the validity of this assumption in the present experiment. We did ask the subjects to rate the degree of discernment of the stimulus person. Here, we found a faint glimmer of support. There was some tendency for the subjects in the Negative-Positive condition to rate the stimulus person higher (M = 6.75) than did the subjects in the Positive-Positive condition (M = 5.35), but this difference was not statistically significant ($t = 1.40$, $p < .15$). There was no difference in the ratings made by the subjects in the other two conditions.

Alternative Explanations

Flattery. Recent work by Jones (1964) on flattery and ingratiation suggests the possibility that a person who makes exclusively positive statements might be suspected of using flattery in order to manipulate the subject, and therefore might be liked less than someone whose evaluations include negative statements. However, this is not a compelling explanation of the results of the present experiment because the subject was led to believe that the confederate was unaware that she (the subject) was eavesdropping during the evaluation. One cannot easily attribute these ulterior motives to a person who says nice things about us in our absence.

Contrast. Another possible alternative explanation involves the phenomenon of contrast (Helson, 1964). After several negative and neutral statements, a positive evaluation may seem more positive than the same statement preceded by other positive statements. Similarly, a negative evaluation following several positive and neutral statements may appear to be more negative than one that formed part of a series of uniformly negative statements. Thus, a contrast effect, if operative, could have contributed to our results. At the same time, it should be noted that in the Neutral-Positive condition, where some degree of contrast should also occur, there is little evidence of the existence of this phenomenon. Specifically, the mean liking score in the Neutral-Positive condition was almost identical to that in the Positive-Positive condition and quite different from that in the Negative-Positive condition ($p < .07$). These data suggest that, although a contrast effect could conceivably have contributed to the results, it is doubtful that such an effect was strong enough, in this experimental situation, to have generated the results in and of itself.

Competence. In the Negative-Positive condition the subject has succeeded in showing the confederate that he (the subject) is not a dull clod but is, in fact, a bright and interesting person. This is no mean accomplishment and therefore might lead the subject to experience a feeling of competence or efficacy (White, 1959). Thus, in this condition, part of the reason for O's great attractiveness may be due to the fact that he has provided the subject with a success experience. Indeed, during the interview many subjects in this condition spontaneously mentioned that, after hearing O describe them as dull and stupid, they tried hard to make interesting and intelligent statements in subsequent encounters with O. It is reasonable to suspect that they were gratified to find that these efforts paid off by inducing a change in O's evaluations. This raises an interesting theoretical question; it may be that the feeling of competence is not only a contributing factor to the "gain" effect but may actually be a necessary condition. This possibility could be tested in future experimentation by manipulating the extent to which the subject feels that O's change in evaluation is contingent upon the subject's actual behavior.

Possible Implications

One of the implications of the gain-loss notion is that "you always hurt the one you love," i.e., once we have grown certain of the good will (rewarding behavior) of a person (e.g., a mother, a spouse, a close friend), that person may become less potent as a source of reward than a stranger. If we are correct in our assumption that a gain in esteem is a more potent reward than the absolute level of the esteem itself, then it follows that a close friend (by definition) is operating near ceiling level and therefore cannot provide us with a gain. To put it another way, since we have learned to expect love, favors, praise, etc. from a friend, such behavior cannot possibly represent a gain in his esteem for us. On the other hand, the constant friend and rewarder has great potential as a punisher. The closer the friend, the greater the past history of invariant esteem and reward, the more devastating is its withdrawal. Such withdrawal, by definition, constitutes a loss of esteem.

An example may help clarify this point. After ten years of marriage, if a doting husband compliments his wife on her appearance, it may mean very little to her. She already knows that her husband thinks she's attractive. A sincere compliment from a relative stranger may be much more effective, however, since it constitutes a gain in esteem. On the other hand, if the doting husband (who used to think that his wife was attractive) were to tell his wife that he had decided that she was actually quite ugly, this would cause a great deal of pain since it represents a distinct loss of esteem.

This reasoning is consistent with previous experimental findings. Harvey (1962) found a tendency for subjects to react more positively to a stranger than a friend when they were listed as sources of a relatively positive evaluation of the subject. Moreover, subjects tended to react more negatively to a friend than a stranger when they were listed as sources of negative evaluations of the subject. Similarly, experiments with children indicate that strangers are more effective as agents of social reinforcement than parents, and that strangers are also more effective than more familiar people (Shallenberger and Zigler, 1961; Stevenson and Knights, 1962; Stevenson, Keen, and Knights, 1963). It is reasonable to assume that children are accustomed to receiving approval from parents and familiar people. Therefore, additional approval from them does not represent much of a gain. However, approval from a stranger *is* a gain and, according to the gain-loss notion, should result in a greater improvement in performance. These latter results add credence to our speculations regarding one of the underlying causes of the gain-loss effect. Specifically, children probably experience greater social anxiety in the presence of a stranger than a familiar person. Therefore, social approval from a stranger may be reducing a greater drive than social approval from a friend. As previously noted, this reasoning is identical to that of Walters and his colleagues regarding the effect of prior anxiety on subsequent performance (Walters and Ray, 1960; Walters and Foote, 1962).

SUMMARY

In a laboratory experiment, coeds interacted in two-person groups over a series of brief meetings. After each meeting the subjects were allowed to eavesdrop on a conversation between the experimenter and her partner in which the latter (actually a confederate) evaluated the subject. There were four major experimental conditions: (1) the evaluations were all highly positive; (2) the evaluations were all quite negative; (3) the first few evaluations were negative but gradually became positive; (4) the first few evaluations were positive but gradually became negative.

The major results showed that the subjects liked the confederate best when her evaluations moved from positive to negative. The results were predicted and discussed in terms of a "gain-loss" notion of interpersonal attractiveness.

References

ARONSON, E., AND MILLS, J. The effect of severity of initiation on liking for a group. *J. abnorm. soc. Psychol.,* 1959, **59,** 177–181.

BYRNE, D. Interpersonal attraction and attitude similarity. *J. abnorm. soc. Psychol.,* 1961, **62,** 713–715.

BYRNE, D., AND WONG, T. J. Racial prejudice, interpersonal attraction, and assumed dissimilarity of attitudes. *J. abnorm. soc. Psychol.,* 1962, **65,** 246–253.

GERARD, H. B., AND GREENBAUM, C. W. Attitudes toward an agent of uncertainty reduction. *J. Pers.,* 1962, **30,** 485–495.

GEWIRTZ, J. L., AND BAER, D. M. The effect of brief social deprivation on behaviors for a social reinforcer. *J. abnorm. soc. Psychol.,* 1958, **56,** 49–56.

HARVEY, O. J. Personality factors in resolution of conceptual incongruities. *Sociometry,* 1962, **25,** 336–352.

HELSON, H. Current trends and issues in adaptation-level theory. *Amer. Psychologist,* 1964, **19,** 26–38.

HOMANS, G. *Social behavior: Its elementary forms.* New York: Harcourt, Brace, and World, 1961.

JONES, E. E. *Ingratiation: A social psychological analysis.* New York: Appleton, Century, Crofts, 1964.

NEWCOMB, T. M. *The acquaintance process.* New York: Holt, Rinehart, and Winston, 1961.

NEWCOMB, T. M. The prediction of interpersonal attraction. *Amer. Psychologist,* 1956, **11,** 575–586.

SHALLENBERGER, PATRICIA, AND ZIGLER, E. Rigidity, negative reaction tendencies and cosatiation effects in normal and feebleminded children. *J. abnorm. soc. Psychol.,* 1961, **63,** 20–26.

SPINOZA, B. *The ethics.* New York: Dover Press, 1955. Prop. 44, p. 159.

STEVENSON, H. W., KEEN, RACHEL, AND KNIGHTS, R. M. Parents and strangers as reinforcing agents for children's performance. *J. abnorm. soc. Psychol.,* 1963, **67,** 183–185.

STEVENSON, H. W., AND KNIGHTS, R. M. Social reinforcement with normal and retarded children as a function of pretraining, sex of E, and sex of S. *Amer. J. ment. Defic.,* 1962, **66,** 866–871.

THIBAUT, J., AND KELLEY, H. H. *The social psychology of groups.* New York: Wiley, 1959.

WALTERS, R. H., AND FOOTE, ANN. A study of reinforcer effectiveness with children. *Merrill-Palmer quart. Behav. Develpm.,* 1962, **8,** 149–157.

WALTERS, R. H., AND RAY, E. Anxiety, social isolation, and reinforcer effectiveness. *J. Pers.,* 1960, **28,** 258–267.

WHITE, R. W. Motivation reconsidered: the concept of competence. *Psychol. Rev.,* 1959, **66,** 297–334.

28

The Effect of Self-Esteem
on Romantic Liking

Elaine Walster

Does a person's momentary self-esteem affect his receptivity to the love
and affection proffered by another? Does a person like an affectionate other
more when his own self-esteem is high or when it is low?

The author hypothesized that when a person's self-esteem was *low* he
would be more receptive to (better like) a person offering affection than
when his self-esteem was high. The rationale for this prediction was two-
fold.

First, a person with high self-esteem (who feels he has much to offer
another) is likely to feel that he, in turn, deserves a more attractive, more
personable friend than does a person with low self-regard. [Goffman (1952)
makes a proposal consistent with this notion: "A proposal of marriage in our
society tends to be a way in which a man sums up his social attributes and
suggests to a woman that hers are not so much better as to preclude a merger

---

Reprinted with permission from the author and *The Journal of Experimental Social Psychology,* Vol. 1, 1965. Copyright 1965 by Academic Press, Inc.

This study was conducted at Stanford University, under a Ford Foundation grant. The help
and support of Dr. Leon Festinger, administrator of this grant, is very greatly appreciated.

or partnership in these matters."] In other words, the more highly a man evaluates himself and his own social attributes, the more perfection he'll feel a woman must possess before she is acceptable as his friend or lover. If the above propositions are true, a given woman should appear more "acceptable" and desirable, and should be better liked by a man, when his self-esteem (and requirements) are *low* that when his self-esteem (and requirements) are high.

Second, a lowering of one's self-regard probably produces an increased *need* for the affection and regard of others. Thus, any affection offered by another person, and thus this person himself, should be more attractive to an individual when his self-esteem is low than when it is high. (A similar proposal made by Dittes (1959) will be discussed in detail later.)

Can we find any support for the above notions in the research literature? Information providing unequivocal support or rejection is not available.

Nearly all the literature treats self-esteem as an invariant. Authors speak of high self-esteem and low self-esteem *people*. The fact that self-esteem can fluctuate, and the effect of these fluctuations, are discussed only by Reik (1944).

In order to find any relevant data, we must temporarily make the assumption that when a person's self-esteem is lowered (or raised) he behaves like the person whose self-esteem is habitually low (or high). Even then, we find that the theoretical literature offers conflicting suggestions as to the nature of the relationship between self-esteem and liking.

1. A very small portion of the literature suggests that people low in self-esteem are in special need of affection, and thus are especially receptive to, and especially prone to, like others. Reik (1944) says that it is when our feelings of self-dislike increase that we are especially susceptible to falling in love; Reik indicates that people are much more likely to fall in love after a rejection.

2. A far greater number of articles suggest that it is the *high* self-esteem person who will be most receptive to another's love.

For example, Rogers (1951) says that the person who accepts himself will have better interpersonal relations with others. Adler (1926) adds that those who themselves feel inferior depreciate others. Horney (1936) views love as a capacity. She sees love of self and love of others as positively related. Fromm (1939) too, agrees with this notion.

Studies supporting a positive relationship between self-esteem and liking or acceptance for others are reported in Berger (1952), Maslow (1942), Omwake (1954), and Stock (1949).

These studies demonstrate a relationship between self-esteem and liking opposite to the one we predicted. Do these data disconfirm our hypothesis, or are there reasons why, in these studies, the relationship existing between self-esteem and liking should be quite different from the one we expect? The situation with which these authors deal is dissimilar to the one we specified in three ways:

First, in these studies, a subject's "liking" or "acceptance" or "sexual love" is assessed by summing his responses to a number of questions. Sometimes these questions do seem to be measuring "liking," but often they seem to be measuring something quite different (e.g., general permissiveness). Since it is the total index that is correlated with self-esteem, it is always difficult to decide if the index is "mostly" measuring liking or not.

Second, all of these studies are correlational. Commonly the subject's self-rating on a test is correlated with his rating of others on either the same or a similar test. Both measures were made in the same place, at the same time. It is not possible to tell how much of the correlated variance is due to the "positive" effect of self-esteem on liking (or acceptance for others) and how much of the correlation is an artifact of the fact that the same situational and personal "sets" partially determined responses to both sets of questions.

Finally, the kind of person the subjects had in mind when rating the "other" was never assessed. (The authors' interests were naturally enough different from ours.) It seems plausible to argue that the low self-esteem people might well be socially inept individuals, not usually offered love and affection by others. Thus, when asked to rate "others" they might very well be visualizing fairly unresponsive individuals. At the same time, the more socially skilled high self-esteem people might envision quite a different collection of individuals (warm, friendly, and responsive) when asked to evaluate "others."

Since we are interested in (a) the *effect* of a momentarily high or low self-esteem on liking for another (b) when that other is *proffering affection*, it is clear that the correlational studies differ from the situation we are considering in crucial ways.

3. The best support for our hypothesis comes from the group cohesiveness literature. Dittes (1959) suggests that self-esteem is sometimes positively and sometimes negatively correlated with amount of liking and attraction felt toward others (a group). Whether a positive or a negative correlation exists between self-esteem and liking for a group is said to depend on whether or not the group is perceived as accepting or rejecting. If the group is seen as accepting, the low self-esteem person is predicted to like the group better than a high self-esteem person would. If the group is seen as rejecting, the low self-esteem person is predicted to dislike the group more than a high self-esteem person would.

Although Dittes is, of course, referring to the effect of stable individual differences in self-esteem on liking, his rationale is similar to the one we proposed when discussing the effect of momentary gains or losses in self-esteem on liking. He says: "A person's attraction toward membership in a group . . . may be considered a function of two determinants: (a) the extent to which his needs are satisfied by the group, and (b) the strength of his needs."

Dittes assumes that the lower the level of one's own self-esteem, the greater one's *need* for *acceptance from others*. From this assumption, Dittes' predictions can be clearly derived: 1. When the other person is accepting, he satisfies a greater need in the low self-esteem person than in the high self-esteem person. Thus, the accepting person is better liked by the low self-esteem individual. 2. When the other person is rejecting, he frustrates a greater need in the low self-esteem person than in the high self-esteem person. Thus, the rejecting person is less well liked by the low self-esteem individual. An experimental study provides support for Dittes' proposals.

It is clear that the above literature does not provide a definitive answer to our specific question as to how a person's self-esteem at any time affects his receptivity to the affection offered by another. Therefore, an experimental design was set up in which we could test the following two relationships: I. The relationship between raised or lowered self-esteem and the liking for an affectionate other. (This was, of course, our main concern.) To assess this relationship, it was necessary to: (1) Introduce a female subject to a male confederate who would make clear his interest in and affection for the subject. (2) Experimentally raise the self-esteem of one half of the subjects by giving them authoritative positive information about themselves. (3) Ask subjects to rate the male confederate under conditions which would encourage them to give honest, frank replies. II. The relationship between *measured* ("stable") self-esteem and liking for various others. This was not our primary interest, but in order to get some information about this relationship, we needed to administer the California Personality Inventory to our subjects. This would allow us to correlate the subjects' esteem scores with their rating of the confederate and some less accepting others.

METHOD

Subjects were 20 women from Stanford University and 17 women from Foothill Junior College. Nearly all *S*s were 18 or 19 years old. All *S*s were paid for their participation, with the exception of 7 Stanford women, who participated in fulfillment of an Introductory Psychology course requirement.

A few weeks before the experimental session, *S*s were told that Stanford was conducting a research project on "personality and the therapy process."

As part of this imaginary project, Foothill *S*s were asked to complete the California Personality Inventory (CPI), and then to make a one and one-half hour appointment to permit further testing and interviewing. Since all Stanford students had taken the Minnesota Multiphasic Personality Inventory shortly before *E* contacted them, Stanford *S*s were not asked to complete the CPI before making an interview appointment. However, the CPI was administered to nearly all the Stanford subjects seven weeks after the experiment.[1]

Introducing Subject to the Confederate

Before *S*'s self-esteem was affected in any way, we wanted to introduce her to a man we hoped she would perceive as an accepting, affectionate male friend. This "introduction" was effected in the following way: When *S* arrived for her interview, *E* was not in the assigned room. A short time after *S*'s arrival, a male confederate (GD) arrived.[2] This confederate was slightly older than our *S*s and quite handsome. He claimed that he had been sent to the interview room by Miss Turner, who was "running another experiment," and had merely been told that Dr. Walster would explain what he was to do when she arrived. After speculating in a friendly way with *S* about what the interviews were like, and why *E* was late, GD began telling *S* a little about himself. (He claimed either to be a former Harvard student now spending a year at Stanford, or a former Foothill student now at Berkeley, as was appropriate.) For approximately 15 minutes, GD talked to *S* with the intention of (1) conveying to *S* that he was personally interested in her, and (2) asking *S* for a dinner and show date in San Francisco, the following week. If *S* was hesitant about accepting a date at any of the proposed times, GD stated that he would call *S* again at a later date.

Self-Esteem Manipulation[3]

Soon after GD and *S* made a date, *E* entered the experimental room, explaining to *S* and GD that she had been held up by the unexpected absence of her co-interviewer, and confusion as to where Miss Turner had sent GD.

Then *E* informed *S* that in addition to the MMPI or CPI test, which she had already taken, she would be given the Word Association and the Rorschach tests. Since "the project required that a different administrator give

---

[1]Patricia Hatfield Rich, Anthropology Department, University of California, Berkeley, administered the test to *S*s, ostensibly as part of an anthropology survey.

[2]The assistance of Gerald Davison, our confederate, and of Gerald Bracy, who worked as a confederate in pretesting, is appreciated.

[3]This esteem manipulation is adapted from material utilized by Dr. Dana Bramel (1962).

each test," *E* asked GD to take the place of her co-interviewer, and read the 15 words that comprised the Word Association test. Then *E* explained that this was the reason GD had been sent down to the experimental room. GD read the words and was then instructed to return to Miss Turner's experiment.

Then *S* was told that her test results would be filed anonymously, but that if she desired *she* could see her CPI results as soon as she finished taking the Rorschach test. Three Rorschach cards were given to *S* and *E* administered the test in the usual way. Once the Rorschach test was completed, *E* handed *S* either an extremely flattering or an extremely disparaging analysis of her personality.

(All *S*s were told that this analysis of their personality was made by a therapist in San Francisco.) Which prepared "analysis" *S* received was randomly determined.

For those *S*s assigned to the Low-esteem condition, the analysis stressed the *S*'s "immaturity" (e.g., "Although she has adopted certain superficial appearances of maturity to enable her to temporarily adjust to life situations, her basically immature drives remain."), her "weak personality, anti-social motives, lack of originality and flexibility, and lack of capacity for successful leadership."

In a sub-section of the report, dealing with conventionality and conformity, *S* was informed that she undoubtedly "lacked openness in her dealings with other people," that her feelings of inadequacy in the presence of others contributed to this lack of openness, that she undoubtedly felt it was necessary to cover her weak points in order to gain social acceptance, and that this led her to consistently over-estimate many of her own characteristics."

For those *S*s assigned to the High-esteem condition, the report stressed *S*'s great maturity and originality, her probable underestimation of her own attributes, and stated that *S* presented "one of the most favorable personality structures analyzed by the staff." The conventionality sub-section stressed *S*'s sensitivity to peers, personal integrity, and originality and freedom of outlook."

While *S* was reading the bogus MMPI report, *E* pretended to score her Rorschach profile. Then *E* explained to *S* how the Rorschach was scored, commenting that the test was a completely objective measure, with results unaffected by the tester's preconceptions.

Then *S* was handed a card which summarized the personality characteristics which the Rorschach indicated she possessed. Low-esteem condition *S*s were given an analysis saying their responses indicated a "constricted and unimaginative mind, and a non-creative approach to life problems." High-esteem condition *S*s received an analysis describing their capabilities for "breaking through the stereotypes and rigidities so common among her peers." Their cognitive freedom and the appropriateness of their responses was also stressed. After *S* had read these reports, *E* told her all testing was complete and her tests were filed away.

Assessing Subject's Emotional and Cognitive Attitudes

When they arrived for interviewing *S*s knew that they were to take some psychological tests *and* be interviewed in connection with a therapy project. Once *S*'s test results were filed away, *E* indicated that she would like to get a little help from *S* in setting up a forthcoming research project.

This project supposedly dealt with small changes that occur in people's attitudes as a result of thinking about things and people in new contexts and new ways. Some studies were cited in which large changes occurred in the attitudes of juvenile delinquents, as a result of "therapy sessions," in which no therapist was present, and in which the delinquents merely expressed their feelings into a tape recorder.

Then *E* explained that *S*'s part in the project was simply to indicate how she presently felt about four people *E* would name; *S* was told that after she completed these ratings, she would be asked to think about one of the four people privately, considering how that person would react in certain novel situations *E* would describe, and indicating whether or not she noticed any changes in her feelings as she thought about that person.

The post-rating portion of the project was described very quickly. Then *E* explained that she knew *S* was probably unclear about exactly what she was to do, but that things would become clear as she went along. (It is only the initial ratings by *S* in which we are interested: the post-ratings were never obtained. The therapy "project" was devised solely to disassociate the ratings from the previous testing and to provide a plausible context for securing honest rating from *S* concerning her feelings toward GD.)

A questionnaire was then handed *S*, who was shown how to indicate her feelings on the rating scales, and told *not* to sign her name or code number. It was very important, *E* explained, that *S*'s answers be anonymous, explaining: "Usually when you ask someone what they think about Joe Smith, and hand them a questionnaire so they can indicate their feelings, they think that they really should tell you how they *ought* to feel about Joe—how it is reasonable or fair to feel—or how they usually feel, even if they don't feel that way right now."

It was stressed by *E* that the project was *not* interested in such cognitive judgments, but in the same kind of honest, spontaneous emotions people express in therapy.

Then *S* was handed a large envelope, told to put the questionnaire in it when she was done, and mail it to the place indicated. *E* reiterated that she would never see it or be able to identify it as *S*'s.

As sort of an afterthought, *E* said "Oh, there's one change we have to make in your booklet. The first person the questionnaire asks about is the therapist who administered the Word Association test. Since he wasn't here tonight, you obviously can't rate him. Instead, rate the fellow from Miss Turner's experiment who administered the Word Association test to you."

Then *E* went to the other side of the room and sat with her back to *S*, so that *S* could answer the questionnaire privately but still ask any questions she might have. The questionnaire asked about *S*'s feelings concerning GD, the "person she was most attracted to at the present time," *E*, a specified teacher, and *S* herself.

Once *S* completed this questionnaire, the actual purpose of the experiment was explained to her. Debriefing was continued for approximately 45 minutes, or until *E* was sure *S* was happy about having participated, and in no way disturbed by the false personality report or the "broken" date.

RESULTS AND DISCUSSION

Effectiveness of the Experimental Induction

On the last page of the questionnaire, the *S* was asked to rate herself on 11 traits. A positive characteristic was indicated on one end of each trait-scale, and its polar opposite on the other end. Thus, a rating was secured of how original, attractive, perfect, optimistic, interesting, mature, independent, competent, cheerful and strong the *S* felt herself to be, and how much "self-esteem" she felt she possessed.

If the self-esteem manipulation was effective, *S*s in the low-esteem condition should see themselves as possessing less maturity and less originality (the traits disparaged in the false personality report) and lower self-esteem than do *S*s in the high esteem condition. This was in fact the case. High-esteem condition *S*s rate themselves significantly higher on a combined measure of these three trait-ratings than do *S*s in the low-esteem condition ($t = 2.98$ with 30 *df*, $p > .01$, 2-tailed). On *all* 11 traits, in fact, low-esteem *S*s place themselves closer to the negative end of the scale than do high-esteem *S*s.

We can now turn to the finding in which we are most interested. How *much* do women in the high-esteem and low-esteem conditions like GD?

As was predicted, women whose self-esteem has been temporarily lowered like GD significantly better than do women whose self-esteem has been temporarily raised. Low-esteem condition women rated GD at 14.8 (in between "I like him extremely much" and "I like him fairly much"). High-esteem condition women rated him at only 13.1 [in between "I like him fairly much" and "I like and dislike him equally"—but much closer to the

TABLE 28.1
Mean liking for GD by women in various self-esteem
conditions

Person rated	Low-esteem condition ($N = 16$)	High-esteem condition ($N = 16$)
Accepting, affectionate confederate (GD)	14.8[a]	13.1
Others		
Female E	15.3	15.8
Teacher	12.1	12.0
Person to whom attracted[b]	8.3	9.3

[a]The higher the number, the more the person indicated is liked by the subject.
[b]This rating scale was scaled differently than the ones on which GD, E, and a teacher were rated, to allow for the inclusion of a "love" designation.

former designation than to the latter (see Table 28.1. $t = 2.9$, 30 *df*, *p* > .01, 2-tailed)].

Initially, this study was run using only 20 Stanford women as *S*s. As in the total group, the Stanford women in the low-esteem condition rated GD significantly higher than did women in the high-esteem condition ($t = 2.5$, 18 *df*, *p* < .02, 2-tailed). Twelve[4] Foothill students were then added to the sample, in order to replicate the Stanford finding with another group of women, and to increase the number of *S*s. Though in both esteem conditions GD was liked slightly less by Foothill women than he had been by Stanford women, the difference between the average rating of GD in the low- and the high-esteem condition is of the same magnitude and in the same direction at both schools. With great consistency, we find greater liking for GD by students whose self-esteem has just been lowered.

Possible Alternative Explanations for the Data

It will be recalled that we hypothesized a negative relationship between self-esteem and liking for an affectionate other for two reasons: (a) A person

---

[4]Actually, 17 Foothill women were run as *S*s. During the first week of Foothill interviewing an attempt was made to follow *exactly* the procedure used with Stanford women—i.e., GD indicated he was from Stanford. To our surprise (since all SU women had accepted dates), 3 of our first 5 subjects refused a date, often questioning GD about *why* he wanted to take them out, and in one case stating to *E* that something must be wrong with GD because he wanted to take her out. For these reasons, the three initial *S*s were discarded, and GD began stating he was from Foothill, talking about his experiences there instead of at Stanford. This change apparently made the situation a more acceptable one for *S*s, since nearly all FC women then began accepting dates. After this procedural change, only two women rejected a date with GD—a high-esteem *S* who liked GD 11.8 and a low-esteem *S* who rated him 13.8. Though GD said he would call these *S*s, they were also excluded from our sample.

probably demands less perfection in an "acceptable" friend when he himself feels imperfect. (b) When a person's self-esteem is low he has an increased need for acceptance and affection. Thus the affectionate other will satisfy a greater need and will therefore be better liked when Ss self-esteem is low.

At this time we were interested only in finding out whether the relationship we hypothesized in fact existed; we did not attempt to secure the additional evidence as to precisely which of these factors produced the effect we hypothesized. However, there were still other possible explanations for our findings that we did want to rule out. Evidence relevant to these alternatives *is* available.

1. It could be argued that since the low-esteem S had failed on so many personality measures, she was probably simply trying to prove to herself, and to E (if the S somehow expected E to see the questionnaire) that at least she was a friendly person who likes others.

However, if this explanation were true, the increased liking that S displayed for GD would have been shown toward any person S was asked to rate.

It will be recalled that in addition to GD, S was asked how much she liked three other people: E, a teacher, and "the person to whom she was most attracted at the present time."[5] When we examine the ratings of these people (Table 28.1) it seems clear that the low self-esteem women are not simply indicating an increased liking for *everyone*. When the ratings of any persons besides GD are considered, the liking indicated by low self-esteem condition women does not differ significantly from that indicated by high self-esteem condition women.

In addition, even when we test the difference between differences (by an analysis of covariance) we find that the between condition difference in liking for GD is significantly greater than the between condition difference in liking for E, the teacher, or the "person to whom most attracted." (For example, the difference between liking for GD in the low-esteem and high-esteem condition controlled for liking for the *teacher* is significant $F = 8.19$, $1/29$ *df, p < .01*.)

2. It could also be argued that the increased liking low-esteem subjects express for GD is a result of dissonance-reduction processes. The dissonance argument goes like this: Subjects come to the experiment with normally high self-esteem. In the low-esteem condition, they succeed with GD,

---

[5] When asked in debriefing about the identity of the person to whom they were most attracted, a very few Ss indicated they had rated cultural heros (e.g., Albert Schweitzer); several indicated they had rated attractive men they had observed in class or at school or athletic events, but had not met; and many indicated they were rating a person they had dated.

but fail on the personality tests. One way of reducing the dissonance arising from this unexpected failure is to convince themselves that the area of their failure (maturity and originality) really isn't very important . . . that the most important skills for a woman are the social ones. Thus, the argument continues, low-esteem condition women exaggerate their abilities as exciting, attractive date-getters, increase the importance of dating, and consequently increase their liking for GD, who is living evidence of their success with men.

If such a hypothesis is correct and is producing our experimental results, we would expect low-esteem women to in fact see themselves as much more interesting, and attractive, or more successful with men (especially GD) than do the high-esteem women.

The data suggest that distortions of this type do *not* take place. On the self-ratings, low-esteem women rate themselves as less "interesting" ($p < .10$) and *less* "attractive" (though not significantly so) than do high-esteem women.

In addition, the questionnaire given to Foothill women contained two questions directly relevant to this alternative explanation: (1) "How much do you think (GD) liked you?" and (2) "How attractive are you to the men that you're interested in?" The six Foothill women in the low self-esteem condition rated themselves as slightly *less* attractive in answer to both questions than did the six high-esteem women (though these differences are not significant).

It is clear then that this dissonance-reduction explantation is not supported by our data. The tendency is for women in the low-esteem condition to see themselves as less personally desirable than they normally would, rather than to exaggerate their attractiveness.

Additional Comments on the Correlation Between "Stable" Self-Esteem and Liking for Others

When working with fairly global personality variables such as self-esteem, one usually has to choose between two unacceptable alternatives: one can try to measure the variable as it exists in the world, accepting the fact that the crucial variable will be confounded with several others; *or* one can try to manipulate the variable in the laboratory, making the somewhat peculiar assumption than the state produced in one hour in the laboratory is isomorphic with its more slowly developing counterpart.

For our experiment, which examined only the effect of *temporary* self-esteem on liking for others, it was unnecessary for us to make the second assumption (that manipulated self-esteem is essentially identical to more slowly developing self-esteem). But it could be argued that we might well have made that assumption; that our experiment could well be considered as an experimental replication and extension of the Dittes proposals. Our data do, in every way, fit neatly into the Dittes framework.

But there are other data and another formulation (Berger, 1952, and others) indicating that self-esteem is positively related to liking for others. Is the situation totally chaotic? If our results had come out in the opposite direction, could it have as easily been said that the results fit "neatly" into the Berger et al. framework? If there is not predictive chaos, how do we decide when the Dittes predictions are to be applied, and when the predictions of Berger et al. should be applied? The crucial variable in deciding which formulation should be applied in a give situation seems to be whether or not the subject knows how the other he is rating feels about *him*.

The Dittes formulation would lead us to expect a negative relationship between a person's self-esteem and his liking for anyone who clearly accepts him. When the other is seen as rejecting, a positive relationship between self-esteem and liking is expected. Naturally, if the other was seen as midway between acceptance and rejection, call such a state "neutrality" or what you will, a zero correlation between self-esteem and liking would be expected by Dittes.

But what about when one does not know whether or not the other accepts or rejects him? It is just such situations with which Berger et al. inevitably deal, and it is just this situation that Dittes does not discuss. (It is very unlikely that Dittes would want to say that when people are unaware of how others feel toward them, that they assume that the other person is neutral.)

We suggested earlier that the most reasonable guess would seem to be that under ambiguous conditions, the high self-esteem person would expect more acceptance and less rejection than would the low self-esteem person. And the more one expects another to like and accept him, the more one would be expected to "reciprocate" liking for that other. Thus, under conditions when S has no information as to whether or not the other accepts him, and must guess, the Dittes formulation is inapplicable, and the Berger et al. formulation that there is a positive relationship between self-esteem and liking seems most reasonable.

A possible reconciling proposal, then, would be when the other's acceptance or rejection is *unspecified,* or when the other rejects S, self-esteem will be positively correlated with liking. When the other makes clear his acceptance of S, self-esteem will be negatively related to liking.

We have no data with which to definitively test the above proposal. We do have some data, however, which might give us some very weak evidence as to whether or not the above proposal seems to be reasonable.

We can compute a measure of "stable" self-esteem for all our subjects. And, we do have ratings by S of several people whose acceptance of S is either clearly known, or unknown to S. GD, for example, was clearly accepting of *S*. According to the above proposal we should expect a *negative* relationship between stable self-esteem and liking for him.

The degree to which the *E* and a *specified teacher* accept *S* should be quite ambiguous. We know *E* made no statements to *S* of her personal feelings toward her; it is also unlikely that the teacher did so. Thus, according to the above proposal, we should expect a *positive* relationship between *S*'s self-esteem and liking for *E* and the teacher.[6]

Computing Stable Self-Esteem

All our *S*s had taken the CPI either some weeks before, or some weeks after, their participation in our experimental situation. From the CPI responses, a measure of stable self-esteem was computed in the following way.

First the girls' CPIs were scored by Jerold Jecker, a student, who was not informed of our research interests.

Then, the *S*'s raw scores on the six CPI measures of Poise, Ascendency, and Self-Assurance (1. Dominance, 2. Capacity for Status, 3. Sociability, 4. Social presence, 5. Self-Acceptance, 6. Sense of Well-Being) were standardized and averaged together. The higher this average, the higher the *S*s stable self-esteem was said to be.

RESULTS

From Table 28.2 we can see that there is some support, though certainly very weak support, for our reconciling proposal. The correlation between stable self-esteem and liking for GD *is* negative, as predicted, but it is not significant. The relationship between stable self-esteem and liking for the *E* and the teacher, as predicted, is positive and significant ($p < .02$, 2-tailed). The correlations between *S*'s self-esteem and liking for GD ($-.17$) is different from the correlation between self-esteem and liking for the teacher ($+.30$), $p < .07$ level, 2-tailed, and is significantly different from the correlation between *S*'s self-esteem and liking for the *E* [($+.49$), $p < .002$ level, 2-tailed].

---

[6]We have no information as to whether the person to whom the *S* was "most attracted" was accepting, rejecting, or neutral in his behavior toward the *S*. We can probably assume that those choosing a former date as the person to whom they are most attracted perceive themselves as being accepted by this person. However, those who choose a cultural hero or a school hero they had not met, might expect either neutrality or rejection from these attractive persons. For this reason, no prediction could be made as to how the *S*'s liking for the person to whom she was most attracted would correlate with the *S*'s self-esteem. For the reader's interest, the correlation between the *S*'s self-esteem and liking for the "attracted to" person is .08.

TABLE 28.2
Correlations between stable self-esteem and liking for others

Person rated	Average correlation[a] between self-esteem and liking	p level[b]
Accepting confederate ($N = 29$)	−.17	$p < .38$
Teacher	.30	$p < .11$
E	.49	$p < .01$

[a]Product moment correlations between self-esteem and liking for others were computed separately for each experimental condition, and the two resulting correlations averaged together. This technique was used to prevent between-condition (or experimentally caused) differences in the ratings from influencing the correlation.
[b]All p levels are 2-tailed.

It should be reiterated that these results are only suggestive. We do not know for sure that students at various esteem levels did not receive information from their teacher as to how much he accepted them. We have no measure to demonstrate that all Ss saw GD as accepting, and that the E and the teacher were perceived as less accepting by low self-esteem students than by high self-esteem students, as we have suggested they would be. Furthermore, it is obvious that E, GD, and the teacher differ in many ways other than on amount of "acceptingness"—E, for example, is a woman. To make any reasonable test of the reconciling proposition, obviously a second experiment would have to be conducted.

SUMMARY

It was proposed that a person's momentary self-esteem affects his receptivity to the affection offered by another. People whose self-esteem was temporarily *low* were expected to like an affectionate, accepting other more than those whose self-esteem was momentarily high.

An experimental study was conducted to test this proposal. The self-esteem of one half of the Ss was raised by giving them false personality information; the self-esteem of the other half of the Ss was lowered by the same technique. Women then rated a male confederate, who had earlier asked them for a date. The Ss in the low self-esteem condition expressed significantly more liking for the confederate than did Ss in the high self-esteem condition.

The relationship between "stable" (or measured) self-esteem and liking for others was also discussed.

References

ADLER, A. *The neurotic constitution.* New York: Dodd, Mead, 1926.

BERGER, E. M. The relation between expressed acceptance of self and expressed acceptance of others. *J. abnorm. soc. Psychol.,* 1952, **47,** 778–782.

BRAMEL, D. A dissonance theory approach to defensive projection. *J. abnorm. soc. Psychol.,* 1962, **64,** 121–129.

DITTES, J. E. Attractiveness of group as function of self-esteem and acceptance by group. *J. abnorm. soc. Psychol.,* 1959, **59,** 77–82.

FROMM, E. Selfishness and self-love. *Psychiatry,* 1939, **2,** 507–523.

GOFFMAN, E. On cooling the mark out: Some aspects of adaptation to failure. *Psychiatry,* 1952, **15,** 451–463.

HORNEY, KAREN. *New ways in psychoanalysis.* New York: Norton, 1939.

MASLOW, A. H. Self-esteem (dominance feeling) and sexuality in women. *J. soc. Psychol.,* 1942, **16,** 259–294.

OMWAKE, KATHERINE. The relationship between acceptance of self and acceptance of others shown by three personality inventories. *J. consult. Psychol.,* 1954, **18,** 443–446.

REIK, F. *A psychologist looks at love.* New York: Rinehart, 1944.

ROGERS, C. R. *Client-centered therapy.* Boston: Houghton Mifflin, 1951.

STOCK, DOROTHY. An investigation into the intercorrelations between the self-concept and feelings directed toward other persons and groups. *J. consult. Psychol.,* 1949, **13,** 176–180.

29

Physical Attractiveness and Evaluation of Children's Transgressions

Karen K. Dion

Preliminary evidence indicates that effects of a physical attractiveness stereotype may be present at an early childhood developmental level. Several of the mediating processes that may be hypothesized to be responsible for these effects presuppose that adults display differential treatment toward attractive and unattractive children in circumstances in which their behavior is identical. The present study is addressed to the tenability of this assumption in a situation integral to the socialization process, that in which the child has committed a transgression and the socializing adult must evaluate the child's behavior. Within a $2 \times 2 \times 2 \times 2$ design (Attractiveness of Child $\times$ Severity of Transgression $\times$ Sex of Child $\times$ Type of Transgression), support was found for the hypothesis that the severe transgression of an attractive child is less likely to be seen as reflecting an enduring disposition toward antisocial behavior than that of an unattractive child. In addition, the transgression itself tends to be evaluated less negatively when committed by an attractive child. No differences in intensity of advocated punishment were found. These and additional findings are discussed.

Accumulating research indicates that an individual's physical attractiveness is an important social cue used by others as a basis for social evaluation. It has been demonstrated, for example, that physically attractive young adults, both male and female, are assumed to possess more socially desirable personalities and to lead more successful and fulfilling lives than are those of

Reprinted with permission from *Journal of Personality and Social Psychology,* Vol. 24, No. 2, 1973. Copyright 1972 by the American Psychological Association.

This study was completed in partial fulfillment of the requirements of the PhD degree in psychology at the University of Minnesota. The research was facilitated by National Institute of Mental Health Grant 16729 to Ellen Berscheid. The author wishes to express special thanks to her dissertation advisor Ellen Berscheid, and to committee members Karl Weick, Paul Rosenblatt, John Masters, and Raymond Collier for their helpful advice and suggestions. The author also wishes to thank Kenneth Dion for his useful comments and criticisms.

lesser attractiveness (Dion, Berscheid, and Walster, 1972). There is also some suggestion that the effects of a physical attractiveness stereotype may be present at an early developmental level. Examination of sociometric choice behavior in a group of nursery school children revealed that a preschooler's level of physical attractiveness, as judged by adults, bears relationship to the extent to which he is popular with his peers and to the extent to which he is perceived to exhibit certain types of behaviors in interaction with them (Dion and Berscheid, 1971).

Although this preliminary evidence indicates that manifestations of the stereotype may be present at an early age, it is not clear what factors mediate the observed relationships. Among the variety of intervening processes that present themselves for consideration is the possibility that preschoolers have already absorbed the adult cultural stereotype and distort their perception of their peers to fit the stereotype. Another alternative is that affect toward attractive and unattractive peers is generated directly from differential behaviors displayed by these peers in interaction. Each of these possible mediating factors presupposes that adults display differential treatment toward attractive and unattractive children, even under circumstances in which their behavior is identical. The present study investigates the tenability of this assumption in a situation integral to the socialization process, namely, one in which a child has committed a transgression and the socializing adult evaluates the child. One might well expect that certain aspects of the transgression itself, such as its seriousness or severity, would influence an adult's reactions to the child. Indeed there is some evidence that adults assign greater responsibility for an action to a child if the outcomes of his behavior are negative (cf. Shaw and Sulzer, 1964).

It seems plausible, however, that a child's personal characteristics may also influence an adult's evaluations of his behavior. Some derivations from the principle of cognitive consistency suggest that individuals strive for internally consistent impressions of others. Heider (1958), for example, speculated that knowledge of a person's general character may influence how others interpret his behavior. People may interpret an individual's actions in a manner consistent with their knowledge or expectations about his personal dispositions. Thus, if adults believe that children differing in attractiveness typically display different personal characteristics, these expectations may affect their evaluation of an attractive versus an unattractive child's behavior.

In the present study, it was assumed that adults hold a physical attractiveness stereotype of children similar to that held for other adults. If so, adults should expect that physically attractive children typically engage in more socially desirable behavior than do unattractive children. The knowledge that an attractive child has committed a harmful act is obviously inconsistent with these expectations. Reasoning from a general consistency principle, therefore, adults should attempt to resolve the discrepancy between their expectations and the child's behavior.

Various modes of resolution might conceivably be used to reduce the inconsistency, depending on the severity of the transgression. If the offense is relatively mild, judgmental dimensions, such as evaluations of the transgression's undesirability, may be primarily affected. A minor transgression committed by an attractive child may be assimilated into the generally positive stereotype for physically attractive children, and thus be regarded as less serious or less undesirable than the same offense committed by an unattractive child.

It might, however, be more difficult to interpret an action that has serious consequences so that it can be assimilated without difficulty into the prevailing stereotype of attractive children. Presumably a severely harmful act evokes stronger negative reactions than a mild offense; there should be less ambiguity about its undesirability. Consequently, when harm-doing is severe, attributional inferences (cf. Heider, 1958; Jones and Davis, 1965)[1] may be primarily influenced by the child's attractiveness. In the present study, attributional inferences refer to the subjects' expectations concerning the child's character, that is, whether his harmful act is interpreted as reflecting a chronically antisocial disposition or, on the other hand, merely a temporary bad mood. When a serious harmful act occurs, adults may interpret this act as less characteristic of attractive than unattractive children. In such a way, even though the transgression is serious, the positive stereotype of physically attractive children may be retained since the behavior is interpreted as more atypical of the attractive child and less likely to reoccur than when the child is unattractive.

Regardless of the severity of the transgression, less punishment should be advocated for attractive than for unattractive children. If the offense is relatively minor, it should be perceived as less undesirable when the child is attractive than when he is unattractive. When the transgression is severe, attractive children should be viewed as less chronically antisocial than unattractive children. Both of these tendencies should result in adults advocating less punishment for attractive children.

On the basis of these rationales, the following hypotheses were formulated:

1. An attractive child who commits a harmful act will be perceived as less likely to exhibit chronically antisocial behavior than an unattractive child, primarily when the offense is severe. Thus, adults evaluating an attractive child should perceive him as less likely to have committed a similar transgression in the past and less likely to commit one in the future than an unattractive child.

---

[1]This discussion should not be taken as implying that the present study tests Jones and Davis' (1965) theory of attribution.

2. A transgression committed by an attractive child will be evaluated as less socially undesirable than the same act committed by an
unattractive child, particularly for mild offenses. In addition, adults
should advocate less punishment for an attractive child's offense,
regardless of the severity, than they do for an unattractive child committing the same transgression.

To test these hypotheses, undergraduate females received written information describing either a mild or a severe transgression reputedly committed
by a 7-year-old child. This sample was thought to be particularly appropriate, since women of approximately this age group generally constitute
the primary socializing influence in the home and in the elementary school.
Pictures of both male and female children were used to assess the generality of effects across sex of children. In addition, impersonal and interpersonal aggression were both represented to assess the generality of effects
across more than one type of transgression. No predictions were made for
type of transgression, and no differences were expected.

The aforementioned hypotheses were tested within a $2 \times 2 \times 2 \times 2$ factorial design in which the independent variables were (*a*) physical attractiveness of the child (attractive versus unattractive); (*b*) severity of the offense
(mild versus severe); (*c*) sex of the child (male versus female); and (*d*) type
of offense (impersonal versus interpersonal).

METHOD

Subjects

Two hundred and forty-three undergraduate females at the University
of Minnesota participated in this study. One hundred and eighty-three subjects were recruited from the subject pool of the psychology department and
received experimental points in return for participation. Sixty subjects were
obtained from introductory sociology classes and were paid $1.50 for par-
ticipation.

Procedure

After greeting each subject and seating her in an individual, partitioned
cubicle, the experimenter gave her a large envelope containing stimulus
materials appropriate to 1 of the 16 cells of the design. The subjects were
randomly assigned to conditions.

The first material presented to all of the subjects was an introduction to
the study, which was described as one concerning person perception. The

subjects were told that the present investigation focused on "adults' evaluations of children's behavior, specifically the behavior of 7-year-old children." The behavioral descriptions that were to be provided for their evaluation were alleged to have been randomly selected from teachers' daily journal reports in which various types of classroom and playground disturbances were routinely described. Thus, these descriptions were said to have been formulated by those who were present when the behavior actually occurred.

As a rationale for the evaluation procedure, the subjects were further told that some theorists hypothesized that observers who are actually immersed in real-life situations tend to give "richer judgments of the behavior segments observed." On the other hand, other theorists had hypothesized that those not present when the behavior segment actually took place "tend to gain a perspective that adds an extra dimension to their judgments." Accordingly, the subjects were informed that the purpose of the present study was to "determine the dimensions along which judgments in these two situations (i.e., direct observation of a behavior segment versus written information about a behavior segment) are likely to differ." All subjects were to take part, of course, in the "written information" condition.

Following this introduction, the subjects were instructed to remove the behavioral description page from the envelope, to read it carefully once, and to then place it back in the envelope. They were told that this procedure simulated real-life observation of events, where the "instant replay" of behavior segments afforded by television is not possible. The behavioral description page included, in addition to the written description of the child's behavior, his name, age, and a small photo glued to one corner. It thus presumably included all of "the information the subject would have had had she been actually present when the act occurred."

The black and white photographs of second-grade boys and girls which accompanied the behavioral descriptions were selected from a larger group on the basis of judges' ratings of their physical attractiveness.[2] On the basis of these ratings, each photo was categorized as depicting a child of either high or low physical attractiveness. Four photographs of each sex at each attractiveness level were used in an attempt to ensure that any effects obtained for the attractiveness variable would not be attributable to isolated stimulus characteristics (e.g., light hair, dark eyes, etc.). All of the photographs depicted children of "normal" appearance (i.e., the unattractive category did not include any with physical defects or deformities). No child in any photo wore glasses.

---

[2]The photos were rated on a 5-point scale by nine graduate student judges (five females and four males). The scores ranged from 1 (very unattractive) to 5 (very attractive).

The behavioral description consisted of a very brief written account of a child's transgression. After pretesting with 90 undergraduate females, two types of behavior—interpersonal physical aggression (toward another child) and impersonal physical aggression (toward an animal)—were chosen from a larger group of behaviors.[3] Both a mild and a severe version of each behavior were used. For example, in the severe-impersonal condition, the subjects were told:

> At one corner of the playground a dog was sleeping. Peter stood a short distance from the dog, picked up some sharp stones from the ground, and threw them at the animal. Two of the stones struck the dog and cut its leg. The animal jumped up yelping and limped away. Peter continued to throw rocks at it as it tried to move away from him.

In the mild-impersonal condition, the child was said to have walked up quietly behind a sleeping dog and stepped on its tail causing it to yelp. In the severe-interpersonal condition, the child was said to have packed a sharp piece of ice into a snowball and have aimed it at another child's head resulting in a deep and bleeding cut, while in the mild-interpersonal condition, the child was said to have thrown an ordinary snowball which resulted in a sting to another child's leg.

After returning the stimulus materials to the envelope, the subjects completed the response questionnaire which contained a series of ungraded, 17-centimeter scales with anchor words at each end. Two of these scales assessed the following attributional inferences: (*a*) the likelihood that the child had committed a similar harmful act in the past (ranging from "very unlikely" to "very likely") and (*b*) the probability that he would commit a similar act in the future (ranging from "very improbable" to "very probable"). Two scales assessed the judgment of the child's offense: (*a*) the undesirability of the act itself (ranging from "not undesirable at all" to "extremely undesirable"), and (*b*) the intensity of punishment advocated for the child (ranging from "very mild" to "very strong"). In addition, the subjects were also asked to rate the child on 16 personality trait dimensions. Six of these dimensions were chosen a priori for subsequent analysis: good-bad, aggressive-unaggressive, pleasant-unpleasant, kind-cruel, honest-dishonest, and nice-awful. A seventh dimension, physically attractive-physically unattractive, was included as a manipulation check. The others served as filler items. Finally, on open-ended questions, the subjects were asked to estimate in their own words (*a*) why the child had committed the harmful act and (*b*) how the child usually behaved on a typical day.

---

[3]The original group of behaviors pretested included impersonal physical aggression, interpersonal physical aggression, verbal aggression, personal damage (to another child's property), stealing, and ridicule. To be selected for inclusion in this study, the behavior had to be perceived as intentional and unjustified (i.e., not immediately the result of another's behavior toward the child).

After completing this questionnaire, the experimenter asked all of the subjects to respond to a separate questionnaire which contained several items designed to identify those who misunderstood the instructions or who were suspicious about the true purpose of the study. Three subjects were discarded for failing to follow the experimental instructions, leaving an N of 240.

RESULTS AND DISCUSSION

Manipulation Checks

As mentioned earlier, one item on the response questionnaire asked the subjects to rate the stimulus child's physical attractiveness. Analysis of variance and simple effects analyses (cf. Winer, 1962) performed on these data indicated that the manipulation of physical attractiveness was successful. Children in the attractive conditions were rated as more attractive than children in the unattractive conditions ($F = 93.45$, $df = 1/224$, $p < .001$ for females; $F = 45.31$, $df = 1/224$, $p < .001$ for males).[4] Analyses also indicated a Sex × Attractiveness interaction ($F = 4.29$, $df = 1/224$, $p < .05$) in which unattractive females were rated as more unattractive than unattractive males ($F = 19.38$, $df = 1/224$, $p < .01$),[5] while no difference in perceived attractiveness was found between attractive males and females. Since no predictions were made within unattractive conditions, this finding did not affect test of the major hypotheses.

Because severity of transgression was manipulated across two types of offense, it was important that the subjects perceived the severe form of both types to be more undesirable than the mild form. Analyses of responses to an item assessing the perceived undesirability of the transgression revealed that, as expected, the severe form of both types of offense was perceived as more undesirable than the mild form ($F = 20.74$, $p < .001$ for impersonal aggression; and $F = 62.82$, $p < .001$ for interpersonal aggression). However, analyses also revealed a Severity × Type of Offense interaction ($F = 5.62$, $p < .05$). Mild impersonal aggression was rated more negatively than mild interpersonal aggression ($F = 14.37$, $p < .001$). Since no predictions were made within the mild condition, this signficant contrast did not affect interpretation of the results.

---

[4]These F values refer to the simple effects analyses of the Attractiveness × Sex interaction.
[5]Unless otherwise noted, $df = 1/224$ on all subsequent results.

Tests of Hypotheses

Attributional inferences. It was hypothesized that an attractive child who committed a transgression would be less likely to be perceived as chronically antisocial than an unattractive child who committed the same act, particularly when the offense was severe. Several response measures were relevant to this differential attribution hypothesis.

First, it will be recalled that subjects gave their personal estimates of how the child usually behaved on a typical day on an open-ended questionnaire item. These descriptions were categorized by four naive judges as being predominantly "prosocial," "mixed prosocial and antisocial," or "predominantly antisocial."[6] Two chi-square analyses of the resultant data, one within each level of harm, were performed.[7] No differences were observed in attributional inferences between attractive and unattractive children within the mild harm-doing condition ($\chi^2 = 3.30$, $df = 2$, *ns*). Within the severe transgression condition, however, a significant difference in the predicted direction did emerge as a function of the physical attractiveness of the child. Specifically, more antisocial inferences implying a chronic behavioral disposition were attributed to unattractive than to attractive children ($\chi^2 = 6.26$, $df = 2$, $p < .05$).

In addition, the subjects also estimated the likelihood that the child would transgress in the future as well as the likelihood that he had done so in the past. Analysis of variance conducted on estimates of the probability of future offenses revealed the predicted interaction between attractiveness and severity of offense ($F = 4.33$, $p < .05$). Table 29.1 presents the means relevant to this interaction. An analysis of the simple effects revealed only one significant comparison. As predicted, within the severe condition, attractive children were seen as less likely than unattractive children to commit a similar transgression in the future ($F = 13.78$, $p < .001$). An analysis of variance on estimates of the child's past offenses revealed a slight and nonsignificant main effect trend for attractiveness. Subjects tended to see attractive children as less likely to have similarly transgressed in the past whether the offense was mild or severe ($F = 2.01$, $p = .15$).

---

[6]Prosocial behavior was defined as exhibiting cooperative and positive relations with others (i.e., the child was seen as usually cheerful, friendly, helpful, pleasant, well-adjusted, etc.). In contrast, antisocial behavior was defined as the exhibition of negative reactions to others (i.e., the child was perceived as typically hostile, nasty, difficult, unfriendly, spiteful, maladjusted, etc.).

[7]For the chi-square analyses, $n = 82$ for the mild condition and $n = 90$ for the severe condition. Subjects were not included in these analyses if they failed to provide sufficient information to permit classification of a child's social behavior. For example, in spite of instructions to describe the child's behavior, some subjects focused on details irrelevant to the present classificatory scheme, such as what the child's family was like, how many siblings he had, etc.

TABLE 29.1
Mean ratings by condition for perceived likelihood of
future transgressions

Condition	Mild transgression	Severe transgression
Unattractive child	12.19	13.12
Attractive child	11.73	10.70

Note: The above scale ratings range from 0 (very unlikely) to
17 (very likely).

One may ask why attributional inferences occurred on the subjects' estimates of the child's future behavior but not on their estimates of his past
actions. It is possible that subjects may be more reluctant to make strong inferences about events that reputedly have already occurred, since the accuracy of their inferences could presumably be easily verified. They might
wish to be seen as reasonably accurate assessors of the child's character.
Estimates of future behavior provide a more ambiguous frame of reference
which cannot as immediately be subjected to empirical verification.

On the whole, however, the above results support the hypothesis that
adults' evaluations of a child who commits a serious transgression differ as
a function of the child's physical attractiveness. Specifically, adult evalua-
tors are less likely to attribute a chronic, antisocial behavioral disposition to
attractive than to unattractive children. This result occurred both on the
subjects' free descriptions of the child's typical behavior and on their estimates of the likelihood of future offenses.

Trait ratings. Additional evidence concerning adults' inferences about the
character of attractive and unattractive children was provided by responses
to the six personality scales, described earlier, which tapped dimensions
potentially relevant to evaluations of a child who commits a transgression.
Analyses of these data revealed main effects for attractiveness on two
dimensions—honest-dishonest and pleasant-unpleasant. Unattractive children who transgressed were perceived as being more dishonest ($F = 9.70$,
$p < .01$) and more unpleasant ($F = 4.28$, $p < .05$) than attractive children.
The effect for *honesty* is particularly interesting. Given the ambiguous
circumstances of many transgressions, an unattractive child may operate
at some disadvantage in the "assignment of blame" process. If the unattractive child is seen as more likely to lie than an attractive child, estab-
lishment of his innocence may not be as easy.

These two main effects for attractiveness are in accord with a general
stereotype that physically attractive people, adults or children, are assumed
to possess more socially desirable personalities than less attractive per-

sons. It is possible that the results of these dimensions might have occurred even if children differing in attractiveness engaged in more neutral (i.e., not harmful) behavior. On the other hand, it is also conceivable that certain types of inferences such as those about general *honesty* are elicited most strongly in transgression situations.

On a third personality dimension, good-bad, a three-way interaction, Severity × Attractiveness × Sex, was observed ($F = 5.82, p < .05$). Simple effects analyses revealed significant contrasts within the severe condition. Attractive males were rated more negatively for a severe offense than either unattractive males ($F = 10.29, p < .01$) or attractive females ($F = 4.34, p < .05$). Also, unattractive females who committed a severe offense received a more negative evaluation than did unattractive males ($F = 4.49, p < .05$). These results suggest the possibility of different evaluative standards for attractive males and female children who unambiguously violate adult expectations by committing a severe transgression. This interpretation is speculative, however, since these results occurred on only one personality item. None of the other personality items yielded Severity × Attractiveness × Sex interactions, nor were there any Sex × Attractiveness interactions.[8]

Judgment dimensions. It was also hypothesized that the subjects would evaluate an attractive child's transgression less negatively than that of an unattractive child, particularly for a mild offense. In addition, the subjects were expected to advocate less intense punishment for attractive than for unattractive children, regardless of the severity of the transgression. An analysis of variance performed on the subject's ratings of the undesirability of the child's transgression indicated an attractiveness main effect ($F = 3.60, p = .06$). A transgression, whether mild or severe, when committed by an attractive child, tended to be perceived as less undesirable than the same act committed by an unattractive child.

No support was found for the hypothesis that the intensity of punishment advocated for a given transgression would vary as a function of physical attractiveness ($F = 1.98$, n.s.).[9] Conceivably, parameters of punishment other than intensity (e.g., type of punishment) may be influenced by the

---

[8]On the *agressiveness* dimension, a four-way interaction occurred. Simple effects analysis revealed an ambiguous pattern of results that could not be definitively interpreted either for or against the attractiveness hypothesis. No significant differences were found as a function of attractiveness on the *cruel-kind* or *nice-awful* dimensions.

[9]Though not of primary interest for the present study, a Sex × Severity interaction occurred on both evaluation of the offense ($F = 7.49, p < .01$) and on intensity of punishment advocated ($F = 6.48, p < .05$). Mild transgression by females was perceived as more undesirable than mild transgression by males ($F = 6.48, p < .05$). The subjects advocated less intense punishment for females than for males who committed a severe offense ($F = 3.96, p < .05$).

child's appearance. Also, in the present study, the subjects may have assumed that the term "intensity of punishment" implied physical punishment. Differences might have been obtained if items concerning intensity had been paired with various disciplinary methods, for example, how strongly should the child be scolded, etc. In any event, it would seem unusual if adults' inferences concerning the behavioral dispositions of attractive versus unattractive children who commit a transgression do not affect the process of punishment administration on at least some dimensions.

CONCLUSIONS AND IMPLICATIONS

The present study finds that the physical attractiveness of a child who commits a transgression does indeed influence adults' evaluations of him. Attributional inferences are affected both by the severity of a transgression and the attractiveness of the child who commits the offense. Children's physical attractiveness also tends to influence judgments of the transgression's undesirability, whether the offense is mild or severe.

Given the numerous occasions when adults must deal with children's transgressions, the implications of these results merit further investigation. It seems plausible that adults' assumptions about a child's character, particularly the type of behavior expected from him, may ultimately be communicated to the child, potentially influencing his self-evaluation. If so, one might find differences between attractive and unattractive children in areas such as reactions to their own transgressions as well as the type and frequency of transgression committed. These issues might be particularly interesting for future research.

References

DION, K., AND BERSCHEID, E. Physical attractiveness and sociometric choice in young children. University of Minnesota, 1971. (Mimeo)

DION, K., BERSCHEID, E., AND WALSTER, E. What is beautiful is good. *Journal of Personality and Social Psychology,* 1972, in press.

HEIDER, F. *The psychology of interpersonal relations.* New York: Wiley, 1958.

JONES, E. E., AND DAVIS, K. E. From acts to dispositions: The attribution process in person perception. In L. Berkowitz (Ed.), *Advances in experimental social psychology*. Vol. 2. New York: Academic Press, 1965.

SHAW, M. E., AND SULZER, J. L. An empirical test of Heider's levels in attribution of responsibility, *Journal of Abnormal and Social Psychology*, 1964, **69,** 39–46.

WINER, B. J. *Statistical principles in experimental design*. New York: McGraw-Hill, 1962.

VII

COMMUNICATION IN SENSITIVITY TRAINING GROUPS

30

The Return of the Repressed

Michael Kahn

The Oriental philosophers warn us to be most wary of the opponent just before he is thoroughly vanquished. At that moment in Judo, in Taoism, in the *I Ching,* he may use all your vulnerable stature and strength to bring you crashing to the mat. The "repressed" in my title are William James and Wilhelm Reich. The James-Lange (1884) theory of emotion has suffered badly over the years at the hands of Cannon's descendents, and the Reichian (1945) theories of character armor and physiologically oriented psycho-therapy have suffered even more from the negative halo of Reich's madness. Both sets of theories have been pushed out of the mainstream of psychology, but now the repressed is indeed returning, even bidding fair to take over the intensive group movement. It is not just that there are occasional Reichian-therapy-on-bio-energetic workshops done at Esalen and at Kairos, but rather that all of the growing emphasis on physical acting out in groups stems basically, I believe, from a James-Lange and a Reichian orientation.

This paper was originally prepared for a conference in Intensive Group Process sponsored by the *Foundations Fund for Research in Psychiatry* and held in Dorado, Puerto Rico, in June 1969.

Reich was a student of Freud's who learned to do psychoanalysis in the usual way: he listened to his patients talk and he waited for the resistances to thaw so that the patient would progress. It took a long time. He noted that the psychological resistances were accompanied by certain physical events: postural rigidities or breathing changes or muscular tensions. Everyone assured him that these physical events were mere by-products of the psychological phenomena and that when the talk progressed, the body would loosen up, or, if not, it didn't matter anyway because the subject of concern was the life of the mind. In spite of this advice he began to add to his therapeutic techniques ways of working directly on the body tensions. Gradually, the amount of talk in Reich's therapy diminished as there was a corresponding increase in the body-oriented work. Reich believed that if he could change the breathing and the musculature by dealing with them directly, the corresponding psychological events would necessarily change also.

The theoretical underpinning for this approach and others like it (e.g., Jacobson's [1938] relaxation theory) seem clearly to be the James-Lange theory of emotion. If one holds with Cannon that the bodily correlates are an irrelevant accompaniment to a subjective emotion, that the phenomenological state can exist with or without these bodily events, then there is no sense working on the body to affect the mind. James, however, believed that the somatic changes *are* the emotion, that my heart doesn't race because I'm afraid, but rather that I know I am afraid because I notice my heart racing. If one agrees with James (and his colleague Lange), then there is a good deal of sense in approaching the mind through the muscles.

The goal of this paper is to give some histroy and description of those encounter groups which include a good deal of non-verbal activity. I shall focus on two such, believing them to be the most conceptually advanced versions of the genre. These two are the Esalen "Joy" groups and the Advanced Human Relations or "Personal Growth" (P.G.) groups sponsored by the National Training Laboratories (N.T.L.). There are versions appearing all over the country, but by and large they are imitations of these two. The aforementioned "Joy" groups by no means represent the only activities taking place at the Esalen Institute. There is also a wide range of group experiences which offer psychotherapy, religious instruction, meditative experience, general interest seminars, and specialized approaches to personal freedom. All of these influence each other and all influence the "Joy" groups. Except for a bit of parameter setting, we shall consider only the latter because it alone deals directly with intensive group process.

I would like to set out seven positively correlated variables, each represented by a continuum along which intensive group experiences can be placed:

1. *Passive leader versus active directing leader.*
2. *Focus on group versus focus on individual.*

As has long been recognized by group leaders, very different phenomena result from the leader making his interventions at the group level from those which result from individual level observations. Examples of group level intervention: "I think the issue is what are we going to do about the leader's power"; "It seems the group is using some of its members to help avoid the real issue." Examples of individual level intervention: "It seems Mary has tried twice to get a response from Al and that he hasn't so far been willing to encounter her."

3. *Talk encouraged and action discouraged versus action encouraged and talk discouraged.*
4. *Psychotherapy versus goals other than therapeutic.*

This requires a bit of defining. Frank (1964), Weschler, Massarick, and Tannenbaum (1961), and others have discussed this issue very usefully. I need, however, for the purposes of this paper to employ a somewhat different criterion than is customary. I want to consider psychotherapy the process that results when a client or patient goes to an avowed professional therapist and seeks help with one or more specific psychological problems. I am aware of some of the weaknesses of this definition, but it will help us differentiate between those groups which calmly accept a member who says, e.g., "I am here to get help with my sexual impotence," and those in which such a statement would get him hustled off to a counselor who will advise him to leave the group, go home, and get a therapist. General awareness of existential inadequacies in us and in the culture are not, for our purposes, considered specific psychological problems. It is, of course, recognized how similar in technique and content a "therapy" group and a "non-therapy" group are apt to be.

5. *Cognitive emphasis versus affective emphasis.*

This refers both to goals and to process. In some groups it gets you many points to make smart comments about what the group is now up to and what you are thereby learning about group process. In other groups this will get you scorned as a defensive, mind-ridden coward.

6. *Informed by pro-establishment values versus a socially radical orientation.*

7. *Encouraging members to go home and adjust to their environment versus encouraging them to rebel against it.*

My ratings are somewhat arbitrary and idiosyncratic, but perhaps not entirely. Table 30.1 lists twelve types of groups which might be found under the banner of one of the major organizations working with intensive group process. Traditional group psychotherapy is the only exception, and it is included because of obvious relatedness. Each group is rated on each dimension. It will be seen that the variables are, by my rating, positively correlated and that the two purest cases are the Tavistock study group and the Reichian workshop. Significant interim positions (significant for our purposes) are occupied by the N.T.L. Institute Basic Human Relations (H.R.) groups and the N.T.L. Institute Advanced Human Relations or Personal Growth (P.G.) groups and by the Esalen "Joy" groups. So we might consolidate the table into a chart that looks like this:

	1.6	2.7		4.6	5
Tavistock study groups	N.T.L. Basic H.R. groups	N.T.L. Personal Growth groups		Esalen "Joy" groups	Reichian workshops

Since this paper is concerned with encounter groups involving a considerable amount of non-verbal activity, it will focus on the P.G. and the "Joy" groups, using the Reichian workshop and the Tavistock study group only to set some parameters.

In the Reichian groups (our pure Type 5) everyone but the therapist and one participant sits quietly while the two principals perform. The performance takes the form of the therapist instructing the participant to engage in various activities, mostly non-verbal, designed to help the participant surmount neurotic obstacles to his functioning. The viewers are supposed to receive vicarious help. Often they see themselves as merely waiting their turn and occupying the waiting period by a harmless bit of voyeurism. Occasionally, a very exciting or moving or depressing interaction in the center of the room will galvanize a group feeling something like that shared by a movie audience. But, mostly, very little group feeling or interaction develops. It is considered bad form for a member of the waiting/viewing circle to participate in the central interaction. The overall point of view is conventional Reich, i.e., anti-establishment and anti-adjustment ("Why should I help my patients adjust to a sick society?''). The leader (therapist) is directive to the point of being highly authoritarian and the attitude toward *talk* is impatient and a bit scornful. Actually, the leader is apt to talk rather a lot. The above-mentioned attitude refers to talk by participants. Truth is seen as residing in the breathing or in the pelvic movements, and talk only obscures. Affect is of great concern and cognitive issues are minimized.

The other end of our scale is anchored by the Tavistock study group (our pure Type 1). In this group the participants and the consultant sit in a circle. The group is encouraged to keep the talk flowing around the group and keep many members involved. If two people begin to talk to each other more than briefly, this is seen as an escape from the work of the group. It is considered very *good* form for a momentary onlooker to join an ongoing interaction. The consultant is very passive in that he never directs, only observes and comments (although his observations do, of course, shape the subsequent interaction). The overwhelming focus of the consultant's interventions and, consequently, of the group's interactions is THE GROUP. THE GROUP is seen as having a personality and a sequence of intentions, wishes, fears, etc. Group feeling becomes very intense. There is no attempt to deal with pre-group individual neuroses. The emphasis is on learning— learning about group process through learning about *this* group. Life-enriching emotions and emotion-centered discoveries happen as though by serendipity, the consultant firmly insisting on the cognizing of the movement of the group. The point of view is Kleinian psychoanalytic, THE GROUP being seen as struggling through a transference neurosis. The social point of view is generally pro-establishment and pro-adjustment with a good deal of discussion of corporate and military structure introduced both as model for the group and as potential beneficiaries of the learning. The attitude toward talk is very friendly, indeed, and non-verbal action is seen as unwelcome and unuseful acting out.

These then are our two anchor points and will enable us to specify the area of this paper which briefly will trace out in the history of the American group movement a progression from the Type 1 emphasis toward the Type 5 and will discuss the East Coast and West Coast versions of the groups which represent the current point of that development.

The T-group or study group was independently invented at about the same time (in the mid- or late 1940s) by Bion in England and Lewin and his co-workers in America, but since very little development in the direction of non-verbal activity has happened in England, we will confine our history-tracing to America.

The development of the American T-group has been marked almost from the beginning by an as yet unsynthesized dialectic in which the social psychology position is thesis and the clinical position is antithesis.

TABLE 30.1
How twelve types of groups rate (1–5) on the seven dimensions

Group	Passive leader = 1; active leader = 5	Group focus = 1; individual focus = 5	Talk = 1; action = 5	Non-therapy = 1; therapy = 5	Cognitive emphasis = 1; affective emphasis = 5	Conservative = 1; radical = 5	Encourage adjustment = 1; encourage rebellion = 5
Tavistock study groups	1	1	1	1	1	1	1
N.T.L. Institute Basic Human Relations	1.5	2.5	1.5	1	2.5	1	1
N.T.L. Institute Personal Growth	3.5	2.5	2.5	2	3.5	2.5	2.5
Esalen "Joy" groups	5	5	5	2.5	5	5	5
Gestalt therapy groups	5	5	5	5	3.5	3.5	2.5
Reichian workshops	5	5	5	5	5	5	5
Psychodrama groups	5	5	5	5	5	1	1
Nude body-movement groups	5	5	5	1	5	5	5
Charlotte Selver groups	5	5	5	1	5	3	1
Religious seminars and workshops	5	5	1	1	1	5	2.5
Esalen couples groups	5	5	3.5	3.5	4	4	2
Traditional group therapy	5	3.5	1	5	2.5	1	1

The original National Training Laboratory groups were called Basic Skills Training Groups. The emphasis was on direct training of participants to perform more skillfully in back-home groups, and the trainer's interventions were primarily group-oriented. By 1949 the clinicians were moving away from this position, and by 1962 three of the N.T.L. Californians (Weschler, Massarick, and Tannenbaum, 1961) had announced their movement away from interpersonal skill training and toward the goals of "personal growth" and "total enhancement of the individual." They were no longer making group-level interventions or discussing human relations problems. They were dealing with "management of anger," "ability to express and receive love," and "feelings of loneliness." The clear implication was that if they could enrich their clients' lives, the functioning of those clients in back-home groups would necessarily improve, although that was seen as a goal secondary to life enrichment. The dialectic continued. Important N.T.L. workers such as Bradford and Benne still represented the Lewinian position although both sides were influenced and modified by each other. Still, today, N.T.L. asks its Basic Human Relations Trainers to promise in writing that they won't ignore the old Lewinian goals and be over-clinical lest they violate their clients' needs and expectations. The fact that N.T.L. finds this contract necessary indicates the still unsynthesized state of the dialectic. However, it is not only, or maybe not even primarily, the position represented in the 1961 statement by Weschler et al. which is most acutely responsible for the above-mentioned contract. As the James-Lange/Reich forces began to make themselves felt in the group movement, first in California and then in the East, the split widened. The impatience that the Reichian and Gestalt[1] therapist felt with the Freudian and the Rogerian showed up in trainers who no longer felt justified in waiting for the group to "get there" by itself. These trainers began nudging and then pushing. The impatience of the Reichians and the Gestaltists with *talk* also appeared, and more and more *action* was introduced to circumvent the superficiality and defensiveness of verbal behavior. In 1964 N.T.L. dealt with this new development with characteristic creativity. They instituted in their summer programs a special laboratory for alumni of Basic Human Relations labs, which, by its second year, came to be called the "Personal Growth Laboratory" and was frankly independent of many of the original T-group goals and characteristics. No attention was paid to teaching about group process or organizational structure. The goals were those of Weschler et al., and

---

[1]*Gestalt* here refers to a school of therapy, the best-known exponent of which is Frederick Perls. Perls has made an ingenious blend of Freudian psychoanalysis, Reichian therapy, and J. L. Moreno's Psychodrama (see footnote 2). Gestalt therapy is action-oriented and pays considerable attention to the body. It has had a growing influence, first in California and then throughout the country, and its influence is particularly notable in the encounter group movement.

the techniques were heavily action-laden. Those techniques included body movement, psychodrama,[2] improvised theater, finger painting and sculpting. In the T-group, anger was expressed by wrestling, and affection by embracing. Every important group theme — e.g., trust, openness, encounter, support, inclusion, dominance/submission — had very specific analogical non-verbal exercises which supplemented or replaced theme-related talk. Specifically, therapeutic goals were ruled in bounds.

These groups have turned out to be enormously influential in the subsequent history of the intensive group movement, being the direct forebears of the current Esalen groups as well as primarily responsible for the increasing action orientation throughout the group movement. They are largely the creation of Californians John and Joyce Weir. After World War II when the T-groups were beginning in the East, there was developing in California a series of apparently unrelated events. Teachers of the dance, drama, and art were finding that their speciality had a psychotherapeutic function and began to conduct sessions first for hospital patients and then for out-patients. An easy next step was to utilize their speciality as a life enricher for non-patients.

It was primarily the Weirs who saw that these separate activities could be combined and introduced into the world of intensive group process, and it was they who saw the value of using body movements, graphics, and theater as analogues of the themes which emerged in T-groups.

These new groups became extremely successful and then, in the N.T.L. community, accrued increasingly higher prestige. The points of view and techniques of the P.G. labs began rapidly to diffuse into the other N.T.L. groups. Having set up a lab specifically for these purposes and specifically employing these techniques, N.T.L. then attempted to keep both the new goals and the new techniques to a minimum in the Basic H.R. labs. This was, as we have seen, partly because of the clients' expectations and wishes, but there was another reason too, and it concerns us directly here. The original T-group development was strongly influenced by a passionate conviction common to the early workers that the values of *democracy* were highly desirable, that these values could and should be enhanced by participation in a T-group, and that everything about a T-group ought to *be* democratic since non-democratic process could not teach democracy. This was certainly the Lewinian tradition, and, in addition, the influence of Carl Rogers was marked from the beginning.

---

[2]*Psychodrama* is a technique invented by J. L. Moreno (1946) in which life situations are acted out as though in a stage play. It was originally designed as a therapeutic technique although its uses now include various kinds of education. In spite of its never having received the recognition it deserves, it is the original source of many techniques now proudly claimed by the encounter group movement. Psychodrama has served an important function in translating many of the Reich and the James-Lange insights into techniques which could be employed by other psychotherapies and by the group movement.

One important characteristic demanded by these considerations was the passivity of the trainer. That passivity also produced unique opportunities for learning; for instance, a fine way to learn about the terrors of freedom is to be confronted suddenly with a passive leader. So when the Personal Growth trainers began pushing participants, there was understandable concern on the part of the Lewin-Rogers group. Chris Argyris sounded the alarm in an article called "On the Future of Laboratory Education" (1967) in which he made essentially two points: first, that under the aegis of the P.G. groups slapdash and perhaps irresponsible psychotherapy had infiltrated the T-groups, and, second, that democracy was dead in them. The death of democracy meant to Argyris that no matter how wonderful an experience you gave a participant, it was a destructive failure experience because you *gave* it to him, and a far less wonderful experience would be far more helpful if he felt he did it himself. Many P.G. trainers were made uneasy by both arguments although the first (slapdash psychotherapy) seemed the more remedial of the two. The anti-democratic characteristic seemed an integral part of the new look, and, though it could be reduced some, it seemed as though one would simply have to choose. The P.G. trainers decided, contrary to Argyris, that the benefits were worth it. If two participants are struggling with an issue and getting nowhere, a trainer can wait it out and settle for the tiny progress they may make on their own or he can suggest, say, a non-verbal exercise which will give them a great leap forward. Afterward they may well feel *he* did it for them, but the results are often remarkable. A thoroughly convinced Rogerian would choose the client-generated step. The P.G. trainers have made the other choice.

Let's spend a day with an N.T.L.-P.G. group. (This will be a vaguely modal picture. Each group, each year, each locus presents huge variations.) The groups meet day and evening for fifteen days. This morning it has assembled at 9:00 A.M. with a special trainer (probably female) whose specialty is body movement. There is an acid rock record playing when they arrive, and the trainer is dancing to it. The members begin to dance, and by the time all hands are aboard, the group is deep into a free-style, improvised dance. The trainer takes over and begins leading the group through the day's exercises. She will have fifteen one-and-a-half-hour sessions with each group and has carefully designed a progression of experiences meant to harmonize with their other experiences in the laboratory. She will try during these fifteen days to help them increase their sense awareness ("Feel the skin on your face. Really feel it. How many textures and temperatures can you find?"), to help them loosen the physical character armor ("Let your shoulders flop like a rag doll's"), to help them experience and express emotions ("Pantomime the most aggressive act you can imagine"; "Everyone stand close to Joe and touch him with the most affection that you feel toward him."), to help them with group themes ("Form a circle holding hands and look into the eyes of each member of the group."), and to help them find their way to deep archetypal experiences ("As you lie in the primal substance, a feeling of life begins to stir in you, and when you're ready it will begin to move you. Feel the first stirring of life through the inert state."). From time to time the movement is interrupted, and the participants are encouraged to talk about the engendered feelings.

After the movement session there will be a coffee break. The rule of silence is imposed and participants and staff wander around the grounds singly or in small groups attending to the grass under their feet, stopping to pick up and examine a leaf, occasionally sitting opposite a fellow group member, sipping coffee, and silently watching the other's face.

After the break the group has a talk session. It starts as a T-group, but before long the trainer has suggested a non-verbal exercise ("Why don't you try really breaking into the group instead of talking about it. We'll form a circle and try to keep you out. See if you can fight your way in."), or a psychodrama ("Who feels most like your father? Okay, why don't you say it to him?"), or a guided fantasy ("Imagine you're climbing a mountain. Can you see yourself there? Okay, let it develop and tell it to us as it does."), or a Gestalt exercise ("Go up to each person in turn and tell them how much you need them to love you."). After a while the group is once more acting like a T-group, and the trainer is training more or less like a Basic H.R. trainer—a Basic H.R. trainer who tends to focus more on the individual than on the group.

Lunch is silent with the group sitting in a circle attending to the process of eating and to each other's presence. Two members are working a dependency issue from a previous group meeting. At the trainer's suggestion one of them has been blindfolded for the meal and the other is feeding him. Across the circle a trainer and one participant, high on the silence and on the accumulated impact of the lab, begin throwing peas basketball-style into each other's mouths and wind up in a wild food-slinging which involves four or five others. Some onlookers laugh; others watch thoughtfully.

After lunch the group has a session with finger paints. There is no attempt to make a pretty product, only to experience texture and temperature and color and smell with fine-grain attention. Some members spend the entire session rubbing the paint in a circle, eyes closed, faces rapt. Others work away, watching the colors change and evolve. Two members are carefully painting each other's bodies. Several days from now there will be a general free-for-all smearing of each other with paint and paste. After the session the group will talk about the feelings evoked by the activity.

Time is free until evening when the group meets with the other small groups in the P.G. lab in a large general session. Sometimes this is a large

T-group of the sort used so effectively at Tavistock, but tonight the staff has designed a ritual. The mid-lab break is approaching and a parting ceremony is being conducted. The mood is solemn and the scene seems primitive. The final item of the ritual consists of the entire group standing in a circle, their arms locked and their eyes closed, chanting a Tibetan Buddhist chant.

Yesterday the schedule was much the same except instead of finger painting the afternoon was spent improvising a play.

Perhaps this small sample will convey something of the flavor of these groups. The other type of group of which I would like to provide a sample is the Esalen Joy group. William C. Schutz, the father of these groups, was for some years a trainer in the Bethel P.G. groups and was strongly influenced by John and Joyce Weir.

When Schutz joined the Esalen staff, he took with him much of what he had learned from the Weirs plus an even stronger Reichian bent than theirs. In the far-out, never-never-land climate of Esalen and freed of the restraints of association with establishment-related N.T.L., Schutz's groups moved from the 2.7 that the Weirs P.G. groups occupy on our scale to the 4.6 we have given them. In addition to the Reichian emphasis, Schutz's unique training style and some strongly held convictions made these new groups very different. It was very important to him to encourage the most direct and complete interpersonal confrontations possible. It was equally important to unearth the sources of shame and fear and help his participants to experience their way right into the middle of that shame or fear and out the other side. He developed remarkable ability to risk his participants in a sink-or-swim situation and emerge with all concerned swimming strongly. One of his great contributions to the movement has been his vindicated confidence in the strength and courage of his participants. Schutz no longer runs these groups. Although his influence is still paramount, the groups are now run by his first generation of Esalen students and the current workshops necessarily reflect the fact that they are now in the hands of young and enthusiastic leaders. Let's spend a day in one.

The group may be together for two or for five days. They meet at 9:00 A.M. in a small, carpeted motel-type room on a spectacular cliff over the Pacific. Unlike the P.G. groups, there is not a variety of planned events. Each of the three daily sessions takes place in the same framework. The group sits on the floor or on mattresses in a circle. The leader says, "This is an encounter group. The rules are talk honestly and directly about your feelings with the here and now." He is then silent. A member says he feels uncomfortable about the group. The leader quickly suggests he pick an individual who is making him uncomfortable. The member insists it's the group. The leader repeats the suggestion. The member looks around and picks another man. The leader suggests the two confront each other. The two members talk briefly about feelings of threat and competition, and the leader suggests they find a non-verbal way to explore this. A third member wonders if all this isn't happening too fast and the leader asks him why he feels the need to interfere with what's going on. The encounter proceeds, perhaps into an energetic wrestling match. Afterwards, the participants embrace and tell each other they feel good about each other and about the excitement of having wrestled for the first time since childhood.

There is a silence and the group waits. The third member says he's mad at the leader for putting him down and goes on to say that he doesn't ever get along well with authority and that's what he's here to work on. He falters and stops. A couple of other members suggest exercises. Nothing much happens. The leader wonders if the member would like to try an encounter with his father. Two chairs are found and sit facing each other. The leader directs the member to sit in one. The group rings the chairs, watching. The leader sits close to the chairs. He instructs the member to visualize his father sitting in the empty chair and to speak to him. The member complies. After a time he is instructed to switch seats and take the role of his father replying to the son. The leader carefully directs the scene, sometimes even telling the member what to say ("Tell your father how you felt when he interfered with your marriage; tell him how mad you were."). At a certain point in the exercise the leader puts a cushion on father's chair and instructs the member to kneel in front of it and pound it while shouting out his anger. The member complies. The pounding starts mildly and there are no words. The leader urges him to hit harder. A couple of other members echo the urging. The pounding becomes stronger, the angry words come, and the whole thing crescendos into a screaming paroxysm of rage culminating in weeping and then near collapse. Two of the women hold him and rock him gently, cooing to him and caressing him. After a time he talks briefly about the feelings of release and about his profound astonishment at having found such violence in himself. He smiles ruefully at the leader and embraces him. For now, at least, he seems not to have an "authority problem."

There is more silence, and then a man tells one of the women that he is attracted to her but scared. Several of the men say they are too. One of the other women calls her a cockteaser. There is a general spirited discussion of her attributes and behavior. Four-letter words abound from members and leader alike. Finally, the leader stops the discussion. The woman has gotten a massive and sudden dose of feedback. She has alternated between fighting it off, taking it nondefensively, and berating herself. The leader suggests she might go to each member in turn and share her feelings toward him/her.

She begins cautiously. "I think you're nice . . ." (To the next man) "You make me nervous . . ." The leader interrupts and says that in his view the issue is sex—what lies behind all these double messages? He guides and coaxes and coerces until finally he has her saying to the men: "I really wouldn't want to sleep with you, but I want you to want me." (To the next man) "I don't really give much of a damn about you." (To the next) "I guess you're the guy here that I really want. I hope we can get together." To the women she says, "I'm afraid of you; you're sexier and younger than me and he might prefer you." (To the next who called her a cockteaser) "You can go fuck yourself, dearie." When she's been around the whole group, she sits and talks about the experience, saying that it both terrified and exhilarated her—terrified her because it seemed so dangerous. ("Now I've lost all chance of being loved or wanted by the men I rejected.") She adds that the hardest thing of all was to reject the man who said she was attractive. A couple of the men reassure her, saying that they are really relieved to have an open and straightforward relationship with a woman. She says what exhilarates her is having allowed herself to give up the opaque social sex game for the first time in her life. She feels clean and straight. Her antagonist takes her hand and asks if it isn't nice not to be a cocktease for a change. She starts, bristles, subsides, smiles sheepishly, and buries her head in the other woman's breast. The event is over. The group laughs and relaxes. There is silence and they wait.

There are three sessions—morning, afternoon, and evening—and they all follow this pattern. After the evening session the group adjourns en masse to the baths. It is clear the session is not over. The baths are natural hot sulphur springs outdoors, perched on the edge of a Pacific cliff. There are some small tubs and some large enough to accommodate the entire group. Men and women bathe nude together and walk around the bath area nude together. It is the first such experience for most members. At first they are tense, frightened, and conflicted about staring. Slowly they perceive the calm acceptance of the few experienced people likely to be present, and with enormous relief at beginning to shed some lifelong anxieties, they relax. After a period of getting settled and another period of silent absorption of the remarkable scene, the group goes back to work, and they may work deep into the night. The leader may leave early, but the group will continue without him. The material evoked in this setting is almost invariably sexual. It is an opportunity for members to confront other lifelong anxieties, for instance, those concerning touching and being touched. The encounters are apt to be quite intimate. Mostly, aggression is off limits down here.

And so it goes for the duration of the workshop, the intensity and the intimacy tending to build rapidly over the course of the weekend or the week.

AIMS AND KEY CONCEPTS

We have, I think, seen the methods employed by the two types of groups with which this paper is primarily concerned. I think the aims and key concepts of each are probably clear too, but let's summarize a bit.

Besides the progenitors of the overall group movement — Bion, Lewin, etc. — there are several main theoretical ancestors of the action groups. We have seen that the James-Lange theory of emotion is one such and that Reich's criticisms of Freud and his attempts to find a physiological mode of psychotherapy represent another. Moreno is a hugely important influence. So is Fritz Perls, the founder of Gestalt therapy, and Charlotte Selver, the mother of American sense-awareness training. We shall see others below.

Let's look at the two types of groups separately for a moment.

The Esalen "Joy" Groups

Here are some passages from Bill Schutz's book *Joy*. They lay out aims and key concepts of the Esalen groups better than I can:

> The underlying philosophy behind the human potential thrust is that of openness and honesty. A man must be willing to let himself be known to himself and to others. He must express and explore his feelings and open up areas long dormant and possibly painful, with the faith that in the long run the pain will give way to a release of vast potential for creativity and joy. This is an exhilarating and frightening prospect, one which is often accompanied by agony, but which usually leads to ecstasy.

> To explore the areas needed for the full development of the human potential, it is helpful to know what a man who has developed his full potential — let us call him a fully realized man — looks like. What are the various pressures that can prevent him from realizing this potential? And where, therefore, must methods be devised for overcoming inhibitions facilitating its development? Man is a biological, psychological, and social animal and his joy comes from these sources.

> To begin with, man is a biological organism. His first point of inhibition is in his physical structure. If a man is sickly and weak, if his energy is low or his vital functions are impaired, it is unlikely that he can function at his utmost. The first area of "realization" is the physical structure. Bodily joy comes not simply from an athletic body but from one that functions smoothly, gracefully, without unnecessary strain; a body in which the joints move easily, the muscles are toned, the blood flows vigorously, the breathing is deep and full, food is digested well, the sexual apparatus is in good order, and the nervous system works effectively. . . .

> Joy also arises from the full development of personal functioning. The parts of the body may be taught and trained, exercised and sharpened. The senses

may be made more acute to discriminate smells and sights. Strength and stamina can be increased in the muscles. Sensory awareness and appreciation can be awakened so that more sensitivity to bodily feelings and natural events can be developed. Motor control can be cultivated so that development of mechanical and artistic skills result, and coordination and dexterity improve. The nervous system may be developed through study and the acquisition of knowledge and experience. Logical thinking and the creative potential can be nurtured and brought to fruition. Bodily functions controlling the emotions can also be developed. Awareness of emotions, appropriate expression of feelings (and their relation to other functions such as thinking and action) can be trained. . . .

Thus far our "realized" man has acquired a finely tuned body, and has developed it to its full integrated functioning. If he is to develop further, he must be able to relate to other people in order to achieve the most joy. Since ours is a communal culture, this means functioning in such a way that human interaction is rewarding for all concerned. . . . [pp. 16–18.]

How is joy attained? A large part of the effort, unfortunately, must go into undoing. Guilt, shame, embarrassment, or fear of punishment, failure, success, retribution—all must be overcome. Obstacles to release must be surmounted. Destructive and blocking behavior, thoughts, and feelings must be altered. Talents and abilities must be developed and trained. . . . [p. 20.]

The N.T.L.-P.G. Groups

In addition to the influences we have noted at work here—Reich, Perls, Selver, Moreno—there is a strong Jungian slant among the trainers of these groups. It goes something like this: Everyone contains within himself all the archetypes—the maiden, the warrior, the divine child, the wise old man, the mother, the devil, etc. The culture requires the person to form an identity (in the Ericksonian sense) which permits the full expression of only one or two of these, the rest being totally repressed or drastically attenuated. The goal of the lab is to give participants experiences which will allow them to establish richer and more complete contact with their existent archetypes and to get some kind of contact with others. It is hardly argued that the ideal state is one in which all possible archetypes are juggled—only that a rich psychological life requires that some of the important ones be available. The over-masculine athelete could use some awareness of the child and the mother in him. The discovery by the meek accountant that he is warrior and animal (his *shadow* in Jung talk) can enrich his self-concept and his relationships considerably. Many men have wished their wives could unearth a bit of the courtesan in themselves. The body movement, the finger painting and clay sculpture, the sense-awareness training, the role-playing, the rituals and ceremonies are all meant to open the intrapsychic channels to the archetypal depths and to allow the emergence of new archetypes. It is important to note this point of view relative to the questions about slapdash psychotherapy raised by Argyris in his previously mentioned article. To the extent that the P.G. trainers stick to the archetype conception, the P.G. labs are innocent of the charge.

It is assumed that the personality of the participant got limited by virtue of his being a member of Western society (whatever his personal psychic history, dynamics, and diagnosis) and that it is appropriate to help him increase his access to more of his human birthright. This help is given in a fashion which does not require the trainer to produce a lightning depth insight and a wild bit of depth interpretation. The trainers being human, and usually clinicians to boot, it is true that occasionally they indulge, but as the archetype conception gets more and more deeply built into the lab design and into the attitudes of the trainers, such wild analysis happens less and less.

In an outline for the theoretical section of a book in progress, John Weir lists four major assumptions which underlie the P.G. labs. They are worth mentioning here.

> 1. Talk is symbolization further removed from feeling than are non-verbal behaviors; e.g., "I'm angry" bears a more distant relation to the feeling of anger than does a wrestling match.
>
> 2. Much crucial learning is pre-verbal, and, therefore, relearning must be non-verbal. This is analogous to the theories which argue the difficulty of changing behavior learned under non-repeatable stimulus conditions. It will also be readily seen that this assumption is strongly influenced by the Reichian concept which says that since behavior is so much controlled by the state of the musculature, it's much harder to bring about behavior change verbally than by directly working with the musculature.
>
> 3. The Gestalt notion of isomorphism implies that brain patterns are isomorphic with motor patterns. Therefore, the assumption runs, brain structures can be changed by changing motor patterns.
>
> 4. The limits imposed by the culture restrict the area of expressiveness to the verbal sphere. This, accordingly, restricts the self-image and depresses the self-concept. Freud's "The ego is first and foremost a body ego" means then that ego enhancement would follow the broadening and deepening of non-verbal expressiveness.

It might not be amiss to conclude by pointing out that there are no data bearing on the outcome of this kind of work. We are somewhat in the position of the psychotherapists: our groups *ought* to change subsequent behavior. Those of us who work in this field feel our *own* behavior has been changed by them. Our participants *seem* different at the end of a group. We all know some anecdotes which say there is lasting change. But we really don't know. I trust the movement is now large enough to generate some more definitive studies. I hope so.

POSTSCRIPT

This paper was written in mid-1969 and the world has moved on. Still, it hasn't changed all that much. In spite of some modification, the groups are still recognizable from the descriptions in this paper. Groups on both coasts have become less homogeneous as more and more leaders conduct them. The East Coast and West Coast groups resemble each other more too as Gestalt therapy and Oriental philosophy become progressively more influential at Esalen and N.T.L. The main differences between them remain as they were before: the sexual and aggressive acting-out tends to be more extreme in the West, and, because of the enduring influence of the Rogers-Lewin forces, the N.T.L. leaders tend to be more careful about either telling participants what to do or telling them what they *really* think or feel.

References

ARGYRIS, CHRIS, "Conditions for Competence Acquisition and Therapy," *Journal of Applied Behavioral Science*, 1968, **2**:147–187.

FRANK, JEROME D., "Training and Therapy," in Bradford, L., et al. (eds.) *T-Group Theory and Laboratory Method,* New York, Wiley, 1964.

JACOBSON, EDMUND, *Progressive Relaxation*, Chicago, University of Chicago Press, 1938.

JAMES, WILLIAM, "What Is an Emotion?" *Mind*, 1884, **9**:188–205. Reprinted in James, William, and C. G. Lange, *The Emotions*, Baltimore, Williams & Wilkins, 1922.

MORENO, J. L., *Psychodrama*, New York, Beacon House, 1946.

REICH, WILHELM, *Character Analysis*, New York, Farrar, Straus & Young, 1949.

SCHUTZ, WILLIAM C., *Joy: Expanding Human Awareness*, New York, Grove Press, 1967.

TANNENBAUM, R., I. R. WESCHLER, AND F. MASSARIK, "The Process of Understanding People," *Leadership and Organization*, New York, McGraw-Hill, 1961.

31

Increases in Hypnotizability as a Function of Encounter Group Training: Some Confirming Evidence

Jerrold L. Shapiro and Michael Jay Diamond

The present study was designed to investigate the effects of encounter group experience on hypnotizability. Thirty-four graduate students were assigned to three experimental encounter groups and one no-treatment control group. The encounter groups varied in the amount of interpersonal contact between group members. Equivalent forms of the Stanford Hypnotic Susceptibility Scale were administered before and after the groups. Significant increases in hypnotizability occurred as a result of encounter group experience. Results were interpreted with regard to the interpersonal nature of group participation and with reference to previous findings. The value of hypnotic susceptibility as a measure of interpersonal behavioral change was considered.

Tart (1970) has suggested that hypnotizability can be increased through exposure to a wide variety of therapeutic experience. He measured changes in hypnotizability scores for seven Resident Fellows at Esalen Institute over a nine-month period. These Fellows were engaged in a program which included bioenergetic analysis, directed imagery, sensitivity and encounter groups, Gestalt therapy, psychodrama, and sensory awareness. Tart reported moderate increases on the Stanford Hypnotic Susceptibility Scale, Form C (Weitzenhoffer and Hilgard, 1962) and attributed these changes to the Esalen program.

Reprinted with permission from the authors and *The Journal of Abnormal Psychology,* Vol. 79, No. 1, 1972. Copyright 1972 by the American Psychological Association.

This study was supported in part by University of Hawaii Innovation Grant G–70–001–F–206–0–008. The authors wish to express their gratitude to Tom Glass, Rene Tillich, and Linda Tillich who served as the group leaders and to the dedicated research assistants of the Laboratory of Cognitive Behavior Control, University of Hawaii. Order of authorship was determined by a coin toss.

Several methodological and conceptual inadequacies detract from Tart's conclusions: (*a*) there was no matched control group; (*b*) demand characteristics were poorly controlled; (*c*) the wide variety of training activities made it impossible to determine which one produced the effects; and (*d*) while the reported changes were significant, they were small and failed to warrant the conclusion that the Esalen Training Program disinhibited a "variety of altered states of consciousness [p. 260]."

Shapiro (1970) has demonstrated that differential cognitive and behavioral effects occurred as a result of different varieties of encounter group training. Three major types of group leadership have produced these changes: (*a*) intrapersonal; (*b*) interpersonal; and (*c*) a combination of intrapersonal and interpersonal leadership (mixed).[1] These three types of groups were compared in this study.

Although both self-report data and independent *O*'s reports have indicated a wide variety of changes occurring as a function of encounter group participation, no data have reliably demonstrated that the cognitive behavior involved in hypnosis could be modified as a result of such experiences. Tart's conclusions, however, suggest the feasibility of such changes.

The present study was designed to confirm and extend Tart's conclusions with a more adequate methodology. A matched control group was included, the hypnosis scales were not presented as though they were dependent measures for group experiences, and only encounter group training was included.

There were three hypotheses. First, significant increases in hypnotic susceptibility were expected to occur as a function of encounter group training. Second, based on Shapiro and Gust's (1971) data indicating that cognitive change is positively correlated with the interaction between members, the greatest increases in susceptibility were expected for the interpersonal group (B) and the smallest changes were anticipated for the intrapersonal group (A). Finally, no significant increases in susceptibility were expected for the control group *S*s.

METHOD

Subjects

Thirty volunteer University of Hawaii graduate students in one class in counseling psychology were matched for age, sex, and counseling experience and randomly assigned in equal numbers to three experimental groups.

---

[1] An extensive examination of the variety of group leadership patterns and a comparison of these three types can be found elsewhere and will not be reported here. The full report is available from the authors.

Ten volunteer students, matched for age, sex, and counseling experience, from an equivalent class, but not involved in any group experience during this time, were assigned to the control condition. Since there were no pre-test differences between experimental and control Ss, and since experimental and control Ss had equivalent graduate training and desire for group experience, it was presumed that there were no systematic differences between these groups. In support of the contention of equal motivation for group experience, it can be noted that 9 of the 10 control Ss volunteered to participate in groups within one semester of the pretest.

Unfortunately, 4 of these individuals began their group experience during the experimental phase of this study. Hence, they had to be eliminated from the posttest data analysis. In addition, posttest data were unavailable for two experimental group Ss. Final numbers for the groups were: for Group A, $n = 9$; for Group B, $n = 10$; for Group C, $n = 9$; and for Group D (control), $n = 6$ (total $n = 34$).

Procedure

Prior to any group experiences, all Ss were individually administered the Stanford Hypnotic Susceptibility Scale, Form A (Weitzenhoffer and Hilgard, 1959) by an experienced hypnotist. The hypnotist was unaware of the purposes and experimental conditions of the study. Similarly, Ss were not aware that the hypnotic sessions were related to their group participation and assured that they were volunteering their time in an unrelated experiment.

Each experimental group consisted of eight two-hour weekly sessions and one ten-hour marathon session in an eleven-week period. No member of the control group received any group experience during this period.

Three expert group leaders typifying different approaches to encounter groups were each chosen to lead one group. Since it was impossible to find one leader equally skilled in the techniques involved in all three approaches, it was decided that leader technique was a more important variable to control than was leader personality.

Group A was typified by an approach emphasizing the intrapersonal problems of the group's members. Personal defense patterns were analyzed and all interactions were focused through the group leader.

Group B was typified by an approach emphasizing the interpersonal problems of the group members within the group setting. Interactional patterns were analyzed, and the leader encouraged communication between members.

Group C was typified by an approach combining the intrapersonal orientation to the interpersonal problems of the group members within the group setting. Group interaction patterns were encouraged and personal defense patterns were analyzed within the context of the group settings. Group interaction patterns were focused through the leader, who, to a large extent, functioned as a group member.

In order to clarify the differences between these three approaches, a common process episode, the development of sexual feelings, is presented. Sexual feelings between members were expressed in each of the three groups. The resolution of these feelings was handled in a substantially different way by each of the three leaders. In Group A (intrapersonal), the pertinence of these sexual feelings for the individual's feelings for the individual's personality patterns was discussed. The individual was asked to examine such sexual feelings as an intrapsychic conflict in need of resolution. The leader assumed the role of *therapist* in helping each individual "work through" these sexual conflicts.

By contrast, in Group B (interpersonal), the sexual feelings were treated as an inevitable function of people working closely together in groups. Members were encouraged to express these feelings to one another. The leader reinforced such sharing of personal feeling and assisted members in working out interpersonal conflicts that arose. Thus, the leader in Group B was primarily a *facilitator* of group process rather than a *therapist*.

Finally, when sexual feelings arose in Group C (mixed), the leader asked the member to examine these feelings in terms of his (her) own life style. In this regard, the leader acted as *therapist*. However, once this examination was well underway, the group member was encouraged to confront these feelings as they occurred with regard to other group members. At this time, the leader became a group member and in this way *facilitated* interpersonal interaction.

All groups met in a 12 × 16 ft. room that contained only a rug and pillows. In addition, each session was videotaped.

After the conclusion of the groups, all Ss were individually administered the Stanford Hypnotic Susceptibility Scale, Form B (Weitzenhoffer and Hilgard, 1959). Debriefing occurred after all Ss had completed this scale. There was no evidence that any S became aware of the true purpose of the hypnosis scales prior to debriefing.

RESULTS AND DISCUSSION

Analysis of variance of pretest scores indicated no significant differences in hypnotizability between groups ($F < 1.$). However, there was a significant posttest difference between groups ($F = 4.72$, $df = 3/30$, $p < .01$). Pretest and posttest means on the 34 Ss are presented in Table 31.1.

TABLE 31.1
Comparison of mean hypnotizability scores

Group	Pretest, Form A	Posttest, Form B	t
A (intrapersonal)	4.3	5.6	1.21
B (interpersonal)	7.7	10.0	3.73**
C (mixed)	5.3	7.7	2.69*
Experimental (A, B, C)	5.8	7.8	4.16**
D (control)	4.3	5.2	1.39

*$p < .05.$ **$p < .001.$

Multiple comparisons via Scheffé's test (Ferguson, 1959) indicated significant differences between Groups B and A ($F = 10.83, p < .001$), B and D ($F = 9.68, p < .001$), and B and C ($F = 2.93, p < .05$). The differences between Groups C and D also approached significance ($F = 2.59, .05 < p < .10$).

In addition to these between-group differences, several within-group differences were also indicated and are presented in Table 31.1. There was a significant overall pretest to posttest difference for Ss in the experimental groups ($t = 4.16, p < .001$). This difference represents a mean increase in susceptibility of two points for all Ss receiving encounter group training. While the pretest to posttest increases for control Ss averaged nearly one point (as a result of practice alone), these increases were not significant.

These results provide support for Tart's conclusion that hypnotic susceptibility can increase as a result of therapeutic experiences. While his conclusions were made on the basis of a nine-month program of great variability, the present findings can be specifically attributed to encounter groups of twenty-six hour cumulative duration.

The highest scores were obtained by Ss in the group allowing for the greatest interpersonal interaction (Group B). These Ss scored significantly higher than Ss in any of the other groups. While the absolute scores were lower for Ss in Group C (mixed), these Ss' mean increases were of the same magnitude as those for Ss in Group B (interpersonal). There were no significant differences between Ss in Group A (intrapersonal) and control group Ss.

Despite the replication of Tart's findings of significant increases in hypnotizability, a conclusion that certain states of consciousness were disinhibited by the therapeutic experience is unwarranted. A more parsimonious explanation is that increased interpersonal trust, a well-supported concomitant of successful encounter groups (Golembiewski and Blumberg, 1970; Rueveni, Swift, and Bell, 1969), was responsible for these changes. This is consistent with the evidence suggesting that hypnotic susceptibility is in part a function of the S's trust of the hypnotist (e.g., Balaschak, Blocker, Rossiter, and Perin, 1970; Small and Kramer, 1969). By increasing S's trust of the hypnotist, it is conceivable that *S* will become more willing to engage in the kinds of behavior involved in hypnosis. Consistent with this contention is the finding that Group B, which maximized opportunities for interpersonal trust, was most effective. The only other group to demonstrate significant increases in hypnotizability (Group C) was also somewhat interpersonally oriented. The failure of Group A *S*s to demonstrate increases is seen as a function of the group's intrapersonal orientation. An intrapersonal orientation allows for minimal interaction and hence produces less trust between members.

Regardless of theoretical biases, all investigators in the field agree that hypnosis is at least an interpersonal influence situation. It is possible that the kinds of interpersonal skills learned in the effective encounter groups transfer to this kind of interpersonal situation outside of the group.

This use of hypnotizability has heuristic value as a measure of generalizable interpersonal behavior changes that occur as a result of therapeutic experiences. Research is now being conducted in our laboratories aimed at isolating the cognitive mechanisms involved in producing these changes.

References

BALASCHAK, B., BLOCKER, K., ROSSITER, T., AND PERIN, C. T. Influence of race and expressed experience of the hypnotist on hypnotic susceptibility. *Proceedings of the 78th Annual Convention of the American Psychological Association, 5, 835–836.*

FERGUSON, G. A. *Statistical analysis in psychology and education.* New York: McGraw-Hill, 1959.

GOLEMBIEWSKI, R. T., AND BLUMBERG, A. (eds.) *Sensitivity training and the laboratory.* Itasca, Ill.: Peacock, 1970.

RUEVENI, V., SWIFT, M., AND BELL, A. A. Sensitivity training: its impact on mental health workers. *Journal of Applied Behavioral Science,* 1969, **5,** 600–601.

SHAPIRO, J. L. An investigation into the effectiveness of sensitivity training. Unpublished doctoral dissertation, University of Waterloo, 1970.

SHAPIRO, J. L., AND GUST, T. Pre-practicum: An innovative program in training counselors. Unpublished paper, University of Hawaii, 1971.

SMALL, M., AND KRAMER, E. Hypnotic susceptibility as a function of the prestige of the hypnotist. *International Journal of Clinical and Experimental Hypnosis,* 1969, **17,** 251–256.

TART, C. T. Increases in hypnotizability resulting from a prolonged program for enhancing personal growth. *Journal of Abnormal Psychology, 1970,* **75,** 260–266.

WEITZENHOFFER, A. M., AND HILGARD, E. R. *Stanford Hypnotic Susceptibility Scale, Forms A and B.* Palo Alto. Calif.: Consulting Psychologists Press, 1959.

WEITZENHOFFER, A. M., AND HILGARD, E. R. *Stanford Hypnotic Susceptibility Scale, Form C.* Palo Alto, Calif,: Consulting Psychologists Press, 1962.

32

The Reduction of Prejudice
Through Laboratory Training

Irwin Rubin[1]

An experiment was conducted to test the hypothesis that increases in self-acceptance, resulting from sensitivity training, have the theoretically predictable but indirect effect of reducing an individual's level of ethnic prejudice. The role of an individual's level of psychological anomy,[2] hypothesized to condition the influences of sensitivity training, was also examined. The results suggest that sensitivity training may well be a powerful technique in the reduction of ethnic prejudice, particularly among those who are low in psychological anomy.

INTRODUCTION

Robert Kahn has stated (1963, p. 14), "The theory of T Groups implies that reduction in prejudice should be one of the results of a general increase in sensitivity to the needs of others and insight into one's own motives and behavior as it affects others. No research is available, however, to test this prediction."

Prior research (Bunker, 1963, 1965; Gordon, 1950) has shown that one of the effects of sensitivity training is an increased level of self-acceptance among the participants. In addition, it has been demonstrated that the way a person feels about himself is positively related to the way he feels about others (e.g., Stock, 1949; Sheerer, 1949). These two factors, when combined, suggest the following question:

---

[1]The author is grateful to Professors Edgar Schein and William McKelvey and to David Meredith, all of M.I.T., for their many helpful comments on various drafts of this paper.

[2]For the definition of this term, see pp. 416–417.

Reprinted with permission from the author and *The Journal of Applied Behavioral Science*, Vol. 3, No. 1, 1967.

This research was supported by a Ford Foundation Dissertation Fellowship in Business Administration.

Does raising a person's level of self-acceptance have the theoretically predictable but indirect effect of raising his level of acceptance-of-others?

The crux of this experiment is not that sensitivity training per se can be demonstrated to increase acceptance-of-others. The salient point to be tested is that demonstrated changes in a theoretically related variable (self-acceptance) produce this effect.

A second area of interest concerns the factors that might condition the kinds of learning an individual experiences as a result of sensitivity training. Certain personality types may be more susceptible than others to the influences of sensitivity training (Miles, 1960; Steele, 1965). The personality variable chosen for investigation in this study was psychological anomy. The rationale for this choice will be discussed in detail later.

HYPOTHESES

1. As a result of sensitivity training, an individual's level of self-acceptance will increase.

a. An individual's focus during the T-Group sessions (as determined by trainer ratings), leaning toward more personal areas, will be associated with increased self-acceptance.

2. As a result of sensitivity training, an individual's level of acceptance-of-others will increase.

3. Those low in anomy will increase more in self-acceptance and acceptance-of-others than those high in anomy.

a. An individual's level of anomy will be unaffected by sensitivity training.

4. Those who increase in self-acceptance will increase more in acceptance-of-others than those who do not change or decrease in self-acceptance.

5. Changes in self-acceptance *will lead* to changes in acceptance-of-others.

DEFINITION OF VARIABLES

Sensitivity Training

The major independent variable in this study is what has come to be known as sensitivity training or laboratory training.[3] In a broad sense, it can be defined as

> . . . an educational strategy which is based primarily on the experiences generated in various social encounters by the learners themselves and aims to influence attitudes and develop competencies toward learning about human interactions (Schein and Bennis, 1965, p. 4).

---

[3]For a complete discussion of all that is involved in a sensitivity training experience, see Schein and Bennis (1965).

Many phenomena occur within the T Group, and it is not within the scope of this study to examine the differential impact of each of these upon the variables of "self-acceptance" and "acceptance-of-others." An attempt, however, was made to control for the effect of two specific aspects of all that occurred within the T Group. The trainers involved were asked to provide *for each individual*—at the end of the laboratory—the following information: (1) To what extent did the person explicitly discuss the topic of race relations (on a scale from "not at all" to "very much," i.e., 50 percent of the time)? (2) What was the nature of the individual's focus during the T Group (on a 7-point scale from Group Process = 1 to Personal Development = 7)?

Self-Acceptance

The term "self-acceptance," as it is used in this paper, involves a willingness to confront ego-alien as well as ego-syntonic aspects of the self and to accept rather than deny their existence. Implicitly, it connotes some sense of rationality or "realistic acceptance" as opposed to, for example, a person's claim, "I am superman. I accept myself as superman. Therefore all of you are underlings!"

The Dorris, Levinson, Hanfmann Sentence Completion Test (S.C.T.) (Dorris, R. J., Levinson, D., and Hanfmann, E., 1954) was used to measure the effect of sensitivity training upon an individual's level of self-acceptance. The S.C.T. includes 50 sentence stems. Half the stems use first-person pronouns and half, a third-person pronoun or proper name.[4] The first- and third-person items are matched in content;[5] e.g.,

---
When he gets angry he

When I get angry I

The measure of self-acceptance used in this study was derived in the following manner: Individual stem completions were coded[6] for ego-threaten-

---

[4]First- and third-person items randomly distributed rather than appearing sequentially.

[5]The person is instructed to complete each of the stems as quickly as he can, using more than one word. After finishing all the items, he is asked to go back, reread his responses, and place a (+) sign next to those sentences that he feels refer to some personal experience or that reflect the way he might feel or act under the specified circumstances. If a sentence has no personal relevance, a (−) sign is used. In introducing the self-reference technique, the authors assumed that the denial of self-reference may be indicative of the subject's lack of awareness of the personal tendency expressed in the completion.

[6]Each pair of items was copied on separate pieces of paper. The respondent's identification number was placed on the *reverse side*. This procedure made it impossible for the coders to know whether the response was "pre" or "post." It also eliminated the halo effect that might have been created by reading an individual's total record.

ing content.[7] The term, "ego-threatening," was defined as follows: "Any item which states or strongly implies any attitude, feelings, or action, which if accepted by[8] —— as *applying to oneself,* would involve confronting at least a mild degree of psychological pain." For example, expression of fears, socially unacceptable responses, admission of inferiority or incompetence, extreme hostility or aggression, and so on were coded as threatening.

The assumption was then made that the more willing a person is to admit the personal relevance of ego-threatening material, the greater his level of self-acceptance. Therefore, the number of ego-threatening responses next to which the respondent placed a (+), divided by the total number of ego-threatening responses (#ET), yields the measure of self-acceptance (ETA)[9] used in this study.

It is important to note that, by this definition, self-acceptance (ETA) can increase because the numerator increases or the denominator decreases. To clarify this point, it is hypothesized that the absolute number of statements coded as being ego-threatening will *not* change as a result of sensitivity training. The rationale here is that sensitivity training will not rid a person of his basic conflicts and anxieties nor does it attempt to help him make light of his times of crises. Instead, in some ideal sense, sensitivity training may help a person to find in himself the natural tools that enable him to effectively cope with these things. This will result, for example, from positive, nonevaluative feedback, the opportunity to test ideas and beliefs (increased "reality testing" about oneself), and a high level of trust and openness resulting in greater authenticity. An environment is created within which there should be a reduction of an individual's need to use projective defense mechanisms which act to distort his perception of himself and others.

Acceptance-of-Others

Harding and Schuman (1961) conceptualize prejudice as the departure from or failure to adhere to three ideal norms of behavior: the norm of rationality, the norm of justice, and the norm of human-heartedness. In this ex-

---

[7]The correlation coefficient between two independently coded samples was 0.89. (See Johnson, 1949, p. 97, for the formula used to compute this coefficient.) The author gratefully acknowledges the assistance provided by his colleague, Tim Hall, in this phase of the study.

[8]For the females, the phrase, "the majority of women associated with the nursing profession," was inserted because virtually all the females in the experimental population fell into that category. For the males, who were more heterogeneous, the phrase, "the average male in our culture," was inserted. Two forms of the scale—male and female—were used for this research.

[9]Throughout the remainder of this paper, the following symbols will be used:
  1. ET means ego-threatening.
  2. #ET means absolute number of sentences scored as ego-threatening.
  3. ETA means self-acceptance as defined above.

periment it was decided to focus upon the norm of human-heartedness (HH)[10] which enjoins a person's emotional *acceptance-of-others* in terms of their common humanity, no matter how different they may seem from oneself. The major dependent variable in this study, in other words, is not prejudice per se but only the affective component of the individual's attitude.

The scale is made up of 15 items[11] of the following type:

> The white school board in a community builds two new schools and fixes the school lines so that almost all the Negro children go to one new school and all the white children to the other new school. How do you suppose most of the Negroes in the community would react to this?
> ———a. While there are some exceptions, many Negroes are mainly concerned with getting money for food, rent, and other things, and so do not have too much interest in the matter of school one way or the other.
> ———b. Every community is different, and it is almost impossible for someone not living in it to know enough about the situation to judge.
> ———c. The average Negro parent would not like what the school board has done about drawing school lines.
> ———d. The average Negro parent would simply be pleased to have a new school for his children, especially if it were equal to the white school in every way.

The measure of human-heartedness used in this study was derived in this manner: The respondent was asked to rank each of the four choices following an item from *1* ("most likely reaction") to *4* ("least likely reaction"). Each respondent's series of ranks was then compared with a theoretically ideal set of ranks[12] and the absolute difference between ranks was computed. The sum of these differences across the 15 experimental items yielded the respondent's human-heartedness score (HH). This score could range from 0–120 (i.e., 15 items times a maximum difference of 8 points for any item).

Psychological Anomy

The personality variable chosen for investigation in this research was psychological anomy,[13] defined as a sense of normlessness, "the feeling that

---

[10]Throughout the remainder of this paper, the symbol HH is used to represent an index of a person's level of acceptance-of-others.

[11]In addition, four control items are included to check on the extent to which response set is operating.

[12]Howard Schuman and the writer *independently* ranked all items as to how the "most human-hearted person" would assign his ranks. We agreed on 100 percent of the first and second ranks and 88 percent of the third and fourth ranks, yielding an overall percent agreement of 94 percent.

[13]The scale used to measure this variable is a nine-item Guttman scale developed by McClosky and Schaar (1965). The items are of the following form:

a. People were better off in the old days when everyone knew just how he was expected to act.

b. It seems to me that other people find it easier to decide what is right than I do.

the world and oneself are adrift, wandering, lacking in clear rules and stable moorings . . . a feeling of moral emptiness" (McClosky and Schaar, 1965, p. 14). This definition is analogous to Seeman's second major usage of the alienation concept—*meaninglessness* wherein "the individual is unclear as to what he ought to believe—when the individual's minimal standards for clarity in decision making are not met" (Coser and Rosenberg, 1964, p. 530).

McClosky and Schaar (1965) present evidence to suggest that anomic responses are powerfully governed by cognitive and personality factors independent of or in combination with social influences. They conclude that anomy "results from impediments to interaction, communication, and learning, and is a sign of impaired socialization." In other words, given that anomic feelings result from a lack of learning, "whatever interferes with one's ability to learn a community's norms, or weakens one's socialization into its central patterns of belief, must be considered among the determinants of anomy" (p. 20).

In a real sense, the T Group represents for its members a new community or society with a set of norms unlike those to which the members have become accustomed. The individual participant, if he is to benefit from sensitivity training, must be able to see and understand the norms of this new culture. Only then will he be able to decide rationally[14] whether they are personally relevant and functional and if so, to truly internalize these new learnings.

The highly anomic person might experience difficulty in understanding and internalizing the dominant norms of the T Group. Furthermore, due to the relatively short duration (two weeks) of the experiment and the here-and-now focus of the T Group, no change was expected in a person's level of anomy.

THE STUDY

Subjects

The laboratory population studied in this research were the participants in the Osgood Hill[15] 1965 summer program in sensitivity training. The program was two weeks in length (June 25-July 7), and the participants "lived

---

[14]Bennis, W. G., Schein, E. H., Berlew, D. E., and Steele, F. I. (1964) discuss this point in terms of a possible meta-goal of sensitivity training—"expanded consciousness and sense of choice."

[15]Osgood Hill is in Andover, Massachusetts. It is owned and operated by Boston University. The author wishes to acknowledge the cooperation and assistance provided by the entire staff group of Osgood Hill in the successful completion of this study.

in" in the sense that they slept on the premises and ate virtually all their meals together.

There were 50 participants — 30 females and 20 males. They ranged in age from 23 to 59, with a mean age of 33 years. The majority had at least a B.S. degree and a few had advanced degrees. The majority came from the New England area, but several came from Miami, Cleveland, and Chicago. There were eight Negroes in the population, and the trainers made certain that each of the five T Groups[16] that were formed had at least one Negro and an even proportion of males and females.

Occupationally, the males were a relatively heterogeneous group that included several businessmen, teachers, policemen, clerics, graduate students, government employees, a male nurse, and a dentist. The females were much more homogeneous, the majority of them being associated with the nursing profession (students, teachers, practicing nurses, and nursing supervisors).

Experimental Design and Procedure

One of the problems facing the researcher interested in evaluating the effects of sensitivity training is that of finding a relevant control group. The participants in a laboratory are, in one sense, a self-selected group — a circumstance which negates the relevance, for control purposes, of just any group of warm bodies.

Thus the experimental design utilized in this study was one in which the subjects served as their own controls. Herbert Hyman (Hyman, H., Wright, C. R., and Hopkins, T. K., 1962, p. 42) utilized this approach in his evaluation of the effects of citizenship camps, as did Carl Rogers in his attempts to evaluate the effects of psychotherapy. As Hyman points out:

> With such a procedure, matching of experimental subjects and controls presents no difficulty, for the same persons constitute both groups. By determining how much instability there is in the group's attitudes, opinions, or other characteristics *during a normal period of time* we could then estimate how much of the change manifested during the experimental period exceeds the normal change resulting from other factors.

Within this design, the total available experimental group (N = 50) was randomly split into two groups of unequal size. The smaller group (N = 14) was tested (0_{1C}) via mail questionnaires two weeks prior to their arrival at

---

[16]Two of the trainers were females — one of whom was a Negro — and the remaining four were males. (One group had two trainers.)

Osgood Hill. The entire group was then tested (for controls: 0_{2C} and for experimentals: 0_{1E}) upon their arrival, but before the first T-Group session. The final "after" measures (for controls: 0_{3C} and for experimentals: 0_{2E}) were obtained the morning of the next-to-last day of the laboratory.[17] This timing was necessary in order to provide a feedback session to all participants prior to their departure at the end of the laboratory.

This design can be depicted in the following manner:[18]

June 11	*June 25*	*July 5*
$0_{1C}\dfrac{\text{controls}}{\text{2 weeks}}$	$0_{2C}\dfrac{\text{controls}}{\text{T Group}}$	0_{3C}
(N = 11)		
	$0_{1E}\dfrac{\text{experimentals}}{\text{T Group}}$	0_{2E}
	(N = 30)	

RESULTS

Control Groups

Table 32.1 presents the test-retest scores for the control group (0_{1C}, 0_{2C}) and the initial test scores for the experimental group (0_{1E}). A series of t tests were performed that compared scores for 0_{1E} versus 0_{1C} and 0_{2C} in order to determine empirically the degree of similarity between experimentals and controls. None of the resulting t's reached statistical significance, with p's being greater than 0.50. On the basis of these results, it is assumed that the members of the control group represent a population comparable with the experimentals on the major variables.

It can also be seen from Table 32.1 that among the members of the control group $\overline{Ap}$ increased slightly, $\overline{\#ET}$ increased slightly, and $\overline{ETA}$ and $\overline{HH}$ both decreased slightly. In using a t test for dependent samples (Blalock, 1960), it was observed that none of the resulting t's reached the 0.60 level of significance. On the basis of these results, it is assumed that the controls do not change significantly from 0_{1C} to 0_{2C} on any of the major variables. It is assumed, therefore, that any changes found among experimentals cannot be attributable to the main effects of instrument instability and/or practice.

---

[17] All administrations, other than 0_{1C}, were conducted by the author on a group basis.

[18] Of the available control group of 14, two persons never arrived and one returned an unusable questionnaire, leaving a final control group of 11. Of the available experimental group of 36, one missed the pretest and five returned unusable questionnaires, leaving 30 for the final experimental group.

TABLE 32.1
Before-after scores for control group (0_{1C}, 0_{2C}) and
before scores for experimental group (0_{1E})

0_{1C} (N = 11)	0_{2C}*	0_{1E}* (N = 30)
(a) $\overline{Ap} = 5.5$	$\overline{Ap} = 5.8$	$\overline{Ap} = 6.5$
(b) $\overline{\#ET} = 11.0$	$\overline{\#ET} = 12.0$	$\overline{\#ET} = 13.5$
(c) $\overline{ETA} = 66.0$	$\overline{ETA} = 65.0$	$\overline{ETA} = 55.0$
(d) $\overline{HH} = 46.5$	$\overline{HH} = 47.5$	$\overline{HH} = 46.2$

(a) $\overline{Ap}$ represents mean level of anomy. Scores ranged from 1–10, with a low score representing a low level of anomy.
(b) $\overline{\#ET}$ represents the mean absolute number of statements scored as being ego-threatening, with the range from 5 to 23.
(c) $\overline{ETA}$ represents mean level of self-acceptance, i.e., the number of ego-threatening statements accepted divided by absolute number of ego-threatening statements. Scores ranged from 0 to 100 percent, with a low score indicating a low level of self-acceptance.
(d) $\overline{HH}$ represents mean level of human-heartedness. Scores ranged from a low of 18 to a high of 80. The lower the score, the closer the respondent's set of ranks was to the theoretically perfect set of ranks and, therefore, the higher his level of human-heartedness.
*$0_{2C} + 0_{1E}$ were gathered at the same point in time, just prior to the first T-Group session.

Experimental Group

It was hypothesized that $\overline{Ap}$ and $\overline{\#ET}$ would not change as a result of sensitivity training. Examination of Table 32.2 reveals that $\overline{Ap}$ and $\overline{\#ET}$ decreased slightly over this two-week period. Using a t test for dependent samples, it was found that for $\Delta \overline{Ap}$ (change in $\overline{Ap}$), t = 0.84 with an associated p < 0.40 two-tail (N = 30); and for $\Delta \#ET$ (change in #ET), t = 0.70 with an associated p < 0.45 two-tail (N = 30). We are unable to reject the null hypothesis of no difference and can therefore assume that sensitivity training had no appreciable effect upon an individual's level of anomy (Ap) or upon the absolute number of ego-threatening statements generated by an individual on our sentence completion test.

The next major hypothesis concerns ΔETA[19] (change in self-acceptance). The prediction here was that self-acceptance would increase as a result of sensitivity training. Examination of Table 32.3 reveals that ETA went from a mean of 55.0 percent to a mean of 67.0 percent. The differences between these means (t test for dependent samples) is significant at the 0.01 level one-tail (N = 30, t = 2.58, p < 0.01). It is therefore concluded that as a result of

---

[19] Δ ETA refers to change in self-acceptance score — ETA score after the laboratory, minus ETA score before the laboratory.

TABLE 32.2
Scores for experimental group
(N = 30) before (0_{1E}) and after
(0_{2E}) a 2-week T Group

	0_{1E}	0_{2E}
	$\overline{Ap} = 6.5$	$\overline{Ap} = 5.9$
	$\overline{\#ET} = 13.5$	$\overline{\#ET} = 13.2$
	$\overline{ETA} = 55.0$	$\overline{ETA} = 67.0$
	$\overline{HH} = 47.2$	$\overline{HH} = 42.0$

sensitivity training, an individual exhibits a greater willingness to accept the personal relevance of ego-threatening material; i.e., his ETA increases.

With respect to Δ HH[20] (change in human-heartedness), it was predicted that an individual's level of human-heartedness would increase. Operationally, this means that his "after HH score should be lower than his "before" HH score. Table 32.2 reveals that HH decreased from 47.2 to 42.0. The difference between these means (t test for dependent samples) is significant at the 0.01 level one-tail (N = 30, t = 2.54, p < 0.01). In other words, the rankings an individual assigned after the laboratory corresponded more closely with expert rankings than those he assigned before the laboratory — he was found to be more human-hearted.[21]

Conditioning Influence of Anomy

We turn now to an examination of the conditioning influence of anomy with respect to the observed changes in ETA and HH. It was predicted that those E's low in anomy (Ap) would change more on ETA and HH than those high in anomy (Ap). The skewed nature of the distribution of Ap scores (the majority of respondents scored either 1 or 8, 9, 10, with virtually no scores in the middle) suggested that the most relevant test of these hypotheses would be to split the group at the median Ap score and to compare the magnitude and direction of ETA and HH differences among groups.

---

[20] Δ HH refers to change in human-heartedness score — HH score after the laboratory minus HH score before the laboratory.

[21] The critical test here is whether Δ ETA and Δ HH among the experimentals differ from Δ ETA and Δ HH among the controls. A Mann-Whitney U-Test (Siegel, 1956, pp. 116–127) was therefore performed on the difference between the changes. This analysis yielded a Z = 1.76 for the Δ ETA's ($N_1 = 11$, $N_2 = 30$, p < .05 one-tail) and a Z = 1.76 for the Δ HH's ($N_1 = 11$, $N_2 = 30$, p < .04 one-tail). In other words, *not only* do the experimentals change while the controls do not, but the *experimentals also change significantly more* than the controls.

Utilizing the Mann-Whitney U-Test, it is observed that those below the median in Ap increased significantly more on ETA than those above the median in Ap ($N_1 = 19$, $N_2 = 19$,[22] $Z = 1.77$, $p < .04$ one-tail). A similar trend was found with respect to HH scores ($N_1 = 19$, $N_2 = 19$, $Z = 1.56$, $p < .06$ one-tail). In absolute terms, those low in Ap increased 17 percent on the average. With respect to HH, those low in Ap decreased six points on the average, while the high Ap's decreased only two points. In summary, strong support is provided for the hypothesized conditioning influence of Ap on changes in self-acceptance (ETA), and marginal support is provided with respect to changes in human-heartedness (HH).

Central Hypotheses

In the light of the results of these preliminary analyses, we are now in a position to examine the central hypotheses of this study:

> 1. Those who increase in self-acceptance will increase more in human-heartedness than those who either do not change or decrease in self-acceptance.[23]
> 2. Changes in self-acceptance will lead to change in human-heartedness.

With respect to the first, of the 38 members of the total experimental group, 23 increased on ETA, six did not change, and nine decreased in ETA. The sample was therefore split into $+ \Delta$ ETA (positive changers in self-acceptance, $N = 23$) and 0Δ ETA (zero or negative changers in self-acceptance, $N = 15$). On the average, the $+\Delta$ ETA group decreased five points in HH, a result which is statistically significant at the $p < .01$ level one-tail ($N = 23$, $t = 2.80$). The 0Δ ETA group also decreased in HH an average of three points, but this change does not reach significance ($N = 15$, $t = 1.03$, $p < 0.20$ one-tail). However, the difference between these changes is *not* significant (Mann-Whitney U-Test, $N_1 = 15$, $N_2 = 23$, $Z = 1.0$, $p < .16$ one-tail). The hypothesis in its present form cannot be unequivocally supported.

In order to shed some light on the reasons for this result, individual change scores on ETA were examined more closely. There appeared to be a sharp discontinuity in the distribution of scores. Several persons increased a moderate amount in ETA (8 to 14 percent), but then the next highest change was 21 percent. There were 13 persons who increased 21 percent or more in self-

[22]For the purposes of this and the following analyses, the eight of 11 control group members who returned usable responses after the laboratory (0_{3c}) were added to the 30 experimentals. These eight persons changed as much (percentage-wise) in ETA and HH after the laboratory as did the experimentals. In addition, like the experimentals, they did not change in Ap or #ET. This raises our available population from $N = 30$ to $N = 38$.

[23]The *initial* correlation between ETA versus HH was $R = -0.32$ ($N = 41$, $p < .05$ one-tail). The minus sign is explained by the fact that a high level of HH is represented by a low score.

acceptance. When we examined this group of high $+\Delta$ ETA's versus the remainder of the sample, the following results emerged: The high $+\Delta$ ETA group decreased an average of 8.0 points on HH (N = 13, t = 3.0, p < .01 one-tail), while the remainder of the sample decreased an average of 2.0 points on HH (N = 25, t = 1.3, p < .12 one-tail). A Mann-Whitney U-Test on the difference between these differences yielded a Z = 1.76 (N_1 = 13, N_2 = 25, p < .04 one-tail). In other words, those who increase a great deal in self-acceptance (Δ ETA > 21 percent) will increase significantly more in human-heartedness than those who decrease in self-acceptance or increase only a moderate amount.

One way to test the hypothesis that changes in self-acceptance lead to changes in human-heartedness is to utilize the method of partial correlation.[24] The three-variable[25] model to be tested can be depicted in the following manner:

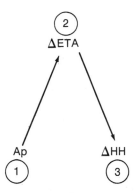

Within the framework of this research, we should like to know the direction of the causal arrow in the relationship between Δ ETA and Δ HH. In order to infer that Δ ETA is causing Δ HH, the following mathematical condition must be satisfied[26] (Simon, 1954; Blalock, 1960):

> The correlation of Ap versus Δ HH with the effect of Δ ETA removed should be less than the zero order correlation of Ap versus Δ HH; i.e., $R_{13.2} < R_{13}$.

---

[24]The utilization of partial correlations to infer causality rests upon several assumptions. In addition, all other possible models must be eliminated. A complete discussion of these assumptions and the methods for eliminating irrelevant models can be found in Simon (1954) and Blalock (1960).

[25]Anomy (AP) was chosen as the third variable because, as discussed earlier, it was unaffected by the training experience but was related both to changes in self-acceptance and changes in human-heartedness. Other ways exist to prove causality but, for these, different experimental designs are required.

[26]Numerical subscripts are used for simplicity.
    1 = Ap
    2 = Δ ETA
    3 = Δ HH

TABLE 32.3
Contingency tables necessary to compute tetrachoric
correlations between Ap, Δ HH, and Δ ETA

A.

	Low Ap	High Ap
High Δ HH	13	10
Low Δ HH	6	9

^{R}Ap, Δ HH = -0.255 (R$_{13}$)

B.

	Low Ap	High Ap
High Δ ETA	13	6
Low Δ ETA	6	13

^{R}Ap, Δ ETA = -0.550 (R$_{12}$)

C.

	High ETA	Low ETA
High Δ HH	15	8
Low Δ HH	4	11

^{R} Δ ETA, Δ HH = 0.575 (R$_{23}$)

Table 32.3 presents the data from which the required zero order correlations are computed. The dichotomous nature of the Ap scores suggested that a tetrachoric correlation method would be most appropriate. Under appropriate conditions (Guilford, 1956), this method "gives a coefficient that is numerically equivalent to a Pearson r and may be regarded as an approximation to it." In every case, the high versus low split was based upon those above and below the median.[27]

Substitution of the zero order correlations into the partial correlation formula (Blalock, 1960) yields an $R_{13.2} = +0.09$ and the mathematical condition stated above is therefore satisfied.[28] It is important to note that this analysis does not enable one to rule out a direct effect of sensitivity training on HH. Nor does it eliminate the possibility that sensitivity training influences another variable which may be termed "feeling-orientation" which, in turn, influences ETA and HH. All it suggests is that some change in HH does result from a change in ETA.[29]

[27]Median Ap = 5.0.
  Median ETA = +8; i.e., 8 percent increase in self-acceptance.
  Median HH = 2.0; i.e., 2-point decrease in HH score.
  [28]A more conservative approach here is to split the total sample at the median ΔETA score and compute the tetrachoric correlation between Ap versus ΔHH within each subsample. The split was made, and the results are almost identical with those obtained when the partial correlation formula was used.
  [29]A Kruskall-Wallis one-way analysis of variance (Siegel, 1956, pp. 184–193) among the five T Groups on all major variables was performed, and none of the resulting HH's reached the 0.50 level of significance two-tail. From this result, it can be assumed that there was no significant trainer effect, nor can the observed changes be attributed to some other factor unique to any one of the T Groups.

Trainer Ratings

Trainers were asked, at the end of the laboratory, to characterize the nature of each individual's participation during the T-Group session on a scale from 1 (Group Process Orientation) to 7 (Personal Development). In addition, the trainers rated, for each individual, the "Salience of the Topic of Race Relations" (i.e., percent of time spent discussing the Topic).

It was hypothesized that changes in self-acceptance (ΔETA) would be associated with an "individual orientation" leaning toward Personal Development. Again, this hypothesis is supported only when we compare the high $+\Delta$ETA group with the remainder of the sample. The average trainer rating for the high $+\Delta$ETA's was 5.2 (i.e., leaning toward Personal Development), as compared with 3.8 (i.e., leaning toward Group Process) for the remainder of the sample. This difference is significant ($N^{30} = 30$, $t = 2.16$, $p < .02$ one-tail).

No directional hypotheses were made concerning the effect of "Salience of the Topic" on an individual's change in human-heartedness. The 20 persons for whom these ratings were available were split into two groups — high (20 to 50 percent of time) versus low (0 to 20 percent) salience, and changes in HH within the two groups were examined. The low-salience group decreases an average of eight points in HH, while the high-salience group decreases an average of only one point in HH ($N_1 = 10$, $N_2 = 10$, $Z = 1.65$, $p < .10$ two-tail, Mann-Whitney U-Test). In other words, there appears to be somewhat of a negative relationship between the amount of time spent discussing the topic of race relations and the change in human-heartedness.[31]

DISCUSSION

Generalizability of Results

One question which comes up immediately is the extent to which the findings of this study are generalizable. It was pointed out earlier that the members of the experimental population all shared a certain level of "motivation to attend a laboratory." It is not yet known what personality variables, for example, differentiate those who are "motivated to attend" from those who are not. Even if knowledge of these parameters did exist, it would then

---

[30]The sample is reduced here because one set of trainer-rating forms was never returned to the researcher.

[31]The correlation between "Salience of Topic" and initial HH score was zero, as was the correlation between "Individual Orientation" and the initial ETA score.

have to be demonstrated that they have relevance in terms of differential learnings resulting from training. This broad issue is beyond the scope of this study. However, several related sub-issues are manageable.

Concerning the distribution of initial self-acceptance scores, a reasonably normal distribution of scores with a mean value close to 50 percent was observed. Unfortunately, no norms exist to indicate what the expected average score might be. Two comparison samples, however, are available: The average ETA score among the college sophomore group studied by Dorris, et al. (1954) was 53 percent, and among a pretest group of 30 Sloan Fellows at M.I.T. (with a simplified index of self-acceptance being used), the mean score was 50 percent. In addition, the results of the present study suggest that even some of those who were initially very low in self-acceptance could be "reached" by sensitivity training.

Concerning human-heartedness scores, Schuman and Harding (1963) found in their main standardization sample that the average HH score (with a simplified measure being used) leaned toward the "unhuman-hearted" end of the scale. The distribution of initial scores observed in this study was skewed in the other direction—toward the human-hearted end of the scale. The atypical[32] educational level of the Osgood Hill sample, with the majority having at least a bachelor's degree, helps to explain this difference. It may be that a certain level of education is a necessary prerequisite to learning via sensitivity training. This proposition is as yet untested empirically.

What Kind of Sensitivity Training

Another question of importance deals with the impact of different emphases in sensitivity training.[33] The results of this study highlight the importance of a "personal development" as opposed to a "group process" orientation. The greatest increasers in self-acceptance and, consequently, in human-heartedness were those whose predominant focus during the T-Group sessions was in more personal areas.

From a pragmatic viewpoint, if one wishes to use sensitivity training as a means to reduce prejudice, then, within the Schein and Bennis (1965) framework, the individual should be viewed as the client, and learning about self and others should be stressed at the levels of awareness and changed atti-

---

[32]The terms "typical" and "atypical," used in this section, have as their frame of reference "a random sample of adults drawn from the general population."

[33]Schein and Bennis (1965) present a three-dimensional schema for classifying the goals of a laboratory in these terms: What is the learning about? Who is the ultimate client? What is the level of learning?

tudes.[34] Furthermore, given the specific goal of prejudice reduction and a personal focus, a shorter laboratory might be feasible. Much research is needed to determine the optimal mix of group process versus personal development orientation, the relative impacts of various kinds of supplementary cognitive inputs, and the effect of laboratory duration on the amount of change observed.

One of the most interesting findings in this study involved the strong conditioning influence of anomy with respect to changes in self-acceptance. The success of sensitivity training as an educational strategy rests upon an individual's ability to see and understand the dominant norms of self-exposure, openness, and feedback which develop with the T Group. What remains to be demonstrated by future research is the role of anomy as a conditioning variable for learning criteria other than increased self-acceptance.

The roles played by discussion of the topic of race relations and the presence of Negroes in the T Group are still unclear. Pure discussion does not help those who are doing the talking. This situation does not mean that the observed changes in human-heartedness could have occurred without any such discussion. The nontalkers[35] may have benefited immensely from listening to the more vocal members of the group. On the other hand, the talkers may have been "intellectualizing"—a technique commonly employed in T Groups to keep the discussion on a less threatening level. This negative effect of participation has been observed by other researchers,[36] and further research is necessary to better understand the dynamics of the relationship between participation (amount and content) and change.

Concerning the effect of racially mixed groups, it may be that for a majority of the white participants the T-Group experience was the first opportunity they ever had to meaningfully interact with a Negro. During the T-Group discussions, many insights may have occurred that served to highlight a feeling of "oneness" of common humanity. For example, "He [a Negro] has feelings and emotions just the same as I!" Research is needed to examine in greater detail the specific patterns of interaction (e.g., Negro to white) and discussion content within a mixed T Group and their effects on the attitudes people have toward one another, as well as the effects of an all-white group.

---

[34]For an excellent description of this form of sensitivity training, see Irving R. Weschler, Fred Massarik, and Robert Tannenbaum, The self in process: A sensitivity training emphasis, in *Issues in human relations training*, No. 5 in NTL's Selected Readings Series. Washington, D.C. National Training Laboratories, 1962. Pp. 33–46.

[35]"Nontalker" does not mean "silent member," but refers instead only to the substance or content of an individual's discussion. The most vocal member, in terms of total participation, may never have mentioned the topic of race relations.

[36]Personal communication from David Kolb of M.I.T. concerning some research he is conducting on individual change within T Groups. 1965.

Change in Self-Acceptance Versus
Change in Human-Heartedness

One of the central hypotheses in this study was that those who increase in self-acceptance will increase more in human-heartedness than those who decrease or do not change in self-acceptance. The data suggest that this hypothesis, in its original form, was too broad. It appears instead that some minimum increase in self-acceptance (20 percent in this study) is necessary in order for any significant change in human-heartedness to be immediately observable.[37] Perhaps, where sensitivity training really "took" (in the sense of great increase in self-acceptance), those involved may have been better able to immediately make the mental transfer from self-acceptance to human-heartedness. The others may have needed some period of incubation in order for this transfer to occur.

Support for this interpretation is provided by Katz (Katz, D., Sarnoff, I., and McClintock, C. M., 1956, 1957) who found that as a result of a self-insight manipulation no changes in prejudice were observed immediately after the experimental induction, but that highly significant shifts occurred several weeks afterwards. In other words, a "sleeper effect" appeared to be operating. The written case study utilized by Katz, et al. (1956) to increase self-insight is certainly less intensive than a two-week sensitivity training laboratory and may well be less powerful. It is possible, therefore, that changes in human-heartedness will persist after the laboratory and, in fact, may become more marked among the group who experienced only moderate increases in self-acceptance.[38] This hypothesis could not be tested because it was necessary to provide a full feedback session[39] for the laboratory participants prior to their departure.

Finally, the reader has undoubtedly noticed that by changing a few words, e.g., "T Group" to "therapy group" and "trainer" to "therapist," this study could have been concerned with the effect of client-centered psychotherapy upon prejudiced attitudes. Both the T Group and the therapy group provide the elements of psychological safety, support, and opportunities for reality testing assumed necessary to effect an increase in an individual's level of self-acceptance and consequently, by our model, to decrease one's level of

---

[37]The risk of maximizing change variations by examining a small subgroup of the total population is reduced considerably by the findings concerning individual focus during the T-Group sessions. The great changers in self-acceptance were also those whose focus during the T Group was in more personal areas.

[38]The Bunker studies (1963, 1965) discussed earlier suggest that many of the learnings derived from sensitivity training *do* remain with an individual over a long period of time.

[39]The reason for this was only partially based upon ethical considerations. Of equal importance was the fact that the data which were fed back to the participants became topics for discussion in the few remaining T-Group session and therefore, hopefully, enhanced the learning value of their training experience.

ethnic prejudice. To the extent that future research and practical experience substantiate the conclusions drawn from the present study, a step has been taken toward solving a problem posed by Adorno (Adorno, T. W., Frenkel-Brunswick, E., Levinson, D. J., and Sanford, R. N., 1950, p. 976) some 17 years ago.

> Although it cannot be claimed that psychological insight (self-insight) is any guarantee of insight into society, there is ample evidence that people who have the greatest difficulty in facing themselves are the least able to see the way the world is made. Resistance to self-insights and resistance to social facts are contrived, most essentially, of the same stuff. It is here that psychology may play its most important role. Techniques for overcoming resistance, developed mainly in the field of individual psychotherapy, can be improved and adapted for use with groups and even for use on a mass scale.

References

ADORNO, T. W., FRENKEL-BRUNSWICK, E., LEVINSON, D. J., AND SANFORD, R. N. *The authoritarian personality.* New York: Harper & Row, 1950.

BENNIS, W. G., SCHEIN, E. H., BERLEW, D. E., AND STEELE, F. I. *Interpersonal dynamics.* Chicago: Dorsey, 1964.

BLALOCK, H. M. *Social statistics.* New York: McGraw-Hill, 1960.

BUNKER, D. The effect of laboratory education upon individual behavior. *Proc. of the 16th Annual Meeting,* Industrial Relat. Res. Ass., December 1963. Pp. 1-13.

BUNKER, D. Individual applications of laboratory training. *J. appl. Behav. Sci.,* 1965, **1** (2), 131-148.

COSER, L. A., AND ROSENBERG, B. (eds.) *Sociological theory—A book of readings.* New York: Macmillan, 1964.

DORRIS, R. J., LEVINSON, D., AND HANFMANN, E. Authoritarian personality studied by a new variation of the sentence completion technique. *J. abnorm. soc. Psychol.,* 1954, **49,** 99-108.

GORDON, T. What is gained by group participation? *Educ. Leadership,* January 1950, 220-226.

GUILFORD, J. P. *Fundamental statistics in psychology and education.* New York: McGraw-Hill, 1956.

HARDING, J., AND SCHUMAN, H. An approach to the definition and measurement of prejudice. Unpublished manuscript, Harvard Univer., January 1961.

HYMAN, H., WRIGHT, C. R., AND HOPKINS, T. K. *Application of methods of evaluation.* Los Angeles: Univer. of California Press, 1962.

JOHNSON, P. C. *Statistical methods in research.* New York: Prentice-Hall, 1949.

KAHN, R. Aspiration and fulfillment: Themes for studies of group relations. Unpublished manuscript, Univer. of Michigan, 1963.

KATZ, D., SARNOFF, I., AND McCLINTOCK, C. M. Ego defense and attitude change. *Human Relat.,* 1956, **9,** 27-45.

KATZ, D., SARNOFF, I., AND McCLINTOCK, C. M. The measurement of ego defense as related to attitude change. *J. Pers.,* 1957, **25,** 465–474.

McCLOSKY, H., AND SCHAAR, J. H. Psychological dimensions of anomy. *Amer. soc. Rev.,* 1965, **30** (1), 14–40.

MILES, M. B. Human relations training: Processes and outcomes. *J. counsel. Psychol.,* 1960, **7** (4), 301–306.

SCHEIN, E. H., AND BENNIS, W. G. *Personal and organizational change through group methods: The laboratory approach.* New York: Wiley, 1965.

SCHUMAN, H., AND HARDING, J. Sympathetic identification with the underdog. *Pub. Opin. Quart.,* Summer 1963, 230–241.

SHEERER, E. T. The relationship between acceptance of self and acceptance of others. *J. consult. Psychol.,* 1949, **13,** 169–175.

SIEGEL, S. *Nonparametric statistics for the behavioral sciences.* New York: McGraw-Hill, 1956.

SIMON, H. A. Spurious correlation: A causal interpretation. *J. Amer. Stat. Ass.,* 1954, **49,** 467–479.

STEELE, F. I. The relationships of personality to changes in interpersonal values effected by laboratory training. Unpublished doctoral dissertation, Masschusetts Institute of Technology, 1965.

STOCK, D. An investigation into the interrelations between the self-concept and feelings directed toward other persons and groups. *J. consult. Psychol.,* 1949, 13.

Author Index

Subject Index